Berlitz HANDBOOK
NEW ZEALAND

Contents

FAMILY FRIENDLY SYMBOL

This symbol is used throughout the Handbook to indicate a sight, hotel, restaurant or activity that is suitable for families with children.

Top 25 Attractions

1 Milford Sound Wild waterfalls and majestic granite peaks tower above the crystal-clear waters of this unforgettable destination *(see p.249)*

2 Wai-O-Tapu Thermal Wonderland Rotorua's most colourful thermal park is home to the bubbling Champagne Pool *(see p.127)*

3 Whale Watching Spot sperm whales and other prolific marine life from the safety of a stable catamaran in Kaikoura *(see p.191)*

4 **Nelson Arts and Crafts Trail** Hop between the studios and galleries of renowned artists *(see p.178)*

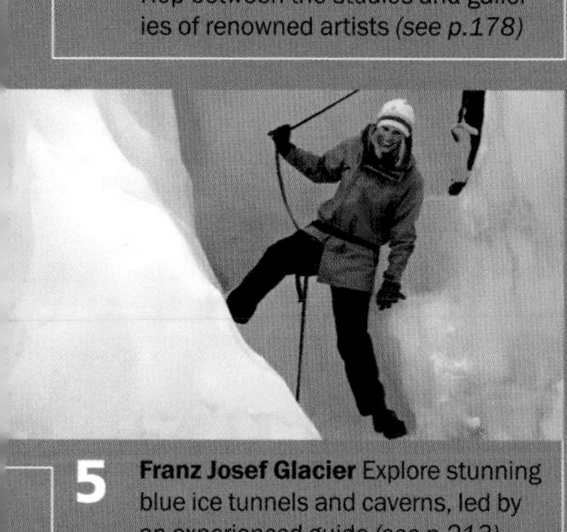

5 **Franz Josef Glacier** Explore stunning blue ice tunnels and caverns, led by an experienced guide *(see p.213)*

6 **Waitomo Caves** This magical underground world of caverns is lit by thousands of glow-worms *(see p.100)*

7 **Ulva Island Open Sanctuary** Watch wild *tokoeka* – Stewart Island kiwi – hunt for grubs *(see p.251)*

8 **Balloon Ride** Drift above the Canterbury Plains between the Southern Alps and the Pacific *(see p.206)*

9 **Te Puia Maori Arts and Crafts Institute** See master carvers and weavers plus the Pohutu Geyser *(see p.121)*

10 **Hump Ridge Jet** Scud at high speeds across Wairaurahiri River rapids in Southland *(see p.248)*

11 **Feilding Stock Saleyards** Rub shoulders with farmers on a tour of this busy saleyard *(see p.143)*

12 **Skyline Gondola, Queenstown** Float up to Bob's Peak for tremendous views *(see p.221)*

13 **White Island** Feel the raw energy of nature on the world's most accessible marine volcano *(see p.110)*

15 Doubtful Sound Listen to the sound of silence in this area of Fiordland National Park *(see p.248)*

14 Auckland War Memorial Museum Peruse the world's finest collection of Maori and Polynesian artefacts *(see p.69)*

16 Waipoua Forest Stroll through this mighty Northland forest to find the oldest living kauri tree *(see p.93)*

17 Mount Cook Scenic Flight Take an unforgettable flight and land on the upper snowfields of the Tasman Glacier *(see p.205)*

18 **Tongariro Crossing** Marvel at volcanic landscapes on New Zealand's greatest day hike *(see p.23)*

19 **Te Paki Sand Dunes** Grab a board and slide down mountainous sand dunes to your heart's content *(see p.92)*

20 **Dance with Dolphins** Duck and dive with Northland's friendly bottlenose dolphins *(see p.97)*

21 **River Valley Rafting** Hit the white waters of the canyon-carving Rangitikei River *(see p.142)*

22 **Te Papa Tongarewa Museum** Experience Maori art and volcanoes in Wellington *(see p.156)*

23 **Hawke's Bay Food and Wine Trail** Sample fine wines and delicious farmers' market fare *(see p.148)*

24 **Central Otago Rail Trail** Cycle a 150km former rail track and stay in old gold-mining towns *(see p.229)*

25 **Sky Tower** Ride to the top for jaw-dropping views of Auckland city, harbour and islands *(see p.68)*

New Zealand Fact File

New Zealand is a land of contrasts, a place of wide-open spaces, magnificent Alpine scenery and lush pastures. Most New Zealanders – commonly dubbed 'Kiwis' throughout its three main isles – live in the nation's five main cities of Auckland, Wellington, Christchurch, Dunedin and Hamilton, while those remaining populate the scattered rural towns in between.

BASICS

Population: 4.3 million
Area: 270,467 sq km
Official languages: English, Maori
Capital city: Wellington
Prime Minister: John Key

National anthems: 'God Defend New Zealand' and 'God Save the Queen'
National symbol: kiwi bird
National sports: rugby, netball
National airline: Air New Zealand
National flag:

TIME ZONE

GMT +13 Sept–Mar
GMT +12 Apr–Oct

In January:

Los Angeles: 3pm
New York: 6pm
London: 11pm
Sydney: 10am
Wellington: noon

In July:

Los Angeles: 5pm
New York: 8pm
London: 1am
Sydney: 10am
Wellington: noon

CURRENCY

New Zealand dollar (NZ$)
NZ$1 = 100 cents (c)

The following figures are approximate:

£1 = NZ$0.46
€1 = NZ$0.52
$1 = NZ$0.71

KEY TELEPHONE NUMBERS

Country code:
+64
International calls:
00 + country code + number

Police: 111
Ambulance: 111
Fire: 111

ELECTRICITY

230 volts, 50 Hertz
Australasian-model three-pin plug

OPENING HOURS

Banks: Mon–Fri 9.30am–4.30pm
Shops: Mon–Fri 9am–5pm, Sat–Sun 10am–1pm, some later. Late-night shopping (until 8pm or 9pm) is common on Thursday or Friday nights and in resorts.
Museums: Mon–Fri 9.30am–4/5pm, Sat–Sun 10am–4/5pm.
Restaurants: outside major towns, most restaurants are closed on Monday evenings.

POSTAL SERVICE

Post Shops: open Mon–Fri 9am–5pm and Sat 9am–noon.
Postboxes: large, rectangular, red and white, mounted on posts.
Domestic post: NZ$0.50c
Airmail: NZ$1.80/NZ$2.30

AGE RESTRICTIONS

Driving: 15
Drinking: 18
Age of Consent: 16

Smoking is banned in restaurants, bars and public buildings.

WHEN TO GO

Climate

New Zealand's climate ranges from subtropical in the northern North Island to temperate/cool in the South Island. Places like Invercargill on the southern coast of the South Island can be bitterly cold in winter, when southerly winds blow up from Antarctica. However, whatever the season, it is essential to bring umbrellas and waterproofs: a typical Auckland day, for example, veers between periods of showers and sun; and on the South Island, Fiordland and the west coast have very high rainfall – Milford Sound gets more than 6m (20ft) of rain a year.

Winds can be strong at any time of year on the Cook Strait, which separates the two main islands, but summer days are generally warm and pleasant in most of the regions. Winters can be cold in the central and southern North Island and coastal districts of the South Island, and can be severe in the central regions of the South Island.

Public Holidays

Jan	New Year (1st and 2nd)
Feb	Waitangi Day (6th)
Apr	Anzac Day (25th), Good Friday, Easter Monday
June	Queen's Birthday (first Monday)
Oct	Labour Day (last Monday)
Dec	Christmas (25th); Boxing Day (26th)

Provincial Anniversaries

Southland (17 Jan), Wellington (22 Jan), Northland (29 Jan), Auckland (29 Jan), Nelson (1 Feb), Otago (23 Mar), Taranaki (31 Mar), South Canterbury (25 Sept), Hawke's Bay (Friday before Labour Day), Marlborough (1 Nov), Canterbury (16 Nov), Westland (1 Dec)

All banks, post offices and some shops close on public holidays. Most nightclubs and bars close at midnight the night before. Tourist attractions remain open except on Christmas Day. Most provincial anniversaries are observed on the closest Monday.

Autumnal colours, Queenstown

Alpine weather is notoriously changeable, so those planning on visiting mountainous areas should bring warm clothing, even in summer.

Summer runs Dec–Feb; autumn Mar–May; winter June–Aug; and spring Sept–Nov. The summer and autumn seasons from December to May are the most settled and sunniest, and the best time for a visit. Unless you are visiting to ski, or plan to travel in Northland, the worst

A surfer makes the most of a fine summer's evening in the Bay of Plenty

time to visit is from July–Oct when most of the country is windy and wet.

The NZ weather service's website, www.metservice.co.nz, has details on weather conditions.

High/Low Season

The high season runs from December through to March and booking ahead is recommended during this period. New Zealanders traditionally take their main family holiday break at Christmas and into January, and advance bookings for accommodation and domestic transport are particularly essential at this time.

The shoulder seasons (Mar–May and Sept–Nov) offer good value and accommodation discounts apply.

The low season (June–Oct) is the cheapest time to travel, however prices remain high at resort towns with ski fields. In other areas some attractions will be closed, though most major attractions remain open year-round.

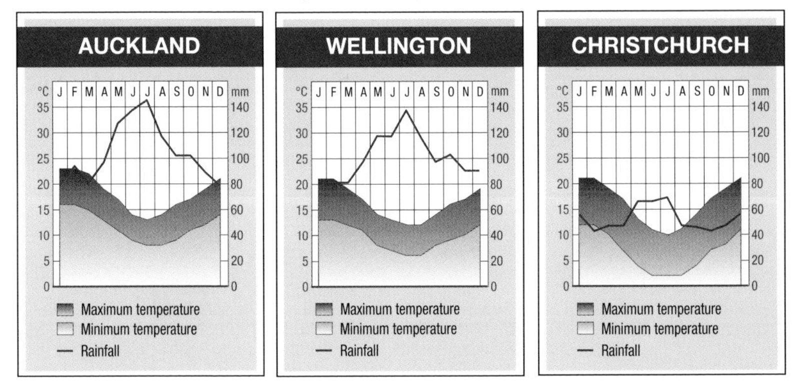

ESSENTIAL EVENTS

Napier Art Deco festival in February

January

Highland Games, 1 January, Waipu
Includes Highland Heavyweight championships and Highland Dancing competition.

Auckland Anniversary Regatta, last Mon of January
Thousands of boats hit the water to celebrate Auckland's public holiday.

International Buskers Festival, throughout Jan, Christchurch
The world's best street acts, with more than 450 live shows city-wide.

February

Marlborough Wine and Food Festival, 2nd weekend February, Blenheim
The biggest of its kind in the country.

Art Deco Festival, 3rd weekend February, Napier
Celebrating the city's Art Deco architecture with 'bubbly' breakfasts, café crawls, celebrity tea parties, and glitzy costume and coiffure competitions.

Waitangi Day, 6 February, Waitangi Treaty Grounds
National day commemorating the Treaty of Waitangi, New Zealand's founding document, which was signed on 6 February 1840.

March

Golden Shears Sheep-Shearing Competition, Masterton
Competitors must be able to shear 410-plus sheep a day to compete in this show.

Wildfoods Festival, mid-March, Hokitika
A one-day celebration of the West Coast's famous bush tucker, from roasted larvae called huhu grubs through to whitebait patties.

Pasifika, Western Springs Auckland
New Zealand's largest festival celebrating the people of the Pacific.

April

Royal New Zealand Easter Show, Easter weekend, Auckland
A one-week event filled with carnival rides, livestock competitions, wine awards, and one of the largest equestrian shows in the southern hemisphere.

May

New Zealand International Comedy Festival, mid-May, Auckland

Held over a period of two weeks, the festival showcases the best local, national and international comedy performers.

June

New Zealand National Agricultural Fieldays, Mystery Creek, Hamilton
A three-day agricultural show and one of the largest in the world, with events including a tractor pull competition.

July

Queenstown Winter Festival, 1st weekend July, Coronet Peak
Celebrity skiers, sheepdog trials, night skiing and all-night partying signal the start of the region's ski season.

August

Christchurch Winter Carnival
A week-long carnival celebrating winter with skiing and snowboarding championships.

September

World of Wearable Art Awards, Wellington
A fashion extravaganza of weird and wonderful designs by national and international designers and artists.

October

Taranaki Rhododendron Festival, mid-October, New Plymouth
Over 60 private gardens open to the public over 10 days.

November

New Zealand Cup and Show Week, Christchurch
Includes New Zealand's largest Agricultural and Pastoral (A&P) show, held over two days, plus horse-racing and fashon events.

December

Festival of Lights, throughout December, New Plymouth
Illuminations in Pukekura Park.

Ushering in the ski season at the Queenstown Winter Festival in July

ITINERARIES

Travelling at a comfortable pace, to see the whole of New Zealand takes four to six weeks. Those travelling to New Zealand for two weeks or less should consider domestic flights between cities to cut down on travel time. Flights are available between the major tourist destinations of Auckland, Rotorua, Wellington, Christchurch and Queenstown.

One Week of Thermal Wonder

***Days 1–2:* Rotorua.** Visit Wai-O-Tapu to see the Lady Knox Geyser erupt, then cruise to the site of the former Pink and White Terraces at Waimangu. Visit the Buried Village, Hell's Gate and Kuirau Park.

***Days 3–5:* Taupo.** Follow the Thermal Explorer Highway to Taupo, stopping at Orakei Korako Thermal Park and Huka Prawn Park where tropical prawns are raised in geothermally heated pools. Take a scenic drive around the volcanoes of Tongariro National Park.

***Days 6–7:* Whakatane.** Visit the shuddering shores of White Island, New Zealand's only active marine volcano, then drive northwest to Mount Edgecumbe and ascend to the top for stunning views.

Lady Knox Geyser

Two Weeks for Wine Lovers

***Days 1–2:* Auckland.** Drop by the vineyards of West Auckland, including Matua Valley Wines, Selaks and Soljans vineyards, then drive north to Matakana for Heron's Flight, Matakana Estate and Ascension vineyards.

***Days 3–5:* Rotorua and Tauranga.** Drive south, calling into Mamaku Blue Winery near Rotorua to sample blueberry wine, then head across to Tauranga to sample wine at Mills Reef.

***Days 6–9:* Hawke's Bay.** Spend three or more days exploring the vineyards and food trail of the Hawke's Bay, sampling farm-fresh cuisine and the wines of Church Road, Mission Estate, Te Mata and Craggy Range.

Martinborough wine tasting

Day 10: **Martinborough.** Head south via Gladstone to Martinborough to sample the region's award-winning Pinot Noir.

Days 11–12: **Marlborough/ Blenheim.** Cross the Cook Strait to Picton and travel south to Blenheim to sample award-winning Sauvignon Blanc and Chardonnay.

Days 13–14: **Waipara.** Wind up in the newest wine region of Waipara Valley.

Ten Days of Impressive Landscapes

Day 1: **Auckland.** Ride to the top of the Sky Tower, and explore Auckland's rugged Waitakere Ranges and awe-inspiring west coast.

Days 2–5: **Rotorua/Tongariro.** Fly or drive to Rotorua to peruse its geothermal landscapes and myriad lakes, then drive south to the vast Tongariro National Park. Ride a chairlift up Mount Ruapehu and hike the volcanically formed Tongariro Crossing.

Day 6: **Marlborough Sounds.** Fly or drive to Wellington and catch the ferry across the Cook Strait to Picton. Join a boat cruise to explore the picturesque Marlborough Sounds.

Days 7–8: **Queenstown.** Fly to Queenstown and ride the Skyline Gondola for outstanding Alpine views. Join a one-day coach/fly tour of Milford or Doubtful Sound.

Days 9–10: **Aoraki Mount Cook.** Drive north to Aoraki Mount Cook. Take a scenic flight around the mountain to the west-coast glaciers of Fox and Franz Josef, and land on the upper snowfields of the Tasman Glacier. Explore the Mackenzie country lakes of Pukaki and Tekapo.

Two Weeks for Snow Bunnies

Days 1–3: **Christchurch.** Visit the club fields of Arthur's Pass, then base yourself in the après-ski Mecca of Methven and enjoy long days at Mount Hutt Ski Field.

Days 4–5: **Tekapo.** Tackle the slopes of Round Hill then toboggan or ice-skate at Tekapo's Winter Park.

Days 6–10: **Wanaka.** Drive south to Wanaka and test your skills at Treble Cone Ski Field and Cardrona, and enjoy Wanaka's laid-back après ski.

Days 11–14: **Queenstown.** Hit the slopes at Coronet Peak Ski Field and The Remarkables Ski Field, and join ice-skaters at Queenstown Gardens.

BEFORE YOU LEAVE

Visas and Entry Requirements

All visitors require passports valid for at least three months after the date they intend to leave the country.

Visas are also required; however, many countries have a reciprocal visa waiver agreement with New Zealand and nationals of these countries can stay in on the visa waiver programme for three months *(see right)*.

Visa requirements differ depending on nationality, purpose of visit and length of stay. Visitors must produce an onward or return ticket and sufficient funds to support themselves during their stay. Check with the New Zealand diplomatic or consular office in your country of residence or at www.immigration.govt.nz.

Nationality	Visa Required		
	Up to 3 months	Up to 6 months	Longer stay
UK	✗	✗	✓
US	✗	✓	✓
Canada	✗	✓	✓
Australia	✗	✗	✗
Ireland	✗	✓	✓
South Africa	✗	✓	✓

Embassies and Consulates

Australia: New Zealand High Commission, Commonwealth Avenue, Canberra, ACT 2600, Australia; tel: 02-6270 4211

Canada: New High Commission, 99 Bank Street, Suite 727, Ottawa, Ontario K1P 6GE, Canada; tel: 613-238 5991

South Africa: New Zealand High Commission Pretoria, 125 Middel Street, New Muckleneuk 0181, South Africa; tel: 12-435 9000

UK/Ireland: New Zealand High Commission, New Zealand House, 80 Haymarket, London SW1Y 4TQ, UK; tel: 020-7930 8422

US: New Zealand Embassy, 37 Observatory Circle, Washington DC 20008, USA; tel: 202-328 4800

Vaccinations

No vaccinations are required by law for entry into New Zealand.

The Tongariro Crossing is New Zealand best one-day hike – don't forget your walking shoes!

Booking in Advance

If you are planning to visit in January, it is essential to book accommodation prior to arrival as this is when New Zealanders are on holiday. It is also advisable to book any key activities that you do not want to miss out on, such as swimming with dolphins with Dolphin Encounter in Kaikoura which tends to fill fast, and tickets for shows and major sporting events.

Tourist Information

The official Tourism New Zealand website, www.newzealand.com, has comprehensive information in several languages. Tourism New Zealand offices abroad include:

Australia: Level 12, 61 York Street, Sydney, NSW; tel: 02-8299 4800

UK: New Zealand House, Level 7, 80 Haymarket, London SW1Y 4TQ; tel: 020-7930 1662

US: 501 Santa Monica Boulevard, Suite 300, Santa Monica, CA 90401; tel: 310-395 7480

Maps and Books

Tourist visitor information centres (i-Sites) and car-hire companies distribute free maps. The New Zealand Automobile Association also produces regional maps and excellent district maps; a nominal sum is charged for North and South Island maps. Hema Maps, Wises Maps and the Shell Road Atlas are also widely available.

Good books to read prior to arriving include the following:

Back from the Brink: the fight to save our endangered birds by Gerard Hutching.

The Bone People by Keri Hulme. British Booker prize for fiction winner.

The Denniston Rose by Jenny Pattrick. A bestselling story of a spirited child in the bleak coal mining settlement of Denniston in the 1880s.

Once Were Warriors by Alan Duff. One of the most talked-about books ever published in New Zealand.

The Penguin History of New Zealand by Michael King. Definitive history.

The Whale Rider by Witi Ihimaera. A beautiful modern tale about a Maori child's struggle to gain recognition as heir to the chiefdom of Ngati Konohi.

Websites

Useful websites for research include:

www.aa.co.nz – driving
www.allblacks.com – rugby
www.aotearoa.co.nz – arts and crafts
www.ecotours.co.nz – eco operators
www.newzealand.com – tourism
www.nzmuseums.co.nz – exhaustive listings across country
www.nzmusic.com – gig guide

Packing List

- Sunglasses, sunhat and sun block
- Swimming costume (togs)
- Flip-flops (jandals)
- Comfortable walking shoes, and hiking boots if you plan to tackle longer walks
- A light raincoat (even during summer)
- Casual clothes like T-shirts and sweaters that can be layered for cooler evenings or brisk days, especially if travelling to regions in the South Island
- Sturdy winter clothing and footwear if travelling to any region except Northland or Auckland during winter
- Dressy attire for arts events, classy restaurants, wine bars and nightclubs

UNIQUE EXPERIENCES

Exploring the National Parks

The vast open landscapes and diverse scenery of New Zealand's national parks, from the high peaks and huge glaciers of the Southern Alps to the cascading waterfalls, fiords and placid wetlands of the coast, provide beautiful backdrops to enjoy a range of invigorating outdoor pursuits.

In terms of accessible wilderness areas, New Zealand is richly endowed. Nearly one third of its landmass (5 million hectares/12.3 million acres) is made up of publicly owned national parks, forest parks, scenic reserves and regional parks, and these are among its greatest attractions.

New Zealanders love the outdoors and are committed to preserving the country's natural heritage. New Zealand's 14 national parks are closely protected by the Department of Conservation (DOC), and each offers a distinct range of landscapes, vegetation and wildlife. In-depth information on each park's geology, flora, fauna, historic sights and conservation initiatives can be found by visiting the DOC visitor centres, located in the parks and all cities.

Together with the national parks, a series of 20 forest parks safeguards the country's indigenous forests, and 4,000 regional parks and scenic reserves protect localised landscapes. Marine reserves, New Zealand's 'national parks of the sea', are where marine life is also fully protected.

Great Walks

Hiking is very popular in the national parks, and people come from all over the world to tackle iconic walks like Fiordland's Milford Track. A particular highlight is the nine multi-day hikes known as 'Great Walks', which are the routes considered to be the country's most significant.

Passes or tickets must be purchased to stay in huts en route, and can be obtained from the DOC.

Admiring the views on the Lake Waikaremoana Track in Te Urewera National Park

Prices range from NZ$7–35 per night for a hut bed, or NZ$5–10 for a serviced campsite. You can choose to hike independently, or join a guided walk. For detailed topographical maps and information on hikes and hiking passes nationwide, see www.doc.govt.nz.

In addition to the Great Walks, there are thousands of short walks where you can hike without seeing a soul; and the national park network provides a broad range of other ways to enjoy life in the great outdoors, from glacier-hiking to kayaking. This is backed up by a host of reputable tour operators with the expertise to safely guide visitors' exploration of New Zealand's wilderness environments.

Hiking the North Island

Summer and the shoulder seasons are the best times to hike in the North Island and the iridescent blue and emerald lakes, steaming crater lakes, old lava flows and vast open landscapes of Tongariro National Park are condensed into a day on the **Tongariro Crossing**, New Zealand's best one-day hike. Other hikes include the Ruapehu summit walk, lead by **Mount Ruapehu Alpine Guides** (tel: 07-892 3738; www.mtruapehu.com; charge), and the 'Great Walks' Tongariro Northern Circuit, which can be hiked independently or with a group by joining **Ruapehu Backcountry Guides** (tel: 06-385 8456).

A challenging hike is to the summit of the 2,515m (8,250ft) volcano, Taranaki, in the **Egmont National Park**, which provides excellent views of Taranaki's lush dairy

Top 5 National Park Experiences

- Cruising Milford or Doubtful Sound
- Spotting wild kiwi on the Rakiura Track
- Glacier-hiking on Fox or Franz Josef glaciers
- Jet-boating Fiordland's Wairaurahiri River
- Scenic flight of Aoraki Mount Cook

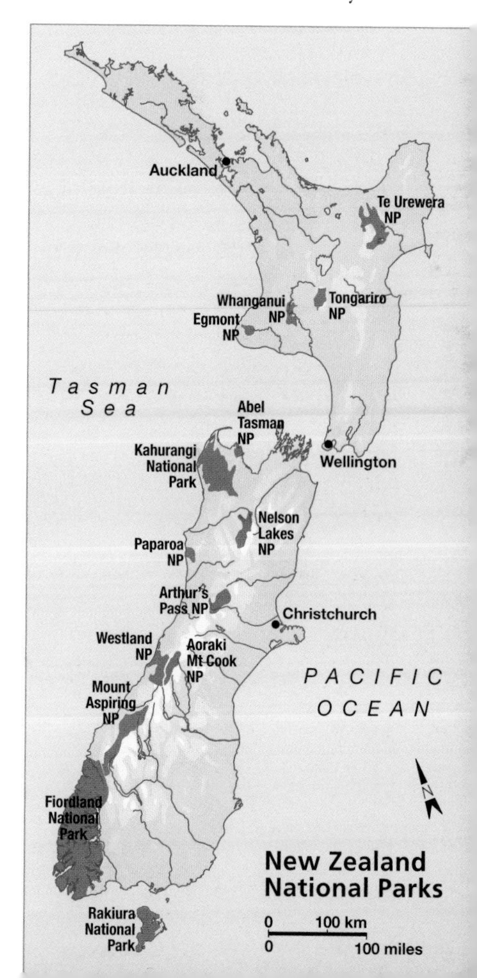

pastures. For safe passage, begin the hike from the **North Egmont Visitor Centre** (top end of Egmont Road; tel: 06-756 0990), where information and detailed maps of Taranaki's other highlights, including the hanging mosses of the Goblin Forest, Dawsons Falls and Wilkies Pools, are found. Alternatively, book in for an informative guided walk with **Mount Taranaki Guided Tours** (tel: 06 765 6234; www.macalpineguides.com).

At 212,000 hectares (524,000 acres), **Te Urewera National Park** is the largest untouched tract of native forest in the North Island. Its mist-shrouded valleys, dramatic bluffs, towering native forests, tumbling waterfalls and shimmering springs are unforgettable. Amid this is Lake Waikaremoana, thick with bush to the water's edge on all but the eastern side, where it is hemmed in by steep cliffs. Hikes here include the Lake Waikaremoana Track, a four-day Great Walks route through vegetation ranging from montane beech forest to dense podocarp rainforest. Short walks such as Aniwaniwa and Mokau falls, Lake Waikareiti and the Lake Kaitawa Fairy Springs Track are equally impressive.

The **Whanganui National Park** encompasses the largest tract of lowland forest and its numerous river valleys provide ideal terrain for those hiking the Whanganui Great Walks route.

Hiking the South Island

At the top of the South Island, the three-day Great Walks Coastal Track in **Abel Tasman** is fast gaining popularity. It follows the coastline past the Tonga Island Marine Reserve, where seals often doze on the rocks. If you are pressed for time, consider catching a water taxi one-way with **Aqua**

Egmont National Park encircles the slopes of Mount Taranaki

Boating on Lake Waikaremoana in Te Urewera National Park

Taxi (tel: 03-527 8083; www.aquataxi.co.nz) and hiking a short section of the track.

In the **Nelson Lakes National Park,** Saint Arnaud provides a good base for hikers heading out to tackle the Lake Rotoiti Circuit, the Mount Robert Loop Track, and the St Arnaud Range Track.

The vast **Kahurangi National Park**, New Zealand's second largest, is a 452,000-hectare (1-million acre) wilderness of native forest and nikau palms, renowned for its limestone and marble outcrops and caves. Track networks allow exploration of its rivers, plateaux, Alpine herb fields and coastal forests. Its most celebrated hike is the 85km (53-mile) -long Heaphy Track, a Great Walks route of four to five days. You can freedom hike carrying your own pack, or join experienced groups such as **Southern Wilderness** (tel: 03-546 7349; www.southernwilderness.com).

A favourite at **Paparoa National Park** is the 20-minute loop walk to the Pancake Rocks and blowholes of Dolomite Point at Punakaiki. Other popular hikes include the Truman Track, and the longer Pororari River Track which leads to an intriguing limestone gorge.

In **Arthur's Pass**, all hikes are carefully graded, from those that provide wheelchair access through to mountain trails requiring specialised equipment. Interesting short walks include the Devil's Punchbowl Waterfall, Bridal Veil Creek, Bealey Valley and the Dobson Nature Walk.

Summer is the only time to hike in **Aoraki Mount Cook National Park** and there is a range of easy half-day and day walks to choose from, including Kea Point, Hooker Valley and the Tasman Glacier Viewpoint tracks. Experienced Alpine hikers can tackle the Mueller, Copland and Ball passes. For guided walks and heli-hiking tours in this region, contact **Discovery Tours** (tel: 03-435 0114; www.discoverytours.co.nz).

Westland Tai Poutini National Park has 110km (68 miles) of walking

Hiking in Abel Tasman

tracks with varied native forest and birdlife, all dominated by the lofty peaks of Cook, Tasman and La Perouse. This trio of mountains is best seen mirrored in Lake Matheson on an early morning walk. The most popular walks lead to the park's famous glaciers, the one-hour return Fox Glacier Valley Walk, and the two-hour return Franz Josef Glacier Hukatere Valley Walk.

Established in 1964, **Mount Aspiring National Park** is home to the Routeburn Track Great Walks route, as well as the multi-day Greenstone Track and Dart/Rees River circuit. These can be completed independently or on a guided tour with **Ultimate Hikes** (tel: 03-450 1940; www.ultimatehikes.co.nz) or **Adventure South** (tel: 03-942 1222; www.advsouth.co.nz). A number of other excellent short walks are found in Haast Pass on State Highway 6.

Fiordland National Park is renowned for its two Great Walks, the Milford Track and the Kepler Track. Of these, the 53.5km (33-mile) Milford Track is the most popular and bookings must be made well in advance with DOC (www.doc.govt.nz) or with a group trekking company like **Ultimate Hikes** (tel: 03-450 1940; www.ultimatehikes.co.nz). **Real Journeys** (tel: 03-249 7416; www.realjourneys.co.nz) offer a taste of the Milford Track on a guided day walk. Alternative multi-day hikes include the Hollyford Valley Track and the Tuatapere Humpridge Track (tel: 03-226 6739, 0800 486 774; www.humpridgetrack.co.nz) at the southeastern end of Fiordland National Park.

Hiking Stewart Island

Rakiura National Park, New Zealand's newest, opened in 2002. The park covers 157,000 hectares (388,000 acres) – approximately 85 percent of the island – and its 245km (150-mile) network of walking tracks, easily accessed from Oban, makes it a paradise for walkers and hikers. Some of the island's least demanding walks take only 15 minutes, while others require a high level of fitness, stamina and self-reliance. The three-day Rakiura Track, a Great Walks route passing through forest, is suitable for anyone with a moderate level of fitness.

Mountaineering and Glacier-Hiking

The South Island's **Aoraki Mount Cook National Park** is where some of the tallest peaks soar, including New Zealand's highest, 3,754m

(12,316ft) -high Aoraki Mount Cook. The park is only 80km (50 miles) long, yet it contains 140 peaks over 2,134m (7,011ft) high as well as 72 glaciers, including five of New Zealand's largest – the Godley, Murchison, Tasman, Hooker and Mueller. Of these, the Tasman Glacier is the southern hemisphere's bulkiest, 27km (17 miles) in length. **Alpine Guides** (tel: 03-435 1834; www.alpineguides.co.nz) operate guided climbs of Aoraki Mount Cook and other peaks during the summer, as well as an intensive mountaineering course.

New Zealand's most famous glaciers reside in the neighbouring **Westland Tai Poutini National Park**, and visitors can choose to explore the deep crevasses and cerulean depths with scenic flights, heli-hiking and glacier-hiking tours. The latter, a budget-friendly option, involves strapping on specialised crampon-like footwear and journeying through a fascinating landscape of stunning, electrifying-blue tunnels that pierce the bright white expanses of snow. Half- and full-day guided glacier walking tours are offered by **Franz Josef Glacier Guides** (tel: 03-752 0763; www.franzjosefglacier.com) and **Fox Glacier Guiding** (tel: 03-751 0825; www.foxguides.co.nz).

Getting out on the Water

Kayaking and canoeing on the Whanganui River is the most popular activity in the North Island's **Whanganui National Park**, and the river offers more than 230km (143 miles) of peaceful paddling. Reputable companies offering kayak and canoe trips include **Wades Landing Outdoors** (tel: 07-895 5995; www.whanganui.co.nz), **Yeti Tours** (tel: 06-385 8197; www.yetitours.co.nz) and **Blazing Paddles** (tel: 07-895 5261). Alternatively, jet-

Glacier-gazing in Aoraki Mount Cook National Park

Kayak trips are a popular way of exploring the bays and lagoons of Abel Tasman

boat tours of the river are offered by **Bridge to Nowhere** (tel: 0800 480 308; www.bridgetonowhere.co.nz) and Wades Landing Outdoors *(see p.27)*. Trips include a visit to the 'Bridge to Nowhere' or, more accurately, a bridge in the middle of nowhere, built to service a new settlement for soldiers after World War I, but subsequently abandoned due to farming difficulties during the 1930s depression.

Abel Tasman National Park, a coastal paradise of golden beaches, large tranquil lagoons, deep-reaching estuaries, forested hills and impossibly clear waters at the top of the South Island, provides a number of ways to enjoy its pristine environment, from sailing with **Abel Tasman Sailing Adventures** (tel: 03-527 8375; www.sailingadventures.co.nz), sea-kayaking (independently or as part of a guided group) with **Abel Tasman Kayaks** (tel: 03-527 8022; www.abeltasmankayaks.co.nz), as well as hiking, swimming, snorkelling and fishing.

The diverse range of landscapes in **Paparoa National Park**, including thick coastal forests and glades of nikau palms, canyons, caves and underground streams, can be explored by kayak or canoe with **River Kayaking** (tel: 03-731 1870; www.riverkayaking.co.nz).

Meanwhile, you can navigate the waterways of **Fiordland National Park**, New Zealand's largest wilderness area, by jet boating on the Wairaurahiri River from Lake Hauroko with **Hump Ridge Jet** (tel: 03-225 8174; www.wildernessjet.co.nz) or by lake- and sea-kayaking with **Adventure Kayak & Cruise** (tel: 03-249 6626; www.fiordlandadventure.co.nz). Organised tours/cruises of Milford Sound are offered by **Southern Discoveries** (tel: 03-441 1137; www.redboats.co.nz), and **Real Journeys** (tel: 03-249 7416; www.realjourneys.co.nz); both companies provide tours of Harrison Cove's Underwater Observatory, and Real Journeys also runs tours/cruises on Doubtful Sound. Kayaking at Milford Sound is an option with **Fiordland Wilderness Experiences** (tel: 03-249 7700; www.fiordlandsea kayak.co.nz).

Mount Aspiring National Park can be viewed on a jet boat excursion with **Dart River Safaris** (tel: 03-442 9992; www.dartriver.co.nz); canoeing excursions and canyoning trips are also available.

A rare encounter awaits visitors at **Aoraki Mount Cook**, where **Glacier Explorers** (tel: 03-435 1641; www. glacierexplorers.com) whisks passengers across the iceberg-littered waters of Tasman Glacier Terminal Lake.

Whitewater rafting is offered on the mid- to lower reaches of the Tongariro River with **Tongariro River Rafting** (tel: 0800 101 024; www.trr.co.nz). Alternatively, cruises are available in many parks; these include guided lake cruises at **Te Urewera National Park** with **Home Bay Water Taxi** (tel: 06-837 3826) – kayaks can also be rented on the lake from **Lake Waikaremoana Motor Camp** (State Highway 38; tel: 06-837 3826; www.lake.co.nz) – and at **Nelson Lakes National Park**, where cruises and rowboat, canoe and kayak hire are available from **Rotoiti Water Taxis** (tel: 03-521 1894; www.rotoiti watertaxis.co.nz).

Safety in the National Parks

Keep safe in New Zealand's National Parks and look after yourself:

- New Zealand's weather can change quickly; make sure you are prepared for unseasonal weather
- Talk to DOC staff or read information guides before departing, and take a topographical map, high-energy foods, sunblock, warm clothing, first-aid kit and wet-weather gear
- Ensure someone knows your plans and time of return. You can sign in with DOC (at Visitor Centres) before starting out and again when you return: a 5-minute job that could save your life
- Boil, chemically treat or filter river water before drinking it

Skiing

During the winter, there's skiing and snow-sports at national park ski fields. Two commercial ski fields operate on Mount Ruapehu in the **Tongariro National Park**. The northwestern slopes of the Whakapapa Ski Field have huge, snow-filled basins with steep shutes, drop-offs and powder stashes, while Turoa Ski Field to the southwest has a wide open bowl with superb conditions throughout October and November.

Arthur's Pass has one popular club field located at Temple Basin. It relies on fresh packed powder to provide perfect conditions and, with its fairly steep terrain and series of basins and shoots, it's a good intermediate-to-advanced field. The down side of skiing here is the vigorous walk up to the field – 30 minutes from the 4WD car park, or otherwise 50 minutes. Although it puts a lot of people off, it does mean there are no queues. There is, however, a goods lift, which makes for an easier hike.

Other club fields are located nearby in the adjoining **Craigieburn Forest**

Park. These include Mount Cheeseman, Broken River and Craigieburn. Contrary to popular belief, you don't have to be invited to club fields; in fact, their main distinction from commercial fields is that there are fewer people. The club fields also have a 'home-based' atmosphere, as most were set up by families in the 1940s and have grown as generation after generation has returned with friends to enjoy the slopes.

At **Aoraki Mount Cook**, snowsports run from July to September. However, as the slopes are accessed by air, this is an expensive affair. **Alpine Guides** (tel: 03-435 1834; www.alpineguides.co.nz) provide a range of heli-skiing options including the exciting Tasman Glacier descent.

Other smaller ski fields located at national parks include the **Manganui Club Ski Field** (tel: 06-759 1119; http://skitaranaki.co.nz) at **East Egmont**, and the small club field at Mount Robert in **Nelson Lakes National Park**; the latter is accessed by a stiff two-hour hike, or weather permitting, you can catch a ride in a helicopter. Both welcome visitors.

Fishing and Hunting

Craggy peaks dominate the **Nelson Lakes National Park** and glistening among them are the trout-laden waters of Lake Rotoiti and Lake Rotoroa. The fishing is renowned here and local guides like **John Gendall Fly Fishing** (tel: 03-548 7892; www.johngendallflyfishing.com) will share their favourite spots, or you can hire a rod in Saint Arnaud

Snowboarding at Whakapapa Ski Field

and head out alone. Fishing is also on offer at **Te Urewera National Park** and equipment can be hired from the store at **Lake Waikaremoana Motor Camp** (SH38; tel: 06-837 3826; www.lake.co.nz). The hunting of introduced animals, such as possums, wild pigs, feral goats and many species of deer, is encouraged in most parks by the DOC. A hunting permit is required if you wish to hunt on conservation land and it pays to hire a professional hunting guide. A complete list of members of the **New Zealand Professional Hunting Guides Association** can be found by visiting www.nzphga.com.

Birdwatching

Visitors to New Zealand's national parks can expect to see all kinds of native birds, and parks provide sanctuary for many rare and endangered species.

There are also opportunities to seek out rare birdlife. For example, the kotuku, or white heron, is found only in the **Okarito Lagoon**, New Zealand's largest natural wetland, covering an area of 3,240 hectares (8,006 acres). Boat trips with **White Heron Sanctuary Tours** (tel: 03-753 4120; www.whiteherontours.co.nz) provide access to the colony, as do guided kayak trips with **Okarito Nature Tours** (tel: 03-573 4014; www.okarito.co.nz).

Ulva Island, an open sanctuary for birds, is the jewel in the crown of **Stewart Island**. This predator-free island, robed in a primeval podocarp forest, is alive with the song of some of New Zealand's most endangered birds. For an in-depth tour join **Ulva's Guided Walks** (tel: 03-219 1216; www.ulva.co.nz).

Stewart Island's three-day Rakiura Track also provides a good introduction to the park's birdlife, including Stewart Island kiwi and the blue penguin. Spotting wild kiwi is common.

The beech forests at **Nelson Lakes National Park**, where short walks include the Bellbird and Honeydew tracks, resound with native birdsong thanks to DOC's intensive management of pests. Displays on the project can be viewed at the DOC Visitor Centre in Saint Arnaud.

A plethora of other birds including tui, robin, kereru (native pigeon) and even the rare saddleback are often seen throughout the national park network. In **Te Urewera National Park** listen for the chatty ki-ki-ki of the kakariki and the rude screech of the kaka, and in **Arthur's Pass** keep an eye on your keys, and your car; removing rubber windscreen seals is something of a rite of passage for young bachelor kea, New Zealand's cheeky green-feathered parrot!

The kaka, a native New Zealand parrot, can be seen (and heard) in Te Urewera National Park

Wildlife Adventures

New Zealand offers marine and land-based wildlife adventures aplenty, from spying upon yellow-eyed penguins and their little blue cousins, swimming with protected marine mammals such as dolphins and seals, watching whales frolic at close range, and participating in conservation efforts to help save kiwi and other endangered birds.

New Zealand is one of the most isolated places in the world. The vast expanse of ocean that has separated these islands from any other appreciable landmass for millions of years has meant that local flora and fauna have evolved in complete isolation from the rest of the world. Prior to the relatively recent arrival of humans, the islands were a haven for flightless birds, and the only terrestrial mammals to be found here were bats. The top predator was a bird – the giant Haast eagle, which preyed on moa up to 20 times heavier than itself.

With Maori settlement came an increased frequency of fires, the removal of forests and the rapid extinction of birdlife. Europeans speeded up the process; large areas of forest were milled or burnt down, and the introduction of grazing animals and farming dramatically altered the landscape. Other introduced species including weasels, stoats, cats and rodents wrought havoc on the native birdlife.

Today, New Zealand's most pressing environmental issue is the conservation of its remaining species. Many of these, including the tuatara, kiwi and kakapo, are bred in captivity while sanctuaries are prepared for their safe return to the wild. Fortunately, over the last 25 years, conservation efforts, including extensive pest eradication programmes and the establishment of sanctuaries on predator-free islands, have rescued many species from the brink of extinction.

Preparing for an expedition to release a rare kakapo back into the wild

New Zealand is now a world leader in conservation management and its protected land and sea-based reserves are extremely successful.

Top 10 Wildlife Encounters

- Whale Watch, Kaikoura
- Ulva Island Bird Sanctuary, Stewart Island
- National Aquarium, Napier
- Kiwi spotting with Footprints Waipoua, Northland
- Penguin Place, Otago Peninsula
- Tiritiri Matangi Island, Auckland
- Tuatara at Southland Museum
- Seal Swim, Kaikoura
- Rainbow Springs Kiwi Wildlife Park, Rotorua
- Swimming with Hector's dolphins, Akaroa

Dolphins off the coast at Kaikoura

Some reserves have no public access to ensure they remain pristine; others are open sanctuaries where licensed tour operators and experienced guides provide a broad range of ways to get up close to New Zealand's native wildlife and marine life.

Whales

Many species of whale frequent the coastline, including eight species of baleen whale and 30 species of toothed whales. New Zealand's waters provide a safe haven as all marine mammals are fully protected by law.

During winter, humpback whales are regularly spotted heading south along the east coast, and also swimming north up the west coast during spring. Occasional beach sightings are also made of southern right whales. Populations of these whales have soared, from 500 at their lowest level in the 1920s, to around 7–8,000 today.

For breathtakingly close encounters with sperm whales, head to Kaikoura, where scheduled **Whale Watch** tours (tel: 0800 655 121; www.whalewatch.co.nz; tours daily 7.15am, 10am, 12.45pm, 3.30pm) make this activity accessible to all. Whales are also often spotted (at a distance) on the inter-island ferry journey across the Cook Strait. And don't be surprised if you find yourself in the midst of a whale rescue team; migrating pilot whales often get stranded in summer – sometimes hundreds at a time – and you may be called upon to help Kiwis refloat them.

Dolphins

Dolphins make the most of their fully protected status in New Zealand and 10 species routinely frolic along the coast. The small and rare Hector's dolphin is endemic to New Zealand and sizeable populations of these dolphins reside in and around the Akaroa Harbour. View them at close range with **Black Cat Cruises** (tel: 03-304 7641;

www.blackcat.co.nz; [family icon]), and swim beside them if you wish. As with all dolphin swimming tours in New Zealand, operators provide wetsuits and general guidelines. Hector's dolphins enjoy riding bow-waves and are often seen in and around Kaikoura, their distinctive rounded dorsal fins and pretty black, grey and white markings making them easily identifiable from others. Kaikoura-based **Dolphin Encounters** (tel: 0800 733 365; www.dolphinencounter.co.nz) offers a chance to get in the water and swim with a number of species.

Further north, the Bay of Islands is a prime location to swim with larger bottlenose and common dolphin. Daily trips depart from Paihia with **Fullers** (tel: 09-402 7421; www.fboi.co.nz) and cruise the bay to swim with various pods.

The Seal Swim Kaikoura tour is recommended

Seals and Sea Lions

New Zealand fur seals reside throughout the country but are prolific throughout the southern half of the North Island and the South Island. Sizeable colonies can be seen along the Southern Wairarapa coastline, Cape Foulwind near Westport, Gillespie Beach near Fox Glacier, and at several points along the Kaikoura coast. On land, it generally pays to keep a distance of 10m (30ft) between you and them; however, in the water they are less vulnerable and a lot more playful. Boat- or land-based seal-snorkelling tours offered by **Seal Swim Kaikoura** (tel: 03-319 6182; www.sealswimkaikoura.co.nz) allow safe encounters with these friendly creatures.

New Zealand sea lions are also often spotted along the southern coastlines of the South Island; sometimes they'll be hanging out with their buddies, the sub-Antarctic elephant seal and the leopard seal. The lighthouse at Waipapa Point in the Catlins is a favourite lounging site, as is the beach at Cannibal Bay.

Sharks

New Zealand is recognised as a hotspot for great white sharks; nevertheless, 66 shark species from the tiny pygmy shark to the 12m (40ft) -long whale shark also make their home here. Encounters with sharks in coastal waters usually occur during warmer months when common threshers sharks, hammerhead sharks and bronze whalers move in-shore to have their pups. However, for a safer encounter head to the **National Aquarium** (Marine Parade; tel: 06-834 1404; www.nationalaquarium.co.nz) in Napier, where fully guided swimming with sharks is an option – if you dare. **Kelly Tarlton's Underwater World** (Tamaki Drive, Okahu Bay; tel: 09-531 5065; www.kellytarltons.co.nz) in Auckland also provides the chance to view sharks through a partially submerged enclosure.

Marine Life

To see a full range of marine life at its finest, you should visit a marine reserve. Of these, New Zealand's most renowned is the **Poor Knights Islands Marine Reserve**, off Northland's Tutukaka coast. Here you will discover a microcosm of underwater life, with 125 species of fish residing among dense kelp forests, sand gardens, giant sea caves, archways and massive underwater caverns. Cnidarians, bryozoans, sponges and ascidians construct intricate scaffoldings amid the kelp, and giant black stingrays gather in archways to meet before they mate. Visitors from warmer climes include Lord Howe coralfish, spotted black and toadstool grouper, yellow banded perch and banded coral shrimp.

A number of charter and tour boats provide access to the islands from Tutukaka, including **Dive Poor Knights** (tel: 0800 693 483) and **Poor Knights Dive Centre** (tel: 09-434 3867; www.diving.co.nz). Full-day sea-kayaking tours with **Pacific Coast Kayaks** (tel: 09-436 1947; www.seakayaking.co.nz) provide an alternative way to explore, as do cruises with **Perfect Day Ocean Cruise** (tel: 0800 288 882; www.aperfectday.co.nz).

Penguins

Southern New Zealand is home to the world's rarest penguin, the hoiho

Yellow-eyed penguin on the Otago Peninsula

(noise shouter), otherwise known as the yellow-eyed penguin. You can view these penguins in the wild at Curio Bay in the Catlins, Monro Beach on the West Coast and Stewart Island. However, be aware that over-eager ecotourists are affecting nest survival rates, so treat these sites with the respect they deserve. Better still, lessen your environmental impact by visiting **Penguin Place** (tel: 03-478 0286; www.penguinplace.co.nz) on Otago Peninsula, where a private landowner has converted his farm to a penguin sanctuary. The penguins can be freely viewed at extremely close range through a unique system of hides and tunnels.

Meanwhile, New Zealand's cute Little Blue penguins can be seen nationwide. However, the best place to view them as they come ashore by the hundred is at **Oamaru Blue Penguin Colony** (tel: 03-433 1195; www.penguins.co.nz) in Otago. Little Blues can also be viewed in an enclosure at the **New Zealand Little Blue Penguin Encounter** (tel: 03-353 7798; www.iceberg.co.nz) at the International Antarctic Centre in Christchurch, while captive king and gentoo penguins can be seen at **Kelly Tarlton's** *(see p.35)* in Auckland.

How You Can Help

With each new visitor comes the risk of a new pest or disease entering New Zealand. These can be bought in on dirty outdoor gear including tramping boots, and on camping or sports equipment. If you enjoy visiting natural areas, whether to picnic or to hike through rainforest, take note of signposts providing guidelines on how to protect native plants and wildlife. Many ecosystems are extremely fragile and can take years to recover from damage.

Birdwatching

New Zealand has many unique birds, including its highly protected national icon, the kiwi. Some, such as the little spotted kiwi, are endangered and only survive on offshore island sanctuaries. These sanctuaries provide a safe haven for a wide range of rare and endangered birdlife, including takahe, kaka, kea, kiwi and saddleback. While some reserves are closed to ensure they remain in a pristine state, others can be visited with licensed operators.

From Auckland, trips to Tiritiri Matangi Island can be organised through **360 Discovery Cruises** (tel: 0800 360 3472; www.360discovery.co.nz). In Wellington, **Kapiti Tours** (tel: 04-237 7965; www.kapititours.co.nz) provide passage to Kapiti Island, while **Dolphin Watch Ecotours** (tel: 03-573 8040; www.naturetours.co.nz) provide tours to the island sanctuary of Motuara Island in the Marlborough Sounds.

Introduced predators are the biggest threat to native birdlife, and the Department of Conservation (DOC) protects wild nests by trapping, shooting and poisoning predators. It also raises chicks in captivity and releases them into the wild. You can see this important conservation work first-hand at captive-breeding facilities. Locations include the

Tuatua at Rainbow Springs Kiwi Wildlife Park

Auckland Zoo (Motions Road, Western Springs; tel: 09-360 3800; www.aucklandzoo.co.nz), Kiwi Encounter at **Rainbow Springs Kiwi Wildlife Park** (Fairy Springs Road; tel: 07-347 9301; www.rainbowsprings.co.nz) in Rotorua, and the **Native Bird Recovery Centre** (SH14, Maunu; tel: 09-438 1457) in Whangarei – to name just a few.

In Northland the large Brown kiwi is widespread, and **Footprints Waipoua** (tel: 09-405 8207; www.footprintswaipoua.com) lead daily twilight kiwi-spotting tours. Stewart Island is also renowned for its prolific populations of Stewart Island kiwi. These can be seen all over the island and at **Ulva Island**, located in the Paterson Inlet, also a haven for numerous other endangered birds.

Tuatara and Others

Biologists come from all over the globe to see New Zealand's tuatara, a medium-sized reptile and the only survivor of the order Sphenodontia, which had many species during the age of the dinosaurs (Mesozoic era). Tuatara once roamed the mainland but now only survive on predator-free island sanctuaries like Kapiti Island. Nonetheless, captive animals and breeding programmes on New Zealand's main islands play an important part in conservation, education and research, and live interaction with tuatara can be enjoyed at **Southland Museum** (Queens Park, Gala Street, Invercargill; tel: 03-219 9069; www.southlandmuseum.com), **Wellington Zoo** (200 Daniell Street, Newtown; tel: 04-381 6755; www.wellingtonzoo.com) and **Auckland Zoo** *(see left)*.

Other noteworthy creatures include bats, New Zealand's only native land mammal, recently bred and successfully translocated by the DOC team at **Pukaha Mount Bruce** (SH2; tel: 06-375 8004; www.mtbruce.org.nz), and a rare native frog *(Leiopeima archeyi)* which resides only on the Coromandel Peninsula and is sometimes seen when hiking.

Maori Cultural Experiences

When the Maori first discovered New Zealand they described its creation in their legends of Maui. Among these, using the South Island as his canoe and Stewart Island as his anchor, Maui fished the North Island out of the sea, giving rise to its name, Te Ika a Maui (the fish of Maui), and the South Island's name Te Waka-o-Maui (Maui's canoe).

Over a thousand years ago, New Zealand's indigenous people, the Maori, arrived in Aotearoa (the land of the long white cloud) by *waka hourua* (voyaging canoes) from their ancestral homeland of Hawaiki. Poetic legends were composed to explain the unique geology they discovered in this rich and diverse new land, and historical sites were given names, many of which still exist today. At first, Maori place names can be confusing for visitors to New Zealand; however, each name provides an insight into significant historical and cultural events.

An example of this is Orakei Korako, which means 'adorning place', as it was in this North Island thermal valley where Maori chiefs once prepared themselves for ceremonies, making use of its 'mirror' pools. The Maori have a strong physical and spiritual connection with this land, and many places are named after ancestors or recall the history of local tribes.

Today, Maori legends and customs are deeply embedded in any New Zealander's psyche; Maori may only make up 14 percent of the population, but their language and culture have

An intricately carved ceremonial *waka* (canoe)

a major impact on all facets of New Zealand life, including New Zealanders' deep affinity with the land. Visitors to the country can learn more about Maori customs through a variety of easily accessible cultural experiences.

Settlements and Architecture

The Maori once lived in fortified villages built upon hills with good vantage points. Good examples of these old *pa* sites can be found all over New Zealand, particularly in the North Island, along with evidence of *kumara* pits (vegetable gardens) and shellfish-filled kitchen middens (rubbish bins). Elaborately carved *wharenui* (meeting houses) also remain, often featuring ancestral *tiki* *(see p.41)* carved on panels supporting the rafters. Examples of beautifully preserved meeting houses can be seen all over New Zealand and accessible ones include the Whare Runanga at **Waitangi National Trust Treaty Grounds** (1 Tau Henare Drive, Paihia; tel: 09-402 7437; www.waitangi.net.nz), the meeting house at **Auckland War Memorial Museum** (Auckland Domain; tel: 09-309 0443; www.aucklandmuseum.com), and **Te Poho-o-Rawiri** (tel: 06-867 2103) at the base of Kaiti Hill in Gisborne. The latter contains impressive *tukutuku* (woven reed) panels and magnificent carvings; visits are available by appointment. Many contemporary meeting houses maintain aspects of the traditional houses in terms of the basic architectural structure and decor (carving, painting and woven panels), but they invariably make use of the wide range of building materials now available.

Speaking Maori

Almost everywhere you travel in New Zealand you will encounter the Maori language as the vast majority of place names are in Maori. For advice on correct pronunciation, *see p.93*. The following is a list of common phrases; while it is by no means necessary to learn every word, try using 'kia ora' (pronounced 'key aura') whenever possible to break the ice.

kia ora	hello
haere mai	welcome
kei te pehea koe?	how's it going?
kei te pai	good
haere ra	farewell
ka kite ano	until I see you again
hei konei ra	see you later
wai	water, drink
kai	food
wahi kai	restaurant/café
heketua	toilet
hikoi	journey
hongi	traditional greeting (nose pressing)
hui	meeting
hapu	extended family
iwi	tribal group
kaumatua	elders
tamariki	children
whanau	family
Maori tanga	Maori culture
pa	fortified living area
tukutuku	woven wall panels
taonga	treasures
wahi tapu	sacred sites
urupa	burial site
wharenui	meeting house
wharekai	cooking and eating house
waiata	song, poetry
waka	traditional canoe

A formal welcome *(powhiri)* to a meeting ground *(marae)*

Marae Visits

A good way to get a feel for traditional Maori culture is by visiting a *marae* (meeting ground). Before entering the *marae*, a specific protocol is followed. This begins with a *powhiri* or formal welcome, followed by a *wero* or challenge. A warrior – perhaps carrying a spear – comes forward from the host tribe and lays down a token (often a small branch) that visitors pick up to show they come in peace. Only then are they called onto the *marae* grounds (in front of the meeting house) by women with a *karanga* (a long wailing call).

It's a riveting experience and there are several operators, particularly in Rotorua, that host *marae* visits, such as **Te Puia** (tel: 07-348 9047; www.tepuia.com). When you join a tour, follow the lead of your tour guide; remember to take off your shoes before entering a meeting house and to greet your hosts with a *hongi* (a touch of noses) to signify friendship. After the *powhiri*, there's usually a cultural performance, and sometimes traditional *kai* (food) is shared, usually cooked in a *hangi* or earth oven.

An excellent place to experience modern Maori culture is at the **Whakarewarewa Thermal Village** (tel: 07-349 3463; www.whakarewarewa.com) in Rotorua. This is an active Maori community so you may find your visit coincides with a tribal gathering or other momentous village event. All the same, you will be guided through the Whare Tupuna (ancestral house) which lies at the heart of village life. The walls of the *wharenui* feature carved and woven panels displaying the genealogy, history and culture of its residents, the local Tuhourangi Ngati Wahiao tribe. Tours include a visit to the village pre-school to hear young children conversing in their native tongue.

In the South Island, **Ko Tane** (60 Hussey Road, Harewood; tel: 03-359 6226; www.kotane.co.nz) at Christchurch provides insights into the culture of the Ngai Tahu people, and a chance to learn the *haka* and *poi* dance. In Kaikoura, small group tours led by **Maori Tours Kaikoura** (tel: 03-319 5567; www.maoritours.co.nz) learn the art of weaving with the native *harakeke* (flax) plant, and explore the traditional uses of trees and plants as food and medicine.

Maori Art Motifs

In Maori artwork the human form, dominant in most compositions, is generally referred to as a *tiki* and represents the first created man of Maori mythology. The nephrite (greenstone) *hei-tiki* pendant is the best known of ornaments. The *manaia*, another major symbol, is a beaked figure rendered in profile with a body that has arms and legs. When it is placed near *tiki* it appears to bite at them about the head and body. Sometimes *manaia* form part of the *tiki* themselves. The *koru*, a well-known symbol based on a curved stalk and a bulb motif, is today often used as a symbol of New Zealand, and also forms Air New Zealand's company logo.

Food and Hangi

If you get the chance to experience a traditional *hangi*, you're in for a real treat. This is a tender and flavour-filled feast in which meat and vegetables (typically pork, lamb, chicken, beef, kumara, potatoes, sweet corn, pumpkins, carrots and cabbages) are packed into baskets and steamed over hot rocks in an earth oven.

Uncovering a *hangi* feast from an earth oven

In order to 'put down a *hangi*', a large hole is dug in the ground. A fire is built in the pit and large stones are placed at the top. After a couple of hours only embers and white-hot rocks remain. Food baskets are placed on top and are sprayed with fresh water to help steam the food. Then everything is covered with clean wet cloths, followed by wet sacks and soil to help seal in any escaping steam. The whole process from beginning to end takes about six hours. Today, stainless-steel baskets are used in place of traditional woven flax baskets, and foil, rather than leaves, is used to wrap food.

Sharing food with family and friends is an important part of the *hangi* tradition, and is considered a means of communicating goodwill. Naturally, home-cooked *hangi* has the edge on that which is commercially prepared, but good experiences are offered by **Te Puia Maori Arts and Crafts Institute** (tel: 07-348 9047; www.tepuia.com) and **Mitai Maori Village** (196 Fairy Springs Road; tel: 07-343 9132; www.mitai.co.nz), both in Rotorua.

Other Maori delicacies worth trying include mutton birds (sooty petrel), freshwater eels and seafood such as paua (abalone), pipi and tuatua (shellfish), and kina (prickly sea urchins), which can be tasted at speciality seafood restaurants and cafés.

Performance, Music and Dance

Maori is an oral culture rich with stories and legends, music, performance and dance. Music has always played a major role in Maori life, and before the arrival of Europeans, instruments were fashioned from wood, whalebone and even stone. Traditional chants and songs *(waiata)* are an important feature of ceremonies such as funerals and weddings. So, too, is Maori dance, which is both rhythmic and physical, with the beat added by the slapping of chest and thighs, foot-stamping or sometimes the hitting of sticks. *Kapa haka* (cultural dance) groups take part in competitions every year to find the best performers, and some of these groups travel internationally to share these cultural arts. For visitors, the best way to experience Maori dance and song is at a cultural show. Accessible venues with good demonstrations include **Auckland War Memorial Museum** *(see p.39)* as well as **Te Puia** and **Mitai Maori Village** *(see left)*.

Be sure to catch a performance of the *kapa haka*

Maori carving on a meeting house in Rotorua

Arts and Crafts

Maori culture has a long tradition of arts and crafts, and traditional rituals such as carving, weaving and tattooing *(moko)* continue today. To see young people learning to carve wood, bone and greenstone, visit **Te Puia Maori Arts and Crafts Institute** in Rotorua *(see left)*. Nationwide, greenstone carving in particular has evolved into an extraordinarily intricate art form, and examples of these works can be found in numerous artisan stores and studios. If you wish to learn to carve your own bone or greenstone pendant, there are many places to do so, including the **Bone Studio** in Whitianga (6B Bryce Street; tel: 07-866 2158; www.carving.co.nz) and **Bonz 'n' Stonz** in Hokitika (16 Hamilton Street; tel: 03-755 6504; www.bonz-n-stonz.co.nz).

In ancient Maori society the traditional indication of rank was through *moko* or facial tattoo; today, it remains a visible expression of the culture. Traditional areas on the body to tattoo include the face, thighs and legs. Tattoo specialists are highly sought-after and *moko* has undergone a renaissance – it's not at all uncommon to see those adorned with this artwork sipping lattes in upmarket cafés.

There are hundreds of Maori artists working in New Zealand today, and their work spans many media. The works of master carvers, such as Pakaariki Harrison, are highly sought-after, and the artists travel nationally and internationally to talk about their work. Several galleries are dedicated solely to Maori art, such as **Kura Gallery** (corner Quay and Lower Albert Street; tel: 09-302 1151; www.kuragallery.co.nz) and **Native Agent** (507b New North Road, Kingsland; tel: 09-845 3289), both in Auckland, as well as the well-priced works sold at studios in and around Ruatoria on the East Cape. However, contemporary Maori art is as diverse as its people, and wherever you travel you will find exhibitions and galleries that reward investigation.

Maori Carving

Prior to the arrival of the Europeans, the Maori used carvings instead of a written language. Each carved item tells a story (*kaupapa*); it is possible to interpret the precise shape and position of various features and patterns to reveal the message within.

Thrillseeker's Paradise

In the adrenaline-pumping realm of extreme sports, New Zealand is the self-styled 'Adventure Capital of the World'. Kiwis love to spend time in the great outdoors, and wherever you travel you will find professional operators who provide a wide range of simply unforgettable experiences.

The tiny nation of New Zealand has a big reputation as nature's theme park of the South Pacific. Here you will discover a dazzling array of achievable sporting and adventure activities – most of which have been devised by passionate New Zealanders – and professional tour operators can be found in almost every town. Enjoy the buzz of shooting whitewater rapids, cycling down steep mountain trails or leaping off bungy platforms into rocky canyons – with or without a river dip. You can skydive over glaciers, join guided hikes through cerulean glacier tunnels, sea kayak through caves, abseil into canyons, hang-glide off cliffs and take part in numerous other thrilling adventures. However, whatever you choose to do, one thing is for sure: your skills and daring will be put to the ultimate test against a backdrop of breathtaking scenery.

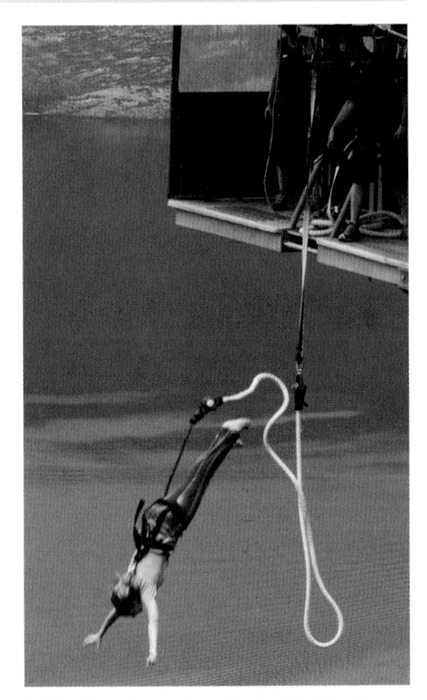

Taking the plunge from the Ledge Bungy on Bob's Peak above Queenstown

Bungy Jumps and Canyon Swings

If your pulse quickens at the thought of jumping off a bridge or platform high above the ground attached only by a single rubber band, then you will be delighted by the range of bungy options offered by **A.J. Hackett** (tel: 0800 286 4958; www.bungy.co.nz) in Queenstown in the South Island. There's the 43m (141ft) Kawarau Suspension Bridge Bungy, where spectators look on from a contemporary Bungy Centre melded into the walls of the canyon; the 47m (154ft) Ledge Bungy perched high on Bob's Peak, 400m (1,300ft) above Queenstown and offering stunning views; the 102m (335ft) Pipeline Bungy accessed by a 4WD expedition through the incredible Skippers Canyon; and the staggering 134m (440ft) Nevis Highwire Bungy.

However, Queenstown does not have a monopoly on the sport. **Mokai Gravity Canyon** (tel: 0800 802 864; www.gravitycanyon.co.nz) near Taihape in the North Island has an 80m (262ft) bungy plunging into its canyon, and the return journey is by way of a water-powered chairlift. Mokai Gravity is also home to the world's most extreme flying fox (zipline). It launches from a ledge 175m (575ft) above the canyon, and whizzes down a 1km (½-mile) wire at speeds of up to 160kmh (100mph). Plus there's a giant bridge swing where you can fly solo or in tandem, kicking off with a 50m (165ft) freefall.

Other adventures in velocity can be found at **Taupo Bungy** (tel: 0800 888 408; www.taupobungy.co.nz), where punters are released from 43m (141ft), to reach speeds of up to 70kmh (40mph). In Rotorua the **Agrodome Adventure Park** (Western Road; tel: 07-357 1050; www.agrodome.co.nz) offers 43m (141ft) bungy jumps.

Skydiving and Other Airborne Adventures

Others take to the sky to 'feel the fear but do it anyway', stepping out into thin air on a tandem skydive. At 3,960m (13,000ft), travelling towards the ground at a mind-blowing 200kmh (125mph), total sensory overload is reached. Qualified jump operators include **NZone** (tel: 0800 376 796; www.nzone.biz), which has two branches, one in Rotorua and one

Tandem skydivers experiencing the ultimate thrill of freefall

in Queenstown. To freefall with views of both North and South islands, try **Skydive Abel Tasman** (tel: 0800 422 899; www.skydive.co.nz). In Franz Josef, **Skydive New Zealand** (tel: 0800 751 0080; www.skydivingnz.co.nz) provides an incredible experience, skydiving over the region's glaciated countryside.

Balloons, hang-gliders and paragliders fill the skies above Queenstown,

Safety Tips

- Always follow the safety advice given by tour operators – they are highly trained and know their sport
- Don't be reckless. Adrenaline-pumping activities are fun but you do want to live to see another day
- Wear all safety equipment provided, including helmets and jackets, and don't take anything off, no matter what

providing alternative means of air-bound exploration. Balloon adventures are operated by **Sunrise Balloons** (tel: 03-442 0781; www.balloningnz.com), and scenic hang-gliding and paragliding can be enjoyed with a number of operators including **Extreme Air** (tel: 0800 727 245; www.extremeair.co.nz). In Canterbury, ballooning is offered through **Aoraki Balloon Safaris** (tel: 03-302 8172; www.nzballooning.com) and **Up Up and Away** (tel: 03-381 4600; ballooning.co.nz).

Whitewater Rafting, Kayaking and Jet-Boating

Water-sports are an exciting way to soak up New Zealand's river and lake scenery. At Lake Rotoiti, near Rotorua, the world's highest commercially rafted waterfall waits to be conquered with **Raftabout** (tel: 07-343 9500; www.raftabout.co.nz). Standing 7m (23ft) high and rated grade five, it's an incredible experience. Or try tandem-kayaking over the same falls with **Kaituna Kayaks** (tel: 07-624 486, www.kaitunakayaks.com).

At Queenstown in the South Island, the rugged beauty and unspoilt grandeur of the upper reaches of the Shotover River provide the setting for extreme whitewater rafting excitement with **Queenstown Rafting** (tel: 03-442 9792; www.rafting.co.nz), while the slightly tamer Kawarau River, taken on by **Raft Challenge** (tel: 0800 723 8464; www.raft.co.nz), offers a great introduction to the sport for first-timers. Alternatively, the Shotover can be tackled with **River Surfing** (tel: 0800 737 4687; www.riversurfing.co.nz), with

Kayaking the Kaituna

Money-saving Tips

- Check out any current promotions online – several companies offer special deals throughout the year.
- Check whether it's cheaper to book activities directly online – many companies offer a 10 percent discount for bookings made using their online system.
- See if combo-deals (combination offers) are available – many operators offer significant discounts if two or more activities are booked together
- If you are travelling with a friend, give them your camera. Photos provided by tour operators are an added extra and can be expensive.

just a body board between you and the torrent.

If pure, engine-throttling speed is more your style, buckle yourself in for a knuckle-clenching ride across the churning Waikato River on the **Huka Falls Jet** (tel: 07-374 8572; www.hukafallsjet.com), or skim past rocky outcrops and narrow canyons with Queenstown's **Shotover Jet** (tel: 0800 746 868; www.shotoverjet.com).

Kayaking offers sedate exploration of New Zealand's sounds, rivers and coastal waterways, and tour operators can be found nationwide. The most popular place to kayak is through the golden bays of Abel Tasman National Park, where **Kahu Kayaks** (tel: 0800 300 101; www.kahukayaks.co.nz) provide freedom rentals and organised guided trips.

Don't overlook Okarito Lagoon on South Island's west coast; **Glacier Country Kayaks** (tel: 0800 423 262; www.glacierkayaks.com) offer tours of this quiet backwater where New Zealand's highest mountain peaks reflect clearly upon its black tannin-filled waters.

Surfing, Windsurfing and Kitesurfing

New Zealand's coastlines and far-reaching harbours provide excellent opportunities for water-board sports. Equipment can be hired from rental shops at all major beach resorts. In Auckland during summer, windsurfers, kitesurfers and jet-ski equipment can be rented from **Mission Bay Watersports** (tel: 09-521 7245 www.windsurfauckland.com) on Tamaki Drive, and lessons are also available. Kitesurfing is currently New Zealand's favourite water sport and there is no better place to learn how than at Auckland's Manukau Harbour with **Ocean Xtreme Kitesurfing** (tel: 09-291 9366; www.oceanxtreme.co.nz).

New Zealand has numerous surf breaks, and many are well known internationally. Surfers flock to Manu Bay in Raglan, Shipwreck Bay near Ahipara and the Taranaki coastline. Surfers and kitesurfers alike love the waves of the Bay of Plenty, where a string of beaches provides outstanding surf. The **New Zealand**

New Zealand has great surfing conditions throughout the country

Discovery Surf School (tel: 027-632 7873; www.discoverysurf.co.nz) at Mount Maunganui provides year-round lessons and equipment.

Rock Climbing and Caving

Rock climbing and abseiling can be experienced with **Climbing Queenstown** (tel: 03-409 2508; www.climbingqueenstown.com), where a series of iron rungs, ladders and wires attached to a mountainside provides a great starting point for first-timers. Meanwhile, at Aoraki Mount Cook village **Alpine Guides** (tel: 03-435 1834; www.alpineguides.co.nz) run rock-climbing expeditions.

Several regions offer caving and canyoning trips; however, for an unbeatable experience, head to the Waitomo District in the North Island, famous for its labyrinthine caves which are wonderful for abseiling, caving, black-water rafting and canyoning with experienced operators like **Waitomo Adventures** (tel: 07-878 7788; www.waitomo.co.nz).

Off-road Driving and Mountain Biking

Still not satisfied? Try heading off-road. At **Off-Road NZ** (tel: 07-332 5748; www.offroadnz.co.nz) near Rotorua you can put your 4WD skills to the test on a bush safari along steep, rough tracks, through muddy waterholes and tunnels, and across precariously positioned bridges, to a luge, a steep 7m (23ft) slope requiring a controlled skid into knee-deep water.

Rotorua is also the place to come to experience mountain biking in the Whakarewarewa Forest, where there's an extensive network of mountain biking trails to suit all levels of ability. **Planet Bike** (tel: 07-346 1717; www.planetbike.co.nz) provides bike and equipment hire, instruction for beginners and a variety of all-inclusive mountain biking tours. Novices can learn all the basics, such as braking and gear

Mountain biking at Ninety Mile Beach

Tackling the landscape in the Zorb

changing, downhill and uphill positioning and how to ride through mud, sand and gravel.

In the South Island the Queenstown-based 4WD company **Nomad Safaris** (tel: 03-442 6699; www.nomadsafaris.co.nz) explores the Skippers Canyon, snaking along a treacherously narrow trail with deep vertical drops to the Shotover River. The company also leads 4WD tours up the Arrow River, where several deep river crossings are negotiated en route to Macetown, a ghost town where hundreds of miners once lived when alluvial gold was discovered here in 1862.

Zorbing and More

New Zealanders, it would seem, are constantly dreaming up whimsical and sometimes downright wacky ways in which to engage with the outdoors. Nowhere is this more apparent than at the **Agrodome** (tel: 07-357 1050; www.agrodome.co.nz) in Rotorua. It's home to a number of extreme sports, including the Zorb, an enormous, clear plastic ball that you climb inside and then roll down a hillside; the Shweeb velodrome, a human-powered monorail racetrack; and the Freefall Extreme where, having been kitted up in a flying suit, goggles and gloves, you'll fly unaided, up to 4m (13ft) high, suspended on a wind tunnel. It takes practice before you can swoop and soar like a pro, and like many activities in New Zealand it should come with a warning: defying gravity is addictive!

Bravery Rating

Activities are rated here from moderately tame (✱) to highly addictive (✱✱✱✱✱). Some feature a range which indicates that these activities can also be enjoyed by beginners.

Activity	Rating
Abseiling	✱–✱✱✱
Ballooning	✱✱✱
Black-water rafting	✱✱✱
Bungy jumping	✱✱✱✱
Canyon swings and high wire	✱✱–✱✱✱
Canyoning	✱–✱✱✱
Caving	✱–✱✱✱
Freefall Extreme	✱✱
Hang-gliding	✱✱✱
Jet boating	✱–✱✱✱
Kayaking	✱–✱✱✱
Mountain biking	✱–✱✱✱
Off-road/4WD	✱–✱✱
Paragliding	✱✱✱
River boarding	✱–✱✱✱
Rock climbing	✱–✱✱✱✱
Surfing	✱–✱✱✱
Shweeb	✱
Tandem sky diving	✱✱✱✱✱
Whitewater rafting	✱–✱✱✱
Windsurfing and kitesurfing	✱–✱✱✱
Zorbing	✱–✱✱

Geothermal Pools and Spas

At the end of a busy day, nothing beats sliding into a soothing thermal pool for a long hot soak. From the resort towns of Rotorua in the north to Hanmer Springs in the south, spa culture has made a comeback in the past decade.

Hot Pool Heaven

Positioned on the 'Ring of Fire', an arc of seismic and volcanic activity around the Pacific Ocean basin, New Zealand's landscape is packed with awe-inspiring natural phenomena, from smouldering volcanoes and bubbling mud pools to wildly colourful thermal lakes and hot springs.

When Maori first arrived here they made good use of what they found. Legends were formed around the origins of springs and mineral pools; some were used to soothe wounds after battles, others were conserved as sites to use for sacred ceremonies.

When the Europeans arrived on the scene in the 1800s they too capitalised on the land's volcanic resources, inviting visitors from far and wide to come and 'take the waters', and in doing so created one of New Zealand's first tourist attractions.

Although long embedded in the psyche of Kiwis, spa culture has made a comeback in the last decade. At major commercial spa resorts, all manner of optional treatments, from detoxification mud masks to massages, are on offer – as well as the obligatory soak in a soothing thermal pool. It's a sure-fire way to relax your muscles and dissolve travel tension.

Enjoying a naturally heated pool in winter at Hanmer Springs

What's more, there is a spa experience to suit everyone. In the major thermal resort towns of Rotorua (North Island), and Hanmer Springs (South Island) you will find public family pools as well as private adults-

Getting muddy at the Wai Ora Spa at Hell's Gate

only mineral spas. Smaller thermal spring towns include Te Aroha, Miranda, Parakai, Waiwera and Okoroire. Additionally, you will have the chance to go all-natural in non-chlorinated, non-commercial pools. These are often set beside, or form part of, a stream amid the towering native forest of a national park or reserve land. Or it could be an idyllic location amid the sands that fringe a lake or the sea. Here visitors can soak in delicious warmth without parting with a single cent.

North Island Spas

Situated on an active volcanic rift, Rotorua is the North Island's epicentre of thermal delight, with spouting geysers, bubbling mud pools and natural thermal springs and spas set amid jewel-like crater lakes. However, spas – family spas, luxury spas, historical spas and natural spas – are found everywhere, particularly in the northern half of the North Island.

Mud Spa

New Zealand's only mud spa is the Wai Ora Spa at **Hell's Gate** (SH30, Tikitere; tel: 07-345 3151; www.hellsgate.co.nz; daily 8.30am–8.30pm), where the local Ngati Rangi Teaorere tell ancient legends about the extraordinary healing powers of the springs, and have operated this area as a public spa since the 1880s.

Slipping into a hot private mud bath to rub thick oozing mud over one's limbs is perhaps the ultimate decadence. The mud itself is completely natural and untreated, but the pH levels are monitored to ensure they remain at a steady 5.0–5.5. To create a comfortable temperature, geothermal water is mixed with cold spring water; or, if heating is required, thermal steam is used. The wash off with cold spring water is at once excruciating and exhilarating.

Top Five Spa Locations

- **Best range of treatments:** Polynesian Spa, Rotorua
- **Best mud treatments:** Wai Ora Spa, Rotorua
- **Best pool slides:** Waiwera Infinity Thermal Spa, Auckland, and Parakai Springs, Auckland
- **Best setting overall:** Maruia Springs Thermal Resort, Lewis Pass
- **Best places to take a natural spa:** Kerosene Creek, Rotorua, and Hot Water Beach, Coromandel

Then it's straight into a sulphur pool for a long hot soak to warm up.

Although Wai Ora Spa is New Zealand's only true mud spa, it is also worth noting that tubes of thermal mud, often combined with honey, can be purchased from most souvenir shops in Rotorua to re-create the experience at home.

Family Bathing

Spas that the whole family will enjoy include **Parakai Hot Springs** (150 Parkhurst Road, Parakai; tel: 09-420 8998; daily 10am–9pm) located in West Auckland, a 45-minute drive from the CBD, and **Waiwera Infinity Thermal Spa** (21 Main Road, Waiwera; tel: 09-427 8800; www.waiwera.co.nz; Sun–Thur 9am–9pm, Fri–Sat until 10pm), a 30-minute drive north. Both parks have hot thermal slides and pools of varying temperatures which are bound to keep older kids amused for hours; little ones can splash about to their heart's content in toddler-only pools. For adults, private spa baths are hired by the half-hour, with complementary treatments including massage available.

Another good choice is **Miranda Hot Springs** (SH25; tel: 07-867 3055; www.mirandahotsprings.co.nz; daily) on the Firth of Thames. It has a super-sized main pool suitable for playing games.

Waikite Valley Thermal Pools (Waikite Valley Road; tel: 07-333 1861; www.hotpools.co.nz; daily) to the south of Rotorua offers a child-friendly main pool as well as a soak beneath rocky ledges in a running hot-water stream, massaged by miniature falls of water.

The **Opal Hot Springs and Holiday Park** (Okauia Springs Road; tel: 07-888 8198; www.opalhotsprings.co.nz; daily), to the east of Hamilton near Matamata, has three large hot mineral pools that can easily accommodate sizeable family groups.

Luxury Spas

An excellent feature of luxury spas in New Zealand is that they are often incorporated into crossover spas where family groups are welcome. A great example of this is the **Polynesian Spa** (Lake End, 1000 Hinemoa Street; tel: 07-348 1328; www.polynesianspa.co.nz; daily 8am–11pm) overlooking Lake Rotorua. It caters for everyone, with family pools, adult-only pools and private pools, as well as a separate adults-only lake spa retreat, where you can enjoy a massage or hydrotherapy treatment then relax in a series of stunningly peaceful rock pools and watch the sun set.

Historic Spas

The eastern Waikato region of North Island offers a wide variety of spa options. Smaller hot pool facilities are found beneath the misty bush-covered slopes of Mount Te Aroha at the **Te Aroha Mineral Spas and Leisure Pools** (Boundary Street; tel: 07-884 8717; www.tearohapools.co.nz; daily 11am–9pm), where an Edwardian bathhouse is set within picturesque gardens. Here the spas' silky smooth waters are sourced from 61m (200ft) below the surface and piped into a series of aromatic kauri-wood tubs. Each is set inside a private room complete with its own toilet, shower and

The Blue Baths at Rotorua occupy a Spanish Mission building

changing facilities. Aromatherapy baths and massage and beauty treatments are also available. This historic complex is also home to the world's only hot soda-water geyser.

Set among ferns on the banks of the Waihou River near Tirau, **Okoroire Hot Springs** have been in existence long before the nearby Okoroire Hot Springs Hotel was built. It is said that in 1808, on the day of his coronation, the famous Maori chief, Waikato Tairea O Ko Huiarau, was anointed with water from these sacred springs. The pools are private and can be hired by the hour at the **Okoroire Hotel** (Sommerville Road; tel: 07-883 4876; http://okohotel.co.nz; daily).

Another worthwhile historic setting is found at Rotorua's geothermally heated **Blue Baths** (Queens Drive, Government Gardens; tel: 07-350 2119; www.bluebaths.co.nz; daily 10am–6pm), where locals and visitors alike have bathed since 1933.

Natural Spa Experiences

The most novel way to toast your tootsies in New Zealand is in a natural setting, and many of these are well-kept secrets. One such place is **Te Wairua** at Lake Tarawera, reached by hiring a Clearwater Charters water taxi from **Tarawera's Landing Café** (Tarawera Road; tel: 07-362 8590; www.thelandinglaketarawera.co.nz). Once there, a two-minute walk along a bush track leads to a natural hot pool set in a tranquil glade. It's a heavenly place to visit for a private hot spa – and an unforgettable experience.

Dig yourself into a hole at Hot Water Beach

Meanwhile, the Coromandel's most famous spa experience is found at **Hot Water Beach** 👪, where, for a couple of hours either side of low tide, you can dig your very own hot spring pool. Try some refreshing hydrotherapy – a hot soak followed by a quick splash about in the sea. This natural pleasure comes free of charge!

South Island Spas

Contrary to popular belief, the North Island does not have a monopoly on thermal pools. At the end of every day, in the pristine resort of Hanmer, a pilgrimage takes place where locals clad in towel turbans and sarongs make their way to join spa visitors at the renowned **Hanmer Springs Thermal Pools and Spa** (Amuri Avenue; tel: 03-315 0000; www.hanmersprings.co.nz; daily 10am–9pm 👪).

Spacious and well set out, these springs offer seven open-air thermal pools, three sulphur pools and four private pools, as well as a sauna, steam rooms, a freshwater heated pool and a family activity pool with two waterslides, as well as a picnic area and licensed café.

The Maori knew of these springs too. Their legends speak of Tamatea, whose canoe was wrecked off the Otago coast. To save his party from freezing he called upon the mountains of Tongariro and Ngauruhoe in the north for help. They sent flames down the Whanganui River and over to Nelson where they rose in the air and landed in Hanmer Springs.

The flames must have also reached deep into the heart of the Lewis Pass, about an hour's drive away from Hanmer. For here lies the **Maruia Springs Thermal Resort** (SH7, Lewis

Pass; tel: 03-523 8840; www.maruia springs.co.nz; daily 8am–8.30pm), where the pools come in various shapes and sizes, but each is a perfectly formed tarn, built from the smoothest of river rocks. Due to its high mineral content the water has healing properties, and no chemicals are added to change its composition so the colour palette of the pools changes daily, ranging from crystal clear to milky to almost black.

For hardy individuals there is a cold plunge pool, and there are private spas as well. An intriguing feature in the main pool area is the Utase-yu, a traditional Japanese method to enjoy hot springs. It's easy to use – you sit under a continuously pouring stream of water and move your body for a massaging effect.

Also located within the Lewis Pass Scenic Reserve is the **Sylvia Flat Hot Springs.** A short walk upstream from the car park of the Department of Conservation-run Sylvia Flat Picnic Area leads to these naturally formed hot thermal pools. Having a soak in a hot pool in a murmuring river surrounded by a dripping beech forest is just about as relaxing as it gets.

Medicinal Minerals

New Zealand's thermal pools have long been revered for their healing qualities and each varies in its mineral composition and restorative benefits. Common minerals include silica, sodium, calcium, potassium and lithium; however, when you soak in natural (non-treated) pools, avoid putting your head underwater in case any dodgy amoebas are lurking. Commercial pools are treated, so they are completely safe; but another word of caution: be sure to remove all jewellery before entering any thermal pools, as their strong mineral compositions are renowned for turning silver and other precious metals black!

Family fun at Hanmer Springs

Rugby and the All Blacks

Ever since the first official match in 1870, rugby has enjoyed a dedicated following in New Zealand; to become an All Black is the ambition of most young lads. In 2011 the Kiwis play host to the Rugby World Cup.

Played with passion for some 140 years and followed today with near religious fervour, rugby has helped shape Kiwis into a proud, sporting nation determined to make its mark in the world. The first rugby game played on New Zealand soil was in May 1870 in Nelson at the top of the South Island, and by 1879 the game's popularity had spread and the first rugby unions were formed in Canterbury and Wellington. Sporting blue jerseys with a golden fern, the first national touring rugby team played and won a series of eight games in New South Wales in Australia in 1884. The first 'All Blacks', wearing the black jersey and silver fern *(see right)*, stormed through Britain and Europe in 1905.

Over the decades, New Zealand's rugby players have gained an international reputation as skilful sportsmen, from George Nepia and the Brownlie brothers in the 1920s and 30s to Colin Meads and Don Clarke in the 1960s, and the national team continues to earn respect wherever it plays. All Black captain Richie McCaw credits the grit of those early men of New Zealand rugby with instilling the pride and passion in today's generation of All Blacks: 'Traditionally we've been an off the land sort of people, pretty strong rugged people ... and when they got out in the field they were tough, hard men. That's why they had success in the earlier years and it's just carried on.'

The love of this fast and physical sporting contest runs deep in

A Saturday afternoon game of rugby at Picton

The All Blacks team of 1924

the Kiwi psyche along with a great sense of national pride for the All Blacks. To wear the hallowed black kit, adorned with New Zealand's silver fern motif, is the ambition of sporting school kids throughout the land. Many clubs, schools, parents and teachers are heavily involved in making the game available to children and the New Zealand Rugby Union supports initiatives to encourage playing from a young age. 'Rippa Rugby' is a non-contact version of the sport developed for primary school children, and 'Small Blacks' has been designed to help young players develop their rugby, making the game as simple and safe as possible for all children, regardless of their age, shape or size.

Today's Small Blacks are being coached to go all the way to becoming All Blacks and Black Ferns (women's national team).

Match Day

The thrill of being amid a victory-hungry crowd at an All Blacks match will leave any sports fan buzzing. It is worth noting that during the New Zealand summer, the team is often touring overseas in the northern

How the All Blacks got their Name

There are a couple of theories as to how the All Blacks got their name. One is that after a big victory in England in 1905 a newspaper that planned to run 'All Backs' as a headline, suggesting that the team's forwards played like backs, accidentally printed the headline 'All Blacks'. The other theory is that the name was coined by a rugby journalist who began referring to the team as All Blacks because of the colour of their kit. No matter which story is true, the name has been synonymous with the great New Zealand team ever since.

hemisphere's winter. Chances of catching a game are a lot higher from April to October, and each of New Zealand's stadiums, mostly located in major cities, has its own method of ticketing. Local New Zealand-based regional teams also play regular matches in Auckland, Wellington, Christchurch and Dunedin in the Super-14 League against teams from Australia and South Africa. I-Site visitor centres will be able to assist you to secure tickets and advise of any matches that are being played locally. Alternatively, visit www.allblacks.co.nz and follow the links to purchase tickets.

There are plenty more opportunities to watch a match, with 26 provincial-based league teams. From late August to late October, the nationwide representative competitions take place, with 14 teams taking part in the Air New Zealand Cup and 12 in the Heartland Championship (fixture details can be found on the All Blacks website).

World Cup Stadiums

Thirteen stadiums will provide venues for Rugby World Cup games. These are located in the following areas:

- **Whangarei, Northland:** The Northland Events Centre:
- **North Shore, Auckland:** North Harbour Stadium
- **Auckland city:** Eden Park
- **Hamilton, Waikato:** Waikato Stadium
- **Rotorua, Bay of Plenty:** The Rotorua International Stadium
- **New Plymouth, Taranaki:** Stadium Taranaki
- **Napier, Hawke's Bay:** Maclean Park
- **Palmerston North, Manawatu:** Arena Manawatu
- **Wellington city:** Wellington Regional Stadium
- **Nelson, Nelson-Tasman:** Trafalgar Park
- **Christchurch, Canterbury:** Stadium Christchurch
- **Dunedin, Otago:** Otago Stadium
- **Invercargill, Southland:** Rugby Park

Waikato Stadium in Hamilton

Find Out More

To learn more about the All Blacks and New Zealand's national sport, visit the **New Zealand Rugby Museum** (87 Cuba Street; tel: 06-358 6947; www.rugbymuseum.co.nz; Mon–Sat 10am–4pm, Sun 1.30–4pm; charge) in Palmerston North. This fascinating collection of photos and memorabilia, from blazers to whistles, will have sports fans lingering for hours.

Another key attraction is the **New Zealand Sports Hall of Fame** (tel: 03-477 7775; www.nzhalloffame.co.nz; daily 10am–4pm; charge), located on the first floor of Dunedin Railway Station. It pays tribute to New Zealand's great obsession with a dizzying array of artefacts and exhibits, including the arm guard All Blacks rugby legend Colin Meads wore when he played a test match with a broken arm.

However, Nelson is considered to be the nation's spiritual home of rugby, as this was where the first game using official rules was played in 1870. Hike up Botanical Hill for outstanding views of the pitch.

Rugby World Cup

The Kiwi's love affair with the oval ball will be taken to new heights in 2011 as the country hosts the Rugby World Cup. When New Zealand co-hosted the inaugural 1987 World Cup, it won not only the trophy but also international praise for the unforgettable show it delivered. Twenty-four years later, the world's third-biggest sporting event returns to New Zealand and some 60,000 visitors from around the globe are expected to attend. The tournament kicks off at Eden Park in Auckland on 9 September 2011, with the final match played at the same venue on 23 October 2011.

With 13 host towns and cities throughout New Zealand, the geographical spread, from Whangarei at the top of the North Island to Invercargill at the bottom of the South Island, reflects the New Zealand Rugby Union's (NZRU) desire to make this tournament a nationally supported event. Group phase games will be played in rugby-mad centres such as Dunedin, Invercargill, Napier, Hamilton and Whangarei, with Christchurch and Wellington both hosting two quarter-finals.

New Zealanders will inject a distinctively Kiwi flavour into the tournament, 'adopting' international teams as their own, hosting their allocated international team in their own cities and towns in a bid to make all players feel at home. The 20 participating national teams will play most of their games out of that area, with provision of top-class training facilities and accommodation, and easy transport links in and out.

For up-to-date information on ticket sales visit www.tickets.rugbyworldcup.com, or for information relating to travel packages, accommodation, stadiums, matches and pools playing in each centre visit www.newzealand.com or www.hospitalitynz2011.co.nz.

The rugby action can also be enjoyed at 'live sites', outdoor venues with big screens and free admission for all.

PLACES

Getting Your Bearings

New Zealand is made up of three main islands, the North Island, the South Island and Stewart Island. Passenger and ferry services provide a link across the Cook Strait between the North and South Islands, while others frequent the waters of the Foveaux Strait, which lies between the South Island and Stewart Island. Great Barrier, New Zealand's fourth-largest isle, is reached by passenger or vehicular ferry from Auckland.

For easy reference when using this guide, each region has a whole chapter dedicated to its exploration, colour coded for quick navigation. In the North Island the regions are divided into Auckland; Northland; Waikato, Coromandel; Bay of Plenty and East Cape; Rotorua and the Central Plateau; Taranaki, Manawatu-Wanganui and Hawke's Bay; and Wellington. In the South Island the areas are divided into Marlborough, Nelson and Tasman; Canterbury; the West Coast; Otago; while Southland, Fiordland and Stewart Island are combined to form one chapter. Detailed regional maps are found at the beginning of each chapter.

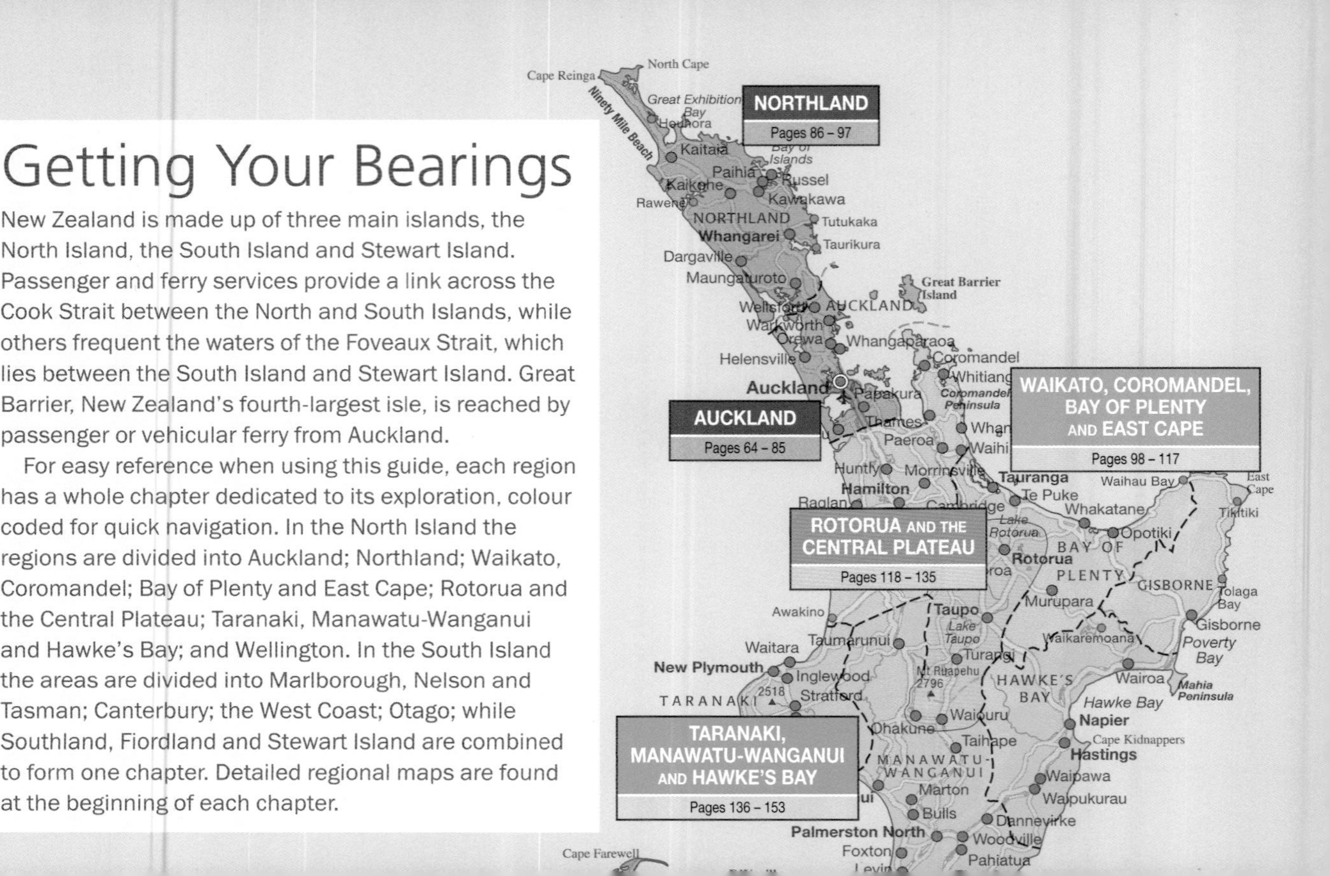

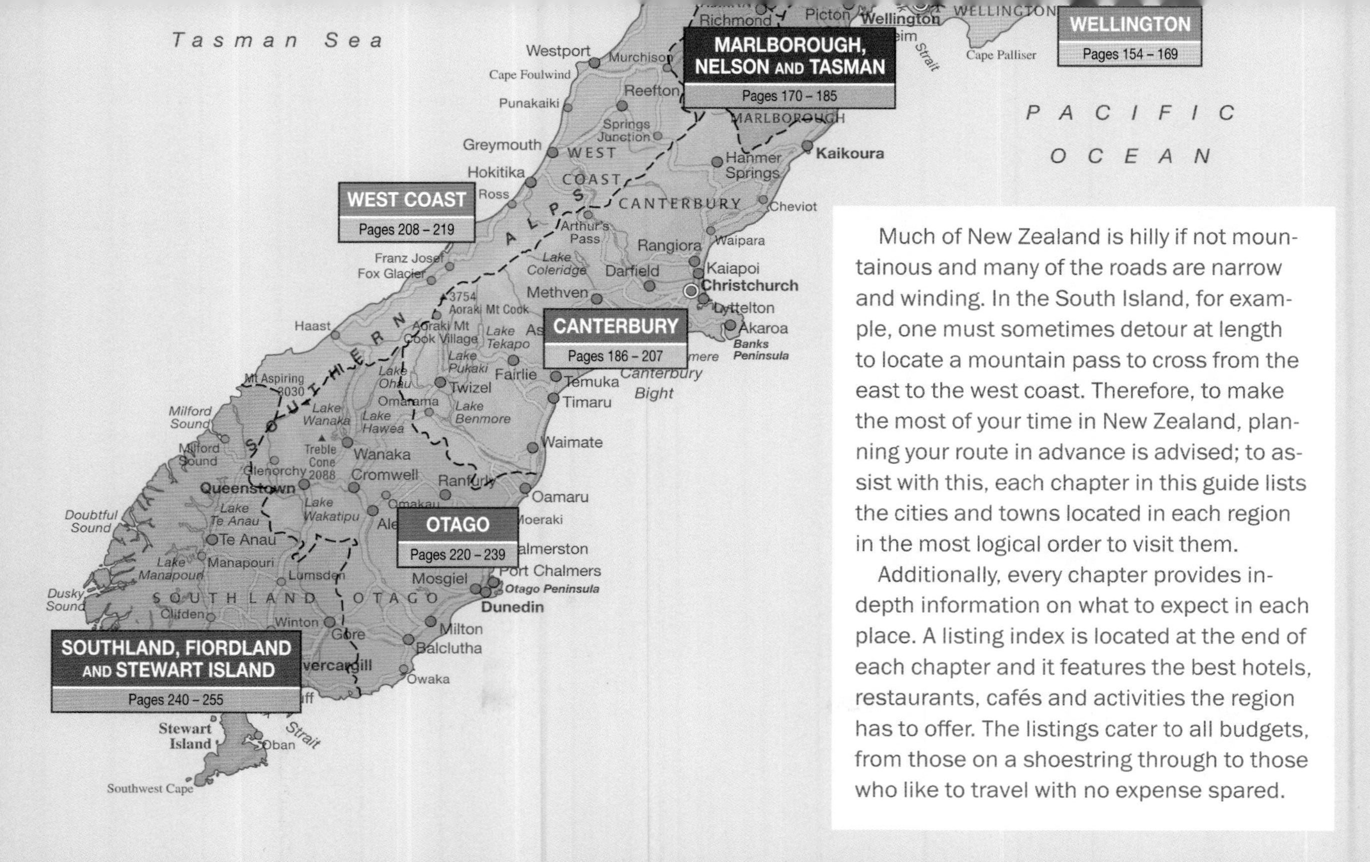

Much of New Zealand is hilly if not mountainous and many of the roads are narrow and winding. In the South Island, for example, one must sometimes detour at length to locate a mountain pass to cross from the east to the west coast. Therefore, to make the most of your time in New Zealand, planning your route in advance is advised; to assist with this, each chapter in this guide lists the cities and towns located in each region in the most logical order to visit them.

Additionally, every chapter provides in-depth information on what to expect in each place. A listing index is located at the end of each chapter and it features the best hotels, restaurants, cafés and activities the region has to offer. The listings cater to all budgets, from those on a shoestring through to those who like to travel with no expense spared.

Auckland

Built on 48 extinct volcanoes and sandwiched between two shimmering harbours, Auckland is one of the world's most sprawling cities, yet with a population of just 1.3 million. Accessible beaches and waterways abound here – little wonder then that the ownership of recreational boats is reputedly the highest per capita in the world.

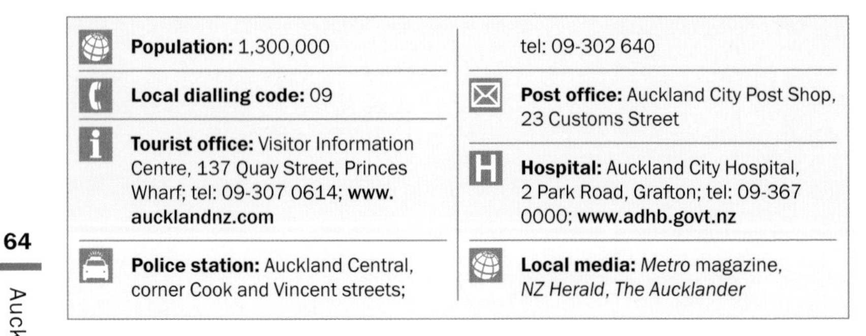

Population: 1,300,000

Local dialling code: 09

Tourist office: Visitor Information Centre, 137 Quay Street, Princes Wharf; tel: 09-307 0614; **www.aucklandnz.com**

Police station: Auckland Central, corner Cook and Vincent streets; tel: 09-302 640

Post office: Auckland City Post Shop, 23 Customs Street

Hospital: Auckland City Hospital, 2 Park Road, Grafton; tel: 09-367 0000; **www.adhb.govt.nz**

Local media: *Metro* magazine, *NZ Herald, The Aucklander*

The city of Auckland straddles an isthmus of land between two glistening harbours, ensuring that a beautiful beach is never far away. So insistent is the sea – nosing up creeks and estuaries and lapping on the shores of a hundred bays – that less than 2km (1 mile) of terra firma stops it from cutting Auckland completely adrift.

Auckland is sprinkled with extinct volcanoes and harbour views; to the Maori people, the area was Tamaki-makau-rau, 'the place of a hundred lovers.' Alas, British administrators, with deplorable lack of flair, renamed it after an English admiral. Nevertheless, Auckland has long since dropped its colonial sobriquet of 'Queen City' and now is known to the world as the 'City of Sails.'

The city's population topped 1 million a few years ago, and it is expected to reach 2 million by the year 2036. Auckland has the largest Polynesian population of any city in the world and an increasing Asian presence, further evolving the fusion of food to sample in its restaurants.

This sophisticated city offers a wonderful lifestyle for visitors and residents alike, and is jam-packed with unique shopping opportunities, restaurants and cafés. And yet, it is only a stone's throw from tranquil country drives, such as the journey north through the vineyards of Matakana or south through the lush fields of Clevedon.

Sailing towards Auckland Harbour Bridge

Central Auckland

Urban sprawl has made getting around the Auckland isthmus something of a challenge. Taxis are expensive by world standards, but there is an increasingly efficient system of buses and ferries throughout the city and its inner suburbs. The city centre's main historic highlights are, however, easy to reach on foot.

Viaduct Harbour and Central Wharves

A good place to start an exploration of the city is at its wharves. All manner of craft berth at **Westhaven Marina**, while international superyachts choose to dock at the **Viaduct Harbour**, a fashionable waterfront restaurant and bar precinct, built when the city hosted the America's Cup in 2000. To experience those heady days, hop aboard the *NZL40* and *NZL41* at **Sail NZ** *(see p.84)*, or visit the **Voyager New Zealand Maritime Museum** Ⓐ (www.nzmaritime.org; daily, 9am–5pm; charge) on Princes Wharf, which showcases New Zealand's seafaring history and provides historic steamboat harbour cruises. Cafés and restaurants line Princes Wharf, and at its tip is the **Auckland Hilton**, intriguingly designed to suggest a cruise liner. Further east on Quay Street is the **Ferry Building** Ⓑ, built in 1912. Once for officials, it now houses two restaurants; ferries to the suburbs and islands depart from behind it.

Bustling Queen Street

Queen Street

Across the way is **Queen Elizabeth Square**, dominated by the city's main transport hub, **Britomart**, housed in the former Chief Post Office. Also of interest is the 1889 **Old Customhouse** Ⓒ; its French Renaissance facade faces Customs Street where it once served as Auckland's financial heart.

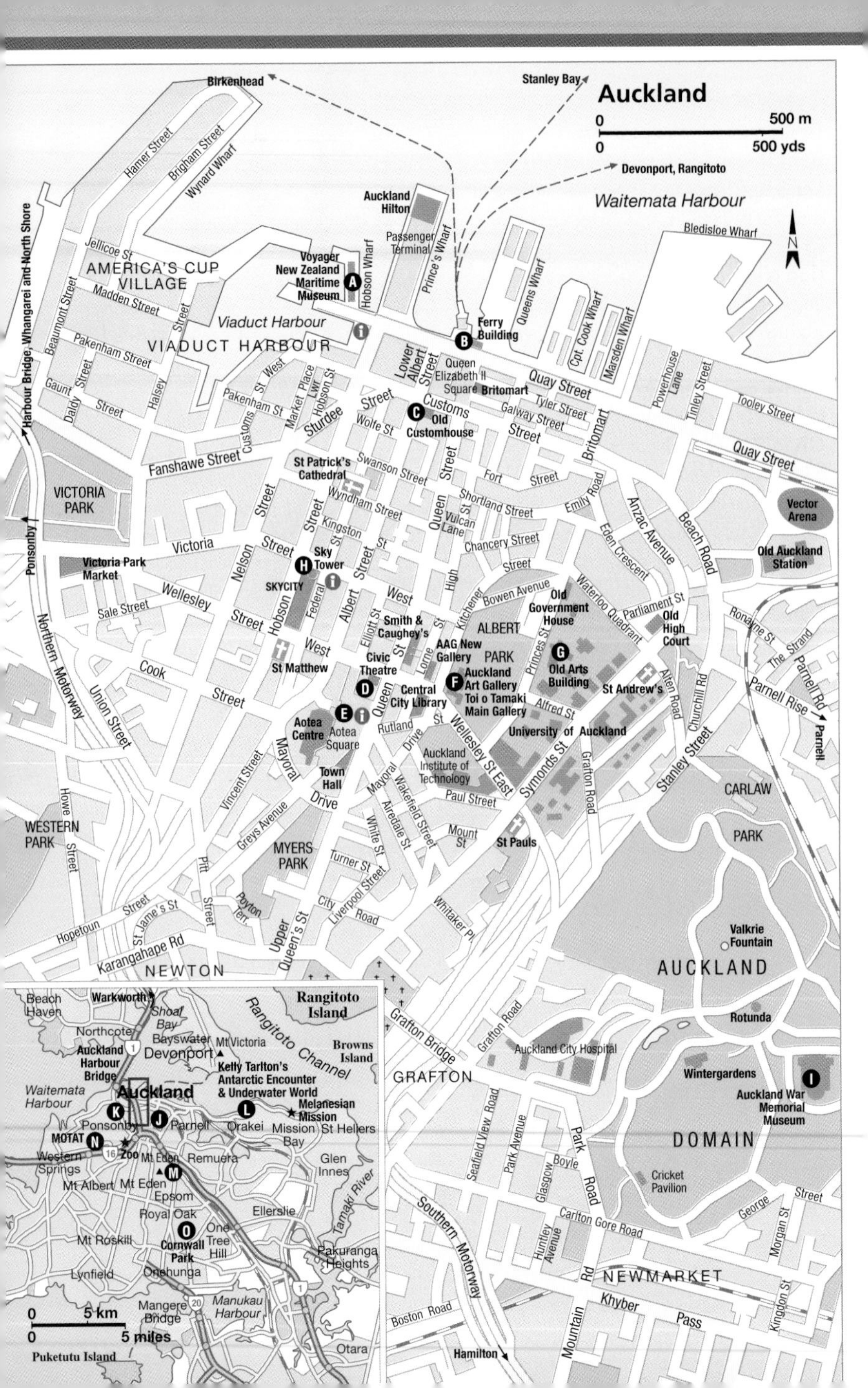

Auckland
0 500 m
0 500 yds
Waitemata Harbour
Birkenhead
Stanley Bay
Devonport, Rangitoto
AMERICA'S CUP VILLAGE
VIADUCT HARBOUR
Viaduct Harbour
Auckland Hilton
Voyager New Zealand Maritime Museum
Passenger Terminal
Ferry Building
Queen Elizabeth II Square
Britomart
Old Customhouse
St Patrick's Cathedral
VICTORIA PARK
Victoria Park Market
Sky Tower
SKYCITY
Smith & Caughey's
AAG New Gallery
ALBERT PARK
Old Government House
Old High Court
Old Arts Building
St Andrew's
Civic Theatre
Central City Library
Auckland Art Gallery Toi o Tamaki Main Gallery
University of Auckland
Aotea Centre
Aotea Square
Town Hall
Auckland Institute of Technology
St Matthew
St Pauls
MYERS PARK
WESTERN PARK
NEWTON
GRAFTON
CARLAW PARK
Vector Arena
Old Auckland Station
Valkrie Fountain
AUCKLAND DOMAIN
Rotunda
Wintergardens
Auckland War Memorial Museum
Cricket Pavilion
Auckland City Hospital
NEWMARKET
Harbour Bridge, Whangarei and North Shore
Ponsonby
Parnell
Hamilton
Northern Motorway
Southern Motorway
Grafton Bridge
Quay Street
Customs Street
Fanshawe Street
Victoria Street
Wellesley Street
Cook Street
Karangahape Rd
Symonds St
Khyber Pass
Beach Road
Anzac Avenue
Warkworth
Rangitoto Island
Rangitoto Channel
Browns Island
Beach Haven
Northcote
Shoal Bay
Bayswater
Mt Victoria
Devonport
Auckland Harbour Bridge
Waitemata Harbour
Kelly Tarlton's Antarctic Encounter & Underwater World
Melanesian Mission
Orakei
Mission Bay
St Heliers
MOTAT
Western Springs
Zoo
Mt Eden
Remuera
Glen Innes
Mt Albert
Epsom
Royal Oak
Ellerslie
Tamaki River
Mt Roskill
Cornwall Park
One Tree Hill
Pakuranga Heights
Lynfield
Onehunga
Mangere Bridge
Manukau Harbour
Otara
Puketutu Island
0 5 km
0 5 miles

Queen Street is a jumble of late-opening souvenir stores, cheap noodle houses, internet cafés, up-market boutiques, designer fashion stores and corporate headquarters. Things to look out for include the intersection of Queen and Fort streets where waves once lapped before reclamation, **Smith & Caughey's** (253–61 Queen Street; www.smithandcaughey.co.nz), Auckland's long-running department store, and the historic **Civic Theatre** Ⓓ on the corner of Wellesley Street, which hosts Auckland's premier events *(see p.83)*. Built in 1929, its interior is one of the city's finest sights.

Aotea Square

About half way up Queen Street an elaborately carved Maori *waharoa* (gateway) provides access to **Aotea Square** Ⓔ, home to the **Aotea Centre** *(see p.83)*, the city's main cultural venue. Inside, a ticket counter provides information on all events. The **Aotea Market** is held in the square on Friday and Saturday from 10am–6pm; stalls sell street-wear, jewellery, food and bric-a-brac. Bordering the square are the City Council buildings, including the renovated **Town Hall**, recognisable by its clock tower.

A block to the east on Lorne Street is the **Central City Library** (Mon–Fri 9am–8pm, Sat–Sun 10am–4pm) which contains some surprises, such as a Shakespeare First Folio (1623) and the largest collection of manuscripts by Alexandre Dumas Père outside the Bibliothèque Nationale in Paris.

Around Albert Park

Across the road on Wellesley Street East, the **Auckland Art Gallery Toi**

Auckland Transport

Airport: Auckland International Airport; tel: 09-275 0789; **www.auckland-airport.co.nz.** Bus services depart every 30 minutes for the CBD. Shuttles/buses cost NZ$18–35 and take one hour; taxis cost NZ$60 plus and take 30 minutes.

Buses: A NZ$13 Auckland Discovery Day Pass (tel: 09-366 6400; **www.maxx.co.nz**) provides unlimited rides on buses, trains and ferries for one day. The inner-city Link bus travels clockwise and anticlockwise in a loop through Ponsonby, K Road and the CBD. A ride costs NZ$1.60.

Trains: Connex, tel: 09-366 6400; **www.maxx.co.nz**; links the city to western and southern suburbs

Ferries: Fullers Cruise Centre, Pier 1, Ferry Building, 99 Quay Street; tel: 09-367 9111; **www.fullers.co.nz**; daily 6am–11.30pm; for travel to North Shore suburbs and Gulf islands; return tickets NZ$10–32

Taxis: Auckland Co-operative Taxis; tel: 09-300 3000; **www.cooptaxi.co.nz**

Car hire: Apex Car Rentals; tel: 09-257 0292; **www.apexrentals.co.nz**

Parking: Parking is available in city car parks and costs NZ$5–15 per hour for casual parking

o Tamaki **F** (www.aucklandartgallery.govt.nz; daily 10am–5pm; free) exhibits New Zealand works. On the hilly slopes between the gallery and the grounds of Auckland University is **Albert Park,** an Edwardian-style public garden displaying eclectic contemporary sculpture. Above the park on Princes Street, the university's central attraction is the **Old Arts Building** **G** – easily spotted by its intricate clock tower. This Gothic-style building was completed in 1926 and was immediately dubbed 'The Wedding Cake' by locals because of its decorative pinnacled white-stone construction.

At the corner of Princes Street and Waterloo Quadrant is the **Old Government House**, built in 1856 for the Governor-General of New Zealand, and the **Supreme Court** (1868), complete with turrets and gargoyles.

Sky Tower

To the west, Auckland's most striking modern landmark is the **Sky Tower** **H** (www.skycity.co.nz; daily 8.30am–10pm, Fri–Sat until 10.30am; charge for viewing decks) which looms over the city. Its base on Victoria Street is well worth a visit to see a free audio-visual on Auckland's history. For a charge, glass-fronted lifts whisk visitors to the enclosed decks at the top of the tower for panoramic 360-degree views. At the top are various dining experiences including one restaurant that turns steadily at one revolution per hour. Those not prone to vertigo might like to consider the 192m (630ft) -high base jump off the tower to **SKYCITY**, New Zealand's largest casino, below.

Auckland Domain

The **Domain**, a leafy area of playing fields and gardens to the southeast of the city, is Auckland's premier green

Cricket practice in full swing in Auckland Domain

Sky Tower, a prime spot for bungy jumping

space *(see also p.70)*. Here the **Auckland War Memorial Museum** ❶ (www.aucklandmuseum.com; daily 10am–5pm; charge 👪), provides an excellent overview of the natural, cultural and social history of New Zealand. For the first-time visitor it is also a superb introduction to Maori culture with artefacts that include a raised storehouse, a carved meeting house and a Maori war canoe. There are daily performances featuring traditional Maori song and dance, and the 'Scars on the Heart' display tells the story of New Zealand in World Wars I and II.

Inner Suburbs

The fringe suburbs of Auckland are edgy and culturally diverse. Traditionally, those to the east are the city's more affluent, while to the west traces of the city's Pacific connections are found in shops displaying brilliantly coloured floral cloth, alongside taro, yam, papaya and other tropical foods.

Parnell

Parnell ❶ is located to the east of the centre past the park known as **Constitution Hill**. The hill was named after the fact that businessmen took a 'constitutional' walk up its steep slope from their Parnell homes to their city offices. It's a peculiarity of the city's history that the suburbs east of Queen Street have always been the city's more affluent – some say it's because the upper classes didn't like the sun in their eyes on the way to and from work in the city. And so it's no accident that Parnell oozes a refined style *(see pp.70–1)*. It's also the gateway to **Newmarket**, a busy shopping strip which is home to some of fashion's big-name outlets, and **Remuera**, where the serious old money lives.

Ponsonby

West of the city centre is **Ponsonby** ❶, centred upon the snake-like stretch of Ponsonby Road. It offers the best selection of restaurants of all ethnic persuasions, plus high-fashion clothing and design stores. Once the domain of students and whole streets of Pacific Island immigrant families, Ponsonby is now filled with refurbished turn-of-the-century villas which fetch high prices at auction, and its streets are filled with arty and elegant individuals. Many of the city's creative types, including its designers, live on its narrow streets selling their wares from tiny studios.

THE DOMAIN AND PARNELL

Discover the city's relaxed side on a half-day walking tour of its parks, museums, historical buildings and churches, and the stylish inner-city suburb of Parnell.

Begin this tour at **Auckland Domain**, New Zealand's oldest park. If you arrive by taxi, ask the driver to point out the Wintergardens along the way. If you are on foot, head into the park from Park Road. If you are on the bus, get off on Parnell Road, slightly further southeast.

The main sight in the Domain, the imposing **Auckland War Memorial Museum** *(see p.69)*, enjoys a prime location with panoramic city and harbour views. The museum has a café, but for a treat walk down to **Sugar & Spice Cafe** *(see p.81)* at the **Wintergardens**. After a snack, stroll through the conservatory, which houses 10,000 exotic plants.

From the Wintergardens, follow the path that runs southeast and out to Parnell Road. Turn left and walk for 15 minutes to **Parnell**, a vibrant inner-city suburb known for its boutique shopping and eateries, such as **Trinity** or **Verve** cafés *(see p.81)*. But first look out on your right for **St Mary's Church**, one of New Zealand's finest wooden Gothic buildings, and for the newer **Holy Trinity Cathedral**.

As you stroll down the hill past the St Stephen's Avenue intersection, Parnell's designer shops begin to appear. Visit the character-filled wooden villas of the **Parnell Village** complex, restored for retail purposes. Verandas and bridges provide access to the shops.

Now either hail a taxi or enjoy a half-hour walk to your final destination, the Auckland Art Gallery.

If you're on foot, veer left down Parnell Rise, walk under the rail bridge and cross the Grafton motorway, then tackle the hill on the other side. A path leads from Churchill Road to the junction of Symonds Street and Alten Road, and the Romanesque columns of the Presbyterian **St Andrew's Church**.

Cross over, head west along the Waterloo Quadrant and, on your right, you will see the old **High Court**, with its historic 1865 chamber and courtrooms joined to a modern extension. Moving on, at 12 Princes Street is the **Old Government House**, completed in 1856. Cross the road and stroll through the grounds alongside the building, now owned by Auckland University. On the left you will see the **Old Arts Building**, opened in 1926.

Opposite the Old Arts Building is **Albert Park** *(see p.68)*, a beautifully maintained inner-city sanctum featuring a floral clock, a statue of Queen Victoria and a band rotunda.

Tour Tips

- Distance: 3½km (2 miles)
- Time: half day
- Begin the tour at the Auckland Domain. To get there catch a taxi, the public Link bus from Queen Street or the Auckland Explorer Bus, a hop-on/hop-off tour which departs from the Ferry Building on Quay Street and runs hourly from 9am throughout the day.

Now take any path downhill to Kitchener Street. On the corner of Wellesley Street is the **Auckland Art Gallery Toi o Tamaki**, heralded in 1888 as 'the first permanent art gallery in the Dominion'. Today, it is New Zealand's largest art institution, with a collection of over 12,500 works from 1376 to the present. The Main Gallery displays historical and European art collections, while the New Gallery, accessed through a courtyard, showcases cutting-edge contemporary art.

Parnell is known for its trendy café scene

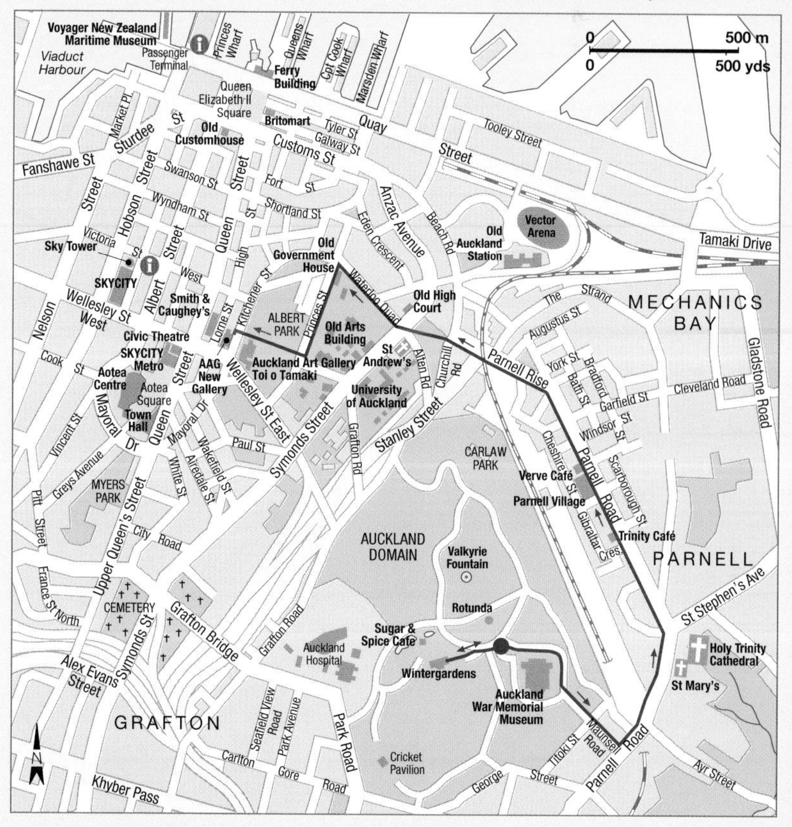

Tamaki Drive Bays

A pleasant drive east along waterfront-skirting Tamaki Drive takes in **Okahu Bay**, **Michael Savage Memorial Park**, named after the country's first Labour prime minister, and **Mission Bay**, a good place to swim at high tide. From here, bikes, boats and windsurfers can be hired to explore the inner harbour.

For a close encounter with local marine life, head to **Kelly Tarlton's Antarctic Encounter and Underwater World** **L** (www.kellytarltons.co.nz; daily 9am–6pm) at Orakei Wharf, near Okahu Bay. Here moving walkways transport visitors through tunnels for an undersea view of sharks, rays, fish and other marine creatures. Highlights include shark feeding and the Snow Cat ride through the 'Antarctic' to view a colony of king and gentoo penguins.

Mount Eden and Western Springs

Directly south of the CBD is the volcanic cone of **Mount Eden** **M**, Auckland's highest point at 196m (643ft). It was once the site of a fortified Maori village, but today it offers excellent views from its summit and heady floral displays at **Eden Garden** (24 Omana Avenue; www.edengarden.co.nz; charge), including a large collection of camellias. To the west is the lake and parklands of **Western Springs** where the **Museum of Transport and Technology** **N** (MOTAT; Great North Road; www.motat.org.nz; daily 10am–5pm) attracts machinery and invention enthusiasts. The museum also has an aircraft built by New Zealander Richard Pearse, who, some claim, flew in March 1903, before the Wright Brothers. Within walking distance is **Auckland Zoo** (Motions Road, Western Springs; www.aucklandzoo.co.nz; daily 9.30am–5.30pm), where kiwi can be viewed, as well as native tuatara, a lizard-like reptile that has survived unaltered since the time of the dinosaurs.

Watching the sharks at Kelly Tarlton's Underwater World

Sailing in front of the uninhabited Rangitoto Island

Cornwall Park

About 3km (2 miles) southeast of the city, the 135-hectare (334-acre) estate of **Cornwall Park** ⓪ surrounds the volcanic cone of **One Tree Hill** (Te Totara-i-ahua). Drive or hike to the top for panoramic views and to see the obelisk and tomb of Sir John Logan Campbell, who gifted the park to Auckland. Other attractions include the city's oldest remaining building, **Acacia Cottage**, built in 1841, and the **Stardome Observatory** (www.stardome.org.nz; Mon 9am–5pm, Tue–Fri 9am–9.30pm, Sat–Sun 1–9.30pm), with regular shows depicting the southern hemisphere's star constellations. The sacred totara tree that once stood at the summit was replaced by settlers in 1852 with a single pine tree. This was subsequently cut down in 2002 in a counter-attack by a Maori activist.

North Auckland

Curving over the harbour, **Auckland Harbour Bridge** links the city to the North Shore suburbs. You can drive over the bridge or take the ferry *(see p.67)* to the suburban North Shore City and the marine playground of Devonport, where a succession of beaches loops northwards up the east coast. For a bird's-eye view of commuters and extraordinary views join an **Auckland Bridge Climb** tour, with an optional bungy jump *(see p.84)*.

North Shore Bays

Affluent **Devonport** ❶ sports grand Victorian houses, antiques stores and galleries, and a plethora of bars and cafés. If the weather is good, hike up **Mount Victoria** or **North Head** for

Auckland Harbour Bridge

The opening of the Auckland Harbour Bridge in 1959 changed Greater Auckland's status overnight. What had been a string of sleepy seaside settlements backed by rolling pastureland became part of Auckland thanks to this 1,020m (3,350ft) structure stretching across the harbour from Fanshawe Street to Northcote Point. Today, the bridge carries an average of 150,000 vehicles a day and is best avoided during rush hour – a daily affair and a time when Aucklanders dub their city the 'city of snails' in jest of its true title.

unobstructed views, or relax and swim at **Cheltenham Beach**. From here, the sheltered coves and white-sand beaches leading north include **Takapuna**, a popular beach overlooking Rangitoto Island *(see p.77)* with decent shopping options and cafés, and **Long Bay Regional Park**, a marine reserve with several good hikes.

Hibiscus Coast

Beyond the North Shore lie the Hibiscus Coast suburbs of **Orewa** and **Whangaparaoa** ❷, which offer safe swimming and pleasant picnic spots. Highlights include the walks of **Shakespear Regional Park** at the tip of Whangaparaoa Peninsula and the scenic cruise *(see p.84)* to the open wildlife sanctuary of **Tiritiri Matangi Island**, which departs from the peninsula's Gulf Harbour Marina. The island is a haven for many species of endangered New Zealand birdlife, including the kiwi and takahe.

Six km (4 miles) north of Orewa is **Waiwera Infinity Thermal Spa Resort** *(see p.52)*, one of two thermal areas in Auckland. From here it's a short drive to **Puhoi**, an early Catholic Bohemian settlement, and old-world **Puhoi Tavern**, with pictures of its early Bohemian migrants and farming paraphernalia on display.

Warkworth and Coast

Beyond the Puhoi Junction, the countryside begins to open up. At the **Honey Centre**, 4km (2½ miles) south of Warkworth, bees can be seen making honey behind the glass walls of a working hive. Closer to town, **Parry Kauri Park** is the site of an 800-year-old kauri tree. Pretty riverside

Kite surfing at Orewa on the Hibiscus Coast

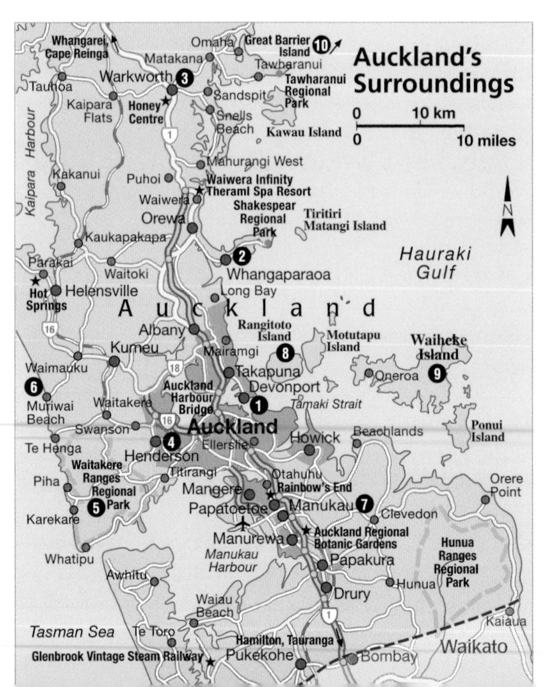

Dense forests cover the Waitakere Ranges

Warkworth ❸ marks the northern boundary of the Auckland region and is the gateway to the wine-growing area of **Matakana** and several excellent beaches including **Tawharanui**, where – on a weekday at least – you will have a white-sand beach all to yourself.

West Auckland

Whatever pace you like to set, West Auckland will have something to suit, from roughing it on the west coast beaches with their black sand and pounding surf, to taking a leisurely drive through the Waitakere Ranges. And then there are the wineries, where you can while away an afternoon sipping the region's award-winning varieties.

Henderson and Environs

The thriving wine industry centres on **Henderson** ❹, reached via the Western Motorway (SH16), exiting at the Lincoln Road turn-off. The region was settled by Dalmatian and Croatian wine growers and today their dynasties are commemorated in street names. Many are studded with vineyards, some world-class, others old family operations whose red wines are still sold in half-gallon flagons. Many wineries offer a cellar door experience, such as at **Lincoln Wines** (130 Lincoln Road). Another 20km (12½ miles) northwest is **Kumeu**, filled with large lifestyle properties, small farm enterprises, market gardens and substantial vineyard operations like Kumeu River, Nobilo and Matua Valley.

Waitakere Ranges

A short drive west of downtown Auckland lie the thickly forested **Waitakere Ranges.** With more than 16,000 hectares (39,500 acres) of native rainforest, waterfalls and wild black-sand surf beaches, it's hard to know which part of 'the Waitaks' to take on first. This is where **Arataki Visitor Centre** (300 Scenic Drive; daily 9am–5pm) comes in handy, with displays on the region's flora and fauna, a plant identification trail, knowledgeable staff, and sweeping views of Manukau Harbour, Nihotupu Dam and the Waitakere Ranges.

Despite early years of logging and farming, the **Waitakere Ranges Regional Park** ❺ boasts large stands of kauri, rimu and kahikatea trees, and

Watercare's **Rain Forest Express** (tel: 09-302 8028; www.watercare.co.nz) utilises the old logging tramways to transport ecotourists from Jacobson's Depot, 5km (3 miles) west of Titirangi, to the Upper Nihotupu Dam. By road the ranges are easily explored by following the **Scenic Drive** (SH24) which runs for 28km (17 miles) along their spine from Titirangi to Swanson.

West Coast Beaches

Beyond the ranges, the west gets truly wild, its black-sand surf beaches moulded by the prevailing winds and Tasman Sea. The northernmost beach, 32km (20-mile) -long **Muriwai** ❻, has a gannet colony which, seen up close from viewing platforms, is one of the region's great sights. The southernmost beach of **Whatipu**, where the sea pours into the tidal Manukau Harbour, has a walking route that leads to sea caves that sheltered early Maori and were later refashioned into a ballroom for 1920s timber workers. Between these two beaches lies **Piha**, where Lion Rock splits the beach right down the middle, creating a steady swell.

West Coast Safety

All of New Zealand's West Coast beaches, including those found in West Auckland, are very dangerous for swimming and the death toll has included many unwary tourists. Beaches in West Auckland are patrolled during the summer months and for your own safety it is wise to swim between the flags. Also, if you are exploring rock pools or fishing, be wary of rogue waves that regularly pluck hikers and fisherfolk from the rocks.

A 40-minute hike from here leads to **Kitekite Falls**, perfect for cool swims on hot summer days. Tracks run south of here along the cliff tops to **Karekare**, where the spectacular opening sequence of Jane Campion's *The Piano* (1993) was filmed.

South Auckland

The suburbs strung on each side of the southern motorway beyond **Otahuhu** *(see right)* unquestionably include some the region's most economically depressed, although parts of Manukau are extremely affluent. The towns are

The gannet colony of Muriwai

Manukau grandmas

among New Zealand's most culturally diverse and so it is little wonder that fusion cooking here is superb.

Manukau

Standing in the midst of the large multicultural community of **Manukau** ❼ is **Mangere Mount**, which rises 100m (328ft) and overlooks Manukau Harbour and **Ambury Farm Park**, a good place to spot a variety of wading birds. While **Manukau Harbour** lacks the scenic charm of the east coast's Waitemata Harbour (its mudflats stretch for many kilometres at low tide), it's uncrowded and pollution-free – the clean-up has been a triumph of conservation planning. Other highlights include **Rainbow's End** (corner of Wiri Station and Great South roads; www.rainbowsend.co.nz; daily 10am–5pm), the country's premier theme park with crazy rides you won't find anywhere else, and the **Auckland Regional Botanic Gardens** (Hill Road, Manurewa; www.auckland botanicgardens.co.nz; daily 8am–6pm), which has a dazzling variety of species, both native and exotic.

Auckland Harbour and Gulf

Some say you haven't experienced Auckland if you haven't ventured onto the waters of the beautiful island-dotted Hauraki Gulf, a vast area of sheltered water lying between the Auckland coastline and Coromandel Peninsula. Dozens of islands lie within this maritime park and can be reached by ferry from Quay Street.

Rangitoto Island

The most striking island to visit is **Rangitoto Island** ❽, the 600-year-old dormant volcano which dominates Auckland's skyline and was purchased by the government in 1854. The summit walk is not hugely demanding but if you choose to hike wear stout shoes as Rangitoto's rough lava pathways make short work of fancy leather. Alternatively,

Souvenirs at Otahuhu and Otara

For a culturally intriguing shopping experience head to Otahuhu, about 15km (9 miles) south of Auckland's CBD. A short jaunt down its main street reveals Asian and Pacific traders jostling cheek-by-jowl as they clamour for the attention of passers-by. Another 3km (2 miles) further south, the colourful and noisy Otara Market held on Newbury Street in the Otara Shopping Centre on Saturdays from 6am–noon should not be missed. This is the place to shop for souvenirs, not just because they are better value for money than the shops in the tourist traps but because of the obvious authenticity.

there's the option of a fully guided trip aboard a **Fullers Tractor-trailer Tour** *(see p.84)*; its 260m (850ft) summit offers spectacular 360-degree views of the city, the northern bays and the Hauraki Gulf. A causeway joins Rangitoto with **Motutapu Island**, once the site of a Maori village, and now farmed.

Waiheke Island

Waiheke Island ❾ is the most populated of the gulf islands, with beautiful beaches, walking tracks, vineyards, olive groves, world-class arts and crafts, native bush and laid-back seaside villages. Options for exploring include hiring a mountain bike, buying a hop-on/hop-off bus pass, or joining a Explorer Tour or Vineyard Tour through Fullers *(see p.84)*. The island's bus service is infrequent – it's tied to the ferry timetable – but the taxis and rental cars are cheap and walking is pleasant.

Waiheke has a burgeoning wine industry and chic cafés line the high street of **Oneroa**, its main settlement.

Great Barrier Island

Lying 90km (56 miles) northeast of Auckland, **Great Barrier Island** ❿ is the gulf's largest and most remote. Its small population of 700 islanders live here without mains power; electricity is supplied by private generators or alternative sources. The beaches are unspoilt, much of the native forest is virgin and the island is home to several unique plant and bird species. There are good day walks and the island is also a

Rangitoto Island

popular destination for diving, fishing, surfing and camping.

Great Barrier is accessible by light aircraft and linked by regular ferry services, including a car ferry. Bringing or hiring a vehicle to explore is essential, and while camping is the traditional accommodation option, there are a number of motels and lodges.

Clevedon Farmers' Market

Beyond the bustle of Manukau turn east off SH1 to the forest-clad Hunua Ranges Regional Park, a great place to take time out or enjoy a picnic at Hunua Falls before driving northwards through lush meadows to Clevedon. Pop in to the Clevedon Farmers' Market to stock up on venison salami, hand-crafted cheeses and artisan breads. Add some warm fillets of freshly smoked fish, some oysters on the half-shell and an organic lemon or two, and you can bring the flavours of South Auckland's farms and coast back to enjoy in the city.

ACCOMMODATION

Auckland has a wide range of accommodation, but at the budget end the choice is fairly limited as this region tends to be pricier than anywhere else in New Zealand, especially during the peak summer period.

Central Auckland

Empire Backpackers
21 Whitaker Place
Tel: 09-950 9000
www.aucklandbackpackers.co.nz
Classy, apartment-style hostel with a café and internet facilities onsite. **$$**

Heritage Auckland
35 Hobson Street
Tel: 09-379 8553
www.heritagehotels.co.nz
Large, landmark hotel with spacious rooms located within easy walking distance of the America's Cup Village. Restaurants, bar, pool, sauna, spa and gym. **$$$$**

Hilton Auckland
147 Quay Street, Princes Wharf
Tel: 09-978 2000
www.hilton.com
This contemporary hotel takes prime position on Princes Wharf and all rooms have clear views of the harbour. **$$$$$**

YHA Auckland International
5 Turner Street
Tel: 09-302 8200
www.yha.co.nz
This five-star hostel offers safe, clean and comfortable accommodation in multishare rooms, as well as twin, double and en-suite rooms. **$**

Inner Suburbs

Barrycourt Suites Hotel
10–20 Gladstone Road, Parnell
Tel: 09-303 3789
www.barrycourt.co.nz
Close to the city and the beach, this hotel has a range of guest rooms, motel units and pricier serviced rooms, many with sea views. Licensed restaurant, bar and spa. **$$$**

Accommodation Price Categories

Prices are for one night's accommodation in a standard double room (unless otherwise specified).

$ = below NZ$30
$$ = NZ$30–75
$$$ = NZ$75–150
$$$$ = NZ$150–350
$$$$$ = over NZ$350

The Great Ponsonby Bed and Breakfast
30 Ponsonby Terrace, Ponsonby
Tel: 09-376 5989
www.greatpons.co.nz
Small boutique bed and breakfast with tidy rooms in an atmospheric 1898 villa. **$$$$**

South Auckland

Airport Goldstar Motel
255 Kirkbride Road, Mangere
Tel: 09-275 8199
www.airportgoldstar.co.nz
Comfortable, clean and tidy accommodation within easy access of the airport. **$$$**

West Auckland

Lincoln Court Motel
58 Lincoln Road, Henderson
Tel: 09-836 0326
www.lincolncourtmotel.co.nz
Quiet motel ideally located for exploring the Waitakere Ranges. **$$$**

Hilton Auckland

Piha Domain Camp
The Domain, Piha
Tel: 09-812 8815
www.pihabeach.co.nz
This camping ground is fairly basic, in the best Kiwi tradition, but the beach is a two-minute walk away and families and surfers flock here. As well as camping facilities, there are simple beach-hut abodes for rent. **$**

North Auckland

Anchor Lodge Motel
436 Hibiscus Coast Highway, Orewa
Tel: 09-427 0690
www.anchorlodge.co.nz
Only steps away from Orewa Beach, Anchor Lodge has comfortable rooms and offers excellent rates for longer stays. **$$**

Peace and Plenty Inn
6 Flagstaff Terrace
Tel: 09-445 2925
www.peaceandplenty.co.nz
Bed and breakfast accommodation in a lovingly restored waterfront Victorian villa. Spacious guest rooms, en-suite bathrooms and modern conveniences including Wi-fi. **$$$$**

Auckland Harbour and Gulf

Beachside Lodge
48 Kiwi Street, Oneroa
Tel: 09-372 9884
www.beachsidelodge.co.nz
Self-contained apartments or bed and breakfast, near the beach. **$$$$**

Medlands Beach Backpackers
Masons Road, Great Barrier
Tel: 09-429 0320
www.medlandsbeach.com
Comfortable family accommodation with great views. **$**

RESTAURANTS

Auckland's cuisine is a fusion of its multicultural make-up, and each cultural group has added its own flavours to the mix.

Central Auckland

Cima Cafe & Bar
56–58 High Street
Tel: 09-303 1971
This busy espresso café and bar is ideal after perusing the Auckland Art Gallery. **$**

Dine by Peter Gordon
Skycity, 90 Federal Street
Tel: 09-363 7030
www.skycitygrand.co.nz
Fusion fare from an exciting menu, plus an excellent level of service seldom found in New Zealand. **$$$$**

Harbourside Seafood Bar and Grill
1st Floor, Ferry Building, 99 Quay Street
Tel: 09-307 0556
www.harboursiderestaurant.co.nz
Superb range of seafood dishes cooked with flair, and great harbour views from all tables. **$$**

Restaurant Price Categories

Prices are for a standard meal for one.

$ = below NZ$15
$$ = NZ$15–30
$$$ = NZ$30–50
$$$$ = over NZ$50

Dine by Peter Gordon

Harbourside Seafood Bar and Grill

Soul Bar and Bistro
Viaduct Harbour
Tel: 09-356 7249
www.soulbar.co.nz
Right on the Viaduct, Soul is a popular choice with locals. Water views and cuisine are among the best in the city. **$$$$**

Sugar & Spice Cafe
Auckland Domain
Tel: 09-303 0627
A lovely setting for a light snack, with views over the duck ponds of the Domain. **$**

Inner Suburbs

Rocco
23 Ponsonby Road, Ponsonby
Tel: 09-360 6262
www.rocco.co.nz
A long-running favourite, serving fresh, healthy cuisine. **$$$**

Trinity Café
107 Parnell Road
Tel: 09-300 3042
Sleek and comfortable café, and a great place to people-watch on busy Parnell Road. **$**

Verve Café
311 Parnell Road
Tel: 09-379 2860
Classic café fare served alfresco. **$–$$**

South Auckland

Broncos Steak House
712 Great South Road, Manukau
Tel: 09-262 2850
This is the place to come for reliably good steaks, served with fresh salads and crispy fries. **$$**

West Auckland

Beesonline Honey Centre and Café
791 SH16, Waimauku
Tel: 09-411 7953
www.beesonline.co.nz
A stylish licensed café that serves first-class food with an emphasis on fresh organic produce, local ingredients and, of course, honey. **$$$**

North Auckland

Kaizen Café
350 Hibiscus Coast Highway, Orewa
Tel: 09-427 5633
www.kaizencafe.co.nz
Super Italian-style food made with organic and free-range produce wherever possible. **$$**

Manuka Restaurant
49 Victoria Road, Devonport
Tel: 09-445 7732
Pizzas (lunch only), pastas, salads, fish of the day and steak served in a relaxed and friendly atmosphere. **$$**

Auckland Harbour and Gulf

Currach Irish Pub
Pah Beach, Stonewall, Tryphena
Tel: 09-429 0211
Authentic Irish atmosphere with Guinness and Kilkenny on tap. Good pub fare including fish and chips, and hearty steaks. **$$**

Vino Vino Restaurant
3/153 Ocean View Road, Oneroa
Tel: 09-372 9888
www.vinovino.co.nz
Stunning views of Oneroa Bay are offered from the deck of this popular Mediterranean-style café. **$$$$**

NIGHTLIFE

In the central city and fringe, music pulsates from almost every door along Ponsonby Road, K' Road, and throughout the Viaduct. Most clubs have dress codes and you won't get in wearing shorts or gym shoes. Some clubs are discreetly hidden away up staircases or down alleyways, and only locals know they are there; just follow the music to find them.

Bar and bistro on Ponsonby Road

Caluzzi
461–463 Karangahape Road, CBD
www.caluzzi.co.nz
Disco, DJs and an interactive show by award-winning drag artistes.

Clooney
33 Sales Street, CBD
Set inside a converted warehouse, this bar has an extensive cocktail list.

Danny Dollans
Viaduct Harbour, 204 Quay Street, CBD
Popular Irish bar in a good location. Decor includes a confessional box.

Fu/Zen Bar
166 Queen Street
Fu Bar is a relaxed hideaway with friendly staff, attracting drum-and-bass fans.

Khuja Lounge
3rd Floor, 536 Queen Street
An intimate Moroccan-themed bar with great DJs and soulful jazz.

Ruby
484 New North Road, Kingsland
Up-market bar filled with an interesting and offbeat crowd. Well worth the taxi ride.

The Wine Cellar
St Kevin's Arcade, K' Road
A hip hang-out for creative types who come here to enjoy wines from the Coromandel in an unpretentious environment. Live acoustic entertainment Sat–Sun.

ENTERTAINMENT

Auckland city has a wide range of entertainment venues and the main concert and opera venues are the modern Aotea Centre and the Town Hall, also part of the Aotea Centre.

Dance

Black Grace
10 Customs Street East
Tel: 09-358 0552
www.blackgrace.co.nz
An all-male dance company featuring some of New Zealand's most respected contemporary dancers.

Theatre

Aotea Centre Complex
Aotea Square
Tel: 09-309 2677
www.the-edge.co.nz
The city's main cultural venue and home to the Herald Theatre and the ASB Auditorium.

Auckland Theatre Company
108 Quay Street
Tel: 09-309 3395
www.atc.co.nz
This is the largest professional theatre company in New Zealand and is currently the most popular producer of professional theatre in Auckland. Audiences come from throughout Auckland to its season of seven or eight plays.

Civic Theatre
Corner Queen Street and Wellesley Street
Tel: 09-309 2677
www.civictheatre.co.nz
Touring musicals and shows play this atmospheric theatre built in 1929.

Maidment Theatre
Corner Princes and Alfred Streets
Tel: 09-308 2383
www.maidment.auckland.ac.nz
Popular venue for drama.

Silo Theatre
Lower Greys Avenue
Tel: 09-366 0339
www.silotheatre.co.nz
Auckland's boutique theatre experience.

Film

SkyCity Metro
291–297 Queen Street
Tel: 09-369 2400
www.skycitycinemas.co.nz
Where the latest blockbusters are shown.

SPORTS AND ACTIVITIES

Hurl yourself off the Sky Tower, or even off the Auckland Harbour Bridge if you wish, or take a ride along Auckland's waterfront on Tamaki Drive, or sail across the sparkling waters of Waitemata Harbour.

Bicycle Hire

Bike Central
3 Britomart Place, Auckland
Tel: 09-365 1768
www.bikecentral.co.nz
Bike hire, maintenance and repairs, and café. Ideal location from which to explore Tamaki Drive and bays.

Cycle Auckland
Shop 6, Devonport Wharf
Tel: 09-445 1189
www.cycleauckland.co.nz
Bike hire company, well placed to explore Devonport and North Shore Bays.

Bungy Jumping

Auckland Bridge Climb/Bungy
Curran Street, Westhaven Reserve
Tel: 09-361 2000
www.aucklandbridgeclimb.co.nz
Guided 1½-hour climb of Auckland Harbour Bridge, with an optional bungy jump.

Bungy jumping off the Sky Tower

Skyjump
Sky Tower, Auckland
Tel: 09-368 1835
www.skyjump.co.nz
See the sights from the Sky Tower, then take a 192m (630ft) -high base jump off it from a platform.

Sailing

Sail NZ
Viaduct Harbour
Tel: 09-359 5987
www.sailingnz.co.nz
Thrilling sailing trips aboard – sit back and enjoy the sights or take the helm and give it a blast on the grinders.

Spectator Sports

Auckland Racing Club
Ellerslie Racecourse, Ellerslie
Tel: 09-524 4069
www.ellerslie.co.nz
Twenty-six throughbred horse-racing events are held here throughout the year, including Auckland Cup Week in March.

Eden Park Stadium
Reimers Avenue, Kingsland
Tel: 09-815 5551
www.edenpark.co.nz
The country's largest stadium, with rugby in the winter and cricket in the summer. Rugby World Cup venue.

TOURS

A range of tours will help you to explore Auckland's key attractions, but to really experience the city you should get out on the water.

Bus Tours

Auckland Explorer Bus
Quay Street, Auckland
Tel: 09-524 7929
www.explorerbus.co.nz
A daily hop-on/hop-off tour departing from the Ferry Building on Quay Street. The bus runs hourly from 9am and stops at major attractions including Kelly Tarlton's.

Boat Trips

360 Discovery Cruises
Gulf Harbour Marina, Whangaparaoa
Tel: 0800-360 3472
www.360discovery.co.nz
Cruises on stable catamarans to the bird sanctuary of Tiritiri Matangi Island. Guided tours of the island are also available.

Fullers Cruise Centre
Pier 1, Ferry Building, 99 Quay Street
Tel: 09-367 9111
www.fullers.co.nz
Cruises from Auckland to Devonport and islands of the Hauraki Gulf, including Rangitoto Island and Waiheke Island. Also provides tractor-trailer rides to the summit of Rangitoto and a range of tours on Waiheke Island.

The view towards the Ferry Building

Walking Tours

Auckland Guided Tours
2A Byron Avenue, Takapuna
Tel: 09-446 6677
www.aucklandguidedtours.com
Various walking and wilderness walks including half-day, full-day and overnight hikes. Fishing and kayaking also available.

Wine Tours

Auckland Scenic Wine Tasting Tours
11 Pentland Avenue, Mount Eden
Tel: 09-630 1540
www.winetrailtours.co.nz
Small-group half-day and full-day guided tours of Auckland's key wine-growing regions.

FESTIVALS AND EVENTS

Due to its large population, events in Auckland are always well attended and several regularly attract international attention and attendance.

Pasifika Festival

January

Auckland Anniversary Regatta
Waitemata Harbour/Hauraki Gulf
www.regatta.org.nz
Fabulous celebration of the Auckland Anniversary, a regional public holiday.

February

Mission Bay Jazz and Blues Fest
Tamaki Drive, Mission Bay
www.jazzandbluesstreetfest.co.nz
With bands playing out in the street.

Devonport Food & Wine Festival
www.devonportwinefestival.co.nz
Two-day highlight of the Auckland calendar.

March

Pasifika Festival
Western Springs Park
Celebrating the people of the Pacific with live bands, cultural performances and food.

April

Royal Easter Show
ASB Showgrounds, Greenlane
www.royaleastershow.co.nz
A week of carnival rides, livestock competitions, wine awards and one of the southern hemisphere's largest equestrian shows.

May

New Zealand International Comedy Festival
Auckland City
www.comedyfestival.co.nz
A two-week showcase of the best local, national and international comedians.

July

Matariki Festival
Auckland-wide
www.matarikifestival.org.nz
The Maori New Year is marked by the rising of Matariki, the group of stars also known as the Pleiades or Seven Sisters, and the sighting of the new moon. Concerts, performances, tree plantings, art exhibitions and workshops are held city-wide.

September

New Zealand Fashion Week
Viaduct Harbour
www.nzfashionweek.co.nz
Starring New Zealand's best fashion designers, this one-week event with catwalk shows and a trade exhibition is well attended.

Northland

When you stand on a deserted beach in Northland, you can imagine what how the land must have appeared to the first Polynesian settlers who landed here in their great ocean-going canoes after the explorations of the legendary navigator Kupe. The region remains an unspoilt idyll where subtropical waters lap against golden beaches.

Whangarei

Population: 68,000

Local dialling code: 09

Tourist office: Bay of Islands i-Site; tel: 09-402 7345; **www.northlandnz.com**

Main police station: Whangarei Central Police; Lower Cameron Street; tel: 09-430 4500

Main post office: Central Post Office; 16 Rathbone Street, Whangarei

Main hospital: Whangarei Hospital, Maunu Road; tel: 09-430 4100; **www.northlanddhb.org.nz**

Media: *Northern Advocate*; *Whangarei Leader*

Main transport hubs: Whangarei Airport, Handforth Street, Onerahi; tel: 09-436 0047; **www.whangareiairport.co.nz**

Car hire companies: Northland Rentals; tel: 09-408 1905; **www.northlandrentals.co.nz.** Go Birdz Rentals; tel: 09-402 7043; **www.gobirdz.co.nz.**

Taxi companies: Kiwi Carlton Cabs; tel: 0800 455 555. Phoenix Cabs; tel: 09-438 9933.

Northland has a special allure which lies in its endless string of sheltered bays, each fringed with honey-tinged sands, and in its tranquil harbours where mist rises slowly every morning; it's also found among the ancient kauri forests and in the fragrant manuka-covered headlands of the wind-whipped west coast. The region stretches 350km (220 miles) north of Auckland to Cape Reinga, where the Pacific Ocean and Tasman Sea collide in a maelstrom of churning waves and spume. Its western shores comprise two of the nation's longest beaches – both driveable and used as public highways – while the east coast features masses of coves, some only accessible by boat. Game fishing is a big attraction here, as is scuba diving, especially around the Poor Knights Islands. A good approach to touring the region is to head north by way of Whangarei on SH1, returning via the west coast townships of Opononi, Dargaville and Matakohe.

Whangarei and Around

At the top of the winding Brynderwyn Hills, the spectacular panorama of Bream Bay, from its sweeping white-sand surf beach framed by the jagged silhouette of Whangarei Heads to the dramatic peaks of the Hen and Chicken Islands, signals the beginnings of Whangarei's striking coastline.

Waipu

Set back from Bream Bay on sunny plains lies the Scottish outpost of **Waipu** ❶, where the **Waipu Museum** (36 The Centre; www.waipumuseum.com; daily 9.30am–4.30pm; charge) highlights the extraordinary journey of the bay's original settlers. Those with stout shoes and a torch can explore the limestone formations of **Waipu Caves** (14km/8½ miles west via Shoemaker Road; 👪 ; *see p.103*), while highly endangered fairy terns are a highlight of **Waipu Cove Wildlife Refuge**

Unspoilt view of Bream Bay

(Johnson Point Road; free 👪) en route to **Waipu Cove**, a safe place to swim, fish and surf.

Whangarei City and Environs

From Waipu, it's 56km (38 miles) north to **Whangarei** ❷, Northland's largest town and deep sea port. The Town Basin area on the waterfront draws visitors to its cafés and galleries, and **Claphams Clocks** (www.claphamclocks.co.nz; daily 9am–5pm; charge 👪), a vast display of timepieces. In the northern suburb of Tikipunga, **Whangarei Falls** plummets 25m (80ft) into a deep bush-fringed pool and a loop track provides excellent viewing. A 10-minute drive west of Whangarei leads to the **Native Bird Recovery Centre** (SH14, Maunu; www.whangareinativebirdrecovery.org.nz; charge 👪) where kids will delight in the antics of its permanent residents – Sparky the one-legged kiwi and Woof-Woof the talking tui. From Whangarei, you can make side-trips out to the coast – take the scenic drive to Whangarei Heads and hike up Mount Manaia for

Whangarei Falls

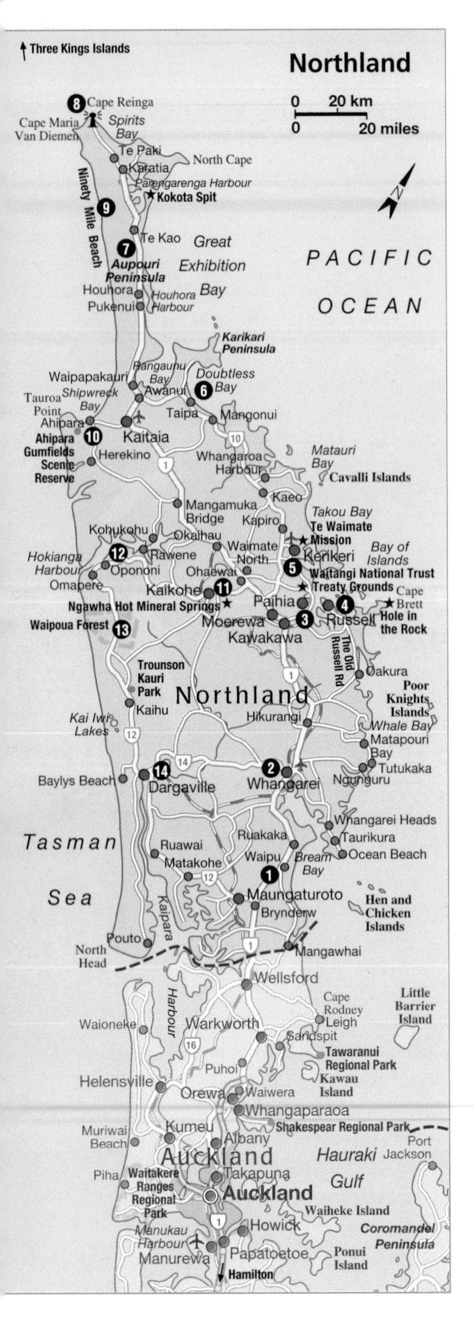

excellent views of **Bream Bay** and the **Hen and Chicken Islands**; or drive to **Tutukaka**, gateway to the **Poor Knights Islands** and some of the best diving, snorkelling *(see p.96)* and game fishing in the world, plus sea-based activities such as speed-boat trips to **Riko Riko**, the world's largest sea cave.

Bay of Islands

The Bay of Islands has long been renowned for its dramatic seascapes, and, rich in Maori and European history, it is often dubbed the birthplace of the nation. Here you can walk in the footsteps of the mighty warrior Hone Heke, visit the first seat of government and stand in the place where New Zealand's founding document, the Treaty of Waitangi, was signed in 1840.

Around Paihia

Surprisingly, it is the public toilets of **Kawakawa** that put it on the tourist map, as they are the last works of renowned Austrian-born artist Friedrich Hundertwasser. Historic train tracks run the length of Kawakawa's main street, recalling the old days of milling and coal mining; these run to Opua, where vehicular ferries provide transport to Russell.

The hub of the Bay of Islands is **Paihia ❸**. It's a good base for excursions and tours to explore the bay's 144 islands, which depart frequently from the wharf. **Fullers Bay of Islands** *(see p.97)* operate a range of cruises, including trips to the **Hole in the Rock**, a naturally formed rock arch on Piercy Island, off Cape Brett. Historical sights, including Captain Cook's 1769 anchorage and the cove

Ngatoki Matawhaorua, a Maori canoe at the Waitangi National Trust Treaty Grounds

where French explorer Marion du Fresne was slain by Maori in 1772, are pointed out en route, and some trips disembark at **Urupukapuka Island**, to explore *pa* sites (fortified living areas).

Waitangi

A river separates Paihia from **Waitangi National Trust Treaty Grounds** (www.waitangi.net.nz; daily 9am–5pm; charge 👪), where the Treaty of Waitangi was signed on 6 February 1840. On behalf of Queen Victoria, Governor William Hobson signed this pact to end the conflict, guarantee the Maori land rights, give them and the colonists Crown protection, and admit New Zealand to the British Empire. Attractions here include the **Treaty House**, the ornately carved *whare runanga* (meeting house), and Ngatoki Matawhaorua, an impressive 35m (115ft) canoe. A highlight of a visit is the modern Maori cultural performance held every evening by Culture North *(see p.96)*.

Russell

Across the bay is **Russell** ❹, where colonists first arrived in 1809, making it New Zealand's first white settlement. Once a lawless and dangerous port, Russell is now a peaceful and compact haven, reached by passenger ferry from Paihia. A good starting point for an exploration is the grand, colonial **Duke of Marlborough Hotel**, which holds the oldest liquor licence in the country. The police station next door was built in 1870, after fire destroyed most of the town's oldest buildings.

At the southern end of the bay are two survivors, the Roman Catholic **Pompallier House** (The Strand; www.pompallier.co.nz; daily 10am–5pm; charge), originally built as a print shop for Bishop Jean-Baptiste-François Pompallier, and the Anglican **Christ Church**, the country's oldest, built in 1836; the bullet holes in its walls are grim reminders of the siege of 1845.

Matauri Bay

On the coast north of Kerikeri the intriguing rock formations of Tauranga Bay give way to the deep bottle-green waters of Matauri Bay, the final resting place of the *Rainbow Warrior*, a Greenpeace ship, bombed by French agents in 1985. The threaded boulders of the memorial form a symbolic rainbow on the cliffs overlooking the Cavalli Islands, and can be reached via a series of staircases, a hike considered a pilgrimage by many New Zealanders.

Local history is on display at the **Russell Museum** (www.russellmuseum.org.nz; daily 10am–4pm; charge) on York Street; here you can learn about the defiant antics of Chief Hone Heke who felled the British flag four times. This is best followed up with a hike up **Flagstaff (Maiki) Hill** for stunning views of the bay.

Peaceful Russell, once a lawless port known as the 'hell-hole of the Pacific'

Kerikeri and Waimate

Kerikeri ❺, 23km (14 miles) northwest of Paihia, also has a rich backdrop of early Maori and European colonial history. **Kemp House** (daily 10am–5pm; charge), built on the Kerikeri Inlet in 1822, is New Zealand's oldest house, while the old **Stone Store** next door once served as a munitions store for troops fighting Hone Heke; these days, it's a shop/museum. Just to the south, a walkway leads to the site of **Kororipa Pa**, once the base of Chief Hongi Hika. Across the river is **Rewa's Village** (daily 9.30am–4.30pm; charge), a replica 18th-century Maori fishing village, while a 20-minute hike upriver () reveals the impressive 27m (88ft) cascade of **Rainbow Falls.**

About 15km (9 miles) southwest of Kerikeri is **Te Waimate Mission** (Nov–Apr daily 10am–5pm, May–Oct Mon, Wed, Sat 10am–4pm; charge), built in 1831–2 for George Augustus Selwyn, New Zealand's first Anglican bishop.

The Far North

Cape Reinga and the Far North is a region of great spiritual significance to Maori. They believe it is 'the place of the leaping', where the souls of the dead gather before they enter the next world. According to Maori traditions, the spirits of the departed leap from an 800-year-old pohutukawa tree on the cape to begin the voyage back to their ancestral homeland of Hawaiki.

Doubtless Bay

Captain Cook named this section of the coast in 1769 when he said it was 'doubtless a bay'. At the southern end of **Doubtless Bay** ❻ is **Mangonui**, once an important whaling port and now known for its fish and chip shop *(see p.95)*, the **Butler Point Whaling Museum** (Marchant Road; www.butlerpoint.co.nz; charge) and hilltop **Rangikapiti Pa Historic Reserve** (Rangikapiti Road; free) which affords expansive views of Doubtless Bay's sandy white beaches. At the northern end of these is the small seaside settlement of **Taipa**, where **Matthews Vintage Collection** (SH10; www.matthewsvintage.com; daily 9am–5pm; charge) displays eclectic memorabilia including vintage cars. The turn-off to **Karikari Peninsula**, 8km (5 miles) from Taipa, gives access to the bay's pristine northern beaches.

Aupouri Peninsula

The **Aupouri Peninsula** ❼ stretches up to Northland's tip. At its base is **Awanui**, where at the **Ancient Kauri Kingdom** (229 SH1; www.ancientkauri.co.nz; daily 9am–5pm; free) 30,000–50,000-year-old swamp kauri logs are crafted into homewares, and at **Gumdiggers Park** (171 Heath Road, Paparore; www.gumdiggerspark.co.nz; daily 9am–5pm; charge) a hundred-year-old gumfield remains testament to the days when settlers dug for kauri gum to make varnish.

Stop to see the 1860 **Subritsky Homestead**, plastered with a paste of powdered seashells at **Houhora Heads**, and at **Pukenui wharf** to see fishermen pulling in snapper. Mammoth ice creams are rolled at **Te Kao** store, and kayak tours with **Cape Reinga Adventures** depart from **Karatia**, crossing the Parengarenga Harbour to the dunes of Kokota Spit, the last landfall for migratory godwits flying to the Arctic.

Re-created Maori dwellings at Rewa's Village

Cape Reinga to Ahipara

At **Cape Reinga** ❽ a lighthouse, an 800-year-old pohutukawa tree, black rocks and screaming gulls mark land's end. Rippling into the distance is the turbulent meeting place of the Tasman Sea and the Pacific Ocean; beyond lie the **Three Kings Islands**. To the east is Spirits Bay, while Cape Maria Van Diemen and secluded Te Werahi and Twilight Beach lie to the west. Steep trails lead down to these; alternatively, take the road to **Tauputaputa Beach**.

The return trip south is best enjoyed on a drive along **Ninety Mile Beach** ❾ (4WD vehicle recommended). Stretching for some 103km (64 miles), this misnamed beach is flanked by the **Aupouri Forest**,

A lighthouse marks land's end at Cape Reinga

populated by bands of wild horses. Entry is via the Te Paki Stream where old boogie-boards can be rented from an on-site caravan to slide down the giant **Te Paki Dunes** 👪. Normal vehicles should return south on SH1; 4WD vehicles can follow the beach south to the ramp exits at Waipapakauri or Ahipara.

Ahipara and Environs

At the base of Ninety Mile Beach is **Kaitaia**, New Zealand's northernmost town, and the seaside village of **Ahipara** ❿, known for its shellfish – the succulent but protected toheroa, and the tuatua which may be freely gathered. Surfers come from all over the world to catch the waves here and at adjacent **Shipwreck Bay**. The nearby **Ahipara Gumfields Scenic Reserve** is a wilderness area where prospectors once excavated kauri gum from the sand. Hike or join a quad-bike adventure with **Tuatua Tours** *(see p.97)* to explore the reserve and the shanties of **Tauroa Point**.

The Hokianga and West Coast

When you first set your eyes upon the magnificent expanse of the Hokianga estuary, you can almost imagine the great Polynesian navigator Kupe gathering his canoes here for the return voyage to Hawaiki. To the north, enormous ochre dunes dominate the skyline, flanked by the misty kauri-coated peaks of the Warawara Forest. To the south lies Waipoua Forest, domain of Tane Mahuta, the country's oldest kauri tree.

Kaikohe to Opononi

Kaikohe ⓫, a large township servicing local farms, is the gateway to the Hokianga. Look out for the hilltop monument to Chief Hone Heke (at the top end of Monument Road; the route is signposted from SH12) which gives views of both coasts. **Ngawha Hot Mineral Springs** (Ngawha Springs Road; daily 9am–9.30pm; charge 👪) provides a tempting thermal soak.

To the west in **Rawene**, displays of colonial life can be seen at **Clendon**

House (8 Clendon Esplanade; summer Mon–Sat 10am–4pm, winter Mon–Tue 10am–4pm; charge). It was at the police station in 1898 that local Maori refused to pay dog tax, marking New Zealand's last armed conflict.

From Rawene it's a 19km (12-mile) drive west to **Opononi ⓬**, famed as the home of Opo, a friendly bottle-nosed dolphin, who played with children in the summer of 1955–6. Harbour cruises, sport fishing expeditions, kiwi spotting and sand hill sliding on the vast dunes at the harbour's entrance are popular pursuits.

Kauri Country

South of the Hokianga Harbour is **Waipoua Forest ⓭**, where enormous mature kauri trees pack some 2,500 hectares (6,200 acres). There are several walks to enjoy here, including the five-minute stroll on a wheelchair-friendly boardwalk to see 2,000-year-old Tane Mahuta (Lord of the Forest; free), the largest kauri of all. His mighty girth spans 13.8m (45.2ft), while his frame supports a volume of nearly 245 cubic m (8,650 cubic ft). Further south, **Trounson Kauri Park** has more fine specimens, and a 40-minute loop track meanders through thick native bush.

Tane Mahuta in Waipoua Forest

Kia Ora – Gidday!

Visitors to New Zealand quickly become immersed in the Maori language as most place names have Maori origins. At first these are confusing, but once you've grasped the five vowel sounds: a e i o u ('a' as in 'car', 'e' as in 'egg', 'i' like the 'ee' in 'tee', 'o' as in 'four', 'u' like an 'o' in 'to'), and the consonants 'wh' and 'ng' you'll find the language is extremely consistent in its pronunciation.

Around Dargaville

Dargaville ⓮ was founded on the timber and kauri gum trades, and the **Dargaville Museum** (Harding Park; daily 9am–4.30pm; charge) is packed with exhibits including shipwreck artefacts and a pre-Maori carving unearthed from nearby dunes. These dunes run the length of Ripiro Beach on the west coast and popular picnicking points include the nearby **Kai Iwi Lakes** and **Baylys Beach**.

River plains lush with kumara crops surround Dargaville and Ruawai. Here, SH12 turns east towards the **Matakohe Kauri Museum** (5 Church Road; www.kauri-museum.com; daily 9am–5pm; charge), which recounts the west coast's kauri-felling days.

ACCOMMODATION

Northland is blessed with a range of places to stay and many of these are within a short walk of the coast. Accommodation situated right on the waterfront attracts a higher premium, especially in larger tourist towns like Paihia. However, Northland's wealth of holiday parks, many with self-contained motel-like accommodation as well as camping sites, nearly always commands prime beachfront real estate where you can stay for a fraction of the price.

Whangarei District

Bream Bay Motel
67 Bream Bay Drive, Ruakaka
Tel: 09-432 7166
www.breambaymotel.co.nz
Self-contained one- and two-bedroom units set right on a popular surf beach. Sea views from upstairs units. **$$$**

Bay of Islands

Abel Tasman Lodge
Corner Marsden and Bayview Roads, Paihia
Tel: 09-402 7521
www.abeltasmanlodge.co.nz
Twenty-five apartment-style units featuring full kitchen and bathroom facilities; most apartments have sea views. **$$$**

Bay Adventurer Backpackers & Apartments
26–28 Kinds Road, Paihia
Tel: 0800-112 129
www.bayadventurer.co.nz
Secure surroundings and comfortable rooms, ranging from shared dormitories (six beds per room) to two-bedroom apartments. Pool, spa, kayaks, bikes all free to use. **$**

Edgewater Palms Apartments
8–10 Marsden Road, Paihia
Tel: 09-402 0090
www.edgewaterapartments.co.nz
Up-market self-contained apartments with sea views set around an outdoor saltwater pool and spa in a waterfront location. **$$$$$**

Accommodation Price Categories

Prices are for one night's accommodation in a standard double room (unless otherwise specified).

$ = below NZ$30
$$ = NZ$30–75
$$$ = NZ$75–150
$$$$ = NZ$150–350
$$$$$ = over NZ$350

Edgewater Palms Apartments

Russell Top 10 Holiday Park
Longbeach Road, Russell
Tel: 09-403 7826
www.russelltop10.co.nz
From budget-priced tent pitches and standard cabins to studios and one- and two-bedroom motel units, this park offers quality affordable accommodation. **$–$$$**

The Far North

Pukenui Lodge Motel
Corner SH1 and Wharf Rd, Pukenui
Tel: 09-409 8837
www.pukenuilodge.co.nz
A comfortable motel built on the site of a historic homestead which now houses separate backpacker accommodation. **$–$$$**

The Hokianga and West Coast

Copthorne Omapere
SH12, Omapere
Tel: 09-405 8737
www.omapere.co.nz
Relaxing harbourside accommodation with a pool, bar and restaurant. Most rooms offer sea views. **$$$**

RESTAURANTS

Northland's cafés and restaurants cater to variety of tastes, but the clear highlight is waterside Russell, a haven for chefs of international renown, who capitalise on the Bay of Island's abundant fresh seafood.

Restaurant Price Categories

Prices are for a standard meal for one.

$ = below NZ$15
$$ = NZ$15–30
$$$ = NZ$30–50
$$$$ = over NZ$50

Whangarei District

A Deco Restaurant
70 Kamo Road, Kensington, Whangarei
Tel: 09-459 4957
www.a-deco.co.nz
Nationally acclaimed restaurant using Northland's best produce in a stunning Art Deco setting. Reservations essential. **$$$–$$$$**

Reva's on the Waterfront
31 Quay Side, Town Basin Marina, Whangarei
Tel: 09-438 8969
www.revas.co.nz
With a good location right on the harbour, Reva's is a popular choice for pizzas, seafood and Mexican-style dishes. **$$$**

Waipu Cafe & Deli
29 The Centre, Waipu
Tel: 09-432 0990
Fresh sandwiches, rolls and panini and decent coffee, served by friendly staff. **$**

Bay of Islands

Alfrescos
6 Marsden Road, Paihia
Tel: 09-402 6797
A boutique-style café with ample outdoor seating and bay views. The wide-ranging menu includes fresh seafood, slabs of steak, and delicious lamb rump. **$–$$**

Duke of Marlborough Hotel
35 The Strand, Russell
Tel: 09-403 7829
www.theduke.co.nz
Historic hotel located right on the waterfront serving fish and chips, oysters and mussels, straight from the sea. **$$$**

Kamakura
The Strand, Russell
Tel: 09-403 7771
www.kamakura.co.nz
The best waterfront location in Russell, with tables set beneath sprawling pohutukawa trees right by the beach. Oysters – plucked from nearby Orongo Bay daily – are popular here, although the menu is wide-ranging. **$$$$**

The Far North

Mangonui Fish and Chip Shop
Beach Road, Mangonui
Tel: 09-406 0478
This fish-and-chip shop overhangs the Mangonui Harbour and is well known for preparing fresh, locally caught fish. Succulent Blue nose, served with lemon, is the speciality. **$**

The Hokianga and West Coast

The Boatshed Café
8 Clendon Esplanade, Rawene
Tel: 09-405 7728
Situated in a renovated shed on stilts overhanging the harbour, this well-established café has long served fresh home-made New Zealand fare. **$–$$**

Funky Fish Cafe
34 Seaview Road, Baylys Beach
Tel: 09-439 888
A classic Kiwi café offering courtyard garden dining surrounded by sculpture and original artworks. The Pacific oysters, garlic prawns and seafood chowder served here are all very good, as is the succulent Northland beef. **$$**

ENTERTAINMENT AND NIGHTLIFE

Nightlife is pretty relaxed in Northland but there are plenty of bars and pubs. The best places to head are Paihia and the town basin area of Whangarei.

Cultural Show

Culture North

Treaty Grounds, Waitangi

A well-choreographed, modern Maori cultural performance in which the tales of the bay unfold in a musical narrated by a Maori *kaumatua* (elder) to his grandson.

Theatre

Whangarei Theatre Company

Riverbank Centre, Whangarei

Tel: 09-438 3523

www.whangareitheatrecompany.org.nz

This amateur opera and drama society performs three shows a year, including musicals.

SPORTS AND ACTIVITIES

In Northland, activities gravitate around the beaches and marine areas for which the region is famous.

Bicycle Hire

Bay Beach Hire

300m/yds south of Paihia Wharf

Tel: 09-402 6078

www.baybeachhire.co.nz

Bay Beach Hire rent bicycles from $5 an hour plus various boats and beachcraft.

Diving/Snorkelling

Poor Knights Dive Centre

Corner of Marina Road and Marlin Place, Tutukaka

Tel: 09-434 3867

www.diving.co.nz

Snorkelling with the Poor Knights Dive Centre

A range of diving and snorkelling trips, plus speedboat trips to the Poor Knights Islands.

Kayaking

Cape Reinga Adventures

SH1, Karatia

Tel: 09-409 8445

www.capereingaadventures.co.nz

Kayaking tours across the Parengarenga Harbour to the dunes of Kokota Spit.

TOURS

There are plenty of opportunities to talk to friendly local guides about the region's culture, flora and fauna. If you wish to travel on Ninety Mile Beach, a 4WD bus tour is essential as rental cars are not permitted on this sand highway.

Boat Trips

Crossings Hokianga

29 SH12, Opononi

Tel: 09-405 8207

www.crossingshokianga.com

Harbour cruises, sport-fishing expeditions and an on-demand ferry service across the Hokianga Harbour to explore sand dunes.

Fullers Bay of Islands
Maritime Building, Paihia Wharf
Tel: 09-402 7421
www.fboi.co.nz
Fullers' cruises include a trip to the Hole in the Rock, a naturally formed rock arch on Piercy Island, off Cape Brett; weather permitting, vessels will pass through it. Others include the Original Cream Trip (the best of the Bay of Islands), Tall Ship voyages, and swimming with bottlenose dolphins.

Mack-Attack
Maritime Building, Paihia
Tel: 09-402 8180
www.mackattack.co.nz
Mack-Attack operates fast 90-minute trips to the Hole in the Rock, travelling in a powerful speedboat.

Bus Tours

Fullers Bay of Islands
Maritime Building, Paihia Wharf
Tel: 09-402 7421
www.fboi.co.nz
A range of cruises including a 4WD bus tour to Cape Reinga, which includes travelling one-way on Ninety Mile Beach.

Quad Bike Tours

Tuatua Tours
Main Road, Ahipara
Tel: 0800-494 288
www.tuatuatours.com
Quad-bike tours of Shipwreck Bay, the Ahipara Gumfields Scenic Reserve and Tauroa Point. No quad-biking experience is necessary, as training is provided.

Wildlife Tours

Footprints Waipoua
29 State Highway 12, Opononi
Tel: 09-405 8207
www.footprintswaipoua.com
Informative daily tours to Waipoua Forest to spot local kiwi and other native wildlife.

FESTIVALS AND EVENTS

Events are well attended by people living in the Northland region, particularly those which involve walking or boating, or the gathering of large extended family groups.

January

Tall Ships Regatta
Russell
www.aplaceinthesun.co.nz
An annual event for square riggers, two-masted vessels and classic sailing craft.

February

Waitangi Day
Waitangi Treaty Grounds
www.waitangi.net.nz
National day celebrating the Treaty of Waitangi, New Zealand's founding document, signed on 6 February 1840.

April

Helly Hansen Cape Brett Challenge
Cape Brett, Bay of Islands
www.capebrettchallenge.co.nz
Individual, relay team and off-road walking challenge at Cape Brett.

May

Waipoua Forest Fun Run & Walk
Waipoua Forest
www.footprintswaipoua.com/events
An annual 12km (7½-mile) run and walk through Waipoua kauri forest.

September

Northland Seafood Festival
Marsden Cove Marina, Bream Bay
www.nsf.net.nz
Presenting the best of Northland's wine and *kai moana* (seafood), with entertainment and cooking demonstrations.

Waikato, Coromandel, Bay of Plenty and East Cape

Anyone with a penchant for wide-open spaces will love the peaceful rolling countryside of the Waikato, Coromandel, Bay of Plenty and East Cape regions. Fringed with white sandy beaches and brushed with bush-covered ranges, these regions are ideal for long walks and hikes.

Hamilton

Population: 131,000

Local dialling code: 07

Tourist office: Hamilton i-Site, 5 Garden Place; tel: 07-575 2456; **www.visithamilton.co.nz**

Main police station: Hamilton Central, 6 Bridge Street; tel: 07-858 6200

Main post office: Hamilton Post Shop, 36 Bryce Street

Hospital: Waikato Hospital, Pembroke Street; tel: 07-839 8899; **www.waikatodhb.govt.nz**

Local media: *Waikato Times*

Airport: Hamilton Airport, Airport Road; tel: 07-848 9027; **www.hamiltonairport.co.nz**

Buses: Go Bus, tel: 07-846 8717; **www.gobus.co.nz**

Car hire: Avis, tel: 07-839 4915; **www.avis.co.nz.** Budget, tel: 07-838 3585; **www.budget.co.nz.**

Taxis: Red Cabs, tel: 07-839 0500. Hamilton Taxis, tel: 07-847 7477.

The idyllic heartland of the Waikato found fame as The Shire in Peter Jackson's *The Lord of the Rings* trilogy, but rural landscapes are just a part of what this region has to offer. You can take a cruise through the city of Hamilton on New Zealand's longest river, catching a sneak preview of the renowned Hamilton Gardens on its banks; hit the surf at Raglan, home to one of the world's longest left-hand breaks; or wind through the back roads to Kawhia, steeped in Maori history and with legendary fishing and a seldom-visited hot-water beach, and to Waitomo Caves, where fabulous limestone caverns are illuminated by millions of glow-worms. To the northeast lies the scenic Coromandel Peninsula, dominated by dramatic mountain ranges cloaked in native bush; its coast features myriad beaches and islands.

East Cape horses

Continuing along the coastline are the sun-drenched shores of the Bay of Plenty, while the remote region of East Cape is where you can still see horses tied up outside the general store ready to provide a ride home.

Waikato

The central and western region of the North Island was once a wild landscape of dense bush on the hills, with peat swamps and kahikatea (white pine) forests on the lowlands, communally owned by Maori tribes. Following the New Zealand Wars, the natural wilderness was gradually tamed into one of the country's great agricultural areas, where fertile, grassy plains grow in a mild, wet climate and dairy herds graze freely.

Hamilton

Although it is a bustling city – the fourth largest in the country – **Hamilton ❶** sits in a park-like environment on the banks of the Waikato River, New Zealand's longest waterway. It was this river, long a vital Maori transport and trading link to the coast, that first brought Europeans to the area and led to the establishment of Hamilton in the 1860s. The first businesses grew on the river bank, and today the city's commercial hub runs parallel to it on the west bank. The best view is from a **Waikato River cruise** *(see p.117)*.

At the **Waikato Museum** (www.waikatomuseum.org.nz; daily 10am–4.30pm; free) on Victoria Street you can discover 15,000 Tainui (Waikato's Maori tribe) artefacts, including wood and stone carvings, and woven flax garments. Also located within the same building is the **Exscite Centre** (www.exscite.org.nz; charge), an interactive

Italian Renaissance garden at the Hamilton Gardens

science and technology environment with an earthquake simulator.

Just south of the centre on SH1 is the city's most popular attraction, the **Hamilton Gardens** (www.hamiltongardens.co.nz; daily 7.30am–5.30pm, until 8pm in summer; free), where there are various garden 'rooms' to enter including the tranquil Japanese and Indian Char gardens.

Harbour Towns

From Hamilton an easy drive through rolling countryside leads to the harbourside town of **Raglan** ❷ where there are several historical buildings, including the 1866 Harbour View Hotel, the 1874 immigrant cottage at 1 Bow Street and the old school in Stewart Street. However, Raglan is most famous with the surfing crowd for the much vaunted left-hand break at **Manu Bay**. An international surfing competition is held here every year and **Raglan Surfing School** *(see p.116)* provides tuition for beginners through to advanced surfers.

Further south in **Kawhia** ❸, well off the beaten tourist track, you can dig your own hot-water spa pool in the sand on its wild ocean beach. **Kawhia Seafoods**, right on the wharf, is deservedly well known for its delicious fresh fish and chips.

Waitomo

Outcrops of stratified and eroded limestone mark the approach to **Waitomo**, where the land is honeycombed with caves. These include

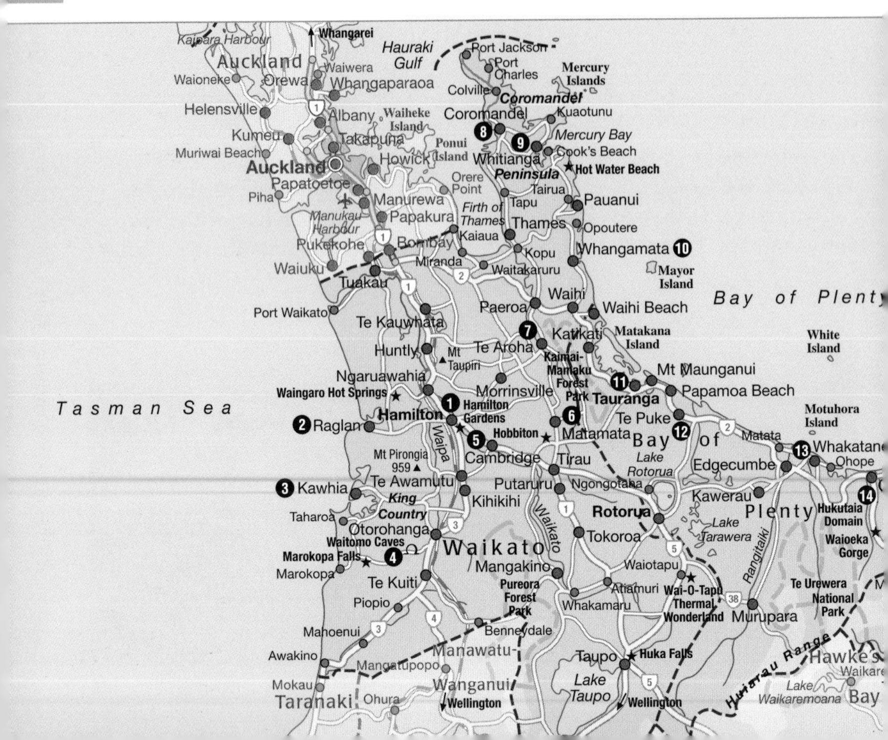

St Benedict's Cavern at Waitomo

the **Waitomo Caves** ❹, where guided tours lead down to the 14m (46ft) -high 'Cathedral', adorned with stalactites and stalagmites. But the highlight comes at the end: an awe-inspiring boat ride through enormous caverns, guided by the radiant light of millions of tiny glowworms. To learn more about them, visit the **Waitomo Caves Discovery Centre** (www.waitomocaves.com; daily Dec–Feb 8.30am–7pm, Feb–May 8.30am–5.30pm, June–Nov 9am–5pm; charge) by the i-Site Visitor Centre, where informative displays explain the biology, geography and history of the region *(see below)*. Other well-known underground chambers in the vicinity include the **Ruakuri and Aranui caves** *(see p.116)*.

What Lies Beneath?

If you can, aim to visit the Waitomo Caves Discovery Centre first to enhance your experience underground. Displays here include:

- Information about Waitomo's karst (eroded limestone) landscapes, how they were formed and the different types of cave formations, plus fossilised bones of bats, moa and kiwi
- A multimedia show, *Arachnocampa Luminosa*, which tells the story of the New Zealand glow-worm and other cave dwellers
- A history of early exploration of the area
- A cave crawl, involving a tight squeeze through a cunningly constructed rock wall

Waikato, Coromandel, Bay of Plenty and East Cape

THE UNDERWORLD

New Zealand offers some of the most challenging and spectacular caving in the world, both guided and unguided. You can opt for a dreamy drift through a glow-worm-festooned grotto to a daring tube race over waterfalls and rapids. Or descend into the underworld on an abseiling rope – passionate local guides will lead you into otherwise unseen river gorges and caverns, dropping down behind giant cascades to witness the grandeur of rock sculptures formed by millions of years of water erosion.

Caves are found throughout New Zealand, but the best range of guided activities is found amid the scenic karst landscape of Waitomo *(see p.100)*, a region riddled with 30-million-year-old underground limestone formations, which you can explore by blackwater rafting, abseiling and caving trips.

Curious karst features, stalactite formations and clusters of glow-worms are also a feature of Northland's Kawiti Caves. Here informative cave walks are lead by descendants of Chief Kawiti (they still own the land) who unfold the caves' unique pre-European discovery.

Other guided subterranean tours can be followed at Oparara Caves on the South Island's west coast, and at the Te Anaroa Caves near Golden Bay on the north coast. The latter feature

Admiring the stalactites at Waitomo Caves

delicate icicle-like stalactites and stalagmites, bacon drapes, straws, columns and unique, delicately formed limestone 'gypsum flowers'.

It was pondering the translation of Te Anau, 'the cave with a current of swirling water', that led to the rediscovery of the Te Anau Glow-worm Caves in 1948 by Lawson Burrows. The 35-million-year-old limestone at this accessible cave network continues to be dissolved and moulded by the lake water and the caves echo with the sounds of water at work.

Opportunities to explore New Zealand's cave networks independently abound, with tracks that allow easy access for novice explorers equipped with torches, spare batteries and stout shoes. Good examples can be found at the Mangaone Caves near Wairoa, the Onepoto Caves near Lake Waikaremoana and the Piripiri Caves near Waitomo. At the accessible Waipu Caves in Northland you can undertake a slippery but thrilling hike into its caverns through knee-deep water, and there's also the chance for experienced cavers to 'freestyle' other holes into hourglass caves filled with millions of delicate limestone straw formations.

Proficient cavers will also be thrilled by the challenge of Harwood's Hole near Takaka (Golden Bay). Its 200m (655ft) drop into the Starlight Cave draws abseiling specialists and caving professionals from around the world to tackle the plunge into the southern hemisphere's largest daylight shaft.

Setting off on a blackwater-rafting adventure at Waitomo

Abseiling into the 'Lost World' with Waitomo Adventures

Waitomo makes a splash for its blackwater rafting, which replicates the thrills of the whitewater variety – except underground and in the dark. **Waitomo Adventures** offers a two-hour blackwater journey as well as various abseiling, climbing and caving expeditions.

Provincial Towns

Just over 20km (12 miles) southeast of Hamilton, the rural township of **Cambridge** ❺ lies at the heart of the local equine industry. At **New Zealand Horse Magic**, performances showcase various horse breeds, with riding available at the end of the show *(see p.116)*.

Further east **Matamata** ❻ is also well known for its thoroughbred racehorse stables – as well as its hobbits. Fans of *The Lord of the Rings* should visit **Hobbiton** (tours daily; www.hobbitontours.com) to see hobbit holes still remaining from the film set. Other attractions include the **Firth Tower Historical Museum** (Thur–Mon 10am–4pm; charge), an interactive historical experience, and the hikes of the nearby **Kaimai-Mamaku Forest Park**, including the magnificent Wairere Falls.

To the northeast of Hamilton, **Morrinsville** is a centre for the surrounding dairy land with its own large processing factory. **Te Aroha** ❼ was once a gold town and fashionable Victorian spa; today, it's known for the **Te Aroha Mineral Spas and Leisure Pools** (Boundary Street; www.tearohapools.co.nz; daily 11am–9pm), a complex of public and private pools including an original turn-of-the-20th-century bathhouse. Te Aroha is also the site of the world's only known hot soda-water fountain, the **Mokena Geyser**. The geyser erupts at 30–40-minute intervals, gushing up to 4m (13ft).

Tranquil view close to the tip of the Coromandel Peninsula

Birdwatching at Mercury Bay

Coromandel

The Coromandel Peninsula is dominated by a dramatic mountain range cloaked in native bush. It is one of New Zealand's most ruggedly beautiful regions, with hot-water beaches, sea caves, giant blowholes and marine reserves, as well as forests, waterfalls, spectacular rock formations and beautiful water gardens. The early European settlers who flocked here were bushmen and gold-seekers, and reminders abound in the colonial buildings and old gold-mining shafts. Nowadays, visitors flock to the great outdoors for diving, boating, swimming, fishing, camping and hiking.

Thames and Kauaeranga Valley

At the base of the Coromandel Peninsula is **Thames**, officially declared a goldfield in 1867 *(see p.106)*. About 10km (6 miles) northeast of Thames, the **Kauaeranga Valley** is the site of the **Department of Conservation (DOC) Visitor Centre** (Kauaeranga Valley Road). The first kauri spars were logged here in 1795, and by 1830 kauri trees were being cut in greater numbers. Huge kauri timber dams were built across streams to bank up water and then float the logs to sea; several dams can still be seen today. The valley is popular for camping and tramping, and more than 50km (30 miles) of tracks provide forest access.

Coromandel and Coast

En route along the coast road to Coromandel township, the **Rapaura Watergardens** (www.rapaurawatergardens.co.nz; daily 9am–5pm; charge), 7km (4 miles) along the Tapu-Coroglen Road, is an inspiring side-trip for gardening enthusiasts. This road crosses all the way to the east coast but it is rough going and most travellers prefer to cross at **Coromandel** ❽ *(see also p.106)*.

The town was named when the Royal Navy ship HMS *Coromandel* called into the harbour in 1820 seeking kauri spars. It was the site of New Zealand's first gold find in 1852. Find out more at the **Coromandel Historical Museum** (Mon–Fri 10am–1pm, Sat–Sun 1.30–4pm; charge) on Rings Road, where there is a jailhouse out back.

Beyond Coromandel lies the one-horse town of Colville; from here the

TOUR OF COROMANDEL

This two-day driving tour explores the Coromandel Peninsula's twin coasts, from its old gold-mining townships and mountainous kauri-clad ranges to its sandy surf beaches, resort towns, rock formations and thermal wonders.

Begin at **Thames**, a service town located at the base of the Coromandel Peninsula. Now with a population of just 7,000, Thames had New Zealand's largest population back in its heyday – some 18,000 inhabitants attracted by the gleam of gold. For glimpses of the past, drive down Pollen Street where old mining buildings remain, including **Brian Boru Hotel**, one of a hundred or so hotels that once stood here. These days, **Sola Café** *(see p.115)*, also on Pollen Street, makes a good refreshment stop.

To continue, head north on Pollen Street and turn right back onto SH25, then right again for the **Goldmine Experience** on Moanataiari Road. The original site of the 1868 Gold Crown claim, it now features a photographic exhibition, gold-panning and guided tours of old mine shafts; closed-toe footwear is recommended.

Coromandel Township

Continue north on SH25, travelling along the waterline on a route edged with pohutukawa trees (New Zealand Christmas trees) to **Coromandel** *(see also p.105)*. Take a walk around the town, which has an arty atmosphere, to admire its Victorian buildings and relics from the gold-mining and timber industries. For a bite to eat, visit **Pepper Tree** *(see p.115)* on Kapanga Road. At the **Coromandel Stamper Battery** on Buffalo Road you can see gold-panning, water-wheel and rock-crushing demonstrations. Now return south and turn right for **Driving Creek Railway**, a 30-year-old project evolving under the direction of Barry Brickell, a respected New Zealand potter. A narrow-gauge 15-inch track, with tunnels, spirals and a double-decker viaduct, zigzags uphill past sculptures to the 'Eyeful Tower', a wooden terminus with gorgeous views of the Firth of Thames.

Whitianga

After your exploration of Coromandel township, resume your drive, crossing the Coromandel Ranges on SH25. En route to Whitianga, you could visit the

Whangapoua on the Coromandel coast, with pohutukawa trees and a white-sand beach

beautiful East Coast beaches of **Matarangi**, **Kuaotunu** and **Opito Bay**.

Whitianga is the main hub for marine-based activities departing for the **Te Whanganui A Hei Marine Reserve**. Charter boats such as **Escapade** *(see p.117)* offer game fishing and fishing trips and sightseeing cruises.

Digging thermal pools at Hot Water Beach

Hahei and Hot Water Beach

Be sure to visit the village of **Hahei**, 16km (10 miles) south. Here you can hike the track to **Cathedral Cove**, where a gigantic arched cavern penetrates the headland, join a guided tour with **Cathedral Cove Kayaking** or hop aboard a boat cruise with **Hahei Explorer.**

For a thermal soak in your own freshly dug pool, drive south 10km (6 miles) and turn off, following the signs to **Hot Water Beach**. Hire a spade from Hot Waves Café, then stroll north along the beach to a rocky outcrop which marks where you should begin to dig.

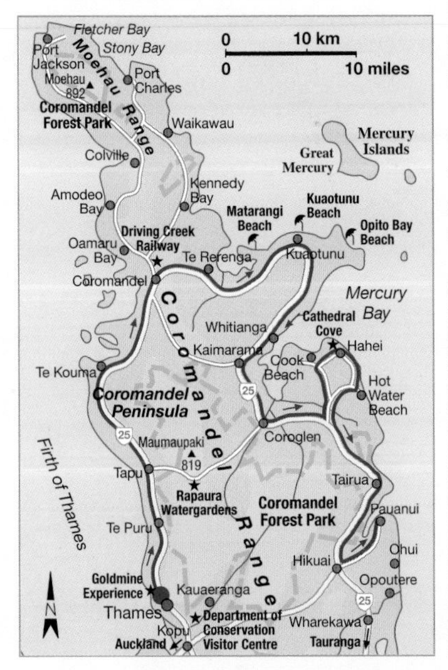

Tairua and Pauanui

Further south on SH25 is the town/resort of **Tairua**. Drive or hike up **Mount Paku** for the best views; Maori legend has it that if you climb to its peak you'll return within seven years.

The neighbouring community of **Pauanui** is a popular playground for wealthy Aucklanders who come for the swimming, surfing, fishing, diving, bush walks and golf.

Tips

- Distance: 452km (281 miles)
- Time: two days
- Begin at Thames
- Take extra care when driving. The road is narrow and winding and often skirts cliffs.
- Pack sturdy shoes for the Goldmine Experience
- Plan to arrive at Hot Water Beach at low tide

road north skirts the Moehau Range, and continues on to the unspoilt beauty of Port Jackson and **Fletcher Bay**. Here, at the end of the road, is the starting point of the **Coromandel Walkway**, a three-hour walk to the east coast's **Stony Bay**.

Whitianga

On the shores of Mercury Bay, **Whitianga** ❾ was once an important gum-shipping port. Several attractions lie within a short drive, including **Cooks Beach** where Captain Cook hoisted the British flag in November 1769 to claim the territory in the name of King George III. While here, he also observed the transit of Mercury; a cairn and plaque at the summit of the dramatic **Shakespeare Cliffs** mark the occasion. Further south is **Hahei**, where a track leads to **Cathedral Cove**, notable for its majestic rock formations. **Hot Water Beach**, another 9km (6 miles) south, provides a thermal soak in a self-dug pool *(see p.107)*.

Tairua to Waihi

The settlement of **Tairua** is dominated by 178m (584ft) **Mount Paku**, from the summit of which there are views of nearby islands. Across the harbour is the affluent resort of **Pauanui**, and 26km (16 miles) further south is **Opoutere**, where a secluded ocean beach and a lagoon are tucked away behind a forest of pines. At the southern end of Opoutere Beach is the **Wharekawa Harbour Wildlife Refuge** (free), a protected breeding area for rare native birds. A short drive south leads to **Whangamata** ❿, a popular family holiday spot with a prime surfing beach. There are lots of land-based activities too, with two good golf courses, mountain biking and walking trails including the Wharekirauponga, Wentworth Valley and Luck at Last Mine tracks. From Whangamata, the road winds inland for 30km (19 miles) to **Waihi**, an old gold-mining town, where a rich gold- and silver-bearing lode was discovered in 1878.

Maori warrior statue and gold mine pumphouse at Waihi

Cricket on the beach at the resort township of Mount Maunganui

Bay of Plenty

From the earliest days of habitation, the sun-favoured shores of the Bay of Plenty have seared themselves into the memories of all who pass by. Maori first made their homes here, surrounded by the irresistibly rich bounty of the seas, forested hills and fertile soils, and today the bay continues to attract new residents.

Tauranga to Mount Maunganui

Often dubbed the 'coast with the most', the bustling cosmopolitan export port of **Tauranga ⓫**, a bridge away from Mount Maunganui's ocean beach charms, boasts sheltered harbour waters. The first missionaries arrived in this flax trading town in 1838, and **The Elms Mission House** (www.theelms.org.nz; Wed, Sat–Sun and public holidays 2–4pm; charge) on Mission Street was completed in 1847. Later on, during the New Zealand Wars, Tauranga was the site of fierce fighting during the Battle of Gate Pa. The **Monmouth Redoubt** and the Mission Cemetery hold the remains of the British troops and local Maori.

Across the harbour is the year-round holiday township of **Mount Maunganui**, where sun-bleached holiday-makers with surfboards weave their way to and from its

Tauranga

Population: 116,000

Local dialling code: 07

Tourist office: Bay of Plenty i-Site, Salisbury Avenue; tel: 07-575 5099; **www.bayofplentynz.com**

Police station: Tauranga Central, Monmouth Street; tel: 07-577 4300

Post office: Tauranga Post Shop, 536 Cameron Street

Hospital: Tauranga Hospital, Cameron Road; tel: 07-579 8000; **www.pobdhb.govt.nz**

Local media: *Bay of Plenty Times*

Airport: Tauranga Airport, 73 Jean Batten Drive; tel: 07-575 2456; **www.tauranga-airport.co.nz**

Buses: Bay Bus; tel: 0800-422 928; **www.baybus.co.nz**

Car hire: Tauranga Car Rental; tel: 07-571 1624; **www.taurangacarrental.co.nz**

Taxis: Tauranga Taxis; tel: 07-578 6086; **www.taurangataxis.co.nz**

The Origins of Whakatane

Whakatane takes its name from the arrival of the Mataatua canoe from Hawaiki at the local river mouth. Legend records that the men went ashore and left the women in the canoe, which began to drift away. Though it was *tapu* (forbidden) for women to touch paddles, the captain's daughter, Wairaka, seized one and shouted: 'Kia whakatane au i ahau!' ('I will act as a man!'). Others followed suit and so the canoe was saved and the settlement was named Whakatane – to be manly. A bronze statue of Wairaka now stands on a rock at the river mouth.

A potter near Opotiki on the Bay of Plenty

white sandy surf beach *(see p.116)*. The town is built around the 231m (758ft) extinct volcanic cone of Mount Maunganui. A walkway leads to the mountain's summit, punctuated by seats offering amazing harbour, ocean and city views.

Te Puke to Whakatane

Trundling into **Te Puke** ⓬, the kiwi fruit capital of NZ, located 28km (17 miles) southeast of Tauranga, a huge green plastic slice of the fruit beckons passers-by into **Kiwi 360** (SH2; www.kiwi360.com; kiwikart tours: summer 9am–4pm, winter 10am–3pm, charge; 👪), an orchard park, information centre and restaurant, where 'kiwikarts' take visitors for trips around the park to learn all about kiwi-fruit growing.

Further south is **Whakatane** ⓭ at the mouth of the Whakatane River and the edge of the fertil Rangitaiki Plains. Here there's a host of wonderful river and bush walks, and the chance to dive, hook the 'big one', swim with the dolphins that thrive in the bay or visit terrifying but unmissable **White Island**, New Zealand's only active island volcano, 50km (30 miles) from the shore. Daily boat trips with **White Island Tours** *(see p.117)* include guided walks of its shuddering lunar-like landscape. The island is also known for its thriving colonies of seabirds.

East Cape

The road from Opotiki to Gisborne wraps itself around the East Cape – the country's most easterly point and one of the first places in the world to see the new day – in a necklace of picturesque bays. The area is a seldom-seen part of New Zealand with its own distinctive personality, and though the scenic route can be driven in a day, its beaches are well worth lingering over.

Opotiki to Hicks Bay

The rural centre and driftwood-strewn coast of **Opotiki** offers beautiful walking both on the beach and at **Hukutaia Domain** ⓮, where a hike leads to a puriri burial tree, named **Taketakerau** and estimated to be more than 2,000 years old. It was discovered in 1913 when a storm broke off one of its branches to reveal numerous human bones that had been interred by Maori. The bones were later re-interred and the *tapu* (sacred or taboo) status lifted from the tree. From Opotiki there are two routes to Gisborne: across or around the cape. The route across is faster, following SH2 through **Waioeka Gorge**.

However, the alternative route, which follows SH35 around East Cape, provides some of the most beautiful coastal driving New Zealand has to offer. Highlights include the old whaling town of **Te Kaha**, with its pretty crescent-shaped beach, and **Raukokore**, where the Anglican Christ Church (1894) leans precariously on a promontory thanks to the Wahine storm of 1968. Whanarua Bay's **Pacific Coast Macadamias** offer delicious scoops of their very own macadamia and manuka honey ice cream, and **Waihau Bay** is a popular place to camp and dive. Several more beautiful bays are passed on the way to **Whangaparaoa**, where Maori canoes landed in AD 1350. Rounding the cape, the next stop is **Hicks Bay**, where horse riding is popular and you can join a 2–3-day horse trek.

Te Araroa to Wainui Beach

Te Araroa ⓯ is noted for its enormous 600-year-old pohutukawa tree, named

Whangara village near Gisborne was used as a setting in the film *Whale Rider*

Traditional Maori wooden sculpture at Gisborne

Te Waha o Rerekohu and believed to be New Zealand's largest, featuring 22 trunks and an overall spread of 37m (122ft). The manuka tree also holds a special place in this community: its leaves are harvested from all over the cape and brought to the Te Araroa Manuka Oil Plant for extraction.

From Te Araroa a turn-off leads to the **East Cape lighthouse**, where the views are spectacular. South of Te Araroa, SH35 runs inland and passes through **Tikitiki,** home to **St Mary's Church**, built in 1924 to honour Maori servicemen killed in World War I, with an intricately carved interior. Just off the highway is **Ruatoria**, centre of the Ngati Porou tribe, where a range of authentic Maori arts can be purchased; further on,

Te Kooti, a Tough Cookie

These days Gisborne is a peaceful place to visit; however, it was once the site of many tribal battles. One of the most intruguing stories concerns the Maori prophet Te Kooti, who led a rebellion against settlers in the 19th century. He was exiled to the distant Chatham Islands, hundreds of kilometres off the east coast of the North Island – but that wasn't the end of him. He masterminded a daring escape back to the mainland and, believing God had appeared to him and promised he would save the Maori as he had saved the Jews, founded a religious movement that still exists called Ringatu ('The Upraised Hand'). Upon learning of his return the government sent an army in pursuit, but Te Kooti proved a formidable enemy, striking back with guerrilla attacks that kept him free and the government harassed. He was eventually pardoned in his old age and was allowed to live with his followers in the King Country area.

the hotel at **Te Puia** has hot springs on site.

At **Tokomaru Bay** the road joins the coast again where it continues on to Gisborne; along the way are several small roads leading off to expansive bays. Notable among these is **Anaura Bay** where there is a campsite, and **Tolaga Bay**, the site of New Zealand's longest wharf.

Closer to Gisborne is **Whangara**, the location used for the 2002 film *Whale Rider*. Approaching Gisborne is **Wainui Beach**, where there is a variety of accommodation. It is close to the city and provides a convenient beach base.

Gisborne

Gisborne ⓰, the 'City of Bridges,' is situated on the banks of the Taruheru and Waimata rivers and Waikanae Creek, which join to form the Turanganui River. On Stout Street, close to the centre, **Tairawhiti Museum** (www.tairawhitimuseum.org.nz; Mon–Fri 10am–4pm, Sat 11am–4pm, Sun 1.30–4pm; free) recounts the history of the city and its coast – Young Nick's Head across the bay was the first land that British explorer Captain James Cook and his crew sighted in 1769, and Cook's landing site was at the foot of **Kaiti Hill**.

Although the city lingers over its association with Cook, the area has earlier historical associations. A wealth of traditional Maori meeting houses line the coast. One of the largest in the country is **Te Poho-o-Rawiri** (tel: 06-867 2103, by appointment only) on Queens Drive; it contains impressive *tukutuku* (woven reed) panels and magnificent carvings.

Inland is sheep and cattle country, citrus, apple and kiwi-fruit orchards, vineyards and market gardens which support a large processing industry. With 15 wineries in the area, it's no surprise that Gisborne's wines – particularly Chardonnay and Gewürztraminer – are among the best in the country; many can be sampled at vineyards open to the public.

Gisborne is noted for its wineries

ACCOMMODATION

The Waikato, Coromandel, Bay of Plenty and East Cape regions offer accommodation to suit all budgets – but book in advance during January when New Zealanders are on holiday.

Accommodation Price Categories

Prices are for one night's accommodation in a standard double room (unless otherwise specified).

$ = below NZ$30
$$ = NZ$30–75
$$$ = NZ$75–150
$$$$ = NZ$150–350
$$$$$ = over NZ$350

Waikato

Port Waikato Top 10 Holiday Park
1158 Maunsell Road, Port Waikato
www.portwaikatoholidaypark.co.nz
Spacious holiday park with camping sites, cabins, kitchen cabins and motels. **$–$$$**

Ventura Inn and Suites Hamilton
23 Clarence Street, Hamilton
Tel: 07-838 0110
www.venturainns.co.nz
Central location; some rooms have king-size beds and spa baths. **$$$**

Waitomo Caves Hotel
Lemon Point Road, Waitomo Village
Tel: 07-878 8204
www.waitomocaveshotel.co.nz
Victorian-style hotel complete with turrets, with accommodation to suit families, couples and backpackers. **$$–$$$$**

Coromandel

Admiralty Lodge Motel
69–71 Buffalo Beach Road, Whitianga
Tel: 07-866 0181
www.admiraltylodge.co.nz
Beachfront apartments, all with sea views. Heated swimming pool. **$$$$**

Waitomo Caves Hotel

Waihi Beach Top 10 Holiday Park
15 Beach Road, Waihi Beach
Tel: 07-863 5504
www.waihibeach.com
Beachfront holiday park in excellent location with campsites, cabins and motel units. **$–$$$$**

Bay of Plenty

Bay Palm Motel
84 Girven Road, Mount Maunganui
Tel: 07-574 5971
www.baypalmmotel.co.nz
Clean, comfortable studio, one- two- and three-bedroom units with spa baths, close to shops and beach. Heated pool. **$$–$$$**

Papamoa Beach Top 10 Holiday Resort
535 Papamoa Beach Road, Papamoa
Tel: 07-572 0816
www.papamoabeach.co.nz
Right on the beach front with a range of options for all budgets. **$–$$$$**

East Cape

Hicks Bay Motel
5198 Te Araroa Road, Hicks Bay
Tel: 06-864 4880
www.hicksbaymotel.co.nz
Campsites, bunk rooms and classic motel rooms. Pool, restaurant and bar. **$$–$$$**

Waikanae Beach Holiday Park
Grey Street, Gisborne
Tel: 06-867 5634
www.gisborneholidaypark.co.nz
Campsites, tourist flats and ranch-style cabins on Waikanae beachfront. **$–$$$$**

RESTAURANTS

Seafood packs the menus on the East Coast, while Waikato eateries are renowned for serving succulent locally raised beef.

Restaurant Price Categories

Prices are for a standard meal for one.

$ = below NZ$15
$$ = NZ$15–30
$$$ = NZ$30–50
$$$$ = over NZ$50

Waikato

The Narrows Landing
431 Airport Road, Hamilton
Tel: 07-858 4001
www.thenarrowslanding.co.nz
Gourmet cuisine with New Zealand and European influences served in an atmospheric, candlelit interior. **$$$–$$$$**

Coromandel

Eggsentric Café and Restaurant
1049 Purangi Road, Flaxmill Bay, Cooks Beach
Tel: 07-866 0307
Small menu of fresh, well-prepared food. Live music nightly and art exhibitions. **$$–$$$**

Pepper Tree
31 Kapanga Road, Coromandel Township
Tel: 07-866 8211
Light, fresh New Zealand fare; local green-lipped mussels are a speciality. **$$–$$$**

Sola Café
720 Pollen Street, Thames
Tel: 07-868 8781
Vegetarian café serving generous portions; offers a wheat- and gluten-free menu. **$**

Bay of Plenty

Sand Rock Café
4 Marine Parade, Mount Maunganui
Tel: 07-574 7554
Beachgoers are kept well fed with coffee and cake, all-day breakfasts, blackboard lunches and à la carte dinners. **$–$$$**

East Cape

Wharf Café Bar and Restaurant
The Waterfront, Gisborne
Tel: 06-868 4876
www.wharfbar.co.nz
Specialises in seafood and local produce, with a superb wine list. Book ahead. **$$–$$$**

NIGHTLIFE AND ENTERTAINMENT

Hamilton's entertainment scene includes live theatre, music and dance. And while Tauranga and Mount Maunganui offer pubs and bars, nightlife on the East Cape is virtually nonexistent – unless you count joining locals on a possum hunt.

Academy of Performing Arts
Knighton Road, Hamilton
Tel: 07-858 5105
Drama and dance performances, art and photography exhibitions, and Maori performing arts, at the University of Waikato campus.

The Baycourt Theatre
38 Durham Street, Tauranga
Tel: 07-577 7198
www.tauranga.govt.nz/baycourt
Stages exhibitions, festivals and events.

Founder Theatre
Corner Tristram Street and Norton Road, Hamilton
Tel: 07-838 6600
Live events from rock to classical, country to comedy and ballads to ballet.

Clarence Street Theatre
Clarence Street, Hamilton
Tel: 07-838 6600
The Clarence hosts drama, comedy and smaller concert events.

SPORTS AND ACTIVITIES

Water sports are popular in this region and there are some unique activities to try too, including caving and land sailing.

Caving

Waitomo Adventures
654 Waitomo Caves Road
Tel: 07-878 7788
www.waitomo.co.nz
Two-hour blackwater journeys, abseiling and caving trips including the seven-hour Lost World adventure, and tours through the spectacular St Benedict's Caverns.

The Waitomo Caves
39 Waitomo Caves Road
Tel: 07-878 8227
www.waitomocaves.co.nz
A 45-minute guided tour through the wonderful Glow-worm Cave. Also provides tours through Ruakuri and Aranui caves.

Diving/Snorkelling

Cathedral Cove Dive
48 Hahei Beach Road, Hahei
Tel: 07-866 3955
www.hahei.co.nz/diving
Dive courses and excursions in a marine reserve, plus hire of diving, snorkelling and fishing gear, body boards and bikes.

Horse Riding

New Zealand Horse Magic
SH1, Cambridge
Tel: 07-827 8118
www.cambridgethoroughbredlodge.co.nz
Performances showcase horse breeds including the Lipizzaner (the only one in New Zealand), New Zealand wild horse, Kaimaniwa, Arabian and Hackney. Visitors can ride a horse at the end of a show.

Kayaking

Cathedral Cove Kayaking
88 Hahei Beach Road, Hahei
Tel: 07-866 3877

Kayaking at Cathedral Cove near Hahei

www.seakayaktours.co.nz
Guided kayak trips (and paddling tuition) to stunning Cathedral Cove, where a gigantic arched cavern penetrates the headland.

KG Kayaks
Fishermans Wharf, Ohope, East Cape
Tel: 07-315 4005
Runs kayaking and canoeing trips at the eastern end of the Bay of Plenty.

Land Sailing

Blokart Heaven
Parton Road, Papamoa
Tel: 07-572 4256
www.blokart.com
A wind-powered Kiwi invention, the 'blokart' is a cross between a go-kart and a land-sailer, with a top recorded speed of 90kph (56mph). Hire one and speed around the tracks.

Surfing

Hibiscus Surf School
Main Beach, Marine Parade,
Mount Maunganui
Tel: 07-575 3792
Surf lessons and hire in the heart of town.

Raglan Surfing School
5b Whaanga Road, Whale Bay, Raglan
Tel: 07-825 7873
www.raglansurfingschool.co.nz
Surf lesson and equipment rental at this internationally renowned surf school.

BOAT TOURS

Boat cruises and tours are popular in this part of the world and you can choose from a gentle float on the Waikato River to a thrilling voyage out to White Island, a live marine volcano.

Cruise Waikato
Memorial Park jetty, Hamilton
Tel: 07-855 5898
www.cruise-waikato.co.nz
River cruises depart daily at 2pm. Booking essential.

Escapade
Whitianga Wharf
Tel: 07-867 1488
www.islandcruise.co.nz
A charter boat offering game fishing trips and sightseeing cruises.

Hahei Explorer
6 Wigmore Crescent, Hahei
Tel: 07-866 3910
www.haheiexplorer.co.nz
Daily cruises at 10am and 2pm to Cathedral Cove and other coastal caves and blowholes.

White Island Tours
15 The Strand East, Whakatane
Tel: 07-308 9588
www.whiteisland.co.nz
A thrilling six-hour adventure to a live marine volcano.

FESTIVALS AND EVENTS

A varied line-up of summer events and festivals in Hamilton draw crowds from all over New Zealand.

February

Hamilton Gardens Summer Festival
Hamilton Gardens
www.hamiltongardens.co.nz
A celebration of opera, theatre, concerts and performing arts.

March

Ngaruawahia Regatta
Waikato River, Ngaruawahia
Maori *waka* (canoe) races.

National Jazz Festival
Tauranga
www.jazz.org.nz
A weekend of jazz throughout Tauranga.

April

Balloons Over Waikato
Hamilton
www.balloonsoverwaikato.co.nz
A five-day event when up to 40 hot-air balloons float over the Waikato region.

National Agricultural Fieldays
Mystery Creek, Hamilton
www.fieldays.co.nz
A three-day agricultural show; one of the largest in the world.

Ngaruawahia Regatta

Rotorua and the Central Plateau

The tranquil landscape of Rotorua and the Central Plateau is punctuated by the hot and steamy thermal activity of geysers and springs. These powerful forces once gave birth to a crater of immense proportions, now New Zealand's greatest lake, and have attracted tourists and health-seekers since Victorian times.

Rotorua

Population: 70,000

Local dialling code: 07

Tourist office: Rotorua i-Site, 1167 Fenton Street; tel: 07-348 5179; **www.rotoruanz.com**

Police station: Rotorua Central, 1190–1214 Fenton Street; tel: 07-348 0099

Post office: Rotorua Post Shop, 1159 Pukuatua Street

Hospital: Rotorua Hospital, corner Arawa and Pukeroa roads; tel: 07-348 1199; **www.lakesdhb.govt.nz**

Local media: *Rotorua Daily Post*

Airport: Rotorua Airport, SH30; tel: 07-345 8800; **www.rotorua-airport.co.nz**

Buses: Bay Bus; tel: 0800-422 928; **www.baybus.co.nz**

Car hire: Avis; tel: 07-839 4915; **www.avis.co.nz**. Budget; tel: 07-838 3585; **www.budget.co.nz**.

Taxis: Fast Taxis; tel: 07-348 2444. Rotorua Taxis; tel: 07-348 1111.

Rotorua is a volcanic wonderland of spouting geysers, bubbling mud pools, fumaroles and natural thermal springs and spas set amid jewel-like crater lakes. It's a place of contrasts where you can watch the Kaituna River cascade over boulders down the Okere Falls – along with white-water rafters and kayakers – or soak in a hot thermal spa. When you've had your fill, the Thermal Explorer Highway leads south to Lake Taupo.

Here the nation's longest river is forced through a gorge and plunges in a tumultuous ice-blue cascade over the Huka Falls on its 425km (264-mile) journey to the sea. Upstream lies the massive expanse of Lake Taupo, New Zealand's largest, nestling beneath the great volcanoes of Tongariro National Park and capturing the sparkling ice-melt that flows down from their imposing slopes.

Rotorua

The distinctive rotten-egg smell of hydrogen sulphide gas heralds your approach to Rotorua. Here steam drifts up from drains and private gardens; even the golf course has thermal hazards. Residents have harnessed some of this natural energy for central heating and swimming pools, while 'steam boxes' in suburban gardens are used for preparing outdoor feasts.

City Centre

Rotorua city is small and compact. At its hub is Lakefront Drive's large adventure playground and jetty, where kids swing energetically amid a steady stream of watercraft, helicopters and sea-planes departing on tours. At 12.30pm daily the PS ***Lakeland Queen*** Ⓐ toots her departure before setting off on a scenic lunch cruise *(see p.135)*.

The Rotorua Museum of Art and History is housed in a Tudor-style former spa building

Bathing in the great expanse of Lake Taupo

Rotorua is well known as a major centre for Maori culture and one third of the city's population is Maori. *Marae* (tribal meeting places) dot the area, including the historic Maori village of **Ohinemutu** Ⓑ, once the main settlement on the lake, a short walk west along the waterfront. Presented to the Maori people of Rotorua for their loyalty to the Crown, the Tudor-style **St Faith's Church**, built in 1910, is notable for its rich carvings, a chancel window depicting Christ wearing the feathered cloak of a Maori chief and positioned so that the figure appears to be walking on the water of the lake, and a bust of Queen Victoria. The adjacent 19th-century **Tamatekapua Meeting House** took 12 years to carve and is named after the captain of the Arawa canoe. It is said that Hine-te-Kakara, the daughter of Ihenga, the Maori discoverer of Rotorua, was murdered and her body thrown into a boiling mud pool. Ihenga subsequently set up a memorial stone, calling it Ohinemutu – 'the place where the young woman was killed.'

Government Gardens

Southeast of the jetty is the Edwardian elegance of the **Government Gardens**, and the impressive facade of **Rotorua Museum of Art and History** **C** (Queens Drive; www.rotoruamuseum.co.nz; daily 9am–8pm; charge), housed in the Tudor Towers (1908), once a fashionable spa centre. As well as art exhibitions, its displays tell the story of the local Te Arawa people and the devastating eruption of Mount Tarawera in 1886.

The popular Lakefront Walk meanders through the gardens, past the boat ramps of Motutara Point and on through the untamed wetlands and lakeside thermal theatrics of the **Sulphur Point Wildlife Sanctuary**.

At the southern end of the park is the **Polynesian Spa** (1000 Hinemoa Street; www.polynesianspa.co.nz; daily 8am–11pm;), where a travelling priest, Father Mahoney, pitched his tent in 1878 and bathed in the warm water until he reportedly obtained complete relief for his arthritis; four years later the spa was established. Now thermal pools of varying temperatures cater for adults and families, and various treatments including massage are available at the on-site Lake Spa Retreat.

Also in the park, on Queens Drive, are the historic **Blue Baths** (www.bluebaths.co.nz; daily 10am–6pm;), geothermally heated freshwater pools located in a stunning Spanish Mission building, first opened in 1933 and beautifully restored in 1999.

Whakarewarewa

While most of Rotorua's thermal parks have an entry fee, at **Kuirau**

Waitukei, a bronze sculpture in Rotorua's Government Gardens

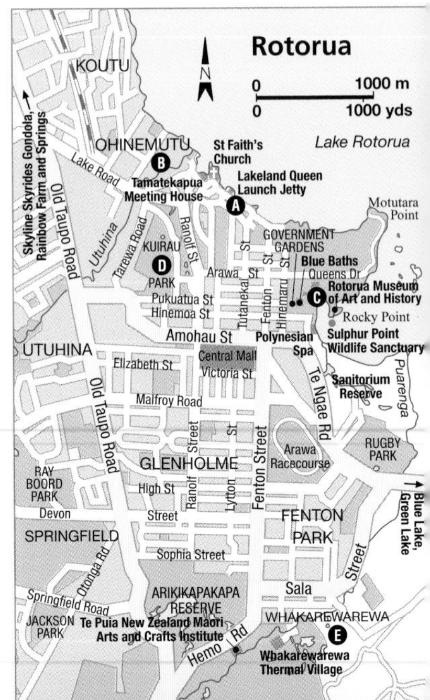

Pohutu geyser at Whakarewarewa

Park Ⓓ on Ranolf Street you can stroll in and watch plopping mud and steam billowing from fumaroles to your heart's content.

At the southern end of Fenton Street is the **Whakarewarewa** thermal area Ⓔ where **Te Puia** *(see p.133)* is home to the famous **Pohutu geyser**, a 30m (100ft) -high spray of boiling water, and the **New Zealand Maori Arts and Crafts Institute** (www.nzmaori.co.nz; daily 8am–6pm; charge), where you can watch Maori carvers and flax weavers at work. Guided tours leave on the hour, and take in the works of the arts institute and the bubbling mud pools, boiling hot springs, and geysers of the thermal park. Also on site is **Rotowhio**, a replica of a traditional Maori village.

An authentic experience awaits at the adjoining **Whakarewarewa Thermal Village** (17 Tryon Street; www.whakarewarewa.com; daily 8.30am–5pm; charge), where you can join a guided tour to meet the Tuhourangi/Ngati Wahiao people who live amid the geothermal activity and make use of the hot springs and steam vents for cooking and communal bathing.

To the south lies **Whakarewarewa Forest**, a popular place to hike and mountain bike.

Around Rotorua

There's no shortage of things to see and do in **Rotorua** ❶, but nothing can beat the beauty of the city's natural surroundings. Spectacular lakes, rivers, waterfalls, forests and volcanoes provide ample opportunities to get away from the crowds.

Shopping in Rotorua

Not surprisingly, the tourist town of Rotorua is one of the best places in New Zealand to purchase souvenirs; the sheer number of stores keeps prices low. Don't miss the Jade Factory (1280 Fenton Street; www.jadefactory.com), where you can buy superbly crafted jewellery and carvings made from New Zealand greenstone, or the Souvenir Centre (1231 Fenton Street; www.thesouvenircentre.co.nz), which stocks a variety of arts and crafts. For the best clothing and fashion stores, head to Tutanekai Street, Hinemoa Street and the shops surrounding City Focus Square.

MAORI LEGENDS

Maori oral culture is a tapestry of legends that go all the way back to the void of pre-existence. Woven into these narratives are elements of religion, spirituality and genealogy that link the living to gods and legendary heroes. As the Maori did not have a written language until the arrival of the missionaries, their legends were passed down orally over many generations.

New Zealand abounds with Maori folklore and legends, and wherever you travel there will be a good story to hear. The legends begin with creation, back when Ranginui, the Sky Father, and Papatuanuku, the Earth Mother, were joined in an amorous embrace, clasping the world in perpetual darkness. Living between them were their sons who each tried to push them apart one by one. Finally, it was the turn of Tane Mahuta, the mighty kauri tree. He rose up, pressing the earth beneath him and the sky far above him until finally the children of *Tane* – the trees, birds and insects of the forest – were able to breathe, see and move.

Further stories describe the origins of New Zealand's mighty landscapes. Many concern Maui, who is responsible for discovering fire and capturing the sun. One of the most famous tales describes how Maui smuggled himself aboard a fishing trip with his brothers and caught a fish of an unimaginable size. As the sun rose, the fish became

Mokoia island in Lake Rotorua, setting for the love story of Hinemoa and Tutanekai

a solid mass underfoot, with a rough and mountainous surface. As time passed by it remained that way and so became known as Te Ika-a-Maui, the fish of Maui – or the North Island as we know it today. According to the legend, the South Island – Te Waka a Maui – was the canoe used by Maui and his brothers, while Stewart Island – Te Punga-a-Maui – was the anchor which held the canoe in place as Maui pulled in the giant fish.

Other tales explain the occurrence of natural phenomena; for example, when the explorer Ngatoro-i-rangi was in danger of freezing to death in the Southern Alps, his fervent prayers for assistance were answered by the fire demons of Hawaiki, who sent flames and created Hanmer's hot springs.

Or else they simply relate unforgettable tales of love and loss, such as the romance of Hinemoa and Tutanekai, set on the island of Mokoia in Lake Rotorua. Hinemoa lived on the mainland and, against her family's wishes, fell in love with Tutanekai, a young island chieftain. Their marriage was forbidden, so the couple secretly planned for Hinemoa to paddle across the lake at night following the sound of Tutanekai's flute. When Hinemoa's family beached the canoe she was forced to swim instead, using gourds to help keep her afloat. When she finally arrived, she warmed herself in a hot pool (which still bears her name), before reuniting with her lover. Today, this site is one of New Zealand's most romantic locations, and is a wonderful place to reflect on the deeply poetic nature of Maori legends.

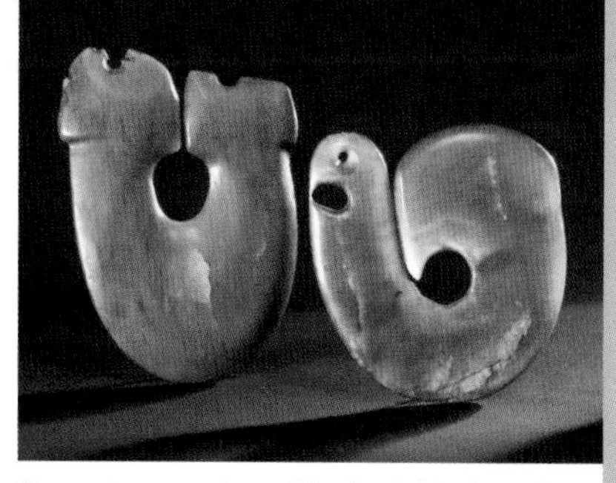

Greenstone carvings of the hook Maui used to catch the fish that became North Island

Tane Mahuta (Lord of the Forest) in Waipoua Forest, Northland

Ngongotaha

Fabulous views of the city and lake can be enjoyed from the 778m (2,552ft) slopes of **Mount Ngongotaha**, accessed by the **Skyline Skyrides Gondola** ❷ on Fairy Springs Road *(see p.134)*. At the top there is a café and restaurant, and luge (three-wheel cart) rides down a 1km (¾-mile) -long track.

A short way further along Fairy Springs Road is **Rainbow Springs Kiwi Wildlife Park** (www.rainbowsprings.co.nz; daily, summer 8am–11pm, winter 8am–10pm; charge), which showcases more than 150 species of native New Zealand fauna set among freshwater springs and pools filled with rainbow and brown trout. These fish, which swim here from Lake Rotorua to spawn, can be hand-fed and viewed through underwater windows. **Kiwi Encounter at Rainbow Springs** (www.kiwiencounter.co.nz; tours daily 10am–4pm) is a unique incubation facility, hatchery and nursery where tours allow you to see kiwis, native geckos and skinks, plus adult and juvenile tuataras, New Zealand's living 'dinosaurs', in a nocturnal house.

On the other side of Fairy Springs Road is the **New Zealand Caterpillar Experience** (www.caterpillarexperience.co.nz; daily 8.30am–5pm; charge), a museum dedicated to an intriguing display of vintage Caterpillar earth-moving machinery.

A couple of kilometres along Western Road, the **Agrodome** ❸ (www.agrodome.co.nz; daily 8.30am–5pm; charge), set on 160 hectares (395 acres) of pasture, tells you all you need to know about New Zealand's sheep

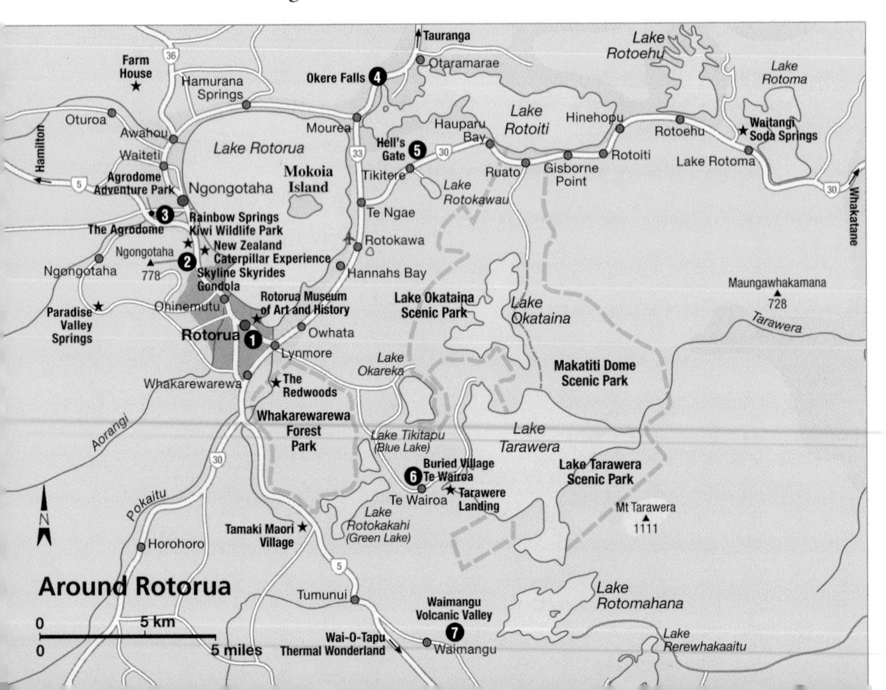

Trout pool at Rainbow Springs

industry in an educational and entertaining performance. Three times a day (9.30am, 11am and 2.30pm), New Zealand's 19 major breeds are put through their paces by well-trained sheepdogs. Children love the chance to bottle-feed lambs and there are a huge number of other activities, including farm tractor tours to feed sheep, deer, alpacas and emus by hand.

The adjacent **Agrodome Adventure Park** offers bungy jumping, jetboat sprint racing and other thrilling activities *(see p.134)*.

Tikitere and Okere Falls

A scenic drive around the northern shores of Lake Rotorua leads to **Okere Falls** ❹ where, after a short walk through native forest, the Kaituna River can be viewed thundering over the **Kaituna Falls** through a narrow chasm into the swirling pool below; join a whitewater rafting trip over the waterfall if you dare *(see p.135)*.

Further south on SH30 is **Hell's Gate** ❺ (www.hellsgate.co.nz; daily 8.30am–8.30pm; 👪), reputedly the most active thermal reserve in Rotorua. The volcanic activity here covers 4 hectares (10 acres), and includes the hot-water **Kakahi Falls**, the largest of its kind in the southern hemisphere. Hell's Gate is also home to the **Wai Ora Spa**, the only place in New Zealand where you can experience the cosmetic benefits of a mud bath *(see p.51)*.

Tarawera and the Buried Village

A pleasant drive to the southeast of Lake Rotorua passes the magnificent **Redwoods** (Long Mile Road; www.redwoods.co.nz), part of Whakarewarewa Forest, to **Lake Tikitapu** (Blue Lake) and **Lake Rotokakahi** (Green Lake), where there are well-

Toast your Tootsies

At least some of your time in this region is likely to be spent soaking in hot mineral water. In 1874 former New Zealand premier Sir William Fox urged the government to 'secure the whole of the Lake Country as a sanatorium owing to the ascertained healing properties of the water'. This immediately sparked off the development of Rotorua into a spa town and the first sanatorium was built in 1880. Some people still believe soaking here is a useful treatment for arthritis and rheumatism, but most simply come to unwind.

marked and graded trails to hike and kayaks available for hire. On a fine day, follow the signs to the lookout points between the lakes to observe the distinct blue and green colouring of the lakes.

The road continues to the larger Lake Tarawera via the eerie **Buried Village Te Wairoa** ❻ (1180 Tarawera Road; www.buriedvillage.co.nz; daily 9am–5pm; charge), destroyed on 10 June 1886 when a devastating eruption of Mount Tarawera blasted rock, lava and ash into the air over a 15,500 sq km (6,000 sq mile) area. It engulfed the villages of Te Wairoa, Te Ariki and Moura, and killed 147 Maori and six Europeans. The Buried Village contains items excavated from Te Wairoa, including the *whare* (hut) of a *tohunga* (priest) who foretold the disaster when he saw a ghostly canoe; he was unearthed alive four days after the eruption.

From the Buried Village, it's a short drive further east to **Lake Tarawera**, tucked snugly beneath the brooding bulk of **Mount Tarawera**. Before the eruption, Victorian tourists were rowed across Lake Tarawera to the fabulous Pink and White Terraces, two huge silica formations which rose 250m (820ft) from the shores of Lake Rotomahana and were billed as an 'eighth wonder of the world'. Today, you can retrace the route to the former site on a cruise departing from the jetty at **Tarawera Landing**. There's also guided trout fishing on offer, and self-drive boats, kayaks and pedal boats can be hired from **The Landing Café**, which also serves good coffee.

Lake Tarawera with Mount Tarawera in the background

Southern Thermal Parks

Twenty km (12 miles) south of Rotorua off SH5 is **Waimangu Volcanic**

Safety in Thermal Parks

For your own safety, never stray off the paths in thermal parks in order to get a better view. In places the ground is nothing but a mere crust, and the water will – to put it bluntly – cook you alive. In addition to this, the pathways are also put into place to protect the environment and New Zealanders take a dim view of visitors who desecrate their natural wonders: some volcanic landscapes have taken thousands of years to evolve and are easily spoilt by footprints.

Orakei Korako thermal park

Valley ❼ (www.waimangu.com; daily 8.30am–5pm), created in 1886 when Mount Tarawera erupted. An easy walk downhill from a tearoom leads past bubbling crater lakes, hot creeks and algae-covered silica terraces to the shores of Lake Rotomahana, where a launch can be taken to the intensively active **Steaming Cliffs** and the former site of the lost Pink and White Terraces.

About 10km (6 miles) further along SH5 is the turn-off to another thermal area, **Wai-O-Tapu Thermal Wonderland** ❽ (Waiotapu Loop Road; www.geyserland.co.nz; daily 8.30am–5pm; charge). Wai-O-Tapu, Maori for 'Sacred Waters,' is home of **Lady Knox Geyser**, which erupts daily at 10.15am. Other attractions include the bubbly **Champagne Pool**, tinted silica terraces and **Bridal Veil Falls**.

As the SH5 continues it passes through tall forests of pine to just north of Waimahana, where a turn-off leads to **Orakei Korako** ❾ on the shores of Lake Ohakuri. Here a boat waits to ferry travellers to a pristine geothermal park surrounded by unique silica terraces, with 35 active geysers, plopping mud pools, fizzing hot springs and an extremely rare geothermal cave.

Taupo

Situated on the crystal-clear waters of New Zealand's largest lake, Taupo offers all kinds of water sport. The fishing is outstanding here, and as Taupo's trout dine on native crayfish, they have a characteristically sweet flavour. Once hooked, keen fisherfolk will disappear for some time.

City Central

Taupo ❿ is the abbreviated version of Taupo-nui-Tia ('the great shoulder cloak of Tia'), given by the Arawa canoe explorer who discovered the region. The township is located in a sheltered northeastern bay of **Lake Taupo**, where the Waikato River begins its 425km (264-mile) journey to the sea. The vast expanse of the lake, which covers some 619 sq km (240 sq miles), may seem serene, but don't be fooled; over the past 27,000 years this crater has erupted 28 times. These days it yields in excess of 500 tonnes of rainbow trout annually and the rivers flowing into it are also well stocked. Taupo offers plenty of activities besides trout fishing, such as boat cruises, kayak trips to see Maori rock carvings, jet-boating, windsurfing, skydiving and bungy jumping over the Waikato River *(see p.134)*. Another highlight is a relaxing soak at **Taupo Hot Springs** (103 Napier-Taupo Highway; www.taupohotsprings.com; daily 7.30am–9.30pm 👪).

Wairakei and Huka Falls

Just north of Taupo is **Wairakei**, a region that once boasted more than 20 geysers. These days the Wairakei Geothermal Field, harnesses the power of about 30,000 tonnes of hot water for a variety of purposes – among them the heating of **Huka Prawn Park** (www.hukaprawnpark.co.nz; daily 9.30am–3.30pm; charge 👪), where you can fish and feast on juicy tropical prawns and admire views of the Waikato River. Nearby is the **Volcanic Activity Centre** (www.volcanoes.co.nz; Mon–Fri 9am–5pm, Sat–Sun 10am–4pm; charge 👪), which has informative displays on the region's geography, and the **Huka Jet**, offering a thrilling spin upriver to the **Huka Falls** *(see p.134)*.

By road, the entrance to these thundering falls is well signposted 2km

Huka Falls

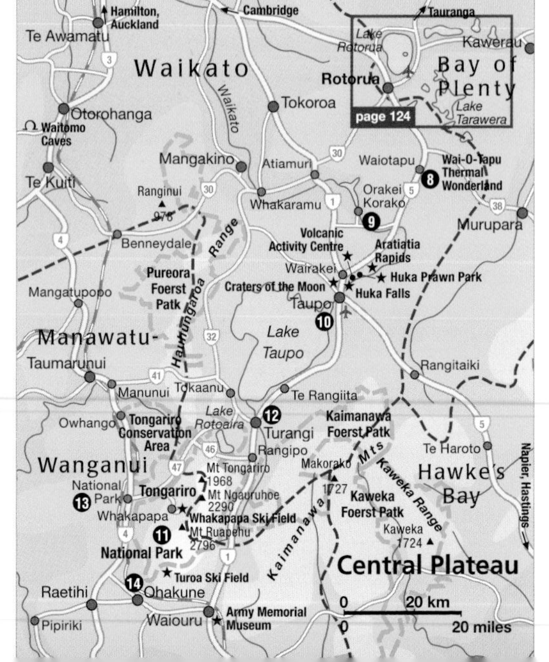

Taupo

Population: 20,500

Local dialling code: 07

Tourist office: Taupo i-Site, Tongariro Street; tel: 07-376 0027; **www.laketauponz.com**

Police station: Taupo Central, 21 Story Place, tel: 07-378 6060

Post office: Taupo Post Shop, 46 Horomatangi Street

Local media: *Taupo Times*

Airport: Taupo Airport, 1105 Anzac Memorial Drive; tel: 07-378 7771; **www.taupoairport.co.nz**

Buses: Bay Bus; tel: 0800-422 928; **www.baybus.co.nz**

Car Hire: A1 Car Rentals Taupo; tel: 07-378 3670. Rent-A-Dent Taupo; tel: 07-378 2740; **www.rentadent.co.nz**

Taxis: Top Cab; tel: 07-378 9250. Taupo Taxis,; tel: 07-378 5100

(1¼ miles) south. A short walk takes you to views of the falls, where up to 270 cubic m (9,535 cubic ft) of water squeezes through a long, narrow gorge before tumbling into a deep pool. There are several good walks in the area, including a riverside walk to the **Aratiatia Rapids**.

Tongariro National Park

A short drive south of Taupo, the Unesco World Heritage Site of **Tongariro National Park** ⓫ straddles the junction of two of the earth's tectonic plates, causing friction that forces steam and hot springs to the earth's surface. Three great volcanic peaks dominate the park. Mounts Tongariro, Ngauruhoe and Ruapehu – considered guardian deities by the Maori – were gifted by a Maori chief in 1887 to create New Zealand's first national park.

Turangi to Whakapapa

The most scenic route from Taupo leaves SH1 at **Turangi** ⓬, where excellent whitewater raft trips exploring the mid- to lower reaches of the river are available through **Tongariro River Rafting** *(see p.135)*.

From Turangi, SH47 winds steeply up through dense native bush into Tongariro National Park, affording views of the red craters of Mount Tongariro (1,968m/6,457ft). Brown windswept plains of toitoi, manuka and flax usher into view the charred cinder cone of **Mount Ngauruhoe** (2,290m/7,513ft), which last erupted in 1975, while Mangatepopo Road provides access to the **Tongariro Crossing**, New Zealand's best one-day hike *(see p.23)*.

The majestic snowy crown of **Mount Ruapehu** (2,796m/9,173ft) dominates the SH48 route to Whakapapa Village, a small ski village servicing the **Whakapapa Ski Field** with a range of accommodation and cafés. The Visitor Centre here provides information on local hikes, including the **Mount Ruapehu summit walk** *(see p.23)*, **Taranaki Falls** and **Tama Lakes**.

The perpetually snowcapped Mount Ruapehu

Of all three mountains, Ruapehu, with its acidic, bubbling crater lake and six small glaciers, is the most volatile – in 1945 it blew clouds of steam and ash over a 90km (56-mile) radius, and more recently closed ski fields when it began puffing again. In December 1953, 151 people died in a train disaster when a *lahar*, or violent discharge of water and mud, roared down the Whangaehu River from its Crater Lake. Fortunately, when the lake burst its banks again in March 2007, an alarm system provided warning before a torrent of mud and debris again poured through the river gorge.

National Park to Waiouru

The township called **National Park** ⓭ at the junction of SH4 and SH47 is a home from home for snow junkies in the winter ski season, with a climbing wall, equipment hire and numerous cosy bars and cafés. However, it's the southern township of **Ohakune** ⓮ on SH49 that is fast becoming a fashionable après-ski hub offering easy access to the slopes of the **Turoa Ski Field** up its picturesque mountain road. **Waiouru**, 36km (22 miles) to the east, is home to the New Zealand Army's largest training camp and the **Army Memorial Museum** (SH1; www.armymuseum.co.nz; daily 9am–4.30pm; charge), where a sensitively curated collection of memorabilia captivates military enthusiasts and civilians alike.

On a Fly

To get away from it all, there is perhaps nothing more relaxing than to team up with a guide for a day's trout fishing. Guides supply all tackle and meet you outside your accommodation or down at the jetty with trailer boats ready for action. Rainbow trout on most lakes around Rotorua and on Lake Taupo average 1.4kg (3lbs); on Lake Tarawera, where they are tougher to catch, fish of 3.5–5.5kg (8–12lbs) are not uncommon. The final hook is having a chef prepare your catch at the end of the day– a service which many guides are used to providing.

ACCOMMODATION

Good value is found year-round in Rotorua and Taupo, and backpackers travelling in pairs will find that it is just as budget-friendly to share a standard motel room.

Rotorua

Acapulco Motel
Corner Malfroy Road and Eason Street
Tel: 07-347 9569
www.acapulcomotel.net.nz
Reasonably priced, in a quiet spot near the centre, with a thermal pool and spa. **$$$**

Cactus Jack Backpackers
1210 Haupapa Street
Tel: 07-348 3121
www.cactusjackbackpackers.co.nz
Dorms, single, twin, double and triple rooms. Spa pool. **$–$$**

Millennium Rotorua
Corner of Eruera and Hinemaru streets
Tel: 07-347 1234
www.millenniumrotorua.co.nz
Luxury hotel in the heart of town with a gym and pool. **$$$$–$$$$$**

Sudima Hotel
1000 Eruera Street
Tel: 07-348 1174
www.sudimahotels.com
Opposite the Polynesian Spa,with restaurant, bar and private thermal spa pools. **$$$**

Around Rotorua

Redwood Holiday Park
5 Tarawera Road, Rotorua
Tel: 07-345 9380
www.redwoodparkrotorua.co.nz
Motel units, tourist flats, cabins, caravans, motorhomes and tent sites, located beside the recreational Redwoods Forest. **$–$$**

Solitaire Lodge
Ronald Road, Lake Tarawera
Tel: 07-362 8208
www.solitairelodge.co.nz
Deluxe lodge with great views of Mount Tarawera and its lake. **$$$$$**

Accommodation Price Categories

Prices are for one night's accommodation in a standard double room (unless otherwise specified).

$ = below NZ$30
$$ = NZ$30–75
$$$ = NZ$75–150
$$$$ = NZ$150–350
$$$$$ = over NZ$350

Taupo

Suncourt Hotel
14 Northcroft Street
Tel: 07-378 8265
www.suncourt.co.nz
Studio, one- and two-bedroom units, most with views of Lake Taupo. **$$$**

Tongariro National Park

Bayview Chateau Tongariro
Whakapapa Village, Central Plateau
Tel: 07-892 3809
www.chateau.co.nz
Historic hotel built in 1929, with comfortable rooms from family-sized to suites. **$$$$–$$$$$**

Tongariro Holiday Park
SH47, Tongariro
Tel: 07-386 8062
www.thp.co.nz
Great-value cabins for up to six, tent and motorhome sites, plus café and spa pool. Transport to Tongariro Crossing. **$–$$$**

Millennium Rotorua

RESTAURANTS

A wealth of unique dining experiences can be found in this region from traditional *hangi (see p.41)* to dining on succulent tropical prawns farmed in thermal waters.

Restaurant Price Categories

Prices are for a standard meal for one.

$ = below NZ$15
$$ = NZ$15–30
$$$ = NZ$30–50
$$$$ = over NZ$50

Rotorua

Bistro 1284
1284 Eruera Street
Tel: 07-346 1284
www.bistro1284.co.nz
Attractively set in a 1930s building, this restaurant continually wins a wide range of awards, including for the quality of the lamb and beef served, and remains one of the top choices in Rotorua for delicious New Zealand and international cuisine. **$$$**

Cableway Restaurant
185 Fairy Springs Road
Tel: 07-347 0027
www.skylineskyrides.co.nz
Aim to be seated in time for sunset. Buffet-style fare is served at this hill-top restaurant reached via the Skyline gondola. **$$$–$$$$**

The Indian Star
1118 Tutanekai Street
Tel: 07-343 6222
www.indianstar.co.nz
If you have been holding out for a decent curry or Tandoori, this is the place to go. There's a licensed bar or you can bring your own. **$$**

Lakeside Café
Memorial Drive, Rotorua
Tel: 07-349 2626
For light lunches and snacks. **$**

Around Rotorua

The Landing Café
The Landing, Lake Tarawera
Tel: 07-362 8595
www.thelandinglaketarawera.co.nz
Fine fare, including gourmet pizzas, served in a lovely lakeside setting. **$$–$$$**

Terraces Café
185 Fairy Springs Road
Tel: 07-347 0027
At the top of the Skyline Gondola, Terraces offers all-day breakfasts, sandwiches, cakes, fish and chips, gourmet pizzas and sushi. **$**

Taupo

Huka Prawn Park Restaurant
Wairakei Tourist Park
Tel: 07-374 8474
www.hukaprawnpark.co.nz/restaurant
Succulent, super-fresh prawns raised on site are served in various delicious ways. **$$$**

Toasting the sunset at the Cableway Restaurant

Salute Deli Café
47 Horomatangi Street
Tel: 07-377 4478
The delicious freshly prepared salads and grilled panini sandwiches make this place popular with locals. **$**

Tongariro National Park

Alpine Restaurant
Corner of Clyde and Miro streets, Ohakune
Tel: 06-385 9183
A smart restaurant serving classic European cuisine. **$$**

Licorice Café
57 SH1, Motuoapa, Turangi
Tel: 07-386 5551
Super popular stop-off point close to Turangi. The menu changes daily and features gluten-free and vegetarian options, plus other home-cooked Kiwi fare. **$–$$**

ENTERTAINMENT AND NIGHTLIFE

Cultural shows are a highlight of a visit to Rotorua; each has its own unique feel and most include a meal.

Cultural Shows

Mitai Maori Village
Fairy Springs Road, Rotorua
Tel: 07-343 9132
www.mitai.co.nz
The cultural performances here provide a good introduction to Maori beliefs and rituals.

Tamaki Maori Village
1220 Hinemaru Street, Rotorua
Tel: 07-349 2999
www.maoriculture.co.nz
Contemporary performances here present the Chronicles of Uitara, a story spanning several generations of a warrior tribe. Tickets include a multi-course meal including *hangi* tasting.

Te Puia
Hemo Road, Rotorua
Tel: 07-348 9047
www.tepuia.com
Marae (tribal meeting- place) visit with *powhiri* (formal welcome) and cultural performances followed by a *hangi* meal.

Nightlife

Barbarella
1263 Pukuatua Street, Rotorua
Tel: 07-347 0409
Live music venue featuring various styles.

A *kapa haka* (cultural dance) performance

Finn MacCuhal's
Corner Tuwharetoa and Tongariro streets, Taupo
Tel: 07378 6165
www.finns.co.nz
Fun Irish bar serving Guinness with live entertainment from Thursday to Saturday.

The Pheasant Plucker
1153 Arawa Street, Rotorua
Tel: 07-343 7071
www.thepheasantplucker.co.nz
Devour a hearty serving from the roast carvery, accompanied by live music most nights with classical jam, jazz, blues, soul, rock and cover bands. Great atmosphere.

Pig and Whistle
Corner Haupapa and Tutanekai streets, Rotorua
Tel: 07-347 3025
www.pigandwhistle.co.nz
Live bands Thursday to Saturday, and big screens to see live sport action.

Theatre

Civic Theatre
1170 Fenton Street, Rotorua
Tel: 07-349 5141
Located within the Rotorua Convention Centre. For current listings refer to local newspapers.

SPORTS AND ACTIVITIES

The Central Plateau region offers sports and activities from the adventurous to the downright wacky, particularly in Rotorua.

Bungy

Agrodome Adventure Park
Western Road, Rotorua
Tel: 07-357 1050
www.agrodome.co.nz
Adjacent to the Agrodome *(see p.124)*, this park features many thrilling experiences including bungy jumping, jet-boat sprint racing, Zorbing, the Shweeb velodrome and Freefall Extreme.

Taupo Bungy
202 Spa Road, Taupo
Tel: 07-377 1135
www.taupobungy.co.nz
Bungy jumps over the Waikato River with an optional 'water touch'. Also the site of the Taupo Cliff Hanger, an extreme swing ride that reaches speeds of up to 70kmh (40mph).

Gondola and Luge Rides

Skyline Skyrides Gondola
Fairy Springs Road, Rotorua
Tel: 07-347 0027
www.skylineskyrides.co.nz
Within minutes of buying a ticket you will be whisked sharply up the 900m (2,953ft) slopes of Mount Ngongotaha for glorious views, with the option of taking a luge (a three-wheel cart) for a spin on an exciting downhill track.

Jet-boating

Huka Jet
Wairakei Park, Taupo
Tel: 07-374 8572
www.hukajet.co.nz
An adrenaline-pumping ride on the Waikato River that is guaranteed to leave you breathless. Departures every half hour.

Scenic Flights

Mountain Air
Corner of SH47/48, Whakapapa
Tel: 07-892 2812
www.mountainair.co.nz
Stunning flights over the Tongariro National Park with views of Lake Taupo.

The Huka Jet whips you along the Waikato River

Whitewater Rafting

Raftabout
811 SH22, Okere Falls, Rotorua
Tel: 07-343 9500
www.raftabout.co.nz
Tackle the highest commercially rafted waterfall in the world.

Tongariro River Rafting
Atirau Road,
Turangi
Tel: 0800-101 024
www.trr.co.nz
Rafting on the Tongariro River is an ideal first-time experience.

TOURS

Tours abound in Rotorua and the Central Plateau, but to take time out from the hustle and bustle join a boat cruise and discover the gentler side of this region.

Boat Cruises

Chris Jolly
14 Rauhoto Street, Taupo
Tel: 0800-252 628
www.chrisjolly.co.nz
Daily Lake Taupo cruises with trips to see Maori rock carvings at Whakaipo Bay.

Lakeland Queen
Lakefront, Rotorua
Tel: 0800-572 784
www.lakelandqueen.com
Paddle steamers on Lake Rotorua with breakfast, lunch and dinner cruises.

Mokoia Island Cruises
Lakefront, Rotorua
Tel: 07-345 7456
www.mokoiaisland.com
Cruises to Mokoia Island in the middle of Lake Rotorua, home to the rare saddleback, stitchbird and North Island robin.

FESTIVALS AND EVENTS

One of the region's most popular cultural events is the Opera in the Pa; however, it is the annual Ironman that draws the largest crowds from all over the nation.

January

Opera in the Pa
Ohinemutu Village, Rotorua
International performances held in the atmospheric and historic lakeside village of Ohinemutu.

March

Ironman New Zealand
Taupo
www.ironman.co.nz
New Zealand's longest endurance event.

Tagged Trout Competition
Rotorua
www.taggedtrout.co.nz
Premier trout-fishing competition held over two days.

July

The Ruapehu Mountain Mardi Gras
Ohakune,
Central Plateau
www.ohakune-mardigras.co.nz
Annual ski mardi gras marking the opening of the local ski fields.

September

Rotorua Trout Festival
Rotorua
One-day event marking the opening of the trout-fishing season.

Taranaki, Manawatu-Wanganui and Hawke's Bay

The less-populated mid- to lower North Island is renowned for its dairy farms, market gardens, orchards and vineyards. From the lush slopes surrounding Mount Taranaki to the rolling hills and flat river plains of Hawke's Bay, it's a landscape of scenic splendour dotted with small and intriguing towns.

New Plymouth

Population: 67,000

Local dialling code: 06

Tourist office: New Plymouth i-Site Visitors Centre, Puke Ariki, 1 Ariki Street; tel: 06-759 6060; **www.pukeariki.com**

Police station: New Plymouth Police Station, Powderhorn Street; tel: 06-759 5500

Post office: New Plymouth Post Shop, 100 Currie Street

Hospital: Taranaki Base Hospital, David Street, New Plymouth; tel: 06-753 6139; **www.tdhb.org.nz**

Local media: *Taranaki Daily News*

Airport: New Plymouth Airport, Airport Drive, New Plymouth; tel: 06-759 6072; **www.taranakiairport.co.nz**

Buses: Citylink and Southlink; tel: 06-757 5783; **www.trc.govt.nz/bus-routes**

Car Hire: Pegasus Rental Cars; tel: 06-757 5255; **www.carrentalsnewplymouth.co.nz**

Taxis: Scotty's Airport Shuttles; tel: 06-769 5974. New Plymouth Taxis; tel: 06-573 000.

Lone Mount Taranaki – often dubbed New Zealand's Mount Fuji after it hosted the star-studded cast of *The Last Samurai* (2003) – is a conical-shaped snowcapped volcano. Its summit rises regally from lush green farmland, heavy with dairy stock, while its lower slopes are robed with impenetrable rainforest. SH45, otherwise known as the Surf Highway, provides a convenient loop to explore the towns at its base. Further south is Wanganui, situated at the mouth of the mighty Whanganui River, which begins its journey to the sea from the Central Plateau. Where these mountains end, the high ridges and peaks of the Ruahine and Tararua ranges begin, forming an almost unbroken spine through the lower north, save

The fertile plains east of Mount Taranaki are ideal for dairy farming

for the Manuwatu Gorge which provides access to an array of quirky Tararua townships before squeezing through the rounded brown hills of the Raukawa and Kaokaoroa ranges and bursting into the ripe wine-making region of Hawke's Bay.

Taranaki

Maori legend has it that the gentle giant, Mount Taranaki, fell in love with a maiden on the Central Plateau whose heart was already set on another. While Ruapehu and Ngauruhoe looked on, Mount Taranaki fled west, his bulk carving the Whanganui River en route, his tears filling it. He settled on the coast in the region that still embraces him.

New Plymouth

Mount Taranaki provides a backdrop to almost every sight in the seaside township of **New Plymouth** ❶, including its beautiful parks and open spaces. Among these are central **Pukekura Park**, with its lakes and fountains; the **Pukeiti Rhododendron Trust** (www.pukeiti.org.nz; daily 9am–5pm; charge), a 320-hectare (791-acre) park showcasing a world-class display of rhododendrons and azaleas, 12km (7 miles) out of town on the Carrington Road; and the **Coastal Walkway**, which runs the length of New Plymouth along a 7km (4-mile) stretch of coast. At the walkway's mid-point is the soaring 45m (148ft) kinetic sculpture *Wind Wand*, designed by Len Lye, a New Zealand artist and film-maker.

A good place to begin exploration of town is at **Puke Ariki** (1 Ariki Street; www.pukeariki.com; Mon–Fri 9am–6pm, Wed until 9pm, Sat–Sun 9am–5pm; free 👪), a combined museum, public library and visitor centre, which also includes the historic **Richmond Cottage**, home of three of the first settler families.

East of Puke Ariki is the **Govett-Brewster Art Gallery** (corner of Queen and King streets; www.govett brewster.com; daily 10am–5pm; free), with a notable collection of contemporary art. New Zealand's oldest stone church, **St Mary's Church** (1846), is nearby on Vivian Street at no. 37, while 8km (5 miles) south on Carrington Road is **Hurworth Cottage** (no. 906; www.historicplaces.org.nz; Sat–Sun 11am–3pm; charge), one of the region's earliest homesteads. From New Plymouth, the hikes of **Egmont National Park** are just a short drive to the south (*see p.23*).

Surf Highway

State Highway 45, known as the **Surf Highway**, follows the spherical

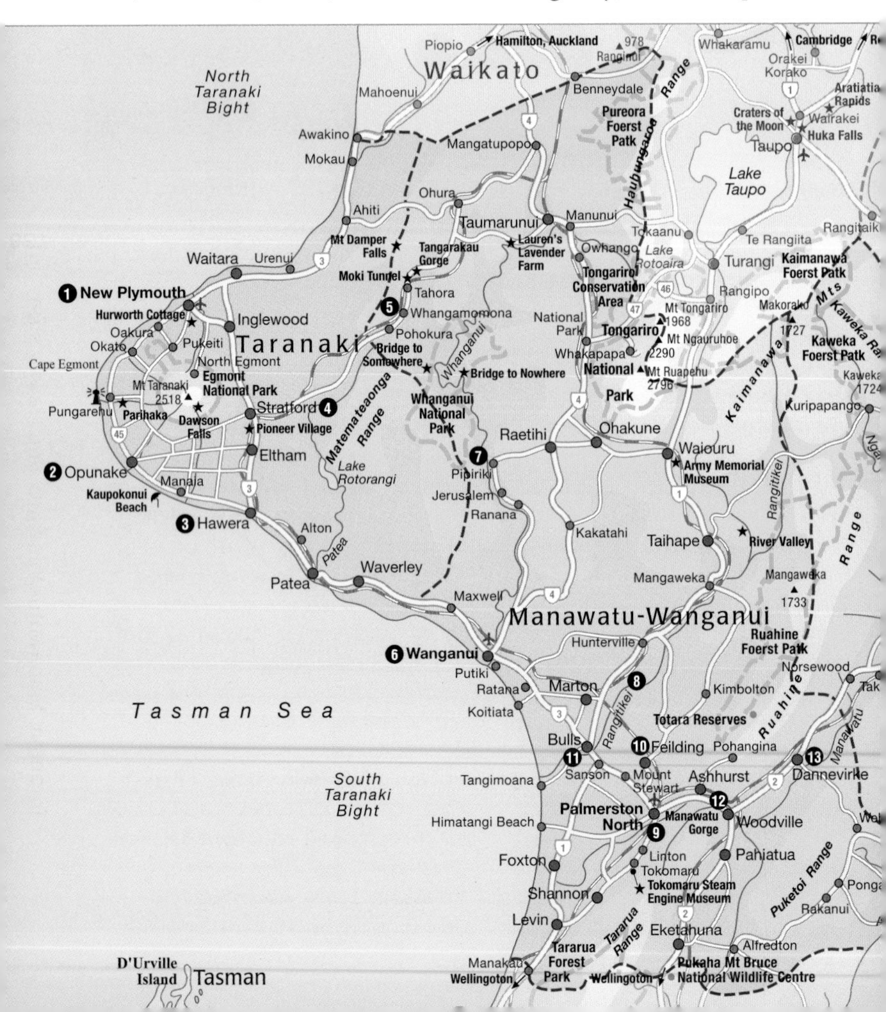

Taranaki coastline from New Plymouth to Hawera, and provides plenty of reasons to dawdle. **Oakura**, 15km (9 miles) southwest of New Plymouth, is a beach outpost with cafés lining its main thoroughfare, while **Cape Egmont lighthouse** (1881) gives beautiful views at **Pungarehu**. A short way further on a drive inland leads to **Parihaka**, the gravesite of the Maori chief Te Whiti-O-Rongomai (*see box below*).

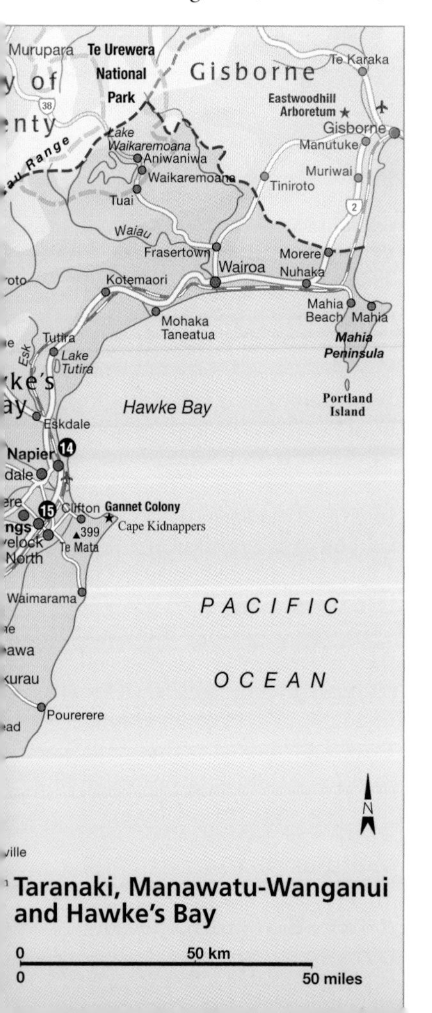

Colourful murals decorate the town of **Opunake** ❷, 65km (40 miles) from New Plymouth, where highlights include the old-time **Everybody's Theatre** and the **Soap Factory** (daily 9am–5pm; free), where boutique lathers are made from scratch.

Further on, the central band rotunda of **Manaia** is surrounded by historic buildings. Two noteworthy roads depart from here: the routes to **Dawson Falls** and to windswept **Kaupokonui Beach**.

In **Hawera** ❸, good views of the countryside can be enjoyed from its old **Water Tower** on High Street. The town has some quirky attractions, including the **Elvis Presley Museum** (51 Argyle Street; www.digitalus.co.nz/elvis; charge), packed from floor to ceiling with King-related memorabilia, and **Tawhiti Museum**

War and Peace

During the 1870s, when Europeans settled on land confiscated from the Maori by the British following the Taranaki Wars, Te Whiti encouraged peaceful protest among his people; but his campaign ended at Parihaka in November 1881 when he was arrested. Earlier that day hundreds of British soldiers and militia marched to the *pa* (Maori fort) ready for battle, but to their surprise they were met by rows of children singing and dancing. As Te Whiti was led away he said to his followers, 'Be you steadfast in all that is peaceful.' Nevertheless, his words had no impact on the troops who, in one of New Zealand's darkest moments, raped and assaulted non-resistant Maori.

(401 Ohangai Road; www.tawhiti museum.co.nz; Fri–Mon 10am–4pm; charge), where local history is told through lifelike models.

Hawera to New Plymouth

From Hawera, SH3 leads north back to New Plymouth, providing a complete circumnavigation of Mount Taranaki. En route it passes through **Eltham** with its wealth of Edwardian and Victorian buildings, and **Stratford** ❹ where a clock tower glockenspiel plays Romeo and Juliet at 10am, 1pm and 3pm daily. Loaded with early settlers' artefacts, the **Pioneer Village** (SH3; www.pioneervillage.co.nz; daily 10am–4pm; charge) just to the south of Stratford is worth a visit, as is the **Fun Ho! National Toy Museum** (25 Rata Street; www.funhotoys.co.nz; daily 10am–4pm; charge) in Inglewood, displaying classic Kiwi toys. From Inglewood it's a short drive to New Plymouth via **Lake Mangamahoe**, where the mirror image of Mount Taranaki reflects perfectly on a clear day.

Stratford's musical clock tower

Forgotten Highway

Winding 155km (96 miles) through isolated hill country between Stratford and Taumarunui is the Forgotten Highway (SH43) heritage trail, passing into the Manawatu-Wanganui province. En route is the feisty settlement of **Whangamomona** ❺, which declared itself a 'republic' after bureaucratic bungling saw it realigned with Wanganui rather than its traditional ally, Taranaki. There are lots of old local photos to see at the **Whangamomona Hotel**, from where quad-bike tours go to the quirkily named **Bridge to Somewhere**.

Further on is **Moki Tunnel**, known locally as the Hobbit's Hole, and the turn-off to **Mount Damper Falls**, a spectacular cascade toppling 85m (278ft) into a deep pool.

The road twists and turns through the **Tangarakau Gorge**, where ancient podocarp forest is riddled with walkways, and on to **Lauren's Lavender Farm**, just 10 minutes' drive from Taumarunui, a good place to unwind after the drive.

Wanganui and Environs

To the southeast of Mount Taranaki, the once-thriving river port of

The 'republic' of Whangamomona

Wanganui ❻ still boasts many of its original villas and bungalows on its wide tree-lined streets. The city is most famous for its river, the Whanganui (note the extra 'h'), the country's longest navigable waterway, and the sooty tooting departure of the PS *Waimarie*, a lovingly restored coal-fired paddle steamer, provides a satisfying window into days of old, when paddle steamers transported river folk to and from town for their weekly shop. Cruises depart daily from the **Whanganui Riverboat Centre** *(see p.153)*.

Other attractions to catch include the **Whanganui Regional Museum** (Watt Street; www.wanganui-museum.org.nz; daily 10am–4.30pm; charge), a treasure trove of Maori artefacts, from art to everyday items; the **Sarjeant Gallery** (Queens Park; www.sarjeant.org.nz; daily 10.30am–4.30pm; free) on the hill above the

Wanganui

Population: 48,000

Local dialling code: 06

Tourist office: Wanganui i-Site Visitors Centre, 101 Guyton Street; tel: 06-349 0508; **www.wanganuinz.com**

Police station: Wanganui Police Station, 10 Bell Street; tel: 06-349 0600

Post office: Wanganui Post Shop, 226 Victoria Street

Hospital: Wanganui Hospital, 100 Heads Road, Wanganui; tel: 06-348 1234; **www.wdhb.org.nz**

Local media: *Wanganui Chronicle*

Airport: Wanganui Airport; tel: 06-349 0543; **www.wanganuiairport.co.nz**

Buses: Horizons; tel: 0508-800 800; **www.horizons.co.nz**

Car hire: Budget; tel: 06-345 5122; **www.budget.co.nz**. Hertz; tel: 06-348 7624; **www.hertz.com**.

Taxis: Wanganui Taxis; tel: 06-343 5555

museum; and **Durie Hill**, where an elevator (daily 8am–6pm) built in 1918 provides access to the **Memorial Tower** for magnificent views of the city and river.

Whanganui River Road

If you have time to spare, the 79km (49-mile) two-hour drive up the **Whanganui River Road** to Pipiriki is a rewarding trip. In **Jerusalem**, where French Catholic missionaries established themselves in 1854, New Zealand poet James K. Baxter set up a commune in the 1960s. **Pipiriki** ❼ is the gateway to **Whanganui National Park**; here you can organise to hike, canoe or jet-boat to the **Bridge to Nowhere** *(see p.28)*.

Rangitikei River Adventures

To the east of Wanganui on SH1, **Taihape** and **Mangaweka** provide access to the swift-flowing, canyon-carving **Rangitikei River** ❽. At **River Valley** near Taihape, gorges of violent white water make for wicked whitewater rafting. Or you can take a 80m (260ft) bungy jump into the river at **Mokai Gravity Canyon** or catch a ride on a flying fox. Meanwhile, the **Mangaweka Adventure Company** offers kayaking and rafting *(see p.152)*.

Manawatu

Manawatu is a region of hill country, plains and quintessential farming townships surrounding Palmerston North, or 'Palmie', a vibrant, cosmopolitan city with sweeping gardens, from the grounds of Massey University to the lawns of classic Manawatu homesteads.

Palmerston North

At the heart of **Palmerston North** ❾ lies **The Square**, a park known in Maori as Te Marae-O-Hine, the

Rafting the Rangitikei River

'Courtyard of the Daughter of Peace', commemorating a female chieftain who sought an end to inter-tribal warfare during the early days of European settlement. On the surrounding grid of streets are **Te Manawa** (396 Main Street; www.temanawa.co.nz; daily 10am–5pm; charge), a museum, art gallery and interactive science centre, and the **New Zealand Rugby Museum** (87 Cuba Street; www.rugbymuseum.co.nz; Mon–Sat 10am–4pm, Sun 1.30–4pm; charge), a must for rugby fans *(see p.59)*. From the centre, Fitzherbert Avenue leads to the Manawatu River and **Victoria Esplanade**, a reserve featuring botanical gardens, a miniature train, a children's playground and an aviary. Across the river is **Massey University**, a number of science research stations, and New Zealand's largest army base, at Linton.

Sculpture outside the Te Manawa gallery and science centre in Palmerston North

Manawatu Towns

Nearby in **Feilding** ❿, reached via SH54, the **Feilding Stock Saleyard Tour** (Information Centre, 10 Manchester Square; tel: 06-323 3318; www.feilding.co.nz; tours Fri 11am)

Palmerston North

Population: 104,000

Local dialling code: 06

Tourist office: Palmerston North i-Site Visitors Centre, 52 The Square; tel: 06-350 1922; **www.manawatunz.co.nz**

Police station: Palmerston North Police Station, 400 Church Street; tel: 06-351 3600

Post office: Palmerston North Central Post Shop, 328 Church Street

Hospital: Palmerston North Hospital, 50 Ruahine Street, Palmerston North; tel: 06-356 9169; **www.midcentraldhb.govt.nz**

Local media: *Manawatu Standard*

Airport: Palmerston North Airport, Airport Drive; tel: 06-351 4415; **www.pnairport.co.nz**

Buses: Horizons; tel: 0508-800 800; **www.horizons.co.nz**

Car hire: Europcar; tel: 06-353 0001; **http://car-rental.europcar.co.nz**. Rent-a-Dent; tel: 06-357 6694; **www.palmerstonnorthcarrentals.co.nz**.

Taxis: Palm Taxi North; tel: 06-355 5333. Gold & Black Taxis; tel: 06-355 5059.

There's a bullish sense of humour in Bulls

soaks up the atmosphere of the busiest saleyards in the southern hemisphere, with the capacity to hold 35,000 sheep and a total turnover of around 1.2 to 1.3 million animals per week.

Northwest of Palmerston North on SH3 is the township of **Bulls** ⓫ where more than a hundred amusing signs entertain passers-by, from 'Cure-a-bull' (the medical centre) through to the 'Consta-bull' police station.

The **Tokomaru Steam Engine Museum** (Makerua Road; www.tokomarusteam.com; Mon–Sat 9am–3.30pm, Sun 10.30am–3.30pm; charge), south of Palmerston North on SH57, displays steam-powered contraptions from steam rollers to sewing machines.

Manawatu Gorge and Woodville

The most dramatic route from Palmerston North leads east through the town of **Ashhurst** – where you can get a good view of **Tararua Wind Farm,** an impressive arrangement of 40m (130ft) -high 660kw turbines – and follows the course of the Manawatu River which winds through the **Manawatu Gorge** ⓬. Activities here include the three- to four-hour gorge walk, kayaking and a thrilling speedboat ride aboard the **Hiwinui Jet** *(see p.152)*. The sprawling gardens of **Beyond the Bridge Café** provide the added bonus of a wagon ride drawn by a team of Clydesdales.

The road emerges at **Woodville**, with a hoard of antiques shops, where the fresh fragrance of lavender wafts from **Graelynn Lavender**'s farm and oil press (1083 Upper Mclean Street).

Old Scandinavian Towns

A dashing Viking sign welcomes visitors to **Dannevirke** ⓭, a town settled by Danish and Norwegian families in 1872. Today a thriving hub for the local farming

Hawke's Bay Quake

Hawke's Bay was where New Zealand's worst earthquake tragedy took place on 3 February 1931. Buildings crumpled under the impact of a 7.9 Richter Scale earthquake. What the shock did not destroy in Napier and Hastings, fire finished off. The resulting death toll of 258 included a number of people killed by falling parapets. The city of Napier was closest to the epicentre, and heroic deeds were performed by rescuers and by naval personnel from the HMS *Veronica*, which happened to be in harbour (along Napier's seafront today there is a colonnade named after the naval sloop).

The 1930s were a time of economic depression, but the Hawke's Bay's post-quake aid fund was well supported and so the city was rebuilt with architecture inspired by the Art Deco movement of the time.

It could be said that Napier today is a kind of memorial to the earthquake. Much of its suburban area, stretching out to the once-independent borough of Taradale in the southwest, is built on the 4,000 hectares (10,000 acres) of former marshland the earthquake pushed up.

community, it offers superb camping at **The Domain**, a 20-hectare (50-acre) park featuring gardens, ponds, aviaries and a deer park, plus playgrounds, paddling pools and a skating rink. The **Dannevirke Fantasy Cave** (High Street; www.fantasycave.net; Sat 10am–12.30pm; charge), a magical grotto crammed full of nursery rhyme scenes, is a great place to take kids. Trolls can be spotted in nearby **Norsewood** on a trail which takes in the town's Scandinavian heritage. Many of its streets bear the original settlers' names, and folk dancing is still taught at the local school.

Hawke's Bay

The Hawke's Bay region has more than 50 wineries and lots of foodie experiences to enjoy, from exquisite vineyard fare to a gourmet trail of

The Dome, an Art Deco building in Napier on Hawke's Bay

Statue of Pania, of Maori legend, in Napier

handcrafted cheese and chocolates, natural (no preservatives or colourings) ice cream and deliciously preserved fruits *(see pp.148–9)*. At the heart of the region is the city of Napier, which flourishes with the zigzags and sunbursts of Art Deco style.

Napier

Looking at the distinctive Art Deco buildings of **Napier** ⓮, it's hard to envisage the destruction wrought by the earthquake of 1931 *(see p.145)*. The city took the opportunity to reinvent itself, and its collection of Art Deco buildings is now internationally recognised thanks to the **Art Deco Trust** which organises many activities, including informative daily walking tours *(see p.153)*. Napier's favourite attractions are found strung along the city's 2km (1¼ mile) -long **Marine Parade**, where a seaside promenade features gardens, fountains and sculptures, including a bronze statue of Pania, a beautiful maiden of local Maori legend. At the **National Aquarium of New Zealand** (Marine Parade; www.nationalaquarium.co.nz; daily 9am–5pm; charge) a moving footpath carries viewers under an

Napier

- **Population:** 57,500
- **Local dialling code:** 06
- **Tourist office:** Napier i-Site Visitors Centre, 100 Marine Parade; tel: 06-834 1911; **www.napiervic.co.nz**
- **Police station:** Napier Police Station, 77 Station Street; tel: 06-831 0700
- **Post office:** Napier Post Shop, 151 Hastings Street
- **Hospital:** Hawke's Bay Hospital, Omahu Road, Hastings; tel: 06-878 8109; **www.hawkesbaydhb.govt.nz**
- **Local media:** *Napier Mail*
- **Airport:** Hawke's Bay Airport, SH2, Westshore; tel: 06-835 3427; **www.hawkesbay-airport.co.nz**
- **Buses:** Go Bus; tel: 06-878 9250; **www.gobus.co.nz**
- **Car hire:** Rent-a-Dent; tel: 06-834 0688; **www.rentadent.co.nz**
- **Taxis:** Star Taxis; tel: 06-835 5511. Napier Taxis; tel: 06-835 7777.

oceanarium filled with sea creatures, while at the **Hawke's Bay Museum** (9 Herschell Street; www.hbmag.co.nz; daily 10am–5pm; charge) the displays include accounts of the earthquake, and exhibits of Maori art and culture.

Hastings and Environs

Some 21km (13 miles) south from Napier is **Hastings** ⓯, an inland city built upon rich alluvial plains. Examples of Art Deco and Spanish mission-style buildings can also be found here, and fruit of all descriptions grows profusely in its Mediterranean-type climate. These can be purchased from road-side stalls, or from the **Sunday Farmers' Market**, along with lots of epicurean treats *(see p.149)*. Other attractions include **Splash Planet**, (Grove Road; www.splashplanet.co.nz; mid-Nov–Jan daily 10am–5.30pm, Feb–Mar Sat–Sun only) a family-friendly water park, and tractor-trailer tours to **Cape Kidnappers**, a gannet colony located 18km (11 miles) from Hastings *(see p.153)*.

From Hastings you can drive 3km (2 miles) southeast across the plains to **Havelock North** and the summit of limestone mountain **Te Mata Peak**, which offers sweeping views. Havelock North is also home to **Arataki Honey** (66 Arataki Road; www.aratakihoneyhb.co.nz; daily 9am–5pm; free), a major honey producer, where a live 'Bee Wall' provides glimpses of an entire colony at work.

The steep cliffs of Cape Kidnappers

FOOD AND WINE TRAIL

There's nowhere else in New Zealand where food and wine are teamed so perfectly together than in Hawke's Bay. The shores of this premier lifestyle destination boast more than 50 wineries, many of which offer a cellar-door experience and have a restaurant on site. At some of the boutique vineyards visitors may even be given the tour by the wine makers themselves. If no one is prepared to be designated driver, then it's no problem to book a winery tour with one of the many operators in Napier or Hastings.

Hawke's Bay is New Zealand's oldest wine-growing region and sees itself as the finest. Certainly, it enjoys ever-increasing recognition for the quality of its Sauvignon Blanc, Chardonnay and Cabernet Sauvignon. Enthusiasts wax lyrical about wineries like **Trinity Hill**, **Te Mata Estate** and Church Road, all of which are 'must dos' on the wine trail. Award-winning **Church Road** (www.churchroad.co.nz), on the outskirts of Napier, is also home to the country's only wine museum, with antiquities from the Mediterranean dating back to 1000BC which can be viewed on a winery tour departing from the cellar door.

Other wine trail highlights include **Craggy Range Vineyard** (253 Waimarama Road, Havelock North; www.craggyrange.com), nestled beneath

Mission Estate Winery, Napier

breathtaking Te Mata Peak, with views of hang-gliders taking flight; and **Mission Estate** (198 Church Road, Napier; www.missionestate.co.nz), established by the Marist Brothers in 1851 and housed inside a former seminary building high upon a plateau.

There are also smaller-scale boutique operations like **Clearview Estate** (194 Clifton Road, Te Awanga; www.clearviewestate.co.nz), where organic wines can be sampled in an atmospheric tasting room. You can enjoy a relaxed lunch among the vines or settle down at an informal dining table built around an 80-year-old olive tree. The towering and symmetrical architecture of Flaxmere's **Sileni Estate** (2016 Maraekakaho Road; www.sileni.co.nz) is designed to impress, as is its well-stocked pantry and cheesery.

This fertile region's Mediterranean microclimate yields a wide range of seasonal fruits and vegetables, and local chefs are spoilt for choice when it comes to creating tempting fare which they expertly match with local wine. As you drive or cycle through the farmland, look out for delicious produce offered at road-side stalls along the way or even stop and pick your own. Or for a great round-up of regionally produced fare, visit the **Hawke's Bay Sunday Farmers' Market** (Hawke's Bay A&P Showgrounds, Kenilworth Road, Hastings; 8.30am–12.30pm) for gourmet meats, artisan breads, handmade cheeses and chocolates, natural ice cream, organic coffee and delicious preserves made from farm-fresh fruits and vegetables.

A Hawke's Bay vineyard with Te Mata Peak in the background

ACCOMMODATION

Somewhat off the beaten tourist track, the regions of Taranaki, Manawatu-Wanganui and Hawke's Bay are renowned for their hospitality.

Taranaki

New Plymouth Top 10 Holiday Park
29 Princes Street, New Plymouth
Tel: 06-758 2566
One-, two- and three-bedroom motel-style units, and cabins for up to eight. Pool, spa, sauna and kids' playground. **$–$$**

Nice Hotel and Restaurant
71 Brougham Street, New Plymouth
Tel: 06-758 6423
www.nicehotel.co.nz
Boutique hotel in the heart of town. Designer bathrooms with double spa baths. Award-winning restaurant. **$$$$**

Tairoa Lodge
3 Puawai Street, Hawera
Tel: 06-278 8603
www.tairoalodge.co.nz
A lovely B&B set on 4 hectares (10 acres) of established gardens. **$$$–$$$$**

Wanganui and Environs

Kings Court Motel
60 Plymouth Street, Wanganui
Tel: 0800-221 222
www.kingscourtmotel.co.nz
Clean, comfortable rooms in a convenient central location. **$$$**

Tamara Backpackers Lodge
24 Somme Parade, Wanganui
Tel: 06-347 6300
www.tamaralodge.co.nz
Doubles, singles and shared rooms with river and garden views. **$–$$**

Manawatu and Tararua

Grandma's Place
123 Grey Street, Palmerston North
Tel: 06-358 6928
www.grandmas-place.com
Comfortable budget accommodation in a 1920s villa with period furniture. **$–$$**

Rose City Motel
120–122 Fitzherbert Avenue, Palmerston North
Tel: 06-356 5388
www.rosecitymotel.co.nz
Modern studio and one- to two-bedroom suites. Sauna, spa pool and squash court. **$$$–$$$$**

Hawke's Bay

Bella Tuscany On Kennedy
371–373 Kennedy Road, Napier
Tel: 06-843 9129
www.bellatuscany.co.nz
Mediterranean-style accommodation with spa bath suites, private courtyards and tasteful furnishings. **$$$–$$$$**

Black Barn
Black Barn Road, RD2, Havelock North
Tel: 06-877 7985
www.blackbarn.co.nz
High-quality accommodation in cottages set on a vineyard. **$$$$$**

Accommodation Price Categories

Prices are for one night's accommodation in a standard double room (unless otherwise specified).

$ = below NZ$30
$$ = NZ$30–75
$$$ = NZ$75–150
$$$$ = NZ$150–350
$$$$$ = over NZ$350

Black Barn cottages

Lawn Cottages
Tel: 06-870 0302
www.lawncottages.co.nz
Supremely stylish cottages set in rural location just 10 minutes' drive to Napier or Hastings. **$$$$**

Omahu Motor Lodge
357 Omahu Road, Hastings
Tel: 06-870 7061
www.omahumotorlodge.co.nz
Modern air-conditioned studio, one- and two-bedroom units, some with spa baths. **$$$–$$$$**

Wallys Backpackers
7 Cathedral Lane, Napier
Tel: 06-833 7930
Budget hostel accommodation with shared rooms and en-suite double rooms. Camping also on-site. BBQ area.
$–$$

RESTAURANTS

Sourcing fresh ingredients direct from its abundant dairy farms, market gardens, orchards and vineyards, this region is renowned for the quality of its cuisine.

Restaurant Price Categories

Prices are for a standard meal for one person.

$ = below NZ$15
$$ = NZ$15–30
$$$ = NZ$30–50
$$$$ = over NZ$50

Taranaki

André L'Escargot Restaurant and Bar
37–41 Brougham Street, New Plymouth
Tel: 06-758 4812
www.andres.co.nz
Run by Frenchman Andre Teissonniere, L'Escargot's signature dishes include roasted quail and eye fillet stroganoff. **$$$**

Table Restaurant
Nice Hotel, 71 Brougham Street, New Plymouth
Tel: 06-758 6423
www.nicehotel.co.nz
This award-winning restaurant is well worth the splurge. A well thought-out menu using the best locally sourced ingredients.
$$$–$$$$

Wanganui and Environs

Redeye Café
96 Guyton Street, Wanganui
Tel: 06-345 5646
Freshly prepared food available from a chilled cabinet and a blackboard menu. **$–$$**

Manawatu and Tararua

Aberdeen Steakhouse
161 Broadway Avenue, Palmerston North
Tel: 06-952 5570
www.aberdeensteakhouse.co.nz
A wide range of dishes, but steak reigns supreme. **$$**

The Herb Farm Café
Grove Road, Ashhurst
Tel: 06-326 7479
www.herbfarm.co.nz
The Herb Farm Café serves beautifully presented, garden-fresh meals in a tranquil rural herb garden setting. **$–$$**

Hawke's Bay

Pacifica Restaurant
209 Marine Parade, Napier
Tel: 06-833 6335
A contemporary seafood/game restaurant with a strong Pacific ambience. **$$$**

Rush Munro's Ice Cream Gardens
704 Heretaunga Street, Hastings
Tel: 06-878 9634
www.rushmunro.co.nz
This all-natural hand-churned ice cream is extraordinarily good. **$**

Terroir
253 Waimarama Road, Havelock North
Tel: 06-873 0143
www.craggyrange.com
The restaurant attached to Craggy Bay winery has an impeccable pedigree and sophisticated cuisine. An excellent children's menu features healthy yet tempting fare. **$$$–$$$$**

Westshore Fish Café
112A Charles Street, Westshore
Tel: 06-834 0227
Delightful, inexpensive fish dishes. **$$–$$$**

ENTERTAINMENT AND NIGHTLIFE

As in many of New Zealand's provincial towns, nightlife is subdued compared to international standards. Your best bet is to make your way to the local pub – there's one to be found in every small town – or head to the local cinema.

Film

Century Cinema
Marine Parade, Napier
Tel: 06-835 7781
www.centurycinema.co.nz
Hawke's Bay's alternative cinema, screening the finest from around the world.

Theatre

Royal Wanganui Opera House
Hill Street, Wanganui
Tel: 06-349 0511
www.royaloperahouse.co.nz
This historical opera house hosts various performances, including local musicians.

SPORTS AND ACTIVITIES

Though the region's rivers are less well known, they still offer some of New Zealand's most thrilling activities.

Bungy Jumping

Mokai Gravity Canyon
Mokai Bridge
Tel: 06-388 9109
www.gravitycanyon.co.nz
A hair-raising 80m (260ft) bungy jump into an enormous river canyon. Other attractions include a canyon swing and a 172m (560ft) -high flying fox. Onlookers can take in all the action from the safety of the viewing deck.

Kayaking

Mangaweka Adventure Company
SH1, Mangaweka
Tel: 06-382 5744
www.rra.co.nz
Whitewater kayaking courses and rafting adventures.

Jet-boating

Hiwinui Jet
Manawatu Gorge
Tel: 06-329 2838
www.hiwinui.co.nz
Thrilling jet-boat tours through the Manawatu Gorge.

Whitewater Rafting

River Valley
RD2,
Taihape
Tel: 06-388 1444
www.rivervalley.co.nz
Whitewater rafting action on the Rangitikei River, where gorges of violent white water, Grade 5 rapids and deep pools make for one of the top whitewater-rafting destinations in the world.

TOURS

You can tour Art Deco Napier, cycle through winelands or even ride a tractor-trailer to a gannet colony.

Bike Tours

Bike D'vine Tours
4 Weathers Road, Taradale
Tel: 06-833 6697
www.bikedevine.com
Winery and sightseeing tours.

Boat Cruises

Whanganui Riverboat Centre
1a Taupo Quay
Tel: 06-347 1863
www.riverboat.co.nz
Daily cruises at 2pm on the PS *Waimarie*.

Tractor-trailer Tours

Gannet Beach Adventures
Clifton Reserve, Hawke's Bay
Tel: 06-875 0898

Cycling through a Hawke's Bay vineyard

www.gannets.com
Eco-friendly beach tour to gannet colony at Cape Kidnappers travelling aboard a cushioned trailer pulled by a tractor.

Walking Tours

Art Deco Trust
163 Tennyson Street, Napier
Tel: 06-835 0022
www.artdeconapier.com
Daily guided walks of Napier's key Art Deco heritage sites.

FESTIVALS AND EVENTS

Events centre on Taranaki and the Hawke's Bay, but the most peculiar festival occurs in Taihape, Gumboot Capital of the World.

February

Art Deco Weekend
Napier
Vintage costumes, café crawls and tea parties.

April

Gumboot Day
Taihape
Rural gumboot-throwing festival.

May

Manawatu Jazz Festival
Palmerston North
Live jazz at venues throughout the region.

September

Hastings Blossom Festival
www.blossomfestival.co.nz
Includes a huge parade, performances by celebrity artists, concerts and fireworks.

October

Hawke's Bay Show
Hawke's Bay Showgrounds
www.hawkesbayshow.co.nz
Agricultural show attracting large crowds.

Taranaki Rhododendron Festival
New Plymouth
www.rhodo.co.nz
Over 60 private gardens open to the public.

December

Festival of Lights
New Plymouth
Illuminations in Pukekura Park.

Wellington

Vibrant Wellington is the seat of New Zealand's government as well as the unofficial cultural centre of the country. The city has long been compared to San Francisco, sharing a superb coastal location with ocean vistas, an abundance of cool, sunny weather, a penchant for colourfully painted old wooden houses and a palpable cosmopolitan buzz.

Wellington

Population: 180,000

Local dialling code: 04

Tourist office: Wellington i-Site Visitor Centre, corner Wakefield Street and Civic Square; tel: 04-802 4860; **www.wellingtonz.com**

Main police station: Wellington Central, 41 Victoria Street; tel: 04-381 2000

Main post office: Thorndon Post Shop, 100 Molesworth Street

Hospital: Wellington Hospital, Riddiford Street, Newtown; tel: 04-385 5999; **www.ccdhb.org.nz**

Local media: *The Dominion Post*

Set on a horseshoe-shaped harbour, **Wellington** ❶ possesses an assurance and an international flair that comes with being the country's artistic and cultural heart as well as its capital city. It is home to the Museum of New Zealand Te Papa Tongarewa, the National Opera, the Royal New Zealand Ballet and the New Zealand Symphony Orchestra, as well as the studios of film-maker Peter Jackson. Leading figures in the worlds of cuisine, art, fashion, academia and politics work here, amid the city's plethora of arty cafés, alternative galleries and theatres, and funky shops. Wellington's charm derives partly from its quirky topography, with wooden turn-of-the-20th-century houses clinging to steep hillsides bristling with native bush and clumps of arum lilies. Streets zigzag downwards to the heart of the city, the harbour and the affluent promenade of Oriental Bay. And just a short drive away is the rugged and desolate south coast, the hip northern beaches of the Kapiti Coast, the roller-coaster of the Rimutakas, the colonial quaintness of Greytown and the Pinot Noir-producing vineyards of Martinborough.

Wellington City

Wellington's great blue bowl of a harbour is only mildly scarred by its port reclamations, and high-rise skyscrapers of steel and glass are set below green hills dotted with white wooden houses. Quaint Victorian two- and three-storey wedding-cake houses and civic buildings like the neo-Baroque St James Theatre on Courtenay Place are well cared for by its residents.

Central

Civic Square Ⓐ, near the Wellington i-Site Visitor Centre, is a good place to begin. Here you will find the **City Gallery** (www.citygallery.org.nz; daily 10am–5pm; free), with contemporary local and international artworks; the refurbished Town Hall; The Michael Fowler Performing Arts Centre; and the **Wellington City Library** (www.wcl.govt.nz; Mon–Thur 9.30am–8.30pm, Fri until 9pm, Sat 9.30am–5pm, Sun 1–4pm; free), decorated with palm-tree pillars. A distinctive bridge, decorated with sculpture, links the square with the waterfront.

Right on the harbour is the popular café precinct of **Queen's Wharf**, where the galleries of the **New Zealand Academy of Fine Arts** Ⓑ (www.nzafa.com; daily 10am–5pm; free) exhibit a range of home-grown arts and crafts. Across the way, housed in the 1892 Bond Store Building, is the **Museum of Wellington City**

High-street and Alternative Shopping

The shopping scene in Wellington is made up of several distinct shopping precincts, including the Lambton Quarter (centred around Lambton Quay) where there are five shopping centres, including the famous Kirkcaldie & Stains, the oldest department store in New Zealand. Head to the Cuba Quarter (around Cuba Street) for more alternative, funky stores and good second-hand shops, and to the Willis Quarter (around Willis Street) for boutique and designer shopping. Antiques-hunters will do well exploring the streets of Thorndon, Wellington's historical district.

Wellington's Civic Square, with the Michael Fowler Performing Arts Centre to the left

Wellington's harbour

and Sea **C** (3 Jervois Quay; www.museumofwellington.co.nz; daily 10am–5pm; free), which has a captivating collection of maritime memorabilia, covering the city's seafaring history from early Maori interaction to the 1900s.

From here, it's a short walk south past the rowing sheds of **Frank Kitts Park** to the monolithic bulk of **Te Papa Tongarewa – Museum of New Zealand** **D** (55 Cable

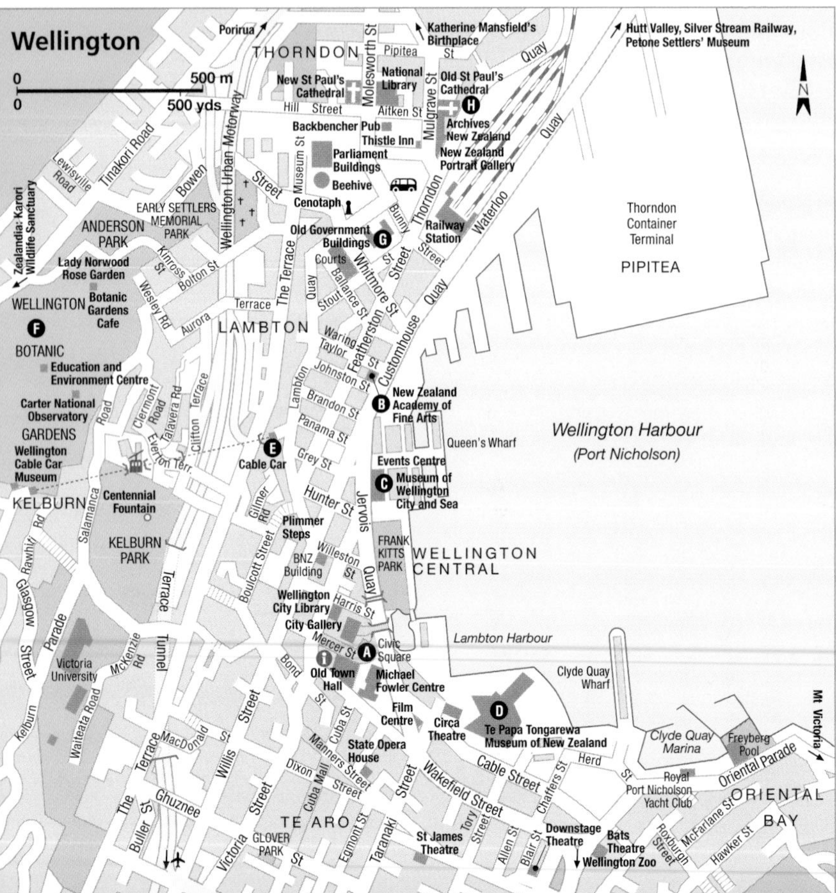

Street; www.tepapa.govt.nz; daily 10am–6pm, Thur until 9pm; free), somewhat revolutionary for a New Zealand museum. Within its well-designed interior are all kinds of interactive technology, such as motion simulators that allow visitors to experience the powerful geological forces that have shaped New Zealand's landscapes like volcanic eruptions and earthquakes. There's a *marae*, or Maori village, here too – and the hands-on activity areas are very popular with children. There are also regular temporary exhibitions of work by eminent New Zealand artists.

South of Te Papa is **Courtney Place**, the city's hip bar and restaurant centre and a hub for the city's liveliest and most innovative professional theatres, including **Circa Theatre**; **Bats Theatre**, an intimate venue and home of the fringe; and **Downstage Theatre**, New Zealand's first professional theatre, offering great shows, a licensed bar and accommodation from its location at the southern end of Courtney Place.

Lambton Quay

Wellington's main commercial street, **Lambton Quay**, used to run along the waterfront, but reclamation has pushed the land out; plaques embedded in the pavement mark the old shoreline. For splendid views over the city and harbour, hop aboard the **Wellington Cable Car** E (www.wellingtoncablecar.

Wellington City Transport

Airport: Wellington Airport, Stewart Duff Drive; tel: 04-385 5100; **www.wellington-airport.co.nz**. The Airport Flyer express bus departs every 15 minutes to the CBD (NZ$8). Taxis to the CBD cost around NZ$30–35; Wellington Combined Taxi group; tel: 04-384 4444; **www.taxis.co.nz**.

Buses: MetLink; tel: 0800-801 700; **www.metlink.org.nz**; buses cover the greater Wellington area.

Trains: MetLink – see details above.

Ferry services: Interislander; tel: 0800-802 802; **www.interislander.co.nz**. Bluebridge; tel: 0800-844 844; **www.bluebridge.co.nz**. These run frequent daily crossings to and from Picton on the South Island, carrying passengers and vehicles including motorhomes. The journey takes around three hours and booking is essential from December to February.
East by West Ferries; tel: 04-499 1282; **www.eastbywest.co.nz**; operate a limited service around Wellington Harbour, from Queens Wharf to Days Bay (for Eastbourne), Petone and Seatoun.

Taxis: Capital Taxis; tel: 04-384 5678; **www.capitaltaxis.co.nz**. Green Cabs; tel: 0508 447 336; **www.greencabs.co.nz**.

Car hire: Apex; tel: 04-385 2163; **www.apexrentals.co.nz**. Pegasus; tel: 0800-354 507; **www.carrentalswellington.co.nz**.

Parking: Parking is available in car parks city-wide and costs NZ$1–10 per hour for casual parking.

co.nz; Mon–Fri 7am–10pm, Sat from 8.30am, Sun from 9am; charge 🚻). It departs every 10 minutes from Cable Car Lane, and travels to an upper terminus. Adjacent is the **Wellington Cable Car Museum** (www.cablecarmuseum.co.nz; daily 9.30am–5pm; free), which tells the story of New Zealand's last operational cable-car system, and the **Wellington Botanic Gardens** F (www.wellington.govt.nz/services/gardens; daily sunrise–sunset; free 🚻), notable for the formal glory of the Lady Norwood Rose Garden

The *marae* exhibit in the Te Papa Tongawera – Museum of New Zealand

and the **Carter National Observatory** (www.carterobservatory.org; tel: 04-910 3140; daily 10am–5pm, Sat until 9pm; charge 🚻) which offers planetarium shows.

Thorndon

Further up Lambton Quay where it meets Molesworth Street in Thorndon is the **Old Government Buildings** G (1876), the second largest wooden building in the world, comprising 9,300 sq m (100,000 sq ft) of timber. Directly opposite, politicians and public officials buzz around the capital's unique circular Cabinet offices, known as **The Beehive.** Built in the late 1970s, the copper-topped Beehive makes a soft contrast with the square marble angles of the adjacent **Parliament Buildings** (www.parliament.nz; Mon–Fri 10am–4pm, Sat 10am–3pm, Sun 11am–3pm; free), completed in 1922, and the neo-Gothic turrets of the **General Assembly Library**, dating back to 1897.

Just to the north of the Beehive and Parliament is the **National Library** (www.natlib.govt.nz; Mon–Fri 9am–5pm, Sat 9am–1pm; free), where the Alexander Turnbull Library houses a remarkable collection of New Zealand and Pacific history. Nearby on Mulgrave Street is **Old St Paul's** H (daily 10am–5pm; free), a small but impressive Gothic Revival-style cathedral made entirely of native timbers. From here, a 10-minute walk further north leads to **Katherine Mansfield's Birthplace** (Tue–Sun 10am–4pm; charge), a two-storey house at 25 Tinakori Road where this famous New Zealand writer was born in 1888.

Katherine Mansfield

The first New Zealand writer to attract significant attention outside her own country was Katherine Mansfield, whose delicate short stories have – despite her own gloomy prediction – survived numerous changes of fashion and can be read with as much pleasure today as when they were written, mostly in the 15 years or so before her death in 1923 at the age of 34. New Zealand in the early 20th century was claustrophobic for the young writer, and in 1908 Mansfield left her country, with some eagerness, in pursuit of a career – first in London and later in Switzerland and the south of France. She never returned.

The Beehive parliament building

Wellington Suburbs

On the fringes of the city centre lie some of Wellington's premier open spaces and nature-based attractions. **Zealandia: Karori Wildlife Sanctuary** (tel: 04-920 9200; www.visitzealandia.com; daily 10am–5pm; charge 👪), 2km (1 mile) west of the city centre, is an oasis where kiwi, weka, ruru (little owls) and tuatara survive in their natural environment; guided night tours are available but booking is essential. South of the city is Newtown, home to the **Wellington Zoo** (200 Daniell Street; www.wellington zoo.com; daily 9.30am–5pm; charge 👪), the oldest zoo in New Zealand, built in 1906, and now run on the natural-habitat conservation model favoured by zoos worldwide.

Wellington Environs

At weekends Wellingtonians head out of the city to enjoy the quiet south-coast beaches, the trendy northern beaches and the marine sanctuary of Kapiti Island.

The Hutt Valley

The Hutt Road (SH2) leads 13km (8 miles) to **Petone** ❷, a recreational area at the northernmost point of the harbour and the site of **Petone Settlers' Museum** (www.petonesettlers.org.nz; Tue–Fri noon–4pm, Sat–Sun 1–5pm; charge) which commemorates the struggles faced by Wellington's earliest pioneers.

To the east is **Wainuiomata**, the gateway to the **Rimutaka Forest Park**, which has several good wilderness hikes, including one track leading to the summit of Mount Matthews.

Further around the harbour is **Eastbourne**, reached by ferry (from Wellington to Days Bay) or a drive around the bays; from here, it is an easy 8km (5-mile) hike around the coastline to view the **Pencarrow Lighthouse ❸**, the country's first permanent lighthouse. This 1859 cast-iron structure was 'manned' at the time by one Mary Jane Bennett, New Zealand's only woman lighthouse keeper.

Kapiti Coast

SH1 heads northwest from Wellington to the **Kapiti Coast** townships of Paraparaumu and Waikanae. Cruises with **Kapiti Tours** *(see p.168)* depart from Paraparaumu bound for the unspoilt native bird sanctuary of **Kapiti Island ❹**. Cats, goats and dogs blighted the native fauna of the island until the Department of Conservation (DOC) embarked on an eradication programme. Today, Kapiti is a valuable sanctuary for several species of native birds such as the kakariki, takahe, kea and kiwi.

Just north of **Paraparaumu**, the **Lindale Centre** (SH1; daily 9am–5pm; free) has a range of epicurean shops including a gourmet cheesery and ice cream shop, and a farm park which gives sheep-shearing and milking demonstrations.

Wairarapa

It takes an hour to drive northeast over the 300m (1,000ft) Rimutaka Range on SH2; cars sometimes need chains to negotiate this route during winter. On the other side lies **Featherston** *(see p.162)*. To the southeast of Featherston is **Martinborough ❺**, which burst onto the world stage in

The Kapiti Coast

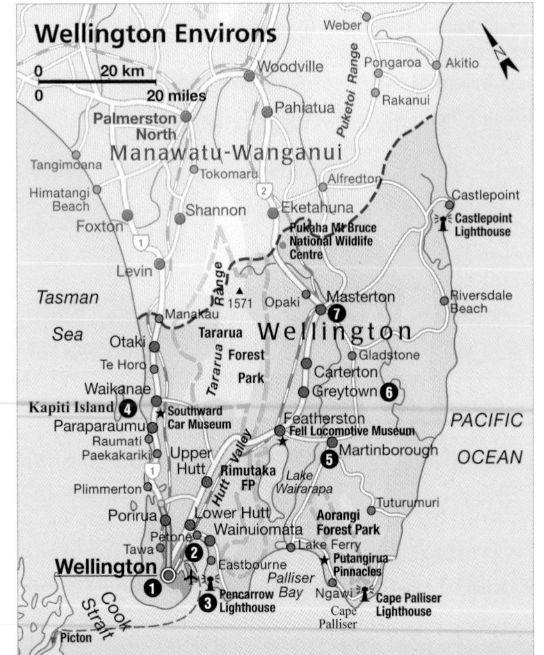

A fresh batch is prepared at Schoc Chocolates in Greytown

the 1990s as a wine producer, particularly for its Pinot Noir.

Greytown ❻ was New Zealand's first inland town and is arguably the prettiest and most Victorian of them all. City folk flock here to indulge in wine trails, antiques, arts, crafts and speciality shops and local produce including the divine organic and preservative-free chocolates and truffles found at **Schoc Chocolates** (177 Main Street; www.chocolatetherapy.com).

Further north on SH2, the eye-catching daffodil capital of **Carterton** has historical buildings to explore, plus **Paua World** (54 Kent Street; www.pauaworld.com; daily; free) with displays and information relating to this shellfish and its uses.

To the west in the **Tararua Forest Park** is the beautiful Waiohine Gorge, where water flows down from the flanks of Arete Peak and Tarn Ridge. There are a number of good hikes here, beginning with a rather precarious-looking swing bridge suspended high above the river, just minutes from the car park.

Masterton and Coast

Life in **Masterton** ❼ centres around **Queen Elizabeth Park** with its historic cemetery, super-sized duck pond, 'Kids' Own' playground, steam train, mini golf and bowls. Masterton hosts the annual **Golden Shears** sheep-shearing competition and at 12 Dixon Street is **Shear Discovery New Zealand** (www.sheardiscovery.co.nz; daily 9am–5pm; charge), with its Golden Shears Hall of Champions, sheep-shearing display, and information about all facets of wool production. Other points of interest include

TOUR OF THE WAIRARAPA

This driving tour explores the southern Wairarapa, a land of wide-open spaces and fertile plains fringed by a brutally handsome coastline, where it's sunnier and less windy than the capital.

Wellington to Featherston

This tour starts in Wellington, at the railway station on Bunny Street. Turn left onto Waterloo Quay, and follow the signs to the Wellington/Hutt motorway. This skirts the Wellington Harbour and travels through Lower Hutt, Stokes Valley and Upper Hutt. From here, SH2 begins its winding climb over the Rimutaka Ranges. Stop at the top for views of the range's bush-clad hills and, beyond, to the plains of the Wairarapa.

A colourful crafts boutique in Greytown

Featherston

A 16km (10-mile) drive brings you to the town of **Featherston**, and the **Fell Engine Museum**, home to the world's last remaining Fell locomotive, built to cope with steep gradients such as the Rimutaka Range.

Another 1km (½ mile) past Featherston is a **POW Memorial**, on the site of a former World War I army training barracks, which also held Japanese soldiers captured in the Solomon Islands during World War II.

Greytown

A further 11km (7-mile) drive on SH2 brings you to Greytown, New Zealand's first planned inland town. Despite its name, it is anything but colourless; its main street is lined with fine examples of early New Zealand wooden Victorian architecture. The **Cobblestones Museum** provides a fascinating insight into the region's past. The atmospheric old coaching stables and cobbled grounds (1857) make it easy to

Tips

- Distance: 202km (125 miles) return, or 346km (214 miles) including the South Coast
- Time: 1–2 days
- Begin this tour in Wellington. For details of car-hire companies, *see p.157*.
- Martinborough is only 81km (50 miles) from Wellington but progress is slow through the Rimutaka Range
- To avoid rush hour, leave before 6.30am or after 9am

imagine old stage coaches pulling up with cargoes of new pioneers.

Spend time browsing Greytown's boutiques, where you can buy anything from an 18th-century chair to locally produced art. The **Main Street Deli** is a good refreshment stop; alternatively, try across the road at **Salute** *(see p.167)*.

Martinborough produces delicious Pinot Noir wines

Martinborough Wine Tour

Any trip to the Wairarapa is incomplete without visiting the wine-growing township of Martinborough, a short drive from Greytown. To get there, drive south down Greytown's Main Street and veer left off SH2. En route vineyards line the roads; with so many to choose from, the **Martinborough Wine Centre** is a good place to try some samples and pick up a Wairarapa and Martinborough wine trail map. About 24 wineries are located within walking distance of the centre, including **Palliser Estate** and **Te Kairanga**. Hold out for lunch, though, at **Café Bloom** on Dry River Road, southeast of Martinborough *(see p.166)*.

Scenic South Coast

The remainder of the day can be spent sampling wine, perusing local arts or discovering the scenic south coast. To do the latter, head south to **Lake Ferry** with its contrasting views over the pounding waves of Palliser Bay and tranquil waters of Lake Onoke.

Continue to the **Putangirua Pinnacles**, huge, organ pipe-like columns that were formed over the past 120,000 years by heavy rain washing away silt and sand to expose the underlying bedrock.

Further on in **Ngawi**, a picturesque fishing village, rows of brightly painted bulldozers – used to launch fishing boats – park on the beach. Keep your eyes peeled for seals.

From Ngawi, it's 6km (4 miles) to **Cape Palliser Lighthouse** (1896). High on a weather-beaten cliff, it marks the southernmost point of the North Island; 258 steep steps lead to the top for magnificent views of the South Island.

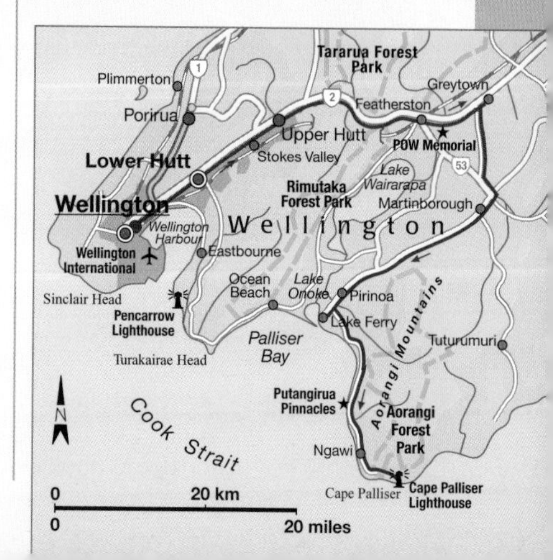

Wairarapa Wine

The Wairarapa region produces about 3,000 cases of wine per year and its success with Pinot Noir is well known. The potential to grow vines in the region was first recognised by William Beetham over a century ago when he planted vines in Masterton in 1883 and successfully managed to produce a quality vintage. A decade later, Beetham added another vineyard at Lansdowne (also in Masterton), which he planted with *vinifera* varietals including pinot noir. In 1905, prohibition brought an end to the Lansdowne vineyards, but in more recent years, riding the wave of Martinborough's success and wider global awareness of New Zealand wines, a flurry of boutique vineyards owned and run by passionate, quality-driven winemakers.

tranquil **Henley Lake**, surrounded by a reserve, and **The Pointon Collection** (2 McKinstrey Road; www.pointoncollection.co.nz; daily 10am–4pm; charge), with its vast aggregation of vintage cars and motorcycles, plus a collection of clothes spanning a hundred years from the 1860s to the 1960s.

Worthwhile excursions from Masterton include the 30km (19-mile) drive north to the **Pukaha Mount Bruce National Wildlife Centre** (SH2; www.mtbruce.org.nz; daily 9am–4.30pm; charge), where threatened species such as the North Island kiwi, the kokako and North Island kaka can be viewed in natural bush aviaries; kaka feeding is held at 3pm. Out on the coast is the **Castlepoint Lighthouse**. It's perched on a craggy wind-blown bluff, and is reached via a rickety causeway.

The Golden Shears sheep-shearing competition is held at Masterton in March

ACCOMMODATION

Like all cities in New Zealand, prices in Wellington are steeper than those quoted in provincial towns, though there are plenty of budget options.

Wellington City

Cambridge Hotel
Corner Cambridge and Alpha streets
Tel: 04-385 8829
www.cambridgehotel.co.nz
Boutique-style bargain-basement rooms including en-suite guest rooms and backpackers' rooms. Kitchen, lounge and cheap bistro breakfasts. **$–$$$**

Duxton Hotel Wellington
170 Wakefield Street
Tel: 04-473 3900
www.duxtonhotels.com
Located in the heart of the CBD, close to the waterfront and Michael Fowler Centre, the Duxton has 192 tastefully appointed rooms. **$$$$–$$$$$**

Intercontinental Wellington
2 Grey Street
Tel: 04-472 2722
www.intercontinental.com/wellington
Right on the waterfront, this hotel has a restaurant, bars, room service and a fitness centre with a pool and sauna. **$$$$$**

Wellywood Backpackers
58 Tory Street
Tel: 04-381 3899
www.wellywoodbackpackers.co.nz
Located in the heart of the city, Wellywood's rooms range from dorm beds, twin and double rooms to larger family rooms. Free spa pool and internet access. **$$**

Wellington Suburbs

Stillwater Lodge
34 Mana Esplanade, Paremata
Tel: 04-233 6628
www.stillwaterlodge.co.nz
A backpackers' beach paradise, 20 minutes north of Wellington on the beachfront. Bunks from NZ$35 and double rooms. **$$**

Accommodation Price Categories

Prices are for one night's accommodation in a standard double room (unless otherwise specified).

$ = below NZ$30
$$ = NZ$30–75
$$$ = NZ$75–150
$$$$ = NZ$150–350
$$$$$ = over NZ$350

Tinakori Lodge Bed & Breakfast
182 Tinakori Road
Tel: 04-939 3478
www.tinakorilodge.co.nz
Situated in historic Thorndon, this B&B offers quality facilities, a restful atmosphere and scrumptious breakfast buffet. **$$$**

Wellington Environs

Kate's Place
7 Cologne Street, Martinborough
Tel: 06-306 9935
www.katesplace.co.nz
Excellent value, with dorm bunk rooms and double rooms. Short walk from Martinborough. **$–$$$**

Peppers Hotel Martinborough
The Square, Martinborough
Tel: 06-306 9350
www.peppers.co.nz/martinborough
An elegant retreat set in a refurbished colonial hotel established in 1882. **$$$$**

The Intercontinental Wellington's restaurant

RESTAURANTS

Wellington is well known for its cafés and restaurants, of which there are more than 300 located throughout the city, offering a high standard of food, wine and coffee.

Restaurant Price Categories

Prices are for a standard meal for one person.

$ = below NZ$15
$$ = NZ$15–30
$$$ = NZ$30–50
$$$$ = over NZ$50

Wellington City

Atlanta
105 The Terrace
Tel: 04-499 5209
Atlanta bar has space for everyone, whether for lunch, coffee or a refreshing cold drink. **$**

Boulcott Street Bistro
99 Boulcott Street
Tel: 04-499 4199
www.boulcottstreetbistro.co.nz
Fine dining in a relaxed atmosphere. Game and seafood are a speciality. **$$–$$$**

Café L'Affare
27 College Street
Tel: 04-385 9748
www.laffare.co.nz
Breakfast is hugely popular here, but the café roasts its own coffee all day long. **$**

Monsoon Poon
12 Blair Street, Courtney Place
Tel: 04-803 3555
www.monsoonpoon.co.nz
A melting-pot of cuisines of the Far East, this richly decorated eatery resembles an Eastern trading house. **$$**

For noodles and curries

One Red Dog
Steamship Building, North Queens Wharf
Tel: 04-918 4723
Cheerful atmosphere, gourmet pizzas and over 50 wines available by the glass. **$$**

Shed 5 Restaurant and Bar
Queens Wharf
Tel: 04-499 9069
www.shed5.co.nz
An atmospheric restaurant housed in an 1800s wool shed serving a range of fine fare, including fresh fish, steak and lamb. **$$$$**

The Tasting Room
2 Courtenay Place
Tel: 04-384 1159
www.thetastingroom.co.nz
This gastro-pub serves traditional pub fare with a twist, plus a wide range of beers. **$–$$$**

Wellington Suburbs

The Flying Burrito Brothers
Corner Cuba and Vivian Street
Tel: 04-385 8811
www.flyingburritobrothers.co.nz
Fun Mexican-style eatery and bar in the Bohemian Cuba quarter, with a good kids' menu. **$$**

Taste
2 Ganges Road, Khandallah
Tel: 04-479 8449
Taste exemplifies the relaxed suburban restaurant with dishes reflecting New Zealand's diverse cultural influences. **$$–$$$**

Wellington Environs

Café Bloom
284 Dry River Road, Martinborough

Tel: 06-306 9165
Located on the terraces of the Murdoch James Vineyard, Café Bloom's fine fare includes tasty platters to share. **$$**

Main Street Deli
88 Main Street, Greytown
Tel: 06-304 9022
Freshly prepared deli-style food and excellent coffee can be enjoyed inside or out, in a pleasant leafy courtyard setting daily from 8am–5pm. **$**

Salute
83 Main Street, Greytown
Tel: 06-304 9825
Recognised as one of the country's best Middle Eastern restaurants, this unpretentious place offers robust flavours and fine wines. **$$–$$$**

NIGHTLIFE

Wellington's cosmopolitan dance clubs attract a young clientele, while the late-night bars hit their stride after midnight.

Havana cocktails

Alice
End of Forresters Lane
Tel: 04-385 2242
www.whiterabbit.co.nz
Creative types flock here for stylish cocktails.

Bodega
101 Ghuznee Street
Tel: 04-384 8212
www.bodega.co.nz
A venue for live music, specialising in New Zealand ale, including the local Tuatara beer.

Boogey Wonderland
25–29 Courtney Place
Tel: 04-385 2242
The place to come for dancing.

Concrete Bar
Level 1, Cable Car Lane
Tel: 04-473 7427
Swish New York style atmosphere and excellent cocktails.

Duke Carvell's Swan Lane Emporium
6 Swan Lane
Tel: 04-385 2240
Restaurant by day, cocktails and tapas by night.

Havana
32 Wigan Street
Tel: 04-384 7039
www.havanabar.co.nz
Live music, rum and coffee.

Motel Bar
Forresters Lane
Tel: 04-384 9084
www.motelbar.co.nz
Discreet cocktail lounge stuck in the 1970s. More vinyl is played here than anywhere else in New Zealand.

Welsh Dragon Bar
Cambridge Terrace
Tel: 04-385 6566
Live music three nights a week, plus impromptu piano performances. Welsh beer served here.

ENTERTAINMENT

Wellington has more screens per capita than anywhere else in the country, showing mainstream, arthouse, international and local films. It's also home to the Royal New Zealand Ballet, New Zealand Symphony Orchestra, String Quartet and Opera, plus all kinds of musical and dance events.

Theatre

Bats Theatre
1 Kent Terrace
Tel: 04-802 4175
www.bats.co.nz
This small, cosy venue has the courage to experiment with lesser-known works; you can often book tickets at short notice.

Circa Theatre
1 Taranaki Street
Tel: 04-801 7992
www.circa.co.nz
Managed by actors, Circa offers stimulating drama in a waterside location by Te Papa.

Downstage Theatre
2 Courtenay Place
Tel: 04-801 6946
www.downstage.co.nz
Modern drama to Shakespeare, plus performances by Maori theatre company, Taki Rua.

Circa Theatre

Film

Embassy Theatre
Courtenay Place
Tel: 04-384 7657
www.embassytheatre.co.nz
Wellington's grandest cinema used for premieres.

St James Theatre
77–87 Courtenay Place
Tel: 04-802 4060
www.stjames.co.nz
The finest lyric theatre in New Zealand. This restored heritage building is *the* Wellington venue for opera, ballet and major musical shows. Also the site of the Ticketek box office agency.

SPORTS, ACTIVITIES AND TOURS

Tours explore the greater Wellington region, with excellent opportunities to walk and cycle. Classic mountain-bike tracks include Mount Victoria, the Rollercoaster from the Wellington wind turbine to Highbury, and the Makarea Peak Mountain Track.

Bicycle and Boat Hire

City Boat and Bike Shed
Frank Kitts Park, Wellington
Tel: 04-499 9295
Mountain bikes, pedal boats, rollerblades/skates and scooters for hire.

Days Bay Boatshed
The Wharf, Days Bay
Mountain bike, kayak and fishing hire. Cycle to the lighthouse or paddle along Days Bay.

Boat Trips

Kapiti Tours
Paraparaumu
Tel: 04-237 7965

www.kapititours.co.nz
Boat tours to Kapiti Island wildlife sanctuary.

Bus Tours

Hammond Wellington Scenic Tours
i-Site Visitor Centre, corner Victoria and Wakefield streets, Wellington
Tel: 04-472 0869
www.wellingtonsightseeingtours.com
Trips to the Kapiti Coast and Palliser Bay, plus the Martinborough Wine Tour which includes a gourmet lunch.

Eco-friendly Tours

Wild About Wellington
Tel: 027 441 9010
www.wildaboutwellington.co.nz
Well-priced guided tours using public transport include 'Sights and Bites', 'Boutique Beer' and 'Wild About Chocolate'.

Kayaking

Fergs Kayaks
Shed 6, Queens Wharf, Wellington
Tel: 04-499 8898
www.fergskayaks.co.nz
Kayak tours and rental. Rents inline skates too.

Seal Safari

Seal Coast Safari
185 Victoria Street, Wellington
Tel: 0800-732 5277
www.sealcoast.com
A three-hour tour to Wellington's seal colonies. Departs from Wellington i-Site Visitor Centre at 10am and 1.30pm daily.

Walking Tours

Wellington Scenic Walks
Wellington Railway Station
Tel: 04-479 7843
Fully guided 6km (4-mile) walk led by locals. Reasonable level of fitness required.

Wine Tours

See also Bus Tours

Martinborough Wine Centre
6 Kitchener Street, Martinborough
Tel: 06-306 9040
www.martinboroughwinecentre.co.nz
Sample wine from local vineyards, then after you've selected your favourites pick up a Wairarapa and Martinborough wine trail map and tailor-make your own walking, cycling or driving tour of the vineyards.

FESTIVALS AND EVENTS

Arts and performing arts festivals are popular in Wellington, the cultural capital of New Zealand.

March

Golden Shears
Masterton
www.goldenshears.co.nz
The world's premier shearing and wool-handling championships.

New Zealand Arts Festival
Wellington
Four-week event featuring national and international acts.

July

International Film Festival
Wellington
The year's best cinematic offerings.

September

World of Wearable Art
Wellington
Weird and wonderful designs by national and international designers and artists.

October

Wellington International Jazz Fest
Wellington
Jazz festival showcasing swing, fusion and experimental jazz music.

Marlborough, Nelson and Tasman

Arriving in the Marlborough Sounds aboard an inter-island ferry is like entering another world; one filled with honey-tinged coves and bays which beckon with blissful hues of greens and blues. It's a fitting introduction to what lies beyond, a sheltered haven of rare native wildlife, vineyards, gourmet food and a vibrant arts scene.

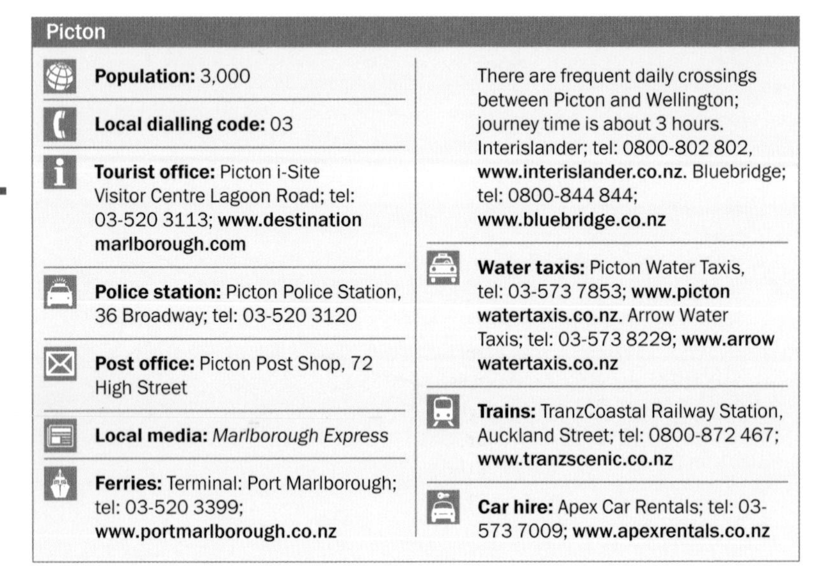

Picton

Population: 3,000

Local dialling code: 03

Tourist office: Picton i-Site Visitor Centre Lagoon Road; tel: 03-520 3113; **www.destinationmarlborough.com**

Police station: Picton Police Station, 36 Broadway; tel: 03-520 3120

Post office: Picton Post Shop, 72 High Street

Local media: *Marlborough Express*

Ferries: Terminal: Port Marlborough; tel: 03-520 3399; **www.portmarlborough.co.nz**

There are frequent daily crossings between Picton and Wellington; journey time is about 3 hours. Interislander; tel: 0800-802 802, **www.interislander.co.nz**. Bluebridge; tel: 0800-844 844; **www.bluebridge.co.nz**

Water taxis: Picton Water Taxis, tel: 03-573 7853; **www.pictonwatertaxis.co.nz.** Arrow Water Taxis; tel: 03-573 8229; **www.arrowwatertaxis.co.nz**

Trains: TranzCoastal Railway Station, Auckland Street; tel: 0800-872 467; **www.tranzscenic.co.nz**

Car hire: Apex Car Rentals; tel: 03-573 7009; **www.apexrentals.co.nz**

Across Cook Strait from Wellington, the provinces of Nelson and Marlborough are the gateway to the South Island for those arriving on the ferry. Cook Strait is a natural funnel for the strong westerly wind known as the Roaring Forties, and on a bad day this can be a pretty stormy stretch of water. But once through the narrows, the breathtaking Tory Channel gives way to the secluded bays of peaceful Queen Charlotte Sound. The ferry journey gives only a glimpse of the glorious scenery beyond.

Encompassing the South Island's northeast corner and providing access to three of New Zealand's 14 National Parks, this is a picturesque

Marlborough Sounds

region with marked differences in scenery, where the dry scrublands of the east contrast dramatically with the dripping rainforests of the west. In the heart of it all are the labyrinthine waterways of the Marlborough Sounds; an immense marine playground, filled with pristine beaches and secluded coves, many only accessible by boat. With so much inspiring scenery and more than its fair share of sunshine it's little wonder that the region produces some of New Zealand's best artists.

Marlborough Sounds

The Sounds are best explored by water and there is an astonishing variety of boats and vessels available to hire, from water taxis to launch charters. Day cruises to historic **Ship Cove** and **Motuara Island**, a thriving wildlife sanctuary, provide an easy way to get around, and kayaking here is rewarding and fun.

Picton

The commercial centre for almost all activity in the Sounds is the attractive town of **Picton** ❶, near the head of Queen Charlotte Sound. As well as being the terminal for the Cook Strait ferry, Picton marks the beginning of the South Island section of both State Highway (SH) 1 and the main trunk railway. It is also the main base for the assorted launches, water taxis and charter boats on which locals and visitors

Pretty Picton, gateway to the South Island

Northern South Island
0
50 km
0
50 miles
N
Mangarak
Paturau River
Heaphy Track
Oparara Basin
National
Karamea
Mt Kenda
1762
Karamea Bight
Mokihinui
Hector
Seddonville
Ngakawau
Westport
Cape Foulwind
Denniston
Buller Gorge
Owen River
Ariki Falls
Inangahua
Buller
Charleston
Tasman Sea
Punakaiki
Paparoa NP
Paparoa Range
Pancake Rocks
Reefton
Victoria Forest Park
Barrytown
Blackball
Grey
Ikamatua
Runanga
Ahaura
Maruia Springs
Springs Junction
Lewis Pass
865
Greymouth
Stillwater
Kumara Junction
Shantytown
Moana
Lake Brunner
Kumara
Lake Sumner Forest Park
Hokitika
Inchbonnie
Lake Sumner
Mt Longfellow
1898
Lake Kaniere
Otira
912
Arthur's Pass National Park
Ross
Kowhitirangi
Mt Rolleston
2271
Arthur's Pass
Puketeraki Range
Hokitika Gorge
Lake Ianthe
2400
Mt Murchison
Abut Head
Harihari
West Coast
ALPS
Okarito Lagoon
Lake Wahapo
Craigieburn Forest Park
Broken River
Waimakariri
Okarito
2644
Mt Whitecombe
Whataroa
Porter's Pass
Oxford
Lake Mapourika
Franz Josef
923
Springfield
Cust
Lake Matheson
Aoraki Mt Cook National Park
2795
Mt Arrowsmith
Sheffield
Gillespie's Beach
SOUTHERN
Rakaia
Mount Hutt
Fox Glacier
3498
Mt Tasman
Darfield
Burnham
Karangarua Bridge Scenic Reserve
3754
Aoraki Mt Cook
Canterbury
Methven
Canterbury Plains
Dunsandel
Westland National Park
Tasman Glacier
Two Thumb Range
Rangitata
Mount Somers
Monro Beach
Lake Paringa
Knights Point
Aoraki Mt Cook Village
1951
Ben McLeod
Rakaia
Lake Moeraki
Paringa
Mayfield
Chertsey
Haast Beach
Haast
Lake Tekapo
Peel Forest Park
Tinwald
Ashburton
Mt John Observatory
Church of Good Shepherd
Jackson Bay
Mount Aspiring National Park
Mt Huxley
2499
Glentanner Park
Ben Ohau Range
Lake Tekapo
Lake Pukaki
Geraldine
Fairlie
Orari
Haast Pass
563
Burke's Pass
Waitohi
Temuka
Canterbury Bight
SOUTHERN ALPS
Albury
Hunters Hills
Lake Ohau
Twizel
Pleasant Point
Makarora
Raincliff Reserve Maori Rock Art
Otago
Kirkliston Range
Lake Benmore
Timaru
3030
Mt Aspiring
Lake Wanaka
Omarama
Pareora
Lake Hawea
Treble Cone
2088
Lindis Pass
971
Wanaka
Queenstown
Waimate
Dunedin

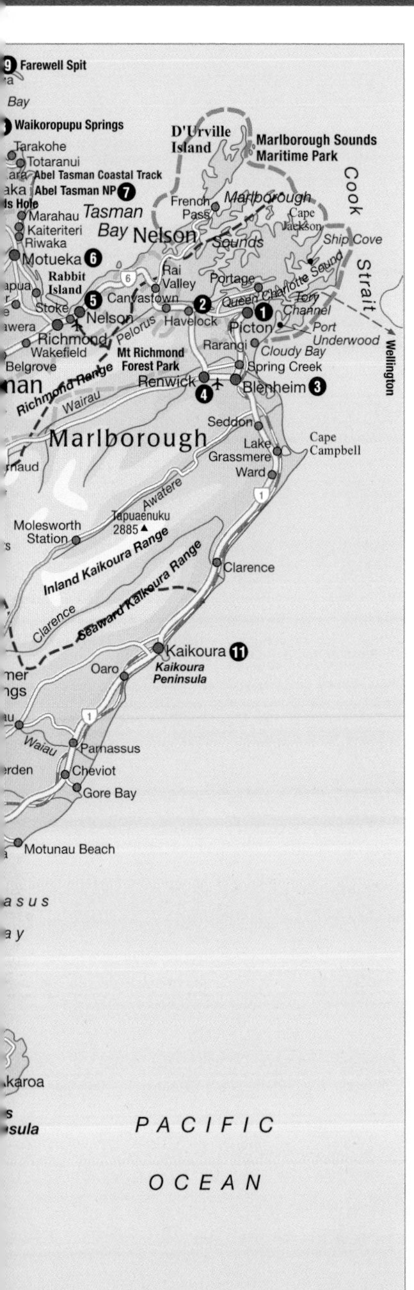

rely for transport. Much of the activity here centres around scenic cruises, kayak trips, and dolphin-watching expeditions. Popular family attractions include the **EcoWorld Aquarium and Wildlife Centre** (Dunbar Wharf; www.ecoworldnz.co.nz; daily 10am–5.30pm; charge), where the feeding habits of native critters can be observed, and the promenade playground with its merry-go-round, 18-hole mini golf course and model yachts. Nearby, the **Edwin Fox Maritime Museum** (Dunbar Wharf; www.edwinfoxsociety.com; daily 9am–5pm; charge) houses the teak hull of the *Edwin Fox*, built in India in 1853, and documents its colourful history.

Half-day and day cruises in the Sounds depart from the Town Wharf, and tours include the popular **Dolphin Watch Ecotour** to Motuara Island bird sanctuary, where once-endangered South Island robins and saddleback can be seen at close range.

Queen Charlotte Track

Salty, seafaring types wait on the pier, ready to whisk passengers by water taxi to various locations; within 30 minutes you can be dining at a resort, or hiking a section of the **Queen Charlotte Track**. If you're reasonably fit you can trek the whole 71km (44 miles) from Ship Cove to Anakiwa over a period of four to five days, traversing bush-clad ridges and idyllic coves. Overnight accommodation caters for all budgets and tastes, and ranges from tent sites and basic rooms with shared facilities, through to well-appointed guest rooms in private lodges.

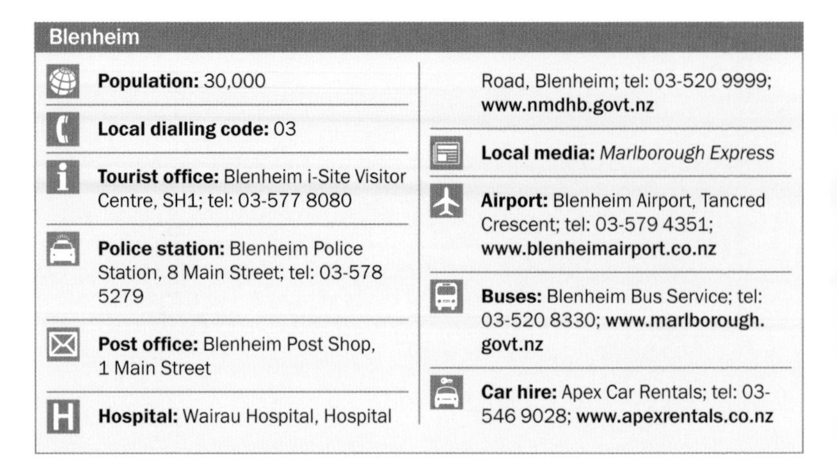

Blenheim

Population: 30,000

Local dialling code: 03

Tourist office: Blenheim i-Site Visitor Centre, SH1; tel: 03-577 8080

Police station: Blenheim Police Station, 8 Main Street; tel: 03-578 5279

Post office: Blenheim Post Shop, 1 Main Street

Hospital: Wairau Hospital, Hospital Road, Blenheim; tel: 03-520 9999; **www.nmdhb.govt.nz**

Local media: *Marlborough Express*

Airport: Blenheim Airport, Tancred Crescent; tel: 03-579 4351; **www.blenheimairport.co.nz**

Buses: Blenheim Bus Service; tel: 03-520 8330; **www.marlborough.govt.nz**

Car hire: Apex Car Rentals; tel: 03-546 9028; **www.apexrentals.co.nz**

Havelock to Canvastown

Reached via the picturesque **Queen Charlotte Drive**, **Havelock** ❷ is a compact fishing settlement which provides easy access to both Pelorus and Kenepuru Sounds. Both Sounds shelter salmon and green-lipped mussel farms. Various tours exploring the Sounds depart from the port including the **Greenshell Mussel Cruise**, which visits mussel farms en route, and matches these tender morsels to local wines. Just beyond Havelock is **Canvastown**, named after the tent village which popped up when gold was discovered on the **Wakamarina River** in the 1860s. The rush is remembered here with a memorial of old mining tools and equipment set in concrete.

Saturday-morning farmers' market, Blenheim

Blenheim and Environs

The Marlborough region – more than any wine-growing region in the nation – has placed New Zealand's wines on the world map. It is home to a wonderful assortment of vineyards and wineries offering tastings to visitors, including Montana and the renowned Cloudy Bay. Other regional staples – grapes, apples, cherries, salmon, mussels and sheep – all take advantage of Marlborough's warmth to grow fat and juicy.

Blenheim

A pleasant 29km (18-mile) drive south of Picton is **Blenheim** ❸, at the hub of sparsely populated Marlborough.

Vineyards and wineries surround the little town of Renwick

Sitting on the Wairau plain, this pleasant rural service town has blossomed since the establishment of the original **Montana** vineyards in 1973. Montana is New Zealand's largest wine maker, producing a bewildering array of wines. One of its wineries, the **Montana Brancott Winery**, is located just south of Blenheim, and a guided tour of the vineyard (daily at 10am, 11am, 1pm and 3pm) is extremely informative.

Vineyards aside, Blenheim has several noteworthy attractions. The **Millennium Public Art Gallery** (corner of Seymour and Alfred Streets; www.marlboroughart.org.nz; Mon–Fri 10am–4.30pm, Sat–Sun 1–4pm; free) is a lively arts venue which exhibits works by artists who have a Marlborough connection, and runs a dynamic programme of exhibitions and events. The history of early settlers is the focus of the **Marlborough Museum** (www.marlboroughmuseum.co.nz; daily 10am–4pm; charge), within the Brayshaw Park museum complex. Here you can also walk the streets of **Beavertown**, a replica pioneer village, and wander into the **Vintage Farm Machinery Museum**, where restored tractors are displayed.

Renwick

Ten km (6 miles) west of Blenheim is **Renwick** ❹, a little town in the Wairu Valley surrounded by vineyards. A pleasant way to tour the vineyards is on a bicycle. **Wine Tours By Bike** is a reputable company that provides everything required, from touring bikes with roomy panniers, to personalised route plans detailing where to find the best wines, olive oils, arts and crafts, and seasonal fruits.

Alternatively, you can make your own pilgrimage from cellar door to cellar door, sampling some of New Zealand's best Sauvignon Blanc, Riesling, Gewürztraminer and Pinot Gris, products of the region's cool, long-ripening season.

Blenheim to Port Underwood

The coast road north of Blenheim to the bay area of **Port Underwood** is very picturesque. It runs first along the cliffs at Rarangi offering wonderful views of the broad sweep of **Cloudy Bay**. From here, a track leads to pretty, sheltered **Whites Bay**, a popular DOC campsite, and a good spot to stop for a swim and a picnic. This coastline is full of history. **Robin Hood Bay** (named after the bay in Yorkshire where Captain Cook acquired his love of the sea) features an old stud and mud cottage, built by a whaler in 1854, and whaling relics dot the shores of **Oyster Bay**, flanked by the towering Robertson Range. Here, a marker commemorates the signing of the Treaty of Waitangi in June 1840, by South Island Maori on Horahora-Kakahu Island (visible from this spot), which effectively handed sovereignty of South Island to the British.

Nelson and Environs

Marlborough and Nelson were once a single province, but the conservative sheep farmers of Marlborough ceded away Nelson in 1859, colonised as it was by progressive artisans and craftspersons perceived as troublemakers. It set the tone for a city unlike any other in New Zealand, a hotbed of creative flair. Today, visitors are drawn to this sunny city on Tasman Bay by its beaches, spectacular sunsets and thriving arts scene – more than 350 artists live and work here – and vibrant café culture.

Vineyards around Nelson are increasing in number, but as well as wine this region contributes a large portion of the nation's production of nashi pears, kiwi fruit, berryfruit and apples. It also produces the entire national crop of hops, grown near Motueka. Forestry, fishing and ship servicing are other big local industries.

Nelson

Population: 43,500

Local dialling code: 03

Tourist office: Nelson i-Site Visitor Centre, 75 Trafalgar Street; tel: 03-546 6228; **www.nelsonnz.com**

Police station: Nelson Police Station, St John Street; tel: 03-546 3840

Post office: Nelson Post Shop, 209 Hardy Street

Hospital: Nelson Hospital, Tipahi Street; tel: 03-546 1800; **www.nmdhb.govt.nz**

Local media: *Nelson Mail*

Airport: Nelson Airport; tel: 03-547 3199; **www.nelsonairport.co.nz**

Buses: Suburban Bus Lines; tel: 03-548 3290; **www.nelsoncoaches.co.nz**

Car hire: Shoestring Rentals; tel: 03-547 2614; **www.nelsonrentalcars.co.nz**. Apex Car Rentals; tel: 03-546 9028.

Taxis: Sun City Taxis; tel: 03-548 2666. Nelson City Taxi; tel: 03-548 8225.

Nelson City

In part, **Nelson** ❺ owes its arty identity to Andrew Suter, Bishop of Nelson from 1867 to 1891. Suter bequeathed a fine collection of early colonial watercolours to the city. These are housed in the **Suter Gallery** (www.thesuter.org.nz; daily 10.30am–4.30pm; charge) on Bridge Street, one of the centres of cultural life, along with the **Theatre Royal** (tel: 03-548 3840) on Rutherford Street, the oldest theatre building in New Zealand. On a rise overlooking the town on Trafalgar Street, **Christ Church Cathedral** is set in pleasantly landscaped grounds at the head of a flight of steps.

For a view over the whole city and Tasman Bay, hike up **Botanical Hill**, and to visit Nelson's best beach, the golden stretch of **Tahunanui**, head 5km (3 miles) southwest along a route lined with trendy seafood cafés.

Shopping for Arts and Crafts

With so many artists and artisans living in the Nelson and Marlborough region, original artworks are easy to find and very affordable. Peruse city galleries, visit artists in their home studios or head to the Nelson Markets in Montgomery Square (Sat 8am–1pm). A select range of local arts is also available at the World of Wearable Art and Classic Cars Museum (www.wowcars.co.nz; daily 10am–5pm; charge for the museum, but entrance to the Gallery Shop and café is free) near the airport. *See also pp.178–9.*

Mapua to Motueka

Northwest of Nelson are the vineyards of **Mapua** and the **Moutere Valley**, where most wineries offer cellar door tastings. Arts and crafts abound in **Motueka** ❻ and numerous boutiques, galleries and studios display work from leading potters, weavers,

Kayaking in Abel Tasman National Park

ARTS TRAIL

The New Zealand art scene is flourishing and deeply rooted in indigenous culture. The practical do-it-yourself tradition of New Zealanders in other fields – notably farming and home renovation – shows through in the work of its artists who frequently incorporate items like corrugated iron and old timber, in what some say is a clever subversion of the 'Kiwi can-do attitude'. Many regions nurture their local artistic talent and there are creative hotspots throughout the country. But Nelson has the highest concentration of artists living, working and exhibiting their talents within its boundaries.

Nelson is renowned for its wealth of talented artisans – painters, potters, sculptors and the like, who make their home here by the sea, forming and becoming part of the creative landscape. The region has more working artists per capita than anywhere else in New Zealand, and so it is relatively easy to visit any number of them in their studios and galleries. For many, a telephone appointment should first be made – the Nelson guide book *Art in its Own Place* provides a comprehensive listing of all those who welcome callers.

Galleries and Boutiques

Nelson's public art gallery, the Suter Te Aratoi o Whakatu *(see p.177)*, is

Classic Cars in the World of Wearable Art Museum, Nelson

central to the local art scene. For more than 100 years a substantial collection of New Zealand artworks has been exhibited here including paintings by C.F. Goldie, D.K. Richmond, Mina Arndt and Frances Hodgkins, among others.

The city also boasts many galleries and arts-and-crafts stores including Element, showcasing Nelson artists, Shine, South Street Gallery, Jewel Beetle, Rome and Catastrophe. The work of artists dedicated to recycling can be viewed at the ingenious ReFinery Gallery.

A few kilometres west of Nelson, along the coast road, is Mapua, a pretty village with its own community of artisans and a cluster of appealing arts-and-crafts boutiques.

World of Wearable Art

Nelson's creative spirit is regularly celebrated through various arts and music festivals, the largest of which ever conceived was the Montana Wearable Art (WOW) Awards. The first show, held in 1987, was the brainchild of local sculptor Suzie Moncrieff. In this annual theatrical extravaganza, designers compete to create the most outlandish garments that encompass it all – fashion, sculpture and art. These days the event is staged in Wellington. However, Nelson remains its birthplace and this is celebrated at the World of Wearable Art and Classic Cars Museum *(see p.177)* where garments from the annual awards show are housed in a unique gallery. The illumination room and audiovisual presentation, which features dramatic excerpts from the show, is riveting, and one cannot help but feel inspired.

The Coolstore gallery, Mapua – a small coastal village with a thriving arts scene

Mapua potter

View of Golden Bay from the top of Takaka Hill

silver workers and glass blowers. Out in the bay the **Motueka Sandspit Scenic Reserve** provides good walking opportunities and the chance to spot a range of coastal and wading birds.

Abel Tasman National Park

Twenty km (12 miles) north of Motueka are the emerald bays and granite-fringed coastline of **Abel Tasman National Park** ❼ *(see p.24)*, whose beauty is best savoured by hiking the **Coastal Track** connecting **Marahau** at its southern end to **Totaranui** in the north. The full walk takes three or four days. Alternatively, there are coastal launch or yacht services from Kaiteriteri or Marahau to a selection of bays along the way. Kayak trips in the park, both guided and unguided, have grown in popularity in recent years. At Tarakohe there is a memorial to Abel Tasman, the 17th-century Dutch navigator who first sighted New Zealand near here.

Golden Bay

Locals say that troubles never follow you over the Takaka Hill, and in **Golden Bay** this seems to be true. People are friendly and creative, and genuinely care about preserving the environment. They also have a passion for art and food, so artistic treasures and fine cafés are guaranteed.

Takaka to Totaranui

The gateway to Golden Bay is the town of **Takaka**, an epicurean and environmental hotspot. The township has a range of excellent wholefood cafés, and treats like tangy home-made salami, home-grown organic fruit and vegetables, and freshly caught salmon can be procured from businesses nearby. Scenic highlights include the craggy limestone outcrops of the **Grove Scenic Reserve** in Clifton, the golden sands at **Pohara** and the 30-minute hike to the thundering **Wainui Falls.** From here it's a short drive to **Totaranui** at the northern end of Abel Tasman National Park, where water taxis can be hired to explore the coastline, and rewarding hikes lead to secluded beaches like Anapai Bay.

Waikoropupu Springs

Just 5km (3 miles) west of Takaka are the **Waikoropupu Springs ❽**. New Zealand's largest freshwater springs, which rise through thick layers of marbled rock, discharge crystal-clear waters giving near perfect underwater visibility for a stunning 62m (200ft). Aquatic plants grow profusely, providing the glorious freshwater equivalent of a coral reef. Early Maori celebrated ceremonial rites in this special place and a sacred aura lingers over the iridescent waters. Further up, at the head of the valley, a car park marks the start of the 2km (1¼-mile) **Pupu Walkway**, which explores the historic water channels and aqueducts built to provide water for gold sluicing back in the region's gold-mining days. Glimpses of the massive expanse of the **Kahurangi National Park** (*see p.25*) are seen en route to the **Mussel Inn** whose owners operate the smallest microbrewery in the country.

Collingwood wharf

Collingwood to Farewell Spit

Golden Bay takes its name from the precious metal that inspired the 1857 Aorere gold rush. Today it is synonymous with the curve of sandy beaches that arch northwest up to **Farewell Spit ❾**. Covered in huge sand dunes and scrub, this unique 35km (22-mile)-long landform curves out across Golden Bay like a giant scimitar, with turbulent waves on one side and vast tidal flats on the other. Built from schist sands washed north along the west coast, the spit is slowly growing, as strong winds and currents continuously shift sand. The Department of Conservation manages the spit and there are strict limits on access. Walking is permitted from the **Puponga Farm Park**, 26km (16 miles) from Collingwood, and **Farewell Spit Eco Tours** operate four-wheel-drive sightseeing trips to its lighthouse and gannet colony.

ACCOMMODATION

During January, Nelson's beaches hum with New Zealand holiday-makers, and, come February, wine-lovers convene in Blenheim for the annual food and wine festival. Midsummer is a busy time to visit, so it's important to book your accommodation well ahead.

Accommodation Price Categories

Prices are for one night's accommodation in a standard double room (unless otherwise specified).

$ = below NZ$30
$$ = NZ$30–75
$$$ = NZ$75–150
$$$$ = NZ$150–350
$$$$$ = over NZ$350

Marlborough Sounds

Harbour View Motel
30 Waikawa Road, Picton
Tel: 03-573 6259
www.harbourviewpicton.co.nz
Twelve tastefully furnished studios with great harbour views. **$$$**

Sennen House
Oxford Street, Picton
Tel: 03-573 5216
www.sennenhouse.co.nz
Historic B&B and self-catering apartments inside a colonial villa. Each apartment is beautifully restored with a private lounge and full kitchen facilities. **$$$$**

The Villa Backpackers Lodge
34 Auckland Street, Picton
Tel: 03-573 6598
www.villa.co.nz
Four- or six-share bunkrooms offer best value but double or twin en-suite rooms are also well priced. Short walk to centre. **$–$$**

Blenheim and Environs

Koanui Lodge
33 Main Street, Blenheim
Tel: 03-578 7487
www.koanui.co.nz
In Maori Koanui means 'a large and happy place to meet' – an apt description for this lodge, with a range of rooms from studio-style en-suite rooms through to three-, four- and six-share dorm rooms. **$–$$$**

Uno Piu
75 Murphys Road, Blenheim
Tel: 03-578 2235
www.unopiu.co.nz
Boutique accommodation set on 1½ hectares (4 acres) of established gardens. Two modern guest suites with en-suite bathrooms, and a self-contained cottage. **$$$$–$$$$$**

Nelson and Environs

The Palace
114 Rutherford Street, Nelson
www.thepalace.co.nz
Cheap accommodation in a heritage building. Dorm beds (no bunks) with duvets. Separate building houses en-suite doubles and self-contained apartment. Solar power and free breakfast. **$–$$$**

Tuscany Gardens Motor Lodge
80 Tahunanui Drive, Nelson
Tel: 03-548 5522
www.tuscanygardens.co.nz
Studio one- and two-bedroom family units have full kitchens. Short walk to beach. **$$$$**

Golden Bay

Collingwood Homestead
Elizabeth Street, Collingwood
Tel: 03-524 8079
www.collingwoodhomestead.co.nz
Boutique B&B set in colonial-style home with impressive outlooks. **$$$$**

Sans Souci Inn
11 Richmond Avenue, Pohara, Golden Bay
Tel: 03-525 8663
www.sanssouciinn.co.nz
An eco-friendly lodge housed in a long, circular, hand-built mud-brick building with turf-insulated ceilings, and spotless composting toilets. **$$$**

RESTAURANTS

The Nelson/Marlborough region provides an incredible range of locally produced gourmet foods including fresh oysters, greenshell mussels, snapper, salmon, scallops, and lots of seasonal fruits, making picnic-packing a breeze. Alternatively, book in at a local café or restaurant; you won't be disappointed.

Restaurant Price Categories

Prices are for a standard meal for one person.

$ = below NZ$15
$$ = NZ$15–30
$$$ = NZ$30–50
$$$$ = over NZ$50

Marlborough Sounds

The Barn Café, Restaurant and Bar
High Street, Picton
Tel: 03-573 7440
Traditional steak, chicken and seafood dishes cater to mainstream tastes. **$$–$$$**

Le Café
14–26 London Quay, Picton
Tel: 03-573 5588
www.lecafepicton.co.nz
Great location on the waterfront; the 'BFS' (Big Fat Salad), which comes served with brie, olives and fresh breads, is a hearty meal. **$–$$**

Blenheim and Environs

Highfield Estate
Brookby Road, Omaka Valley, Blenheim
Tel: 03-572 9244
A vineyard restaurant with a seasonal menu, which excels in matching fresh local produce with its own wines. **$$–$$$**

Rocco's Italian Restaurant
5 Dobson Street, Blenheim
Tel: 03-578 6940
Run by Italians, this place specialises in home-made fresh pasta and prosciutto, as well as New Zealand seafood, lamb and chicken cooked in the traditional Italian way. **$$–$$$**

Nelson and Environs

Boat Shed Café
350 Wakefield Quay, Nelson
Tel: 03-546 9783
www.boatshedcafe.co.nz
There is a great atmosphere at this wharf café/restaurant. Incredible views and imaginative seafood dishes. **$$–$$$**

The Smokehouse Café
Shed Three, Mapua Wharf, Mapua
Tel: 03-540 2280
www.smokehouse.co.nz
A unique smokehouse and café using the freshest local seafood. The menu is based on fish, mussels and vegetables, delicately hot-smoked on site using a traditional brick kiln and manuka shavings. **$$$–$$$$**

Golden Bay

Dangerous Kitchen
46 Commercial Street, Takaka
Tel: 03-525 8686
Organic breads and brick oven gourmet pizzas, with several gluten-free options available. **$–$$**

The Naked Possum Cafe
RD1, Aorere, Collingwood
Tel: 03-524 8433
Wild NZ game foods, fresh garden salads and a variety of home-cooked snacks. Vegetarians are well catered for here. **$–$$**

The laid-back Dangerous Kitchen

ENTERTAINMENT AND NIGHTLIFE

Your best bet for a night out in Nelson/Marlborough is to head to the local pub. Pubs are a great New Zealand institution and you will seldom find yourself short of conversation or an opinion.

Live music at the Mussel Inn, Golden Bay

The Honest Lawyer
1 Point Road, Monaco, Nelson
Tel: 03-547 8850
www.thehonestlawyer.co.nz
Traditional English-style country pub.

Mussel Inn
Onekaka, Golden Bay
Tel: 03-525 9241
www.musselinn.co.nz
This intriguing pub is famous for its steamed mussels and mussel chowder, as well as its own home-brewed beer. Bring in the tail of a possum and you will earn a free pint!

Smugglers Pub
8 Muritai Street, Tahunanui, Nelson
Tel: 03-546 4084
www.smugglerspub.co.nz
Craft ales served in an atmospheric old-world setting.

SPORTS AND ACTIVITIES

With Abel Tasman National Park and a wealth of waterways right on its doorstep, one of the most popular activities in Nelson/Marlborough is coastal kayaking.

Horse Riding

Happy Valley Adventures
194 Cable Bay Road, Nelson
Tel: 03-545 0304
www.happyvalleyadventures.co.nz
Guided horse trekking to suit all levels. Also quad-bike tours and Skywire rides.

Kayaking

Abel Tasman Kayaks
Main Road, Marahau
Tel: 03-527 8022
www.abeltasmankayaks.co.nz
Guided day- and multi-day kayaking trips through Abel Tasman National Park.

Abel Tasman Wilsons Experiences
265 High Street, Motueka
Tel: 03-528 2027
www.abeltasman.co.nz
Single- and multi-day kayak expeditions with a long-established company.

Ocean River
Main Road, Marahau
Tel: 03-527 8266
www.oceanriver.co.nz
Rents kayaks to independent explorers of Abel Tasman National Park. Also provides safe parking and luggage storage.

Swimming with Dolphins

Dolphin Watch Ecotour
Picton Foreshore, Picton
Tel: 03-573 8040
www.naturetours.co.nz
Informative half- and full-day tours including swimming with dolphins and trips to the Motuara Island bird sanctuary to see a host of rare and protected bird species.

TOURS

Nelson/Marlborough is well known for its marine environment and its wine; many tours offer experiences combining both these worlds.

Bus Tours

Farewell Spit Eco Tours
Tel: 03-524 8257
www.farewellspit.com
A variety of tours of Farewell Spit including areas with restricted access.

Boat Trips

Abel Tasman Sailing Adventures
Kaiteriteri
Tel: 03-527 8375
www.sailingadventures.co.nz
Cruises throughout the Abel Tasman National Park.

Marlborough Travel Greenshell Mussel Cruise
Havelock Marina
Tel: 03-577 9997
www.marlboroughtravel.co.nz
Cruise which explores the Pelorus and Kenepuru Sounds, taking in a greenshell mussel farm. The tour includes a dish of mussels and a cool glass of Sauvignon Blanc.

Walking Tours

Southern Wilderness
Nelson
Tel: 03-546 734
www.southernwilderness.com
Combines guided walks in the wilderness with the chance to sample locally produced food and wine.

Wine Tours

Montana Brancott Winery
SH1, Riverlands
Tel: 03-578 2099
www.pernod-ricard-nz.com
A guided tour of the vineyard, which departs from the visitors' centre at 10am, 11am, 1pm and 3pm, takes in several of the winery's highlights, including rare, giant *cuves* made of French oak.

Wine Tours by Bike
191 Bell Road, Blenheim
Tel: 03-577 6954
www.winetoursbybike.co.nz
Leisurely bike tours of the many vineyards in the region. Detailed maps provide personalised itineraries of vineyards, food stops, arts-and-crafts outlets, scenic sights and the pick of seasonal fruit.

FESTIVALS AND EVENTS

Events and festivals in Nelson/Marlborough revolve around food and wine, and the arts. Several smaller arts-and-crafts gatherings are held throughout the year; check events listings in local newspapers for details.

February

Marlborough Wine Festival
Blenheim
www.wine-marlborough-festival.co.nz
Showcases the region's wines and local cuisine through workshops and tastings.

October

Nelson Arts Festival
Nelson
A two-week event showcasing New Zealand artists of all genres.

December

Nelson Jazz Festival
Nelson
A week-long festival of jazz held at various venues.

Canterbury

Canterbury is a marriage of mountain and sea, linked by snow-fed rivers that cut braided courses across patchwork plains. The province encompasses New Zealand's highest mountains, its longest glacier and its widest rivers, set amongst forested hills, extinct volcanoes and sheltered bays. Here, too, is South Island's largest city, Christchurch, which prides itself on its strong English roots.

Christchurch

Population: 350,000

Local dialling code: 03

Tourist offices: Christchurch i-Site Visitor Centre, Cathedral Square; tel: 03-379 9629; **www.christchurchnz.com**. Hurunui i-Site Visitor Centre, 42 Amuri Avenue West; tel: 0800-442 663; **www.visithurunui.com**. Timaru i-Site Visitor Centre, 2 George Street; tel: 03-688 6163; **www.southisland.org.nz**

Main police station: Christchurch Central Police Station, corner Hereford Street and Cambridge Terrace; tel: 03-363 7400

Main post offices: Cathedral Square Post Shop, 736 Colombo Street, Christchurch; Geraldine Post Shop, 26 Talbot Street; Kaikoura Post Shop, West End; Timaru Post Shop, 19 Strathallan Street

Hospital: Christchurch Hospital, Riccarton Avenue; tel: 03-364 0640; **www.cdhb.govt.nz**

Local media: *The Press*, *Canterbury Times*

The popular view of Canterbury as a patchwork plain where lambs frolic under a nor'west sky really does exist. Canterbury lamb, bred for meat and wool, is regarded as the country's best, and the Canterbury nor'wester is a notorious wind that creates warm, dry and blustery conditions as it descends from the high peaks that flank the plains to the west. To the north and south of the region, lakes and golden, tussock-covered hills give way to the Southern Alps, a world of cloud and ice, glacier and rock, mountain streams and Alpine flowers. Here, one mountain towers above the rest – Aoraki Mount Cook, New Zealand's highest peak. Beneath the jagged backbone of the Alps rumbles the Tasman Glacier, the southern hemisphere's longest tongue of ice, and beyond lie the peaceful turquoise waters of Lake Pukaki and Lake Tekapo. The river Waitaki marks the province's southern boundary. Around Canterbury's northern boundaries small rural settlements like Hurunui are set in Alpine countryside. Here, you can soak in Hanmer Springs thermal spas before heading out to the Kaikoura coast to watch for whales, dolphins and seals. *For a map of the Canterbury region, see pp.172–3.*

Christchurch City

Often dubbed the Garden City, **Christchurch ❿** boasts over 700 established parks and gardens. A wealth of early 19th-century architecture gives a distinct air of permanence to this city, which offers a wide range of sophisticated restaurants, cafés, boutique shops, and museums.

Cathedral Square

At the heart of the city is the pedestrian-only Cathedral Square, where the lofty **Christchurch Cathedral Ⓐ** (www.christchurchcathedral.co.nz; daily 8.30am–7pm; tours daily 11am, 2pm; free) takes centre stage. Dating to the mid-19th century, it is one of the southern hemisphere's finest neo-Gothic churches. Construction began in 1864 and wasn't completed until 1904 due to a lack of funds. For a small charge, you can climb the 134 steps up the 63m (208ft) tower for breathtaking city views.

The square is officially regarded as a public-speaking area and its star

Tram tour from Cathedral Square

Earthquake Disaster

On 4 September 2010, an earthquake measuring 7.1 on the Richter Scale hit Christchurch at 4.36am. It was at a depth of 10km (6 miles), centring near Darfield, 40km (25 miles) west of the city. Incredibly, there was no loss of life. However, the city was placed in a state of emergency as much of its infrastructure was affected. Many heritage buildings were damaged and further harm was caused by hundreds of high-magnitude aftershocks in the following weeks. Some buildings will be reconstructed, others will be assessed and demolished as required. Modern architecture in the CBD, built to New Zealand's stringent earthquake building code, stood firm; however, in the suburbs homes were destroyed and residents displaced. Details on pp.187–9 may change; for the latest on the city's reconstruction and other matters relating to the earthquake, see www.ccc.govt.nz.

performer is **The Wizard**, who, after a long absence, is again haranguing bemused crowds from 1–2pm. Dressed in black robes, he delivers an impassioned line on various topics ranging from Queen and country to global warming. Other highlights include the year-round market (Wed–Sat 9am–4pm), and the **Southern Encounter Aquarium** (www.southernencounter.co.nz; daily 9am–5pm; charge), a walk-through aquarium and kiwi display.

Cultural Precinct

For an excellent overview of the city, hop aboard the historic **Christchurch Tram.** It circles the inner city, and

Christchurch City Transport

Airport: Christchurch Airport, Memorial Avenue; tel: 03-358 5029; **www.christchurchairport.co.nz.** Taxis to the city centre take 15–20 minutes and cost NZ$30–50; shuttle buses take 20–30 minutes and cost NZ$15–20 per person. Local buses (numbers 3, 10 and 29) cost just NZ$7.20, but the trip takes 30–40 minutes.

Buses: Metro; tel: 03-668 855; **www.metroinfo.co.nz**; covers all suburbs of Christchurch. Services operate every 15 minutes 6.30am–10.30pm. Tickets start at $2.80 for central city travel; an all-day pass costs $4.20.

Tram: Christchurch Tramway; tel: 03-366 7830; **www.tram.co.nz**; daily, Apr–Oct 9am–6pm, Nov–Mar 9am–9pm. Trams run on a 25-minute loop from Cathedral Square along Worcester Boulevard to the Arts Centre and Christ's College, then back along Armagh Street. Tickets cost $15 adult, $5 child.

Train: TranzScenic; tel: 0800-872 467; **www.tranzscenic.co.nz**; runs trains from Christchurch to Greymouth, and Christchurch to Picton

Taxi: Corporate Cabs; tel: 03-379 5888. Gold Band Taxis; tel: 03-379 5795; **www.goldbandtaxis.co.nz**. Green Cabs; tel: 0508 447 336.

Car hire: Apex Car Rentals; tel: 0800-939 597; **www.apexrentals.co.nz**. Budget New Zealand; tel: 03-357 0231; **www.budget.co.nz**. Thrifty; tel: 03-374 2357; **www.thrifty.co.nz**.

Parking: Parking is available in city car parks and costs NZ$2–10 per hour for casual parking

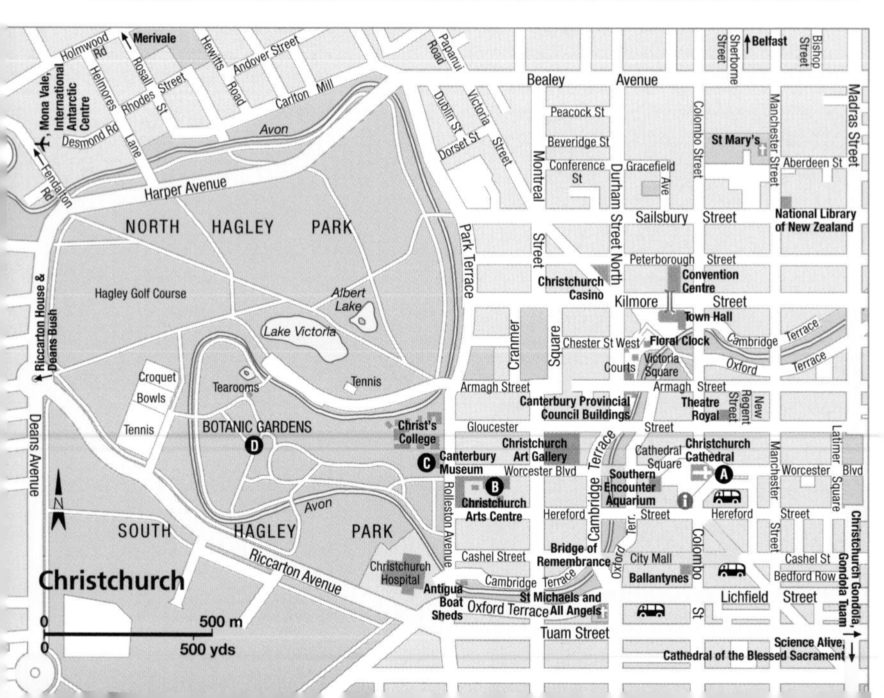

stops at Christchurch's cultural precinct where there are several attractions including the **Christchurch Art Gallery** (www.christchurchartgallery.org.nz; daily 10am–5pm, Wed until 9pm; free), home to an impressive collection of New Zealand art-works. At the heart of the precinct is the **Christchurch Arts Centre** Ⓑ (www.artscentre.org.nz; daily 8.30am–5pm, daily guided tour 11am; free). Housed in the former Canterbury University buildings, the centre boasts galleries, the Arts Centre Cinemas, the professional Court Theatre company, craft workshops and a pottery centre. The whole area comes alive during the weekend market (Sat–Sun 10am–4pm). Another highlight of the precinct is **Canterbury Museum** Ⓒ (www.canterburymuseum.com; daily 9am–5pm; free), which has displays on local history, and a collection of European decorative art and costume. Space is also devoted to the discovery and exploration of Antarctica, and to **Discovery** (charge), the museum's natural history centre for children.

Hagley Park

West of the cultural precinct is **Christ's College**, a private boys' school with landscaped grounds adjoining the city's pride and joy – the 161-hectare (500-acre) **Hagley Park**, planted entirely with deciduous trees from the northern hemisphere – astonishingly lovely in spring and autumn. The park includes a golf course, playing fields, tennis courts, a duck pond and the splendid **Botanic Gardens** Ⓓ (daily 7am–sunset; free). Enclosed within a loop of the Avon River, highlights include English herbaceous borders, native sections, and glasshouses of sub-tropical and desert species.

Port Hills and Suburbs

Further from the city centre the suburbs feature many fine homes. With

Souvenir Shopping

Christchurch has a large selection of designer stores, souvenir shops and nationwide chains. On Colombo Street is Ballantynes department store, where the assistants dress in black and are unfailingly helpful. The Arts Centre in Worcester Street has lots of local craft studios and galleries to peruse, while the Antarctic shop opposite Christchurch Airport sells New Zealand-made products with a wintry theme. For paua jewellery look no further than Canterbury Museum on Rolleston Avenue. It also sells a selection of genuine Maori carvings, pottery, glass and stone.

Botanic Gardens, Hagley Park

View of Christchurch from Port Hills

mature trees and secluded gardens the areas of Fendalton and Merivale, northwest of the city, are easily recognisable as havens for the well-to-do, while other homes such as those situated on Port Hills and clinging to the slopes of Lyttelton Harbour enjoy a clear geographical advantage over the rest of the city. Their elevation lifts them above the winter smog and offers fantastic views.

Fendalton and Merivale

A stone's throw from Hagley Park, with the Avon River burbling through, are the leafy suburbs of Fendalton and Merivale where marriage vows are blessed in the Gothic charm of churches such as **St Barnabas**. On Fendalton Road, the 6-hectare (13-acre) **Mona Vale** (www.monavale.co.nz; daily 9.30am–5pm; free) has beautiful gardens and landscaped lawns sloping to the Avon River and is a real delight, even more so if you have time for a leisurely punt. The Avon also borders **Riccarton House & Deans Bush** (Kahu Road; tel: 03-341 1018; www.riccartonhouse.co.nz; guided tours Sun–Fri 2pm; charge), the former home of the pioneering Deans family. The estate boasts the sole remnant of native kahikatea forest to be found on the Canterbury Plains.

Port Hills and Lyttelton

South of the city lie the Port Hills where the **Summit Road** provides tremendous city, harbour and Southern Alp views, and access to an extensive network of walking tracks. One way to reach the top is on the **Christchurch Gondola** (10 Bridle Path Road; www.gondola.co.nz; daily 10am–6pm; charge 👪), one of the city's big attractions. At the top is a café/restaurant, and mountain bikes can be hired to explore or ride back down.

Lyttelton, 12km (7 miles) to the southeast, and reached via the Lyttelton road tunnel, has a laid-back atmosphere, and is full of quirky cafés. Tour the harbour and its wildlife with **Black Cat Cruises**, or visit the **Time Ball Station** (2 Reserve Terrace; daily 10am–5.30pm; charge) for an insight into the port's history.

Harewood

On the other side of the city, a short distance from the airport, is the fascinating **International Antarctic Centre** (www.iceberg.co.nz; daily 9am–5.30pm, until 7pm in summer; charge), which celebrates Christchurch's history as an embarkation point for expeditions. As part of the 'Snow and Ice Experience', visitors can explore a snow cave and ride snowmobiles. An additional attraction is the **New Zealand Little Blue Penguin Encounter**, which features the world's smallest penguins *(see p.36)*. Harewood is also the site of **Orana Wildlife Park** (www.oranawildlifepark.co.nz; daily 10am–5pm; charge), a large, open-range, safari-style zoo, featuring rhinoceroses, cheetahs, giraffes, zebras and other exotic species. The park also houses New Zealand wildlife including tuatara, and birds such as the kiwi, kereru and kaka.

North Canterbury

Exploration of North Canterbury uncovers a diverse array of activities. On the coast whale-watch cruises depart regularly and seafood is plentiful, especially crayfish (lobster) which teams well with local Waipara wine. Further inland is the hot thermal bliss of Hanmer Springs, where rivers teem with salmon and trout.

Kaikoura

It's ironic that the quaint seaside town of **Kaikoura** ⓫, founded on the killing of whales over a century ago, should find new prosperity showing them off. Whales can be viewed year-round on a cruise with **Whale Watch Kaikoura** *(see p.33)*, or in a light aircraft. As well as sperm whales – Kaikoura's predominant species – other species, such as minke, humpback and the southern right whale, are often sighted not far from shore. Or don flippers and snorkel and join dolphins in their watery world with **Dolphin Encounter. Seal-swimming** tours, which allow bathers equipped with snorkels to frolic with these friendly creatures, are also gaining popularity *(see p.34)*.

Hanmer Springs

Further inland, the compact Alpine village of **Hanmer Springs** ⓬ is a favourite destination for Cantabrians, who come here to soak in the hot mineral pools of the **Hanmer**

Whale Watch Kaikoura offers close encounters with whales all year round

TOUR OF AKAROA

Spend a day discovering the Banks Peninsula and the French-inspired settlement of Akaroa on this driving tour. Take a harbour cruise and enjoy a leisurely lunch overlooking the harbour before returning to Christchurch.

Christchurch to Birdlings Flat

From Cathedral Square in Christchurch, head south along Colombo Street to Moorhouse Avenue. Turn right and travel for five blocks, then turn left into Lincoln Road. After the railway line the road morphs into SH75, travelling through the farmlands of Halswell, Taitapu and Motukarara, before skirting **Lake Ellesmere** (Te Waihora), a wide, shallow coastal lagoon filled with game birds and waterfowl. A sharp corner marks the turn-off for **Birdlings Flat**. Drive out to the beach, where the ocean transforms semiprecious stones into polished gems, and deposits them on the stony beach, ready to fossick. To see examples, visit the local **Gemstone and Fossil Museum** (SH75; tel: 03-329 0812; www.birdlingsmuseum.741.com; Wed–Mon 9.30am–5pm; free).

Looking out over Akaroa

Little River to Barry's Bay

Back on SH75 continue past picturesque Lake Forsyth to the settlement of **Little River**, once a notable stop on the old railway line through Banks Peninsula. The road climbs steeply out of Cooptown up to **Hilltop** and the Hilltop Tavern, whose car park offers grand views of Akaroa Harbour. This was the site of a Maori *pa* (fortified village), built in 1831 by the Ngai Tahu people to stave off a northern tribe.

Descend into Barry's Bay, to sample traditionally home-made produce at **Barry's Bay Cheese** and watch the cheese-making process through glass

Tips

- Distance: 168km (104 miles) return
- Time: 1 day
- Begin this tour in Christchurch. To get there you will need to hire a vehicle. For details of car-hire companies see *p.188*.
- Depart early if you wish to return on a scenic route via Summit Road, Diamond Harbour and Lyttelton
- Akaroa began its European life in 1838 as a French settlement; take time to discover its intriguing history at Akaroa Museum

windows, before travelling on through Duvauchelle and Takamatua to Akaroa.

Akaroa

Park as soon as you enter the town – there's plenty of free parking available – and walk along Rue Lavaud to the **Akaroa Museum** (tel: 03-304 7614; daily 10.30am–4.30pm; charge). Highlights here include Maori *taonga* (treasures), as well as relics from Akaroa's whaling past. A 20-minute audiovisual relates the complete history of the town. The museum also incorporates several important historical buildings, including the Customs House at Daly's Wharf and the **Langlois-Eteveneaux Cottage**, one of the oldest in Canterbury.

Other sights include **St Patrick's Church** (1863) and Settlers Hill, both on Rue Balguerie. From Settlers Hill a track leads to L'Aube Hill Reserve and the **Old French Cemetery**, the first consecrated burial ground in Canterbury. Then head back down to the water following Rue Lavaud to the beachside promenade complete with gardens and a War Memorial.

For a cruise of Akaroa Harbour's sea-filled crater, sign up at the wharf with **Black Cat Cruises** *(see p.33)*. On the two-hour trip to the headlands you will visit a salmon farm and spot dolphins, fur seals and a variety of sea birds, such as the little blue penguin. The company also provides the chance to swim with the Hector's (or NZ) dolphin, one of the world's smallest and rarest dolphin species.

After the cruise, take time out to sample the fresh catch of the day and

Artisan gallery in the historic village of Akaroa on the Banks Peninsula

the excellent local wines at cafés, including **Truby's Bar & Cafe**, by the waterfront.

Back to Christchurch

To return to Christchurch, there are two options: either retrace your route or, for a two-hour scenic drive of Banks Peninsula, return via the attractive port of Lyttelton. To do so, take the signposted and scenic Summit Road via Pigeon Bay, Diamond Harbour and Governor's Bay, and on through the Lyttelton tunnel back to Christchurch city centre.

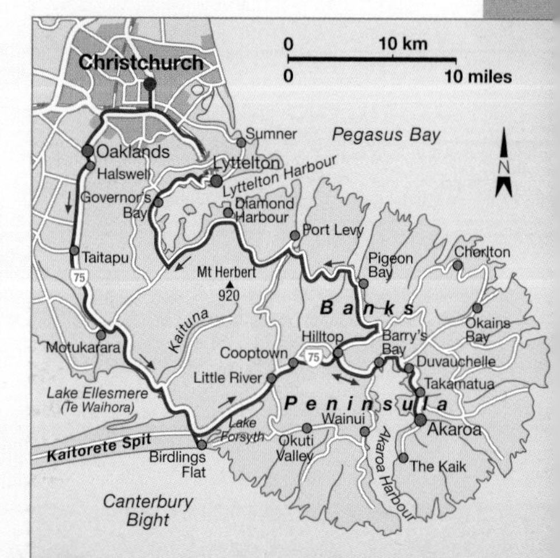

Springs Thermal Resort and Spa (Amuri Avenue; www.hanmersprings.co.nz; *see p.54*). It's also a popular place to walk and cycle along the well-defined paths that meander through **Hanmer Forest Park**. More demanding walks include the 30-minute Zig-Zig Track up **Conical Hill** for fine views over the Hanmer Basin, and the **Mount Isobel Track**, a naturalist's delight, which passes 200 species of sub-Alpine flowering plants and ferns. **Thrillseekers Canyon**, located at the 140-year-old single-lane Waiau Ferry Bridge, offers bungy jumping, jet-boat rides and whitewater rafting trips.

Waipara

To the south is **Waipara Valley**, one of New Zealand's most rapidly growing wine regions where Pinot Noir, Riesling, Chardonnay and Sauvignon Blanc grapes thrive in a warm microclimate just out of reach of the brisk easterly winds that swirl through the foothills. Stop for a tasting at a cellar door, or dine at one of its award-winning wineries, including **Waipara Hills**, The Mudhouse, and Waipara Springs Winery. Or follow the signposts to the highly acclaimed boutique winery of **Pegasus Bay**, where you have a good chance of being introduced to its wines by the passionate wine makers themselves.

Nearby, the **Mount Cass Walkway** offers glorious views from its unusual limestone landscape, while inland there's Maori cave art to discover at **Waikari**, and the historic Weka Pass Railway.

Canterbury Plains

The plains of South Canterbury are seemingly never-ending, a colourful patchwork of fields toiled over by massive irrigators and flanked by the dramatic peaks of the Southern

Canterbury's patchwork plains bordered by the snow-capped peaks of the Southern Alps

Mount Hutt is one of New Zealand's best skiing and snowboarding areas

Alps. This scenery stretches south well beyond Timaru, the metropolitan heart of South Canterbury.

Methven and Mount Hutt

Heading south, long straight roads lead to the Rakaia River and the **Rakaia Gorge**, world-famous for its salmon. Experienced local guides lead back-country fishing excursions, while **Rakaia Gorge Alpine Jet** rides its rapids. Looming above is **Mount Hutt**, Canterbury's most popular ski field, which has excellent skiing and snowboarding. The après ski mecca of **Methven** ⓭ provides access to back-country swimming holes like **Lake Coleridge** where a sparse scattering of high country station homesteads, isolated fishermen's huts and campsites is the only sign of human habitation. Nearby, **Terrace Downs**, a championship 18-hole golf course, provides challenges worthy of such formidable terrain.

Geraldine

The tiny inland country town of **Geraldine** ⓮, 138km (86 miles) southwest of Christchurch, is set on the banks of the Waihi River. It is home to many artisan workshops including the **Giant Jersey**, where gorgeously soft Perendale, mohair and merino wools are crafted into stylish made-to-measure garments, and the **Belanger-Taylor Glass Studio** where you can watch intriguing works of art in the making. Taste buds are creatively tempted at Four Peaks Plaza at the **Talbot Forest Cheese shop** and the aromatic **Barker Fruit Processors**. Other attractions include the **Vintage Car and Machinery Museum**, a must for enthusiasts, and the classic, country-style **Geraldine Cinema**, where arthouse and mainstream films are screened on an old Ernemann 2 projector. There are excellent picnic and fishing spots in the nearby Waihi and Te Moana gorges and Peel Forest Park.

Timaru

The vibrant Edwardian township of **Timaru** ⓯ still has many of its original buildings, constructed of locally sourced bluestone. This, teamed with its striking piazza overlooking **Caroline Bay**, has created a respectable town centre with an air of quiet dignity. The renowned New Zealand artist Colin McCahon was born here,

TOUR OF ARTHUR'S PASS

One of New Zealand's most dramatic drives is the 260km (160 mile) Alpine highway through Arthur's Pass, a startling landscape of mirrored lakes, ridges and valleys, wide shingle river beds and deep gorges.

Christchurch to Lake Lyndon

From Cathedral Square in Christchurch, follow Colombo Street south, and turn right on to Tuam Street. Continue past Christchurch Hospital and cross over into Hagley Park on Riccarton Avenue. Follow this all the way through the suburb of Riccarton, then veer right on to Yaldhurst Road, following the signposts for Arthur's Pass (SH73).

This route travels through the town of **Darfield**, where the Terrace Café and Bar is an option if you're hungry, and on through Sheffield and Springfield (70km/43 miles from Christchurch), before climbing swiftly into the foothills of the Southern Alps. The scenery becomes increasingly dramatic.

Follow the road over Porter's Pass (923m/3,028ft), which passes Lake Lyndon and the turn-off to Porter's Pass ski field, before you go past **Kura Tawhiti** (Castle Hill Reserve). A 10-minute hike leads to some striking limestone rock formations.

Another 6km (4 miles) further on is **Cave Stream Scenic Reserve**, which has a car park with good views of the basin area. Unless you suffer from claustrophobia, spend an hour exploring the 362m (1,188ft) limestone cave here, with its flowing stream and Maori cave art. You will need warm clothes and a torch.

Arthur's Pass Village

SH73 passes **Lake Pearson** (a road on the right provides access), Lake Grassmere and Lake Sarah, before meeting up with the braided Waimakariri River and the **Bealey Hotel**, built when the road opened in 1866 to accommodate passengers on the three-day stagecoach journey to the West Coast.

A further 10km (6-mile) drive leads to **Arthur's Pass Village**, set in a river

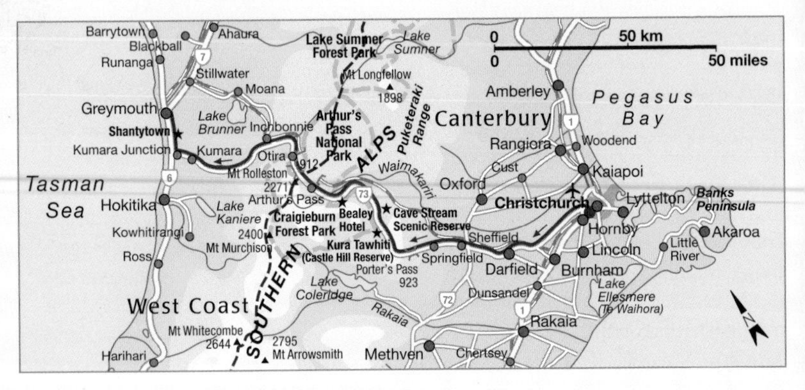

The Alpine highway through Arthur's Pass

valley among the mountains of the Arthur's Pass National Park. The DOC Visitor Centre provides displays on local flora and fauna, and information on local walks. If time permits, hike the 2km (1½-mile) track known as Devil's Punch Bowl, which leads to the base of a 131m (430ft) waterfall.

Otira

From the village, the road climbs steeply to the pass (912m/2,992ft). Stop at the signposted lookout on the right for glorious views in the company of cheeky, green keas (parrots). From here the road descends steeply via the modern Otira Viaduct into the old railway township of **Otira**. You are now on the West Coast, often dubbed the Wild West Coast or the Wet Coast, where locals are rightly proud of the pristine rainforests, and the climate that keeps them that way.

Shantytown

While Maori journeyed to the West Coast for *pounamu* (jade), European settlers came for gold, and Shantytown brings those heady days alive. To get there, follow SH73 through the town of Kumara and on to Kumara Junction. Turn north on SH6, following the signs to Greymouth, turning off at Paroa, and follow the signs to Shantytown. This replica West Coast settlement has more than 30 historic buildings to view, and offers gold panning and steam-train rides aboard the 25-tonne Kaitangata, built in 1897.

Greymouth

It's another 10km (6 miles) north into Greymouth *(see p.211)*, where highlights include the **Jade Boulder Gallery**, a museum that tells the story of this semiprecious stone, and **Monteith's Brewery**, a classic West Coast icon, offering tours of the plant followed by a tasting.

Tips

- Distance: 252km (157miles) one way
- Time: 1 day
- Begin this tour in Christchurch.
- Pack warm clothes, sensible walking shoes and a torch with spare batteries
- In places this historic route (used by Maori to gather jade on the West Coast and later paved when gold was discovered) is steep and windy; drive with caution

and many of his works can be seen at the **Aigantighe Art Gallery** (daily 9am–4pm; free), the third-largest public art gallery in the South Island. Other highlights include the **South Canterbury Museum** (free), with its wealth of local history including Maori cave art, and the **Trevor Griffiths Rose Garden** where 529 old rose varieties can be viewed. Nearby, at **Pleasant Point Museum and Railway** (tel: 03-614 8323; www.pleasantpointrail.org.nz), rides aboard the world's only Ford Model T Railcar depart every hour between 11am and 3pm. Wine tasting can be enjoyed at the café at **Opihi Vineyard** (www.opihi.co.nz; Wed–Sun 11am–4pm), where nearby historical sites include Maori rock art at **Raincliff Reserve** and the memorial to unsung aviation pioneer Richard Pearse, located at Upper Waitohi.

Waimate

Many travellers bypass the turn-off to **Waimate** ⓰ in Southern Canterbury, an 8km (5-mile) side-trip from SH1, missing **EnkleDooVery Korna** (daily Sept–June 10am–5pm; charge), where you can cuddle a wallaby and make friends with orphaned joeys. Wallabies were introduced to this region and are considered a pest – hunting them is seen as a community service. Waimate is renowned for its fresh berries, and mouth-watering morsels can be purchased from the **Berry Barn**, along with home-made strawberry ice cream. Head to Waimate's main street for an architectural flashback to the Edwardian era, but don't leave without tasting the **Savoy Tearooms'** famous wallaby pies, a mix of steak, onion, salt and pepper and plum sauce.

Tekapo and Environs

High in the Mackenzie Country hinterland, amid vast windswept mahogany plains and pleated foothills, a multitude of turquoise lakes fed by the meltwater of glaciers awaits exploration before winter sets in and transforms this colour-filled environment into a white wonderland filled with glistening icicles.

Church of the Good Shepherd on Lake Tekapo

The startlingly blue Lake Pukaki

Fairlie to Lake Tekapo

The small country town of **Fairlie**, reached by travelling through Geraldine or Pleasant Point, has a tiny historical museum. From here SH8 rises with deceptive ease past the colonial homesteads of **Burke's Pass**, and into the great tussocked basin known as **Mackenzie Country**, named after a Scottish shepherd who, in 1855, tried to hide stolen sheep here. Winding across a stark, bronzed landscape, SH8 leads to **Lake Tekapo** ⓱, a great turquoise glacial lake, 710m (2,329ft) above sea level. By the water's edge is the **Church of the Good Shepherd**, built from stone as a memorial to the pioneers of Mackenzie Country, and a solitary **bronze sheepdog**, erected in honour of all high-country mustering dogs. West along the lake is **Alpine Springs Spa & Winter Park** (Lakeside Drive; www.alpinesprings.co.nz), three non-thermal hot pools with an adjoining ice rink and snow tube park. During the winter **Round Hill Ski Field** offers a pleasant drive to gentle, open slopes and cosy club rooms. For stunning views by day and star-gazing tours by night, take the road to **Mount John Observatory**, where telescopes probe these clear skies searching for black holes and distant planets.

Canal Road and Lake Pukaki

Beyond Tekapo there is a choice of two routes, either the main SH8 or the **Canal Road**, a scenic route which follows the course of a man-made canal to the powerhouses of the Waitaki Hydroelectric Scheme on the southern shore of **Lake Pukaki** ⓲. A stunning alternative, this road offers great Alpine views and the chance to hook a fresh fish for dinner at the **Mount Cook Salmon Farm.** Lake Pukaki today is twice the size it was in 1979, prior to the building of its hydroelectric power dam when its waters were allowed to flow unimpeded to Lake Benmore. A lookout provides spectacular views across the lake to Aoraki Mount Cook.

Aoraki Mount Cook National Park

At the southwestern corner of Lake Pukaki, SH80 begins its stunning 55km (34-mile) journey beneath Ben Ohau's textured peaks to **Glentanner Park Centre** (a holiday park/campsite) where the lake meets glacial river rubble. From here a vast valley of earthy tones and charcoal-coloured scree slopes leads to **Aoraki Mount Cook Village** ⓳, gateway to one of New Zealand's best-loved national parks *(see p.26)*. Due to its sacrosanct status within a national park, accommodation in the village has been limited. Nevertheless, in addition to The Hermitage Hotel, there are also self-contained A-frame chalets, a campsite, a well-equipped youth hostel and a new lodge. Well-defined tracks lead from the village up to the surrounding valleys. If you love the great outdoors, there is a lot to do here, so consider staying a few days.

Village and Environs

The Aoraki Mount Cook Alpine region was the training ground for the late Sir Edmund Hillary (1919–2008), the first person to scale Mount Everest. At the **Sir Edmund Hillary Alpine Centre Museum**, the Hillary Gallery depicts his deep connection with this region and showcases its history through displays on transport and climbing. Other attractions include the cinematic **Mount Cook Magic in 3D**, an inspiring experience of the park's highlights, and the **Full Dome Planetarium**, New Zealand's first full-dome, digital Planetarium. The night sky above the village is incredibly clear and star-gazing tours depart every clear evening. For up-to-date weather reports visit the Aoraki Mount Cook DOC Visitor Centre which also has information on the park's geology, climate, flora and fauna.

Aoraki Mount Cook

The **Aoraki Mount Cook National Park** ⓴ is the monarch of New Zealand's parks, where the highest peaks in the land soar above the crest of the Southern Alps. Supreme is Aoraki Mount Cook itself at 3,754m (12,316ft). The mountain, named

Aerial view of Glentanner Park Centre, where Lake Pukaki meets the Tasman River

Aoraki Mount Cook, New Zealand's highest peak, dominates the Southern Alps

Aoraki (Cloud Piercer) by the Maori, is frequently shrouded in cloud, depriving sightseers of its face. But come rain or shine, this Alpine region is ever masterful, ever dramatic, and when the sun does shine, the views of the mountain, especially when the last rays strike its blushing peak in twilight, form the highlight of many a traveller's exploration of Canterbury.

Tasman Glacier and Lake

Although the park extends only 80km (50 miles) along the Alpine spine, it contains 140 peaks over 2,100m (7,000ft), and 72 glaciers. Of these, the **Tasman Glacier** ㉑ is the largest and longest in the southern hemisphere, extending 27km (17 miles) – it has retreated in recent times – and in some places is up to 3km (2 miles) wide. The ice in this glacier can reach over 600m (2,000ft) in depth. A 10-minute drive from the village leads to the start of the 30-minute hike to the **Tasman Glacier Viewpoint**, which provides first-class views. **Aoraki Mount Cook Skiplanes** offer magnificent scenic flights to view the glaciers up close and, on some routes, land on them. Alternatively, join a **Glacier Explorers** boat adventure to see where the glacier yields its ice-melt to the glacier lake, before being washed away downstream.

Cheeky Kea

Among the birdlife seen in the Mount Cook National Park you will no doubt be amused – and possibly peeved – by the antics of the kea, a sizeable green mountain parrot. Kea are the most mischievous ragamuffins you're likely to meet. They steal food, toboggan down roofs, hang around campsites, ransack backpacks for food and gleefully shred or make off with anything in sight. So if kea are about, keep a vigilant eye on your keys, the rubber seals on your car and other possessions.

ACCOMMODATION

Canterbury has a wide range of accommodation, and guest rooms provide good value for money.

Christchurch City

Christchurch YMCA
12 Hereford Street
Tel: 03-365 0502
www.ymcachch.org.nz
Quality accommodation, centrally located.
$–$$

The George
50 Park Terrace
Tel: 03-379 4560
www.thegeorge.com
Contemporary rooms in boutique hotel with park and river views. **$$$$$**

Latimer Hotel and Apartments
30 Latimer Square
Tel: 03-379 6760
www.latimerhotel.co.nz
Good-value rooms, close to the city centre. Café/restaurant and parking. **$$$–$$$$**

Port Hills and Suburbs

Merivale Manor
122 Papanui Road, Merivale
Tel: 03-355 7731
www.merivalemanor.co.nz
Studios, one- and two-bedroom motel apartments. Free breakfast. **$$$–$$$$**

North Canterbury

Albergo Lodge
80 Rippingdale Road, Hanmer Springs
Tel: 03-315 7428
www.albergohanmer.com
Luxury suites set in landscaped gardens and lawns, all with Alpine views. **$$$–$$$$$**

Dylans Country Cottages
268 Postmans Road, Kaikoura
Tel: 03-319 5473
www.lavenderfarm.co.nz
Peaceful, self-contained cottages on a lavender farm. Breakfast included. **$$$**

Accommodation Price Categories

Prices are for one night's accommodation in a standard double room (unless otherwise specified).

$ = below NZ$30
$$ = NZ$30–75
$$$ = NZ$75–150
$$$$ = NZ$150–350
$$$$$ = over NZ$350

Park-view room at The George, Christchurch

Canterbury Plains

Canterbury Hotel (The Brown Pub)
Mount Hutt Village, Methven
Tel: 03-302 8045
www.thebrownpub.co.nz
Historic hotel with a range of basic but comfortable family rooms and a good family restaurant. **$–$$**

Tekapo and Environs

Lake Tekapo Scenic Resort
Main Highway, Tekapo
Tel: 03-680 6808
www.laketekapo.com
Centrally located with good views. Budget bunk rooms also available. **$–$$$$**

Aoraki Mt Cook

The Hermitage Hotel
Terrace Road, Aoraki Mount Cook Village
Tel: 03-435 1809
www.hermitage.co.nz
Luxurious accommodation and amazing views make this worth a splurge. The Hermitage also runs well-priced chalets and motel units, perfect for family groups.
$$$$–$$$$$

RESTAURANTS

Canterbury has an excellent range of eateries, and while you're in this region sample its delectable Canterbury lamb, fresh Mount Cook salmon, and Kaikoura crayfish.

Restaurant Price Categories

Prices are for a standard meal for one.

$ = below NZ$15
$$ = NZ$15–30
$$$ = NZ$30–50
$$$$ = over NZ$50

Christchurch City

Asian Food Court
266 High Street
Tel: 03-377 0151
A melting pot of Asian cuisines including Vietnamese, Thai, Indonesian, Chinese and Malay, all deliciously prepared and cheap. **$**

Boat Shed Cafe
Antigua Boat Sheds, Avon River
Tel: 03-366 6788
Cheap and cheerful steak sandwiches, toasties, chips, nachos and burgers at a casual café on the Avon River. **$**

Piko Piko
14 Cathedral Square
Tel: 03-365 1111
On the ground floor of the Millennium Hotel, Piko Piko uses indigenous ingredients to create contemporary New Zealand fare. **$$$**

Retour
Cambridge Terrace
Tel: 03-365 2888
www.retour.co.nz
In a former band rotunda on the Avon River, ideal for a special occasion. **$$$–$$$$**

Port Hills and Suburbs

Sign of the Takahe
200 Hackthorne Road, Cashmere Hills
Tel: 03-332 4052
www.signofthetakahe.com
Modern and traditional New Zealand cuisine in an atmospheric manor house. **$$$$**

North Canterbury

Malabar Restaurant and Cocktail Bar
5 Conical Hill Road, Hanmer Springs
Tel: 03-315 7745
Asian and Indian cuisine. Popular. **$$–$$$**

Canterbury Plains

Café 131
131 Main Street, Methven
Tel: 03-302 9131
Hearty breakfasts, lunches and snacks. **$**

Terrace Cafe & Bar
20 Main South Terrace, Darfield
Tel: 03-318 7303
Seasonal menu featuring locally reared meat (Canterbury lamb) and salmon. **$$**

Tekapo and Environs

Pepe's Pizza
SH8, Tekapo
Tel: 03-680 6677
Cosy bar and incredibly good pizza. **$–$$**

Aoraki Mount Cook

The Old Mountaineers
Aoraki Mount Cook Village
Tel: 03-435 1890
'Mountain' burgers, steak and chips, and other hearty favourites. **$–$$**

Panorama Restaurant
Hermitage Hotel
Tel: 0800-686 800
Outstanding views, particularly at sunset. World-class cuisine by Chef Paul Doyle. Bookings essential; ask for a window seat. **$$$$**

Sign of the Takahe, Cashmere Hills

NIGHTLIFE

While Auckland and Wellington are busy most nights of the week, Christchurch is quieter until Thursday, Friday and Saturday nights when most pubs have live bands.

The Dux de Lux
299 Montreal Street, Christchurch
Tel: 03-366 6919
www.thedux.co.nz
This trendy, laid-back place has live music, often folk and blues, and brews its own beers.

The Dux de Lux for live music and good beer

The Loaded Hog
Corner of Cashel and Manchester streets, Christchurch
Tel: 03-366 6674
www.loadedhog.co.nz
A busy bar; big, bold and popular.

The Ministry
90 Lichfield Street, Christchurch
Tel: 03-379 2910
www.ministry.co.nz
Big dance floor and latest sounds played to a frequently gay crowd.

ENTERTAINMENT

The theatre and concert scene is varied in Christchurch and up-to-date listings of current events can be found in *The Press*, and the free *Christchurch and Canterbury Visitors Guide* available at i-Site Visitor Centres.

Concert Halls

Convention Centre Town Hall
95 Kilmore Street, Christchurch
Tel: 03-366 8899
www.convention.co.nz
This modern building near the casino hosts major musical events.

Cultural Shows

Ko Tane
60 Hussey Road, Harewood
Tel: 03-359 6226
www.kotane.co.nz
Cultural performance plus the chance to learn the haka and poi dance.

Film

Arts Centre Cinemas
Arts Centre, Christchurch
Tel: 03-366 0167
www.artfilms.co.nz
Home of the arthouse Academy and Cloister Cinemas.

Theatre

Court Theatre
20 Worcester Boulevard, Christchurch
Tel: 03-963 0870
www.courttheatre.org.nz
New Zealand's leading theatre, with a small, high-quality ensemble staging middle-of-the-road modern drama. It's also home to the Southern Ballet and Dance Theatre.

Isaac Theatre Royal
145 Gloucester Street, Christchurch
Tel: 03-366 6326
www.isaactheatreroyal.co.nz
This Edwardian-style theatre hosts concerts, comedy and a range of other arts events.

SPORTS AND ACTIVITIES

Canterbury provides plenty of ways to enjoy the great outdoors from land-based activities like cycling and skiing, to the thrills of bungy jumping and jet-boating and wildlife adventures like whale-watching and swimming with dolphins.

Bicycle Hire

Mountain Bike Adventure Company
68 Waltham Rd, Christchurch
Tel: 0800-343 848
www.cyclehire-tours.co.nz
Bike rentals with the choice of a challenging off-road mountain bike track, a gentle scenic cycle, or a ride to Sumner Beach.

Bungy Jumping

Thrillseekers Canyon
Ferry Bridge, Hanmer Springs
Tel: 03-315 7046
www.thrillseekerscanyon.co.nz
Located at the 140-year-old single-lane Waiau Ferry Bridge, this outfit offers bungy jumping, quad-bike adventures, jet-boat rides, and whitewater rafting trips.

Fishing

Mount Cook Salmon Farm
Canal Road, Lake Pukaki
Tel: 03-435 0085
www.mtcooksalmon.com
Fish for your dinner.

Glacier Adventures

Glacier Explorers
Sir Edmund Hillary Centre
Aoraki Mount Cook
Tel: 03-435 1641
www.glacierexplorers.com
Boat tours of the iceberg-littered waters of Tasman Glacier Terminal Lake.

Mount Cook Ski Planes
SH80, Aoraki Mount Cook
Tel: 03-435 1026
www.mtcookskiplanes.co.nz
Scenic flights using ski planes *(see below)* with specialised equipment for snow landings at the head of Tasman Glacier.

Golf

Terrace Downs Resort
Coleridge Road, Windwhistle
Tel: 03-318 6943
www.terracedowns.co.nz
A challenging 18-hole link-style golf course with eight lakes and 70 bunkers, set against a stunning backdrop of snowcapped mountains.

Ice-skating and Snow-tubing

Winter Park
Lakeside Drive, Tekapo
Tel: 0800-235 382
www.winterpark.co.nz
Ice-skating rink and fun snow park offering tube toboggan rides for all ages.

Jet-boating

Rakaia Gorge Alpine Jet
Zig Zag Road, Rakaia
Tel: 03-318 6574
www.rivertours.co.nz
A thrilling jet-boat ride up the Rakaia Gorge river rapids.

Skiing

Alpine Guides
Sir Edmund Hillary Centre, Aoraki Mount Cook
Tel: 03-435 1834
www.alpineguides.co.nz
'Ski the Tasman' package provides the chance to ski the gentle bowls, open snowfields, towering seracs and icefalls of the national park.

Round Hill Ski Field
Lake Tekapo
Tel: 03-680 6977
www.roundhill.co.nz
Excellent ski field, good for beginners and intermediates. Cosy clubrooms.

Star Gazing

Mount John Observatory
Tel: 03-680 6960
www.earthandsky.co.nz
Star-gazing tours.

Swimming with Dolphins/Seals

Black Cat Cruises
Akaroa Wharf, Akaroa
Tel: 03-304 7641
www.blackcat.co.nz
The only operator licensed to swim with the rare Hector's dolphin.

Dolphin Encounter
96 The Esplanade, Kaikoura
Tel: 03-319 6777
www.dolphin.co.nz
Swim with dolphins or be a spectator. Hugely popular so book in advance during summer.

Seal Swim Kaikoura
58 West End, Kaikoura
Tel: 03-319 6182
www.sealswimkaikoura.co.nz
Boat- or land-based seal-snorkelling tours.

Searching for seals

Whale-watching

Kaikoura Helicopters – World of Whales
Kaikoura Airport, Main South Road
Tel: 03-319 6609
www.worldofwhales.co.nz
Whale-watching by helicopter.

Whale Watch Kaikoura
Railway Road, Kaikoura
Tel: 03-319 6767
www.whalewatch.co.nz
Famous whale-watching boat trips with a 95 percent success rate in finding whales.

Wings Over Whales
Kaikoura Airport, Main South Road
Tel: 03-319 6580
www.whales.co.nz
Aerial views of whales in a light aircraft.

TOURS

Balloon rides are a speciality in Canterbury and are a great way to get views of the Southern Alps, Canterbury's patchwork plains and the coast.

Balloon Rides

Aoraki Balloon Safaris
Methven, Canterbury Plains
Tel: 03-302 8172
www.nzballooning.com
Soar aloft for views of Mount Cook and the National Park mountains, plus a full panorama of the Canterbury plains.

Up Up and Away
31 Stevens Street, Christchurch
Tel: 03-381 4600
www.ballooning.co.nz
Scenic balloon rides operating out of central Christchurch. Balloons depart in the early morning so be prepared to get up at the crack of dawn.

Bus/Tram Tours

Christchurch Tram
Cathedral Square, Christchurch
Tel: 03-366 7830
www.tram.co.nz
Sightseeing tram rides. A complete loop takes approximately 25 minutes.

Boat Trips

Black Cat Cruises
17 Norwich Quay, Lyttelton
Tel: 03-328 9078
www.blackcat.co.nz
Tours of Lyttelton Harbour, Akaroa Harbour and swimming with dolphins.

FESTIVALS AND EVENTS

There is nothing Cantabrians enjoy more than a family day out and this is readily apparent in the range and quality of its major events, shows, carnivals and festivals.

January

Caroline Bay Carnival
Timaru
A celebration of summer in the carnival fairgrounds at Timaru's Caroline Bay.

World Buskers Festival
Christchurch
www.worldbuskersfestival.com
A 10-day event showcasing the world's best street acts and featuring more than 450 live shows city-wide.

February

Coast to Coast
West Coast to Christchurch
www.coasttocoast.co.nz
Longest-running multi-sport event in the world. Competitors run, kayak and cycle a 238km (148-mile) route from the West Coast to Christchurch's Sumner Beach.

Festival of Flowers
Christchurch
www.festivalofflowers.co.nz
Abundant floral displays centred on Christchurch Cathedral.

March

Waipara Wine and Food Celebration
Waipara
An annual event celebrating the region's wines.

April

Christchurch International Jazz Festival
www.jazzfestivalnz.com
New Zealand's biggest jazz fest featuring local and international artists.

August

Christchurch Winter Carnival
A week-long carnival celebrating winter with skiing and snowboarding championships.

November

Royal New Zealand Show
Christchurch
New Zealand's largest Agricultural and Pastoral (A&P) show, held over two days.

December

Strawberry Fare
Waimate
A fun day bringing families together to celebrate Waimate's strawberry harvest.

Competitors in the Coast to Coast race

West Coast

A rugged and primeval region, the West Coast provides fresh inspiration at every turn, with untamed rivers, rampant rainforests, spectacular surf, rugged mountains, icy lakes and glaciers. Gold-mining legends lurk at every corner, and living here is still for the hardy. There are more 'settlements' than towns, and no cities. Along with the mist and the mountains, a pioneering spirit still hangs in the air.

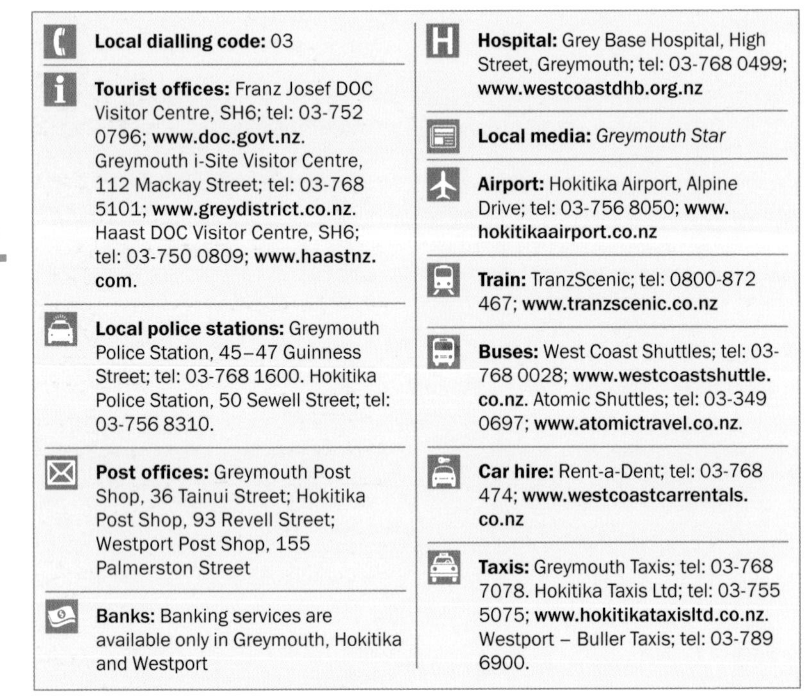

Local dialling code: 03

Tourist offices: Franz Josef DOC Visitor Centre, SH6; tel: 03-752 0796; **www.doc.govt.nz.** Greymouth i-Site Visitor Centre, 112 Mackay Street; tel: 03-768 5101; **www.greydistrict.co.nz.** Haast DOC Visitor Centre, SH6; tel: 03-750 0809; **www.haastnz.com.**

Local police stations: Greymouth Police Station, 45–47 Guinness Street; tel: 03-768 1600. Hokitika Police Station, 50 Sewell Street; tel: 03-756 8310.

Post offices: Greymouth Post Shop, 36 Tainui Street; Hokitika Post Shop, 93 Revell Street; Westport Post Shop, 155 Palmerston Street

Banks: Banking services are available only in Greymouth, Hokitika and Westport

Hospital: Grey Base Hospital, High Street, Greymouth; tel: 03-768 0499; **www.westcoastdhb.org.nz**

Local media: *Greymouth Star*

Airport: Hokitika Airport, Alpine Drive; tel: 03-756 8050; **www.hokitikaairport.co.nz**

Train: TranzScenic; tel: 0800-872 467; **www.tranzscenic.co.nz**

Buses: West Coast Shuttles; tel: 03-768 0028; **www.westcoastshuttle.co.nz.** Atomic Shuttles; tel: 03-349 0697; **www.atomictravel.co.nz.**

Car hire: Rent-a-Dent; tel: 03-768 474; **www.westcoastcarrentals.co.nz**

Taxis: Greymouth Taxis; tel: 03-768 7078. Hokitika Taxis Ltd; tel: 03-755 5075; **www.hokitikataxisltd.co.nz.** Westport – Buller Taxis; tel: 03-789 6900.

The wild west coast of the South Island occupies a special place in the New Zealand psyche. Rugged individualists, eccentrics and wild tales abound. The coast itself is a narrow strip of land wedged between the Tasman Sea and the Southern Alps. No more than 50km (30 miles) wide at any point, it spans glaciers, lush forests and soaring mountain peaks. Sealers were the first Europeans to settle these parts; gold miners descended after the yellow metal was discovered in the 1850s. Its main industries of gold, coal, timber and greenstone all tell stories of rivalry between settlers, set against a background of shanty towns, strong-willed women and quietly spoken, swarthy men. The coast is still strewn with old machinery, tunnels and the creaking remnants of ghost towns. Isolated, irrepressible and individualistic, today's West Coaster adds a touch of irony and humour to the South Island scene.

For a detailed map of the region see pp.172–3.

The Bushman's Centre, Pukekura

Northern West Coast

The West Coast has not always been as accessible. Today 554km (344 miles) of sealed tarmac, beginning in Karamea, dips and curves its way south past pockets of nikau palms and on through rugged and dramatic hills, acres of rainforest and spectacular surf.

Karamea

The west coast's northernmost town, 97km (60 miles) north of Westport, is **Karamea** ㉒, gateway to the vast 4,520 sq km (1,745 sq mile) **Kahurangi National Park** and the rugged route of Heaphy Track *(see p.25)*. Other attractions in the area include gold-mining relics and the **Oparara Basin**, an area of majestic limestone arches and caves northeast of Karamea. Just 1km further up from the Oparara Arch is **Honeycomb Cave**, discovered by cavers in 1980. So far, the bones of 27 extinct species of birds, including giant moa and eagles, have been found in its 17km (11 miles) of passages. Honeycomb Cave, with its delicate straw stalactites, pedestal 'elephant feet' and cascades of rougher flowstone, can be viewed with **Oparara Guided Tours**.

Walking through nikau palms on the Heaphy Track, Kahurangi National Park

Westport and Environs

Further south is **Westport** ㉓, a thriving harbour, where the **Coaltown Museum** (tel: 03-789 8204; daily Oct–Apr 9am–4.30pm, May–Sept 10am–4pm; charge) brings its history alive, with displays on sawmills, gold and coal mines, and an array of related industries which continue to shape Westport today.

About 14km (9 miles) north is the deserted coal-mining town of **Denniston**, once the nation's largest producer of coal. The **Denniston Walkway** climbs the high plateau to the old coal town and provides views of the once breathtakingly steep tramway called the Denniston Incline.

West of the town is **Cape Foulwind**, where a walkway follows the coast for 4km (2 miles). The highlight is a view of a breeding colony of New Zealand fur seals.

Inland Towns

Five km (3 miles) south of Westport, SH6 turns inland (becoming the Buller Gorge Highway) to follow one of South Island's most beautiful rivers, the Buller, through its lower and upper gorges for 84km (52 miles) to Murchison, where **Ultimate Descents** operate a range of thrilling whitewater rafting and kayaking trips. Other activities include panning for gold, jet-boat rides, and hiking along the river to the **Ariki Falls** and the White's Creek fault line, the site of a major earthquake in 1929.

From Inangahua Junction, SH69 traverses one of the most mineralised districts of New Zealand. About 34km (21 miles) south, it enters **Reefton**, named after its famous quartz reefs. This region was once abundant with gold and coal and is excellent walking country.

Westport, a good base for exploring the area

Mine for gold and board an old steam train at Shantytown, a replica West Coast settlement

Punakaiki

Nikau palms cling obstinately to the layered rock escarpments in **Punakaiki ㉔**: a tropical backdrop to the green-blue sea. Here the coastline takes on the extraordinary appearance of a pile of petrified pancakes. The **Pancake Rocks** and their blowholes comprise layers of stratified limestone. Reached by a 20-minute scenic loop walk from SH6, the rocks are best visited at high tide, when the brisk westerly wind causes the tempestuous sea to surge explosively and dramatically into the chasms, spouting spray through a series of blowholes.

Punakaiki is situated on the edge of the **Paparoa National Park** *(see p.25)* where the peculiarities of the limestone landscape continue inland. Here, rainwater has created deep gorges, fluted rocks and cave networks. Take a stroll along the nearby coastal tracks and collect polished quartz, explore one of the inland trails, or maybe even kayak your way along the **Pororari River** to a beautiful limestone gorge with good swimming holes. The visitor information centre at Punakaiki has all the information you need on park trails and local activities.

Greymouth

Greymouth ㉕, the largest town on the West Coast and the terminus of the TranzAlpine train route from

Gleam of Gold

Back in the early days the west coast was so forbidding that European exploration inland did not begin until 1846. It was only in 1860, after favourable reports of huge low-level glaciers in the south and possible routes through the Alps to Canterbury, that the central government purchased the west coast from the Maori for 300 gold sovereigns. Soon after, the discovery of gold attracted miners from all over the world. New strikes were found up and down the coast, in the river gorges and gravels, and even in the black sand of the beaches. The boom did not last long, but the surviving town sites, workings and rusty relics provide glimpses of the past.

Christchurch, is the area's adventure capital. The pioneering spirit still drives tourist ventures that cajole visitors to try their hand at gold mining, four-wheel-drive quad-bike safaris, dolphin-watching and cave rafting.

The **Jade Boulder Gallery** (daily 9am–5.30pm; free) in Guinness Street showcases *pounamu* (NZ greenstone or jade) with innovative displays, while **History House** (27–29 Gresson Street; www.history-house.co.nz; daily 10am–4pm; charge) features old photographs and memorabilia dating back to the 1850s. At **Monteith's Brewery Company** (60 Herbert Street; www.monteiths.co.nz; charge), plant tours are followed by a tasting, while **Shantytown** (Rutherglen Road; www.shantytown.co.nz; daily 8.30am–5pm; charge), 10km (6 miles) south of Greymouth, puts you at the centre of the 1860s gold rush, in a re-created mining settlement. In addition to sawmilling displays, there's the chance to pan for gold and ride on an old steam train.

Central West Coast

The Central West Coast's rugged and inhospitable terrain makes some of its scenic spots difficult to reach: those who persevere will be rewarded with untamed nature at its finest, particularly around the Franz Josef Glacier, where giant tongues of ice grind through temperate rainforest to just 300m (1,000ft) above sea level.

Hokitika

Back in the gold rush days **Hokitika** 26 was a busy, prosperous town with a thriving port. It is much quieter these days, but has regained something of its prosperous feel. It is served by the West Coast's main airfield, and a vibrant artisan community thrives here, with many galleries and studios to peruse. Hokitika's **West Coast Historical Museum** (summer daily 9.30am–5pm, winter Mon–Fri 9.30am–5pm, Sat–Sun 10am–2pm; charge) explores local history and the gold fever that once engulfed this region, while the **National Kiwi Centre** (64 Tancred Street; www.thenationalkiwicentre.co.nz; daily 9am–5pm; charge) offers one of the country's best facilities for viewing these nocturnal birds.

Scenic drives lead inland through pretty countryside to **Lake Kaniere** and the 64m (210ft) drop of Dorothy Falls. Before leaving town visit the

Craftsman shaping greenstone, Hokitika

Okarito Lagoon has the only nesting colony of the rare white heron

glow-worm dell (free) and sample some of Hokitika's legendary wild foods. A celebration of the coast's bush tucker is held every March at the Hokitika Wild Foods Festival.

Ross to Lake Ianthe

The tiny township of **Ross** ㉗ is packed with history and **The Ross Goldfield's Information and Heritage Centre** (4 Aylmer Street; www.ross.org.nz; daily 9am–4pm; charge) is a good place to start. It was here that the largest gold nugget in New Zealand was unearthed in 1909 and given to King George V as a coronation gift. Explore the tailings down by the river, or hire a mining pan from the heritage centre and hunt for a nugget to take home.

From Ross, the Fergusons and Waitaha Scenic Reserves meld into one en route to the **Bushman's Centre** (www.pukekura.co.nz; daily 9am–5pm; charge) in Pukekura. A giant sandfly hangs above the entrance to this museum/café which gives an entertaining insight into the life of the pioneering bushmen of the west coast in the 19th century.

Further on, the forest-lined shores of **Lake Ianthe** are ideal for camping and fly-fishing.

Whataroa and Okarito Lagoon

From Lake Ianthe, SH6 continues on to Whataroa, where **White Heron Sanctuary Tours** run sedate jet-boat trips downriver through towering kahikatea forest to the breeding ground of the rare kotuku or white heron on the **Okarito Lagoon** ㉘, New Zealand's largest natural wetland and a bird-watcher's paradise. Guided kayak trips organised by **Okarito Nature Tours** are an excellent way to explore.

Franz Josef

The streets of **Franz Josef** ㉙, tucked away in the forest beneath the magnificent **Franz Josef Glacier**, are lined with cosy cafés, eateries and accommodation. The visitor centre

Fox Glacier in Westland National Park

has an extremely informative display on the history, geology and ecology of the glacier region. Both Franz Josef Glacier and Fox Glacier *(see below)* are located in **Westland Tai Poutini National Park** *(see p.25)*, with its 88,000 hectares (217,000 acres) of Alpine peaks, snowfields, forests, lakes and rivers. It's an hour's walk along a 4km (2½-mile) track to the base of Franz Josef Glacier. The glacier itself is too slippery and dangerous to explore alone, but guided walks or scenic flights are both excellent ways to experience the glaciers first-hand *(see box right)*.

Back in town, evenings are best spent at the **Glacier Hot Pools** (Cron Street; www.glacierhotpools.co.nz; daily, noon–10pm; charge [M]) where a series of steaming pools is set amid the rainforest.

Fox Glacier

The village of **Fox Glacier** ㉚, 25km (15½ miles) to the south, is smaller than Franz Josef, and it takes only 30 minutes to hike to its glacier's base. Fully guided glacier hiking tours are also available *(see box below)*.

Other excellent hikes in the area include the **Chalet Lookout Walk**, a popular trail with fine views of the lower icefall, and the walk around **Lake Matheson**, which reflects the summit of Mount Cook and Fox Glacier in its mirrored surface. A short detour 19km (12 miles) west leads to **Gillespie's Beach**, noted for its miners' cemetery and seal colony.

Southern West Coast

After a few days on the West Coast it becomes apparent that its rainfall can be fairly extreme. But take away the rain and there would be no lush rainforest. When the sun comes out the scenery is sparkling fresh; rivers

Walking on Ice

Ice hiking is all the rage and the best way to experience the cerulean depths of Westland's glaciers. Guided walks organised by Franz Josef Glacier Guides and Fox Glacier Guiding *(see p.218)* range from a half- to full day. A more expensive option is a heli-hike – a scenic helicopter flight followed by a guided walk. It's wise to dress warmly in layers, although boots, socks and gloves, crampons, a Gore-Tex raincoat and a trekking pole will be provided. If the idea of walking on ice doesn't appeal, hop onto a helicopter or light plane instead for a brief snow landing on a glacier.

flow fast, waterfalls are spectacular, and the smell of the rainforest is rich and earthy.

Lake Moeraki and Lake Paringa

Surf kicks moodily along this coast. At the **Karangarua Bridge Scenic Reserve** the Copland Track winds its way into Westland National Park, leading to the deliciously soothing hot pools at Welcome Flat. SH6 continues to Bruce Bay, before winding inland to the **South Western Salmon Farm** where fishing lines can be hired to secure dinner. Anglers are enticed again at the quiet holiday spot of **Lake Paringa** brimming with brown trout and quinnat salmon.

Kahikatea forests line the road to **Lake Moeraki**, saved from the lumberjack's axe by the lack of road access up until 1965. From here a 45-minute trek leads to **Monro Beach** where Fiordland crested penguins make their homes near a prehistoric headland.

Haast and Environs

Heading south to Haast, the **Knight's Point Lookout** provides typical West Coast views of tumultuous rollers crashing against black cliffs. To reach **Haast**, first you must cross its impressively long one-lane bridge. **Haast River Safaris** provide a leisurely scenic cruise upriver into the **Mount Aspiring National Park**, and the DOC Visitors Centre at Haast Junction has useful displays on the journey through Haast Pass, a stunning drive through the towering peaks and lofty waterfalls of the National Park.

Another lonely corner of New Zealand can be found by taking the 36km (22-mile) road to the fishing village of **Jackson Bay**. This small community swells in size during the spring, when whitebaiters descend en masse to the nearby river mouth, an annual occurrence repeated beside swift-flowing rivers all the way along the West Coast.

Explore one of New Zealand's last frontiers on a Haast River Safari

ACCOMMODATION

Accommodation on the West Coast ranges from well-priced backpacker and holiday park accommodation through to luxury lodges with all mod cons. Franz Josef offers the widest variety and the newest abodes are set amid the rainforest on Cron Street, within walking distance of the Glacier Hot Pools – the perfect antidote to a day on the ice or the rigours of the road.

Accommodation Price Categories

Prices are for one night's accommodation in a standard double room (unless otherwise specified).

$ = below NZ$30
$$ = NZ$30–75
$$$ = NZ$75–150
$$$$ = NZ$150–350
$$$$$ = over NZ$350

Northern West Coast

Blackball Hilton Hotel
26 Hart Street, Blackball
Tel: 03-732 4705
www.blackballhilton.co.nz
Rooms are well priced and comfortable. Expect a candlewick bedspread and hot water bottle. **$$**

Gables Motor Lodge
84 High Street, Greymouth
Tel: 03-768 9991
www.gablesmotorlodge.com
Luxury self-contained studio, one-bedroom and two-bedroom suites, some with spa baths. **$$$**

Karamea River Motels
Bridge Street, Karamea
Tel: 03-782 6955
www.karameamotels.co.nz
One- and two-bedroom self-contained suites on a private farm, with views across the wilderness of Kahurangi National Park. **$$$**

Central West Coast

58 On Cron Motel
58 Cron Street, Franz Josef
Tel: 03-752 0627
www.58oncron.co.nz
Contemporary motel by Glacier Hot Pools. Quality bed linen and spa baths. **$$$$**

Rainforest Motel
15 Cook Flat Road, Fox Glacier
Tel: 03-751 0140
www.rainforestmotel.co.nz

Blackball Hilton Hotel

Perfect for families, this spacious and clean motel comprises studios and one- and (large) two-bedroom units, all with kitchens, en-suite bathrooms and views of the Southern Alps and local rainforest. **$$$**

Rainforest Retreat
46 Cron Street, Franz Josef
Tel: 03-752 0220
www.rainforestholidaypark.co.nz
A premium motel, campsite, motor camp and caravan park complex set amongst lush rainforest. Also home to Rainforest Backpackers, Franz Josef's newest backpacker accommodation with four-bed en-suite rooms, and five-bed dorms, and excellent rates for double share. **$–$$$**

Shining Star Chalets & Accommodation
16 Richards Drive, Hokitika
Tel: 03-755 8921
www.shiningstar.co.nz
A range of accommodation options set right on the beach including camping, cabins,

chalets and apartment-style units. Facilities include a sauna, spa pool, BBQ area and children's playground. **$–$$$$**

Southern West Coast

McGuires Lodge
SH6, Haast
Tel: 03-750 0020
www.mcguireslodge.co.nz
A popular lodge with one of the best eateries to be found in this area serving local specialities such as whitebait, Hereford steak and blue cod. **$$$$**

Wilderness Lodge Lake Moeraki
Tel: 03-750 0881
www.wildernesslodge.co.nz
A tranquil riverside setting, with fantastic bush and coastal walks. Tariff includes bed, breakfast and dinner, and two 'guest-only' tours, plus a range of optional tours including secluded penguin sites. **$$$$$**

RESTAURANTS

Most restaurants on the coast operate as a café by day, serving breakfast, brunch and lunch, then become restaurants/bars by night, changing over to dinner menus at around 5.30pm daily.

Restaurant Price Categories

Prices are for a standard meal for one person.

$ = below NZ$15
$$ = NZ$15–30
$$$ = NZ$30–50
$$$$ = over NZ$50

Northern West Coast

The Bay House Café
Tauranga Bay, Westport
Tel: 03-789 7133
www.thebayhouse.co.nz
Seasonal menu featuring West Coast specialities including whitebait, duck, salmon and beef. **$–$$$**

Café 124 On Mackay
124 Mackay Street, Greymouth
Tel: 03-768 7503
Great food and coffee. Indoor and outdoor dining. **$–$$**

Central West Coast

Blue Ice
SH6, Franz Josef Village
Tel: 03-752 0707
Popular with locals and visitors alike, this restaurant serves Pacific Rim and classic New Zealand dishes plus light meals including pizza. **$$–$$$**

Bushman's Café
SH6, Pukekura
Tel: 03-755 4144
A tongue-in-cheek menu from a Wild West Coast café serving local fare from tasty 'Roadkill Pies' featuring possum, venison, goat and rabbit meat, through to vegetarian 'Grass-eater' sandwiches. **$**

Café de Paris
19–21 Tancred Street, Hokitika
Tel: 03-755 8933
French-inspired café serving good coffee, mouth-watering cakes, and featuring a range of mains and desserts on its blackboard menu. **$–$$**

Wet weather warning at the Bushman's Café

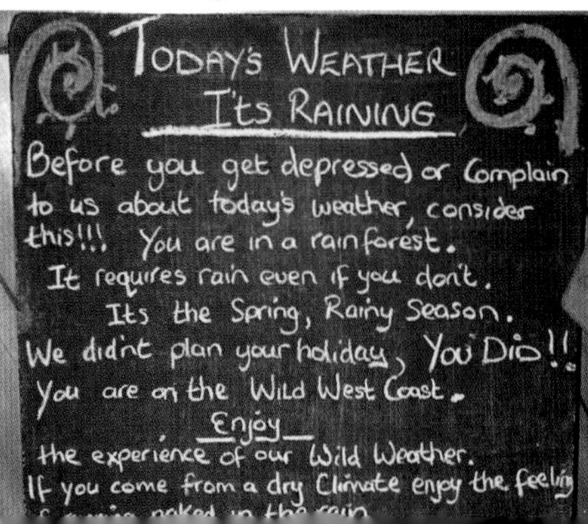

Cafe Neve
Main Road, Fox Glacier
Tel: 03-751 0110
A consistently good café/restaurant serving award-winning beef and lamb, seafood, venison and gourmet pizza. **$$–$$$**

The Landing
SH6, Franz Josef Village
Tel: 03-752 0229
Hearty roast pork dinners are popular here and everybody loves the large portions and reasonable prices. **$–$$**

Southern West Coast

Fantail Café
Corner Mark Road and SH6, Haast
Tel: 03-750 0055
Dine in or get takeaway at this conveniently located café. Fish and chips, pies, vegetarian food and sandwiches. **$–$$**

Salmon Farm Cafe
SH6, Paringa
Tel: 03-751 0837
Freshly hooked farmed salmon (catch your own if you wish!) at this farm café. **$–$$**

ENTERTAINMENT AND NIGHTLIFE

Few people visit the West Coast for the nightlife; however, you will always find a warm welcome at traditional pubs, and many cafés/restaurants become bars by night.

Nightlife

Blackball Hilton Hotel
26 Hart Street, Blackball
Tel: 03-732 4705
www.blackballhilton.co.nz
West Coast beer on tap, garden bar, and a surprising line-up of evening events.

Monsoon Bar
Rainforest Retreat, 26 Cron Street, Franz Josef
Tel: 03-752 0220
www.rainforestholidaypark.co.nz
A great place to meet Kiwi holiday-makers as well as other internationals.

Pioneer Hotel
80 Gibson Quay, Hokitika
Tel: 03-755 8641
Old-style West Coast pub and a good place to meet local farmers and tradespeople. To break the ice, just mention the rugby.

Stumpers Bar And Café
2 Weld Street, Hokitika
Tel: 03-755 6154
www.stumpers.co.nz
Café/bar by day, restaurant/bar by night, this warm and cosy eatery is a great place to hang out in the evening over a quiet pint or glass of New Zealand wine.

SPORTS AND ACTIVITIES

The West Coast is the only region in New Zealand to provide highly accessible ice/glacier hiking experiences at affordable prices.

Caving

Oparara Guided Tours
Market Cross, Karamea
Tel: 03-782 6652
www.oparara.co.nz
Guided tours of the Honeycomb Cave.

Ice/Glacier Hiking

Fox Glacier Guiding
SH6, Fox
Tel: 03-751 0825
www.foxguides.co.nz
Ice hiking tours on Fox Glacier.

Ice hiking on Franz Josef Glacier

Franz Josef Glacier Guides
SH6, Franz Josef
Tel: 03-752 0763
www.franzjosefglacier.com
Half- and full-day guided glacier hiking tours. More adventurous travellers can try their hand at ice climbing or heli-hiking.

Kayaking

Okarito Nature Tours
Main Road, Okarito
Tel: 03-573 4014
www.okarito.co.nz
Guided kayak trips exploring the lagoon and its birdlife including the rare white heron.

River Kayaking
SH6, Punakaiki
Tel: 03-731 1870
www.riverkayaking.co.nz
Guided and non-guided kayak and canoe trips of Paparoa National Park.

Whitewater Rafting

Ultimate Descents
51 Fairfax Street, Murchison
Tel: 03-523 9899
www.rivers.co.nz
Whitewater rafting trips to suit all abilities.

TOURS

Westland is filled with National Park land and scenic reserves, and walking and boat tours exploring the landscape are popular.

Boat Trips

Haast River Safaris
Haast Bridge, Haast
Tel: 03-750 0101
www.haastriver.co.nz
Scenic jet-boat rides up the Haast River.

White Heron Sanctuary Tours
SH6, Whataroa
Tel: 03-753 4120
www.whiteherontours.co.nz
Tours of the White Heron Bird Sanctuary.

Walking Tours

Southern Wilderness
Tel: 03-546 7349
www.southernwilderness.com
Guided hikes of the 85km (53-mile) -long Heaphy Track, a 'Great Walks' route of four/five days, and other tracks on request.

FESTIVALS AND EVENTS

The West Coast is famous for its Wild Foods and the annual Wild Foods Festival draws crowds from all over New Zealand.

March

Hokitika Wild Foods Festival
www.wildfoods.co.nz
A one-day celebration of the coast's bush tucker in mid-March. Sample wild boar, venison, huhu grubs and whitebait patties.

Otago

From sparkling royal-blue lakes and jagged schist tors where vineyards cling picturesquely to rocky hillsides, through to a verdant coastline where ecotourism activities abound and sightings of penguins, albatross, fur seals, sea lions, whales and dolphins are a regular occurrence, Otago is a region of stunning contrasts.

Queenstown

Population: 10,500

Local dialling code: 03

Tourist office: Queenstown i-Site Visitor Centre, Clocktower Building, corner Shotover and Camp streets; tel: 03-442 4100; **www.queenstown-vacation.com**

Police station: Queenstown Police Station, 11 Camp Street; tel: 03-441 1600

Post office: Queenstown Post Shop, 13 Camp Street

Airport: Queenstown Airport, Lucas Place; tel: 03-450 9031; **www.queenstownairport.co.nz**

Buses: Connectabus; tel: 03-441 4471; **www.connectabus.co.nz**

Car hire: Apex Rentals; tel: 03-442 8040; **www.apexrentals.co.nz**

Taxis: Alpine Taxis; tel: 0800-442 6666; **www.alpinetaxis.co.nz.** Queenstown Taxis; tel: 03-442 7788.

The hub of Otago is the jewel in New Zealand's tourism crown. In 30 years, Queenstown has grown from a sleepy lakeside town into a sophisticated all-year tourist resort, a sort of Antipodean St Moritz. This is a place that has been nurtured on tourism, and while other rural towns have struggled to survive, it has flourished. The Otago region possesses a personality quite distinct from other parts of the country. Some of the Southern Alps' most impressive peaks dominate its western flank, towering over deep glacier-gouged lakes. Yet the enduring impact is more subtle, encapsulated in the strange landscape chiselled and shaved from central Otago's plateau of mica schist rock. This was once gold-mining country, and relics from the past still remain. Far to the east is the university city of Dunedin, where a wealth of eco-tourism adventures awaits, while the Southern Scenic Route provides access to the Catlins, a remote and often forgotten corner of New Zealand.

Queenstown

Resting on the shore of Lake Wakatipu, **Queenstown** ❶ in Central Otago is the quintessential year-round holiday resort. Within a radius of only a few kilometres, the ingenuity and mechanical wizardry of New Zealanders have combined with the stunning landscape to provide an unrivalled range of adventure activities. Little wonder, then, that the town is often dubbed the 'Adventure Capital of the World.'

Queenstown adventures

Commercial water adventures on Queenstown's lakes and rivers range from canoeing, sailing, windsurfing and parasailing, through to water-skiing, canyoning, and rafting. Scenic flights also operate from Queenstown, providing access to spectacular lake, Alp and fiord scenery. For those with enough daring to dispense with machines, there is also paragliding, hang-gliding and skydiving, strapped to a guide of course.

Queenstown sits on the shore of Lake Wakatipu, surrounded by mountains

Spectacular views from the Skyline Gondola

Passenger launches take visitors trout fishing, and jet-boat, helicopter and four-wheel-drive excursions transport anglers to various pristine and remote stretches of water. The **i-Site Visitor Centre** (daily 7am–6pm, until 7pm in summer, *see box opposite*) has all the information you need. (*For more about action and adventure options in South Island see pp.44–49.*)

Skyline Gondola and Bob's Peak

One of the best introductions to Queenstown is to admire the magnificent views of the town and surroundings from **Bob's Peak** on the **Skyline Gondola** Ⓐ (Brecon Street; www.skyline.co.nz; daily, summer 10am–9pm, winter 10am–5pm; charge). The chairlift rises some 450m (1,476ft) to a restaurant, café, gift shop and an outdoor deck for views of Queenstown, Lake Wakatipu, The Remarkables mountain range, and Cecil and Walter Peaks.

A walking track leads to **The Ledge**, one of several sites run by bungy pioneer A.J. Hackett. The bungy jump from here offers spectacular views – if you manage to keep your eyes open as you take the plunge. Speed demons can ride the chair-lifts to a higher elevation and ride the **Luge** (daily 10am until late) back down. If you like the idea of flitting between trees, check in at the **Ziptrek Ecotours** tree hut, near the gondola station, to ride a series of flying foxes which 'zip' between treetop platforms built high in the forest canopy.

Back at the gondola station on Brecon Street there are two further attractions: **Caddyshack City** (25 Brecon Street 🚻), an elaborate mini-golf centre, and the **Kiwi Birdlife Park** (Brecon Street; www.kiwibird.co.nz; daily 9am–6pm; charge 🚻), a chance to see kiwis, fantails, bellbirds, tui and other native birdlife, as well as endangered species such as the black stilt and banded rail.

Cavell Mall and the lakefront

Although much of Queenstown's architecture is contemporary, around the waterfront and pedestrian-only **Cavell Mall** shopping area, some of its attractive original buildings still stand, including the **Courthouse** (1876), the buildings lining historical **Cow Lane**, the old **Williams Cottage** (1864) and the former **Eichardts' Pub** (1871) on the foreshore – now a lodge and stylish bar. From the piers at Queenstown Bay, water-craft provide pastimes ranging from parasailing to jet-boat rides.

Northwest of the piers is **Steamer Wharf Village** **B**, full of shops and restaurants, and several vessels including the TSS *Earnslaw*, a grand coal-fuelled steam ship which has graced the waters of **Lake Wakatipu** since 1912, when it was first used to carry

Rees Street and the Skyline Gondola

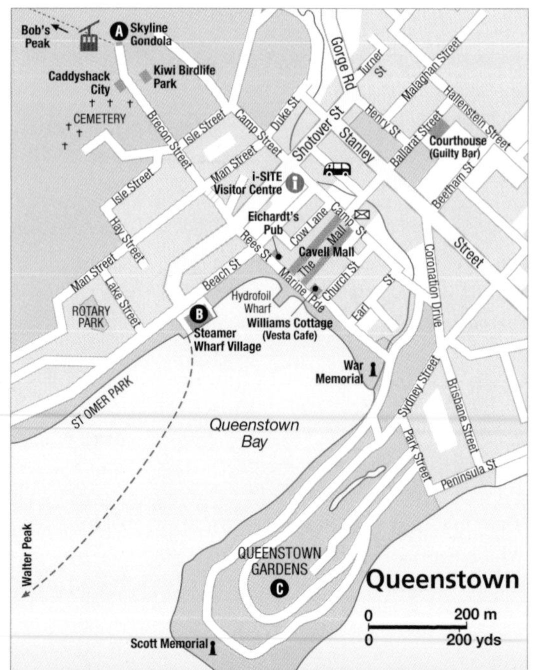

The *TSS Earnslaw* steamship

goods to remote settlements. 'The Lady of the Lake,' as she's known to locals, regularly ferries passengers to **Walter Peak High Country Station**, a working farm in a magnificent location where visitors can enjoy a meal, embark on a station horse trek, and/or experience sheep-shearing displays and agriculture first hand.

Back at the Steamer Wharf, 'land legs' can be regained with a walk in **Queenstown Gardens** ❸ at the far side of the bay. Located on a promontory, pathways explore its broad lawns, fir trees and roses, and lead to a memorial to Antarctic explorer Robert Falcon Scott – a great place to watch the sunset.

Around Queenstown

To enjoy most of the activities for which the area is renowned, you will have to venture a little further from Queenstown itself – either independently or on a guided tour. The region's swift-flowing rivers set the scene for whitewater rafting and jet-boating adventures; and there's the 'Middle Earth' landscape of Mount Aspiring, treacherous Skippers Canyon, ghostly Macetown, picturesque Arrowtown, the historic Kawarau Bridge, and the vineyards of the Gibbston Valley to explore.

Glenorchy

To escape the tourist bustle, take the road west out of Queenstown. For much of the distance, the scenic road follows the shores of the Wakatipu's western arm. Some 42km (26 miles) northwest of Queenstown, at the head of Lake Wakatipu, is **Glenorchy** ❷, an area of exceptional beauty in a region where exceptional beauty seems to be the norm. Although it's quiet, there's plenty to do here. Kayaking, jet-boating, horse riding, fishing, canoeing and canyoning are all popular pursuits here. **Dart River Safaris** leads groups on many of these activities, including jet-boat excursions to Sandy Bluff at the edge of **Mount Aspiring National Park**, and full-day canoe trips. All tours explore the **Dart River**, which passes through scenery from Tolkien's 'Middle Earth.' Dominated by views of **Mount Aspiring** (3,030m/9,941ft), the park also offers excellent hiking on the **Routeburn Track** *(see p.26)* which begins here, and abundant fly-fishing.

Arthur's Point to Coronet Peak

Heading immediately north out of Queenstown, Gorge Road leads to

Climbing Queenstown, a rock-climbing and abseiling centre on the outskirts of town. About 5km (3 miles) further on, in the canyons beneath the **Edith Cavell Bridge** which spans the Shotover River, is **Arthur's Point** where the expert drivers of **Shotover Jets** take passengers on a thrilling ride up and down the river, twisting through narrow canyons, skimming past rocky outcrops and completing full 360-degree turns. The rugged upper reaches of the Shotover River also provide the setting for whitewater rafting excitement; several companies including **Queenstown Rafting** offer trips with bus transfers to the launch point, wetsuits and a brief lesson before you take off.

Just beyond Arthur's Point is the turn-off to Coronet Peak and **Skippers Canyon**, the epicentre of gold-mining activity from the 1860s. The dramatic **Skippers Road**, hand-hewn from solid rock, is an adventure in itself. Self-driving is not recommended, but **Nomad Safaris** offer guided four-wheel-drive tours to the old settlement and **Skippers Canyon Suspension Bridge**, spanning the river 102m (335ft) below. However, **Coronet Peak**, a top-class ski-field in the winter *(see p.227)*, can be accessed on a fully sealed mountain road. No matter the season, it is a superb place to enjoy wide-ranging views.

Arrowtown

Skip the Coronet Peak turn-off and you'll wind up driving past **Millbrook Resort**, a stylish hotel complex with an 18-hole golf course, to **Arrowtown** ❸, the best-preserved gold-mining settlement in Central Otago. **Buckingham**

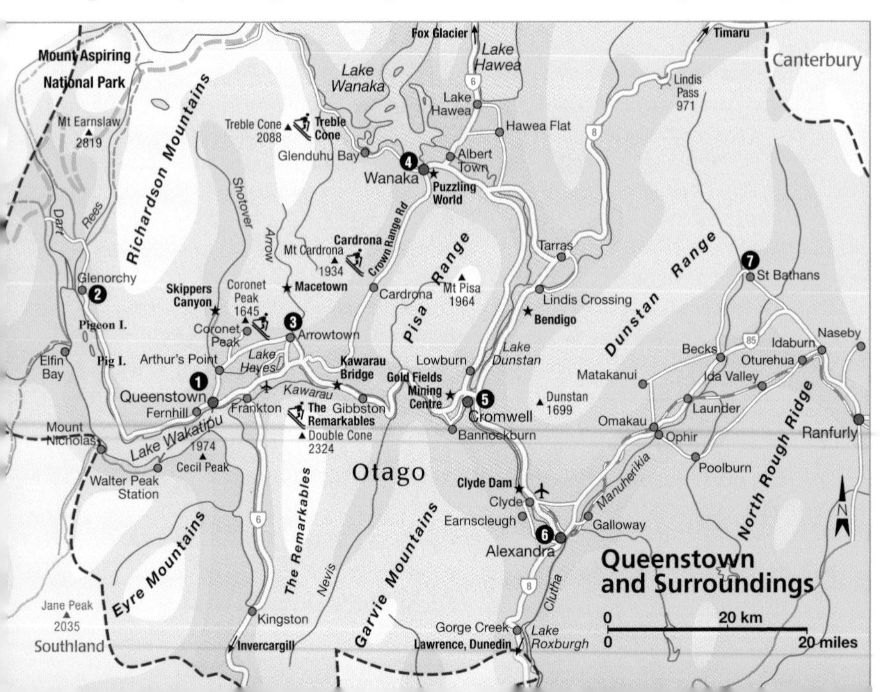

Autumn in Arrowtown

Street, the town's main thoroughfare, is lined with speciality stores and souvenir shops. A number of historic landmarks recall Arrowtown's rich history, including **Chinese Settlement** down by the Arrow River. At the peak of the 1880s gold rush, this sad collection of tiny hillside huts was home to 60 Chinese miners. Their story is told at the **Lakes District Museum** (49 Buckingham Street; www.museumqueenstown.com; daily 8.30am–5pm; charge), exhibiting gold, miners' tools and personal effects, plus a collection of horse-drawn vehicles and a re-created streetscape. For a taste of the old days, hire a pan from the museum and head down to the river to gather a few gold flakes.

Macetown is one of several ghost towns haunting the hills here. You can hike the 15km (9 miles) there and back. Alternatively, **Nomad Safaris** provide tours to its ruins.

Lake Hayes to Gibbston Valley

Leaving Arrowtown, the Arrowtown/Lake Hayes Road passes mirror-like **Lake Hayes** where scenic reserves provide access. At the junction, SH6 leads east to the historic Kawarau Bridge, the site of the first commercial bungy-jump operation, an option for thrillseekers *(see p.44)*. A behind-the-scenes **Secrets of Bungy Tour** takes a look at making a bungy-cord and gives access to viewing decks for those who would rather watch than jump.

From here it's a short drive on to the Gibbston Valley where a number of vineyards offer cellar-door tastings. At **Gibbston Valley Wines**, tours are

Gold Rush

In 1861 the first major gold strike was made in the Tuapeka River, marking the beginning of Central Otago's gold boom. In just four months, 3,000 men were swarming over the valley, searching for alluvial gold. A year later, Tuapeka's population was 11,500, double that of Dunedin. Otago's income trebled in 12 months, and ship arrivals quadrupled. New fields were discovered in quick succession in other valleys – the Clutha at the foot of the Dunstan Range, the Cardrona, Shotover, Arrow and Kawarau. In 1862 the Shotover, then yielding as much as 155g (5oz) of gold by the shovelful, was known as the richest river in the world.

held on the hour and finish with an atmospheric wine tasting held in the deep schist cave-turned-wine-cellar.

Wanaka and Central Otago

Vast, open meadows lead to Wanaka, an affluent settlement nestled amongst golden poplars and deciduous trees on the southern shores of the lake. Here you can keep the thrills coming, with jet-boating, kayaking, rock climbing and whitewater rafting, or follow in the footsteps of those who have gone before, exploring Central Otago's old gold-mining townships.

Crown Range Road to Wanaka

From the outskirts of Arrowtown, the **Crown Range Road** climbs a series of steep switchbacks, and then swoops down through a dry, rounded, tussock landscape into the **Cardrona Valley**. Here the historic **Cardrona Hotel** (1863) offers local hospitality, and there's a range of adventures to be had, including horse riding on well-behaved Appaloosas.

Wanaka ❹, 34km (21 miles) north of Cardrona, is smaller than Queenstown, but with its own lake, ski fields and everything else that's required of a southern playground, it's still a very popular resort. In addition to all the action and adventure on offer, **Rippon Vineyard and Winery** (246 Mt Aspiring Rd; tel: 03-443 8084; www.rippon.co.nz; Dec–Apr 11am–5pm, July–Nov 1.30–5.30pm, closed May–June) will keep wine buffs amused, and families can make a day of it at **Puzzling World** (188 SH84; www.puzzlingworld.co.nz; daily 8.30am–5.30pm; charge), a wacky, fun attraction about 2km (1¼ miles) south of Wanaka, with crazy

Lake Wanaka, New Zealand's fourth-largest lake

Bannockburn vineyards

tilted rooms, a challenging maze and puzzles galore. Another family attraction, the **Transport and Toy Museum** (tel: 03-443 8765; www.nttmuseum.co.nz; daily 8.30am–5pm; charge) has a rare and unusual collection of vehicles and toys from a bygone era. Wanaka's **i-Site Visitor Centre** (100 Ardmore Street; tel: 03-443 1233; www.lakewanaka.co.nz) has all the details you need to plan a stay here.

Bendigo to Bannockburn

Just off the SH8 past Lindis Crossing, **Bendigo** is a near-perfect ghost town, especially when the wind whistles through the tumbledown stone cottages at the bleak crossroads.

The road south of Bendigo runs for 15km (9 miles) to **Cromwell** ❺. This is wine- and fruit-growing country, although Cromwell's greatest asset is **Lake Dunstan**, the body of water on which the town now sits. The lake is used extensively for water sports and has an abundance of birdlife. In 1993 the building of the Clyde Dam resulted in the submersion of the original town of Cromwell. The historic buildings of the old town were relocated to the new township, and are now a major attraction, housing artisans' workshops and cafés. Another interesting attraction is the **Gold Fields Mining Centre** on the outskirts of town, a re-created miners' village complete with a Chinese settlement, which offers the chance to pan for gold.

There's a host of vineyards to explore in nearby **Bannockburn**, and bountiful crops of sun-kissed apples,

Ski Fields of Otago

Otago is a key snowsports centre and four of the largest ski fields in the South Island are located within easy reach of Queenstown and Wanaka. Coronet Peak Ski Field is just 18km (11 miles) by sealed road to the north and is noted for the variety of its terrain and floodlit skiing. The Remarkables Ski Field, 20km (12 miles) east, forms part of the rugged range that is Queenstown's famous backdrop. Its ski runs are popular with beginner and intermediate skiers, although there are some challenging runs for the more experienced. Further afield is the Cardrona Ski Field on the Crown Range Road, midway between Wanaka and Queenstown, and the Treble Cone Ski Field, within easy reach of Wanaka.

nectarines, apricots and peaches also grow here – buy a bag from a roadside stall or pick your own.

The Gold-Town Trail

At its southern end, Lake Dunstan spills over the **Clyde Dam**. A lookout point provides some perspective on this mammoth feat of engineering, which holds back 26.4 sq km (10.2 sq miles) of water. Beneath, the old goldmining town of **Clyde** is worth a visit. Explore the river tailings in the nearby **Earncleugh Dredge Tailing Reserve**, where well-formed tracks crisscross mountains of rock and gravel, all moved here by miners.

Alexandra ❻, 31km (19 miles) southeast of Clyde, distinguishes itself yearly in spring with its colourful blossoms. In winter, ice-skating and curling take place on natural ice on the Manorburn Dam. Follow a track through schist tors to the lookout beside the giant **Alexandra Clock**, for views of the old Shaky Bridge and William Hill Vineyard.

Northeast of Otago is a trio of gold-rush towns. **Ophir**, reached via an old suspension bridge, has a quaint old post office among other historic buildings. **St Bathans** ❼ is one of Otago's best-preserved sites. Among its 19th-century wood, stone and mud-brick buildings is the celebrated **Vulcan Hotel**, built in 1882, famous for its resident ghost. The town stands on the edge of disused goldfields, and the shimmering Blue Lake.

Other worthwhile destinations include **Naseby**, a quaint hillside hamlet with period buildings and a village green, and **Ranfurly**, whose Art Deco buildings stand testimony

Dunedin University, founded in 1869

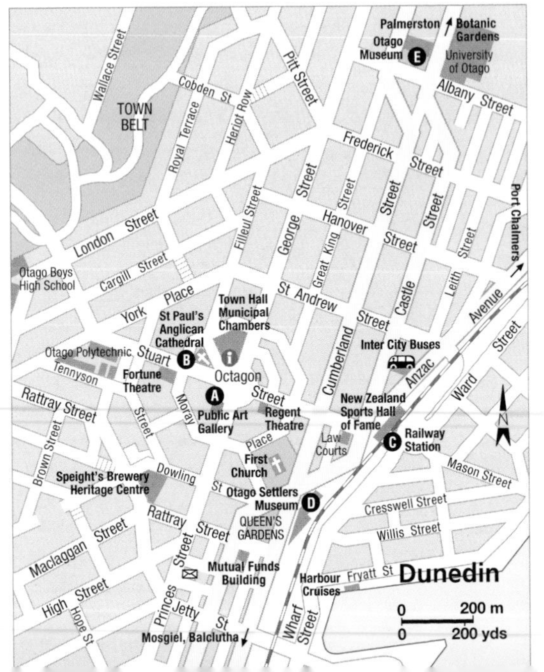

Yellow-eyed penguin mural in the Octagon

to the town's comeback after a devastating fire in the 1930s.

Dunedin

To the east, the charming coastal city of **Dunedin** ❽ reclines, all-embracing at the head of a bay, its southern end spilling into the Otago Peninsula. Behind the solid, sombre facade of a city built by Scots and leavened in gold-rush wealth lies a lively green-belted place of slate and tin-roofed houses, of spires, chimneys and churches, of glorious Victorian and Edwardian buildings, and a community of culture and learning. Here in the deep south is a way of life, a peace and a tranquillity that few cities can match.

Central City

Any exploration of the university city of Dunedin should begin at the **Octagon**, in its heart, where leafy trees border a wealth of historic buildings. These include the **Dunedin Public Art Gallery** Ⓐ (www.dunedin.art.museum; daily 10am–5pm; free), the oldest in New Zealand, housing works by Van der Velden, Frances Hodgkins, Constable, Gainsborough, Monet, Pissarro and Reynolds. Just north of the gallery is **St Paul's Anglican Cathedral** Ⓑ, its Gothic Revival pillars rising 40m (130ft) to support the only stone-vaulted nave roof in New Zealand. Next door are the century-old **Municipal Chambers**, which were designed by the noted colonial architect Robert Lawson, and behind it the **Town Hall**.

Town Belt

However, Dunedin's most photographed building is the **Dunedin**

The Otago Central Rail Trail

Cycle touring in New Zealand offers huge rewards, and some of the best places for cycling are in the South Island, particularly in areas such as Wanaka, Glenorchy and Queenstown. The Otago Central Rail Trail (www.otagocentralrailtrail.co.nz) is a 150km (93-mile) cycle route that runs from Clyde to Middlemarch following an old railway track (resurfaced by the DOC) through the incredible Otago landscape, over old viaducts and bridges and through tunnels, stopping off at historic mining villages. Fair weather and a gentle terrain make this a popular tour. Guided tour operators, such as Off the Rails, supply quality bikes, organise accommodation, and often include a bus to carry your luggage. The whole trail (which can be cycled in either direction) takes four to five days, but sections of it can be cycled on day trips.

Dunedin

Population: 122,000	**Local media:** *Otago Daily Times*
Local dialling code: 03	**Airport:** Dunedin Airport, Miller Road, Momona; tel: 03-486 2879; **www.dnairport.co.nz**
Tourist office: Dunedin i-Site Visitor Centre, 20 Princes Street; tel: 03-474 3300; **www.dunedinnz.com**	**Buses:** Citibus; tel: 03-477 5577; **www.citibus.co.nz**. Taieri Gorge Railway; tel: 03-477 5577; **www.citibus.co.nz/tracktrail.asp**.
Police station: Dunedin Police Station, 25 King Street; tel: 03-471 4800	**Car hire:** Driven Rental Group; tel: 0508 123 7483; **www.drivengroup.co.nz**
Post office: Dunedin Post Shop, 243 Princes Street	**Taxis:** Southern Taxis; tel: 03-476 6300; **www.southerntaxis.co.nz**
Hospital: Dunedin Hospital, 20 Great King Street; tel: 03-474 0999; **www.otagodhb.govt.nz**	

Railway Station ❸. Built between 1904 and 1906 in the Flemish Renaissance style, it has a 37m (121ft) -high square tower, three huge clock faces and a covered carriageway projecting from the arched colonnade. The **Taieri Gorge Railway** train (complete with vintage 1920s wooden carriages) departs from here daily bound for the spectacular Taieri River Gorge.

Dunedin Railway Station, one of the finest stone buildings in New Zealand

The station is also home to the **New Zealand Sports Hall of Fame** (www.nzhalloffame.co.nz; daily 10am–4pm; charge), a national sports museum that pays tribute to New Zealand's most famous sportspeople.

Just south of the station is **Otago Settlers Museum** ❹ (31 Queens Gardens; daily 10am–5pm; charge), established in 1898 and one of New Zealand's finest social history museums. To the north are the campuses of the **University of Otago**, Otago Polytechnic and Dunedin College of Education, dominated by the university's main clock tower. Other attractions include the **Otago Museum** ❺ (Great King Street; www.otagomuseum.govt.nz; daily 10am–5pm; free), loaded with Pacific Island and Maori artefacts, maritime relics and colonial-era collections, and the Dunedin **Botanic Gardens** on Signal Hill, a 65-hectare (160-acre) sea of flowers and rhododendron dells.

A fledgling royal albatross, the world's largest seabird, on Taiaroa Head

Around Dunedin

Visitors to Dunedin should not restrict themselves to the city. To both the north and south and located within easy reach, there are areas of immense natural beauty which are sparsely populated, full of ecotourism possibilities and as yet undiscovered by the masses *(see map on pp.242–3)*.

Otago Peninsula

The first sight you will see along the curving western coast road out of Dunedin is **Glenfalloch Woodland Garden** (tel: 03-476 1006; www.glenfalloch.co.nz; daylight hours), lovely rambling gardens encircling a 1871 homestead with a café on site. The winding road runs along the peninsula coast through the village of **Portobello**, centre of marine life studies, past **Otakou**, a historic Maori site, and on to the tip of the peninsula.

Just before reaching the headland, a farm road leads east to **Penguin Place** ❾ (www.penguinplace.co.nz; daily tours every 30 minutes from 10.15am until sunset; charge). Here the rare yellow-eyed penguins roam free while visitors watch from a hidden network of burrows and hides. The **Royal Albatross Centre** (www.albatross.org.nz; daily 9am–5pm; charge) at Taiaroa Head offers the chance to get up close to these legendary seabirds with their vast 3m (10ft) wingspan. Beneath the headlands NZ fur seals and sea lions laze in the sun. Cruise past on a wildlife boat or kayak, or visit **Nature's Wonders** to see baby seals frolicking in naturally formed rock pools.

On the way back to Dunedin, make a detour to **Larnach Castle** (www.larnachcastle.co.nz; daily 9am–5pm; charge), a century-old baronial manor and New Zealand's only castle complete with carved ceilings, Georgian staircase, princess turret and beautifully tended gardens.

The stunning Tautuku Beach, as seen from Florence Head on the Catlins coast

North Coast

The Otago coast north from Dunedin has many points of interest, too. At **Kaitiki Beach** common dolphins are often spotted, while further north the **Moeraki Boulders**, huge round stones, lie like giant marbles on the seashore.

In **Oamaru** ⑩, you can see the largest collection of protected heritage buildings in New Zealand. Crafted from a creamy local limestone called Oamaru Stone, these exquisitely restored Victorian buildings with their huge columns and extensive ornamentation are a sight to behold. Oamaru's **Harbour and Tyne Historical Precinct** features a rare curved wooden wharf and beneath the headlands beyond is the **Oamaru Blue Penguin Colony** (www.penguins.co.nz; daily, Oct–Mar 9.30am–11pm, Apr–Sept 9.30am–8.30pm; charge), where every evening these little birds ride in on the surf, and waddle back to their cliff-side homes.

The Catlins

To the south lies the **Catlins** coastline. It has a long line-up of natural attractions including the lighthouse at **Nugget Point**, perched upon a high, narrow spur of land. **Owaka** ⑪ is a hub for sport-fishing and hunting, and the leaping point to see Jacks Blowhole, and the **Purakaunui Falls**, which cascade over a series of ledges amid dense forest. **Papatowai** is the starting point for magnificent beach and forest walks including nearby **Tautuku Beach**, smothered to the shoreline with a jungle of native forest. Visit the beach for a dip, or hike to **Lake Wilkie**, or across private farmland to the **Cathedral Caves**, two hours either side of low tide.

At **Waikawa** ⑫ a museum bears evidence of the early days of this once-thriving port, but today its main attraction is found at Curio Bay, where the remains of a 180-million-year-old fossilised forest can be seen at low tide. To the south lies **Waipapa Point**, where a lighthouse guards the memory of New Zealand's worst shipping disaster in 1881. Oblivious to this tragedy, half-tonne New Zealand sea lions regularly sun themselves in the lighthouse car park, joined occasionally by the four-tonne elephant seal.

ACCOMMODATION

Accommodation in and around Queenstown is plentiful, but tends to be either at the luxury or budget end. There are good deals to be had further afield in the less crowded outlying areas.

Queenstown and Lake Wakatipu

Copthorne Lakefront Resort
Corner of Adelaide and Frankton Road
Tel: 03-442 8123
www.millenniumhotels.co.nz
Quality rooms, many with views of the lake and mountains. Not in the centre of Queenstown, but within walking distance of the shopping area. **$$$$–$$$$$**

Nugget Point Boutique Hotel
146 Arthur's Point Road
Tel: 03-441 0288
www.distinctionqueenstown.co.nz
Award-winning boutique hotel with impeccably furnished suites located within 10 minutes' drive of Queenstown. **$$$$$**

YHA Queenstown Lakefront
88–90 Lake Esplanade
Tel: 03-442 8413
www.yha.co.nz
Right on the waterfront among luxury hotels, with a choice of single or shared rooms, there is no other accommodation in Queenstown that offers such good value for money. **$**

Room with a view at the Copthorne Lakefront Resort

Accommodation Price Categories

Prices are for one night's accommodation in a standard double room (unless otherwise specified).

$ = below NZ$30
$$ = NZ$30–75
$$$ = NZ$75–150
$$$$ = NZ$150–350
$$$$$ = over NZ$350

Around Queenstown

Millbrook Resort
Malaghans Road, Arrowtown
Tel: 03-441 7000
www.millbrook.co.nz
Large golf resort with luxurious modern accommodation in restored historic buildings with Alpine views and an award-winning restaurant. **$$$$$**

Settlers Cottage Motel
22 Hertford Street, Arrowtown
Tel: 03-442 1734
www.settlerscottagemotel.co.nz
Boutique motel in a quiet location with cosy, gold-rush themed studios and one- and two-bedroom apartments. **$$$**

Wanaka and Central Otago

Brook Vale Motels
35 Brownston Street, Wanaka
Tel: 0800-438 333
www.brookvale.co.nz
Central but private, with views of the Southern Alps. All units have kitchens, and there's a spa pool, outdoor pool, bbq area and guest laundry. **$$$–$$$$**

The Chalets Holiday Park
102 Barry Avenue, Cromwell
Tel: 03-445 1260
www.cromwell.org.nz/chalets
Cabins for two with linen cost less than a bed at shared backpackers. **$–$$$**

Dunedin

Cargill's Hotel
678 George Street
Tel: 03-477 7983

www.cargills.co.nz
Central hotel with basic but comfortable rooms. Restaurant on site. **$$$**

Hulmes Court Bed and Breakfast
52 Tennyson Street
Tel: 0800-448 563
www.hulmes.co.nz
Clean and comfortable rooms in an 1860s Victorian mansion in the heart of town. Plenty of off-street parking. **$$$–$$$$**

Around Dunedin

Avenue Motel
Thames Street, Oamaru
Tel Ivy House: 03-437 0091
www.avenuemotel.net.nz
Good value for money; rooms are quiet, comfortably furnished and overlook the playing fields of Milner Park. **$$$**

Larnach Lodge
145 Camp Road, Otago Peninsula
Tel: 03-476 1616
www.larnachcastle.co.nz
Twelve individually decorated, period-style bedrooms, each with an ocean view. Lodge guests may dine in the historic castle dining room. Cheaper rooms with shared bathrooms in the converted stable. **$$$–$$$$$**

RESTAURANTS

Eating out in Central Otago is a real treat – fresh local produce is used to create menus that reflect the lifestyle of the region and partner well with locally produced wines.

Restaurant Price Categories

Prices are for a standard meal for one.

$ = below NZ$15
$$ = NZ$15–30
$$$ = NZ$30–50
$$$$ = over NZ$50

Queenstown and Lake Wakatipu

The Bathhouse
15–28 Marine Parade
Tel: 03-442 5625
www.bathhouse.co.nz
Right on the lake, in a converted Victorian bathhouse with scenic waterfront views. The old-world ambience belies its innovative fusion cuisine. **$$–$$$$**

Fergburger
42 Shotover Street
Tel: 03-441 1232
Flavoursome, oversized gourmet burgers and the best chips in town. **$–$$**

Habebes
Wakatipu Arcade, Rees Street
Tel: 03-442 9861
This Lebanese takeaway is a favourite with Queenstowners for its quick lunch-time wraps, yummy vegetarian dishes and super-fresh salads. **$**

Joes Garage
Searle Lane
Tel: 03-442 5282
All-day breakfast/brunch menu. **$–$$**

Pier 19
Steamer Wharf
Tel: 03-442 4006
A swish café/bar right on the lake which often features crayfish (lobster), whitebait and oysters on its menu. **$$–$$$**

Around Queenstown

The Red Tractor
54 Buckingham Street, Arrowtown
Tel: 03-442 0991
A casual and atmospheric pizza restaurant. **$$–$$$**

Gibbston Valley Winery Restaurant
SH6, Queenstown
Tel: 03-442 6910
Dishes team perfectly with Gibbston's superb range of wines. **$$$$**

Wanaka and Central Otago

Kai Whakapai Café and Bar
Lakefront, Wanaka
Tel: 03-443 7795
www.kaiwanaka.co.nz
Panoramic lake views and freshly baked breads, pies, pasta and vegetarian selections. **$–$$**

Speights Ale House
155 Ardmore Street, Wanaka
Tel: 03-443 2920
Fireside dining with great views and varied menu. Excellent kids' meals. **$–$$$**

Dunedin

Bell Pepper Blues
474 Princes Street
Tel: 03-474 0973
www.bellpepperblues.co.nz
Pleasant, high-quality restaurant with a welcoming atmosphere. Always full. **$$$$**

Etrusco at the Savoy
8A Moray Place, Dunedin
Tel: 03-477 3737
www.etrusco.co.nz
An extensive menu of Tuscan favourites – pasta dishes, thin-crust pizzas, Italian breads and *antipasti*, and a good wine list. **$–$$**

Speights Ale House for good, solid pub food

Around Dunedin

Niagara Falls Café
Main Road, Waikawa
Tel: 03-246 8577
A funky café in an old school building. **$–$$**

Whitestone Cheese
3 Torridge Street, Oamaru
Tel: 03-434 8098
www.whitestonecheese.co.nz
Delicious lunch platters featuring Whitestone Cheese made on site. **$–$$**

ENTERTAINMENT AND NIGHTLIFE

Queenstown and Central Otago have lots of good nightspots, particularly wine bars, pubs and nightclubs, while the university city of Dunedin is a hothouse for contemporary and up-and-coming bands.

Bardeaux
Eureka Arcade, Queenstown
Tel: 03-442 8284
Comfy leather armchairs, extensive wine and cocktail lists and a huge open fireplace.

Craft Bar
10 The Octagon, Dunedin
Tel: 03-470 1426
Vibrant mix of live music, poetry readings, and contemporary bands. Open late.

Di Lusso
12 The Octagon, Dunedin
Tel: 03-477 3776
A live and loud music venue that stays open until late.

Dorothy Brown's Cinema, Bar and Bookshop
Buckingham Street, Arrowtown
Tel: 03-442 1964
www.dorothybrowns.com

A quirky movie house, which shows arthouse films in an opulent setting (possum fur armchairs, chandeliers) with an open fire and bar.

Ra Bar
21 The Octagon, Dunedin
Tel: 03-477 6080
DJs and live local bands play here. Happy hour 5–8pm on Fridays.

Stadium Sports Bar
91 St Andrew Street, Dunedin
Tel: 03-477 2029
A good place to catch live sport coverage.

Surreal
7 Rees Street, Queenstown
Tel: 03-441 8492
www.surrealbar.co.nz
Lots of live bands play here and anything goes from house, electro and hip-hop, through to live jazz, rock and dub.

Tardis
Cow Lane, Queenstown
Tel: 03-441 8397
A sleek late-night club and bar on Cow Lane. Renowned for its DJs who play hip-hop; this place is popular and fills fast so go early.

The World Bar
27 Shotover Street, Queenstown
Tel: 03-442 6757
www.theworldbar.com
Always packed to the rafters with a lively crowd who enjoy its extended happy hours.

SPORTS AND ACTIVITIES

As you would expect in the adventure capital of the world, Queenstown offers an astonishing range of adrenaline-pumping outdoor activities. Local operators meet the tourist demand with a high level of professionalism and safety.

Bungy Jumping

Kawarau Bungy Centre
SH6, Queenstown
Tel: 03-442 5356
www.bungy.co.nz
Bungy jumps from the historic Kawarau Bridge. A.J. Hackett also operates the 102m (334ft) Pipeline Bungy, and the staggering 134m (440ft) Nevis Highwire Bungy *(see pp.44–5)*.

The Ledge
Top of Gondola, Brecon Street, Queenstown
Tel: 03-441 8926
www.bungy.co.nz
Spectacular views of Queenstown provide a scenic backdrop for the plunge.

Climbing

Climbing Queenstown
36 Shotover Street, Queenstown
Tel: 03-409 2508
www.climbingqueenstown.com
Climbing courses, tours and instruction for beginners through to advanced climbers.

Flying Fox

Ziptrek Ecotours
Top of Gondola, Brecon Street, Queenstown
Tel: 03-441 2102
www.ziptrek.com
Fly through the treetops on these exhilarating ziptrek ecotours.

Golf

Millbrook Resort
Malaghans Road, Arrowtown
Tel: 03-441 7000
www.millbrook.co.nz
Hotel resort with an 18-hole golf course.

Horse Riding

Moonlight Country Stables
Domain Road, Queenstown
Tel: 03-442 1240
www.moonlightcountry.co.nz

Horse-riding lessons and treks near Arthur's Point for beginners and experienced riders.

Jet-boating

Dart River Safaris
4 Mull Street, Glenorchy
Tel: 03-442 9992
www.dartriver.co.nz
Jet-boat safaris between mountains and glaciers and into Mount Aspiring National Park, as well as Funyak (inflatable canoe) trips on the Dart River.

Shotover Jets
Gorge Road, Arthur's Point
Tel: 03-442 8570
www.shotoverjet.co.nz
Thrilling jet-boat rides on the Shotover River. Courtesy buses from the i-Site Visitor Centre.

Kayaking

Wild Earth Adventures
Dunedin
Tel: 03-489 1951
www.wildearth.co.nz
Kayak tours to see royal albatross and fur seal colonies and lots of other native wildlife including penguins and dolphins.

Paragliding, Paraflights and Hang-gliding

Coronet Peak Tandems Ltd
28 Lake Avenue, Frankton
Tel: 0800-467 325
www.tandemparagliding.com
Tandem paragliding and hang-gliding taking off from 700m (2,300ft) harnessed to an instructor.

Queenstown Hang-gliding
36 Erskine Road, Lake Hayes
Tel: 03-442 5747
www.hangglide.co.nz
Fly in tandem with the world's most experienced pilot-instructors.

Queenstown Para Flights
Queenstown Pier
Tel: 03-441 2242
Take off from a boat on Lake Wakatipu and rise up to 200m/yds before landing back onto the boat.

Wanaka Paragliding
Treble Cone Ski Area
Tel: 0800-359 754
www.wanakaparagliding.co.nz
New Zealand's highest tandem paragliding.

River Surfing/Sledging

Frogz White Water Sledging
39 Camp Street, Queenstown
Tel: 03-441 2318
www.frogz.co.nz
Frogz operate daily trips from Queenstown and Wanaka. Experienced guides teach you how to use your sledge and read the river.

River Surfing
39 Camp Street, Queenstown
Tel: 0800-737 4687
www.riversurfing.co.nz
Extreme action with just a body board between you and the Shotover River torrents.

Skiing and Snowsports

Coronet Peak
Queenstown
Tel: 03-442 4620
www.nzski.com/coronet
The roller-coaster terrain makes this a good pick for intermediate/advanced skiers.

Cardrona
Crown Range Road, Cardrona
Tel: 03-443 7341

Jet-boating on the Shotover River

www.cardrona.co.nz
Excellent snowboarding facilities and challenging terrain. Ski school for all levels, including children aged 5 upwards.

The Remarkables
Queenstown
Tel: 03-442 4615
www.nzski.com/remarkables
Close to town with a free shuttle service from the Queenstown Snow Centre. A good choice for beginners.

Treble Cone
Wanaka
Tel: 03-443 7443
www.treblecone.co.nz
Northwest of Wanaka, Treble Cone has the longest vertical rise in the district.

Skydiving

NZONE
Tel: 03-442 5867
www.nzone.biz
Tandem jumps over Queenstown, priced according to how high you choose to go.

The ski season runs from July to September

Whitewater Rafting

Queenstown Rafting
35 Shotover Street, Queenstown
Tel: 03-442 9792
www.rafting.co.nz
Rafting tours of the Kawarau River (grade 2–3) and Shotover River (grade 3–5).

Raft Challenge
35 Shotover Street, Queenstown
Tel: 0800-723 8464
www.raft.co.nz
A great introduction to rafting on the Kawarau or extreme action on the Shotover River.

TOURS

Wherever you would like to go or whatever you would like to do there is a tour to suit in Central Otago. Wine-tasting tours sampling the region's fine wines are popular, as are fully inclusive bicycle tours on the Central Rail Trail.

Balloon Rides

Sunrise Balloons
Tel: 03-442 0781
www.ballooningnz.com
See the sunrise over lakes and mountains followed by a champagne breakfast.

Bike Tours

Off the Rails
32 Charlemont Street, Ranfurly
Tel: 0800-633 7245
www.offtherails.co.nz
Guided cycling tours in Central Otago including the Central Rail Trail *(see p.228)*. Fully supported with back-up transport provided.

Boat Trips

Monarch Wildlife Cruises
20 Fryatt Street, Dunedin
Tel: 03-477 4276
www.wildlife.co.nz
Cruises Taiaroa Head, Otago Harbour and Peninsula to see seals, penguins and albatross in their natural environment.

TSS *Earnslaw*
Steamer Wharf, Queenstown
Tel: 03-442 7500
www.realjourneys.co.nz
Sightseeing cruises aboard the grand, coal-fuelled steamship depart every two hours for

Walter Peak High Country Station, a working farm, for lunch and an optional guided horse trek.

Driving Tours

Nomad Safaris
37 Shotover Street, Queenstown
Tel: 03-442 6699
www.nomadsafaris.co.nz
Guided four-wheel-drive adventure tours to Skippers Canyon and Macetown, plus a tour of *Lord of the Rings* 'Middle Earth' locations.

Walking Tours

New Zealand Wild Walks
10A Tenby Street, Wanaka
Tel: 03-443 4476
www.wildwalks.co.nz
Specialists in hiking and climbing in Mount Aspiring National Park. Small groups, maximum of five people.

Train Tours

Taieri Gorge Railway
Dunedin Railway Station
Tel: 03-477 4449
www.taieri.co.nz
Excursion from historic Dunedin station to the rugged Taieri Gorge on a vintage train.

Wine Tours

Apellation Central Wine Tours
Tel: 03-442 0246
www.appellationcentral.co.nz
Daily vineyard tours to Gibbston Valley and beyond, departing from Queenstown.

Queenstown Wine Trail
Queenstown
Tel: 03-441 3990
www.queenstownwinetrail.co.nz
Wine tours and wine tasting in Queenstown and Central Otago vineyards.

FESTIVALS AND EVENTS

Here in Central Otago where the seasons are more pronounced than in New Zealand's warmer climes, the coming of each season is celebrated.

April

Arrowtown Autumn Festival
Arrowtown
www.arrowtownautumnfestival.org.nz
In autumn Arrowtown becomes the prettiest town in Central Otago and this is celebrated with parades, performances and markets.

Southern Lakes Festival of Colour
Wanaka
www.festivalofcolour.co.nz
Art, music, theatre and dance make up this annual festival.

July

Queenstown Winter Festival
Coronet Peak, Queenstown
www.winterfestival.co.nz
Every year in early July, Coronet Peak comes alive during the Queenstown Winter Festival, when celebrity skiers, sheepdog trials, night skiing and all-night partying signal the start of the region's ski season.

September

Alexandra Blossom Festival
Central Otago celebrates the coming of spring with a parade, sheep-shearing competitions and garden tours.

Snowboarding display at the Winter Festival

Southland, Fiordland and Stewart Island

The expansiveness of New Zealand's southernmost extremes is striking. Its sprawling stations and vast unpopulated open spaces are filled with flourishing rainforests, massive schist peaks and lofty waterfalls that cascade from rugged foothills layered in carpets of moss, and highlighted with a distinctive quality of bold light.

Invercargill

Population: 50,000

Local dialling code: 03

Tourist office: Invercargill i-Site Visitor Centre, 108 Gala Street; tel: 03-211 0895. Fiordland i-Site Visitor Centre, Lakefront Dr, Te Anau; tel: 03-249 8900; **www.southlandnz.com.**

Main police station: Invercargill Police Station, 117 Don Street; tel: 03-211 0400

Main post office: Invercargill Post Shop, 51 Don Street; Te Anau Post Shop, 100 Town Centre

Hospital: Southland Hospital, Kew Road, Invercargill; tel: 03-214 7224; **www.southlandhealth.co.nz**

Local media: *Southland Times*

Airport: Invercargill Airport, Airport Avenue, Invercargill; tel: 03-214 0571; **www.invercargillairport.co.nz**

Buses: Invercargill Passenger Transport; tel: 03-218 7108. A public bus service operates six days a week covering the inner city and outlying suburbs.

Car hire: Riverside Rentals; tel: 03-214 1030; **www.riversiderentals.co.nz**

Taxis: Invercargill: Blue Star Taxi; tel: 03-217 7777. City Cabs; tel: 03-214 4444. Te Anau: Te Anau Taxis; tel: 03-249 7777.

Most people use Southland and the Fiordland region as a base simply to visit the spectacular Milford Sound. When they get here they find a larger region of hauntingly beautiful wild valleys, soaring schist mountains and startlingly blue waterways also vying for their attention. Fiordland National Park is often said to be New Zealand's most spectacular. Its borders remain sparsely populated and, in parts, it is virtually unexplored. The region is so remote that rumours of 'lost' Maori tribes, never encountered by Europeans, persisted until the 1950s, as did reports of surviving moa birds. The sheer enormity of these southern-most regions is unforgettable; soaring peaks and seemingly endless pastures of cattle and sheep stations fill the spaces between scattered and friendly townships all the way to Invercargill, a genteel south-coast city with a strong Scottish heritage and a legacy of wide tree-lined streets. Beyond lie the pristine shores of Stewart Island, a seldom-explored wilderness of podocarp rainforest, granite peaks, freshwater wetlands and deserted beaches.

Milford Sound, described by Rudyard Kipling as 'the eighth wonder of the world'

Invercargill and the South Coast

In the lee of the west-coast mountains are the two extensive plains on which the province's prosperity has grown to depend. These lowlands surround **Invercargill ⓭**, New Zealand's southernmost city, extending across the South Island to reach the southeastern coastlands. Sealers and whalers first visited these shores but it was the Scots who settled here and made the place their own, building elegant villas and bungalows, richly embellished churches and memorials, neat gardens and tree-lined parks.

The Boer War Memorial, Invercargill Centre

Invercargill

The original town planners of Invercargill were generous in the amount of space devoted to main thoroughfares and public spaces. Today, **Queens Park**, the green heart of the city, provides a wide range of recreational pursuits, from sunken rose gardens and statuary, to a golf course and swimming pool. Invercargill's most popular attraction, the **Southland Museum and Art Gallery** (www.southlandmuseum.com; Mon–Fri 9am–5pm, Sat–Sun 10am–5pm; charge 👪), is located at the Gala Street entrance of the park. There are galleries devoted to local Maori, history and art, but the displays on the sub-Antarctic region – the cluster of islands between New Zealand and the Antarctic – alone make a visit

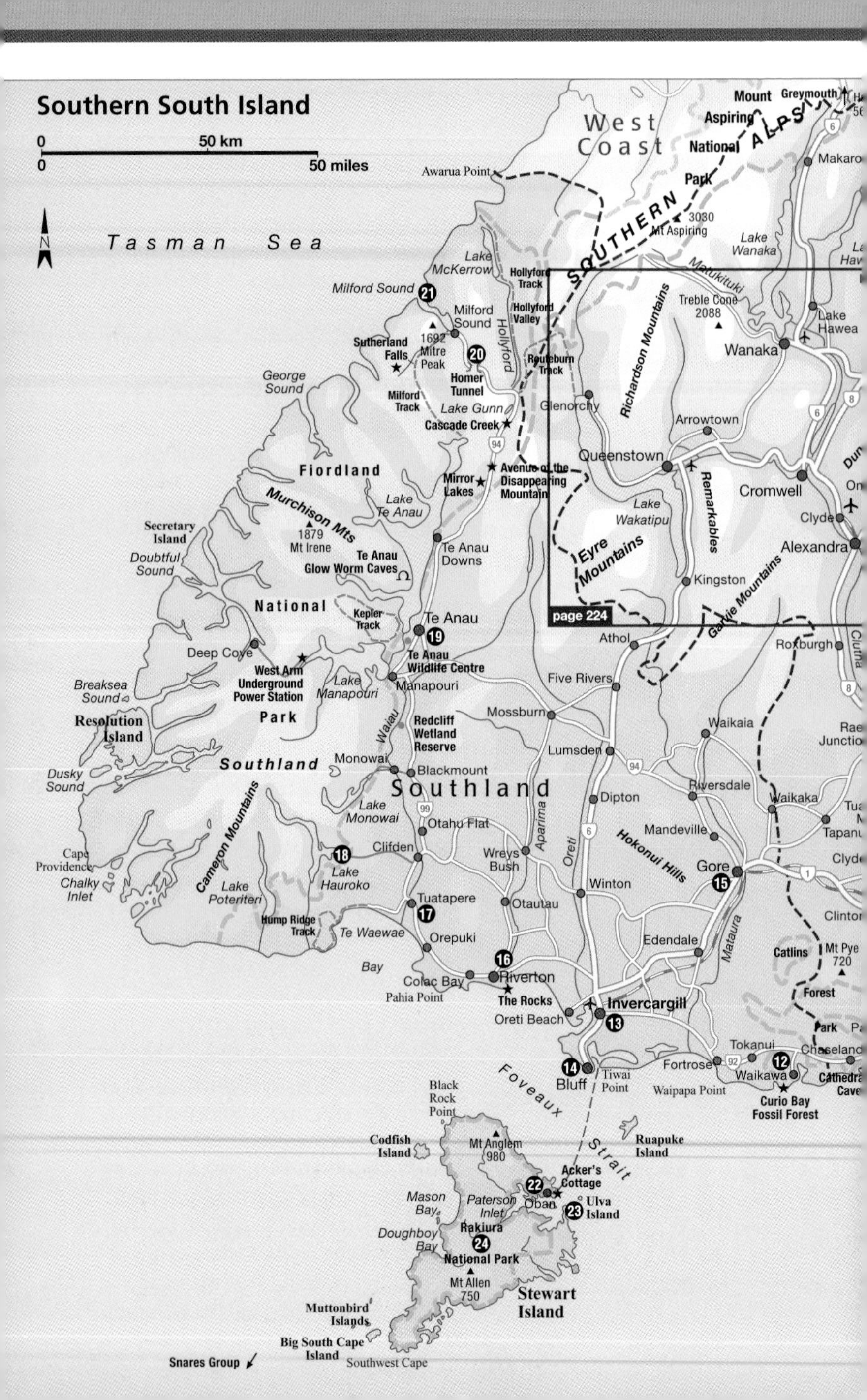

Southern South Island
0
50 km
0
50 miles
Tasman Sea
West Coast
Mount Aspiring National Park
SOUTHERN ALPS
Greymouth
Makaro
Awarua Point
3030
Mt Aspiring
Lake Wanaka
Lake McKerrow
Hollyford Track
Milford Sound
Milford Sound
Hollyford Valley
Hollyford
Treble Cone
2088
Richardson Mountains
Matukituki
Lake Hawea
Wanaka
1692
Mitre Peak
Sutherland Falls
Homer Tunnel
Routeburn Track
George Sound
Milford Track
Lake Gunn
Glenorchy
Cascade Creek
Arrowtown
Queenstown
Fiordland
Mirror Lakes
Avenue of the Disappearing Mountain
Remarkables
Cromwell
Murchison Mts
Lake Te Anau
Lake Wakatipu
Clyde
Secretary Island
1879
Mt Irene
Doubtful Sound
Te Anau Glow Worm Caves
Te Anau Downs
Eyre Mountains
Alexandra
Kingston
Garvie Mountains
National
Kepler Track
Te Anau
page 224
Athol
Roxburgh
Deep Cove
West Arm Underground Power Station
Te Anau Wildlife Centre
Manapouri
Lake Manapouri
Five Rivers
Breaksea Sound
Resolution Island
Park
Waiau
Redcliff Wetland Reserve
Mossburn
Waikaia
Lumsden
Southland
Monowai
Blackmount
Dusky Sound
Southland
Riversdale
Waikaka
Lake Monowai
Otahu Flat
Dipton
Mandeville
Tapanui
Cameron Mountains
Aparima
Oreti
Hokonui Hills
Cape Providence
Clifden
Wreys Bush
Gore
Chalky Inlet
Lake Hauroko
Lake Poteriteri
Winton
Tuatapere
Otautau
Hump Ridge Track
Te Waewae
Orepuki
Edendale
Mataura
Catlins
Mt Pye
720
Bay
Colac Bay
Riverton
Pahia Point
The Rocks
Forest
Invercargill
Oreti Beach
Park
Tokanui
Chaseland
Foveaux
Bluff
Tiwai Point
Fortrose
Waipapa Point
Waikawa
Curio Bay Fossil Forest
Black Rock Point
Strait
Codfish Island
Mt Anglem
980
Ruapuke Island
Acker's Cottage
Mason Bay
Paterson Inlet
Oban
Ulva Island
Doughboy Bay
Rakiura
National Park
Mt Allen
750
Stewart Island
Muttonbird Islands
Big South Cape Island
Southwest Cape
Snares Group

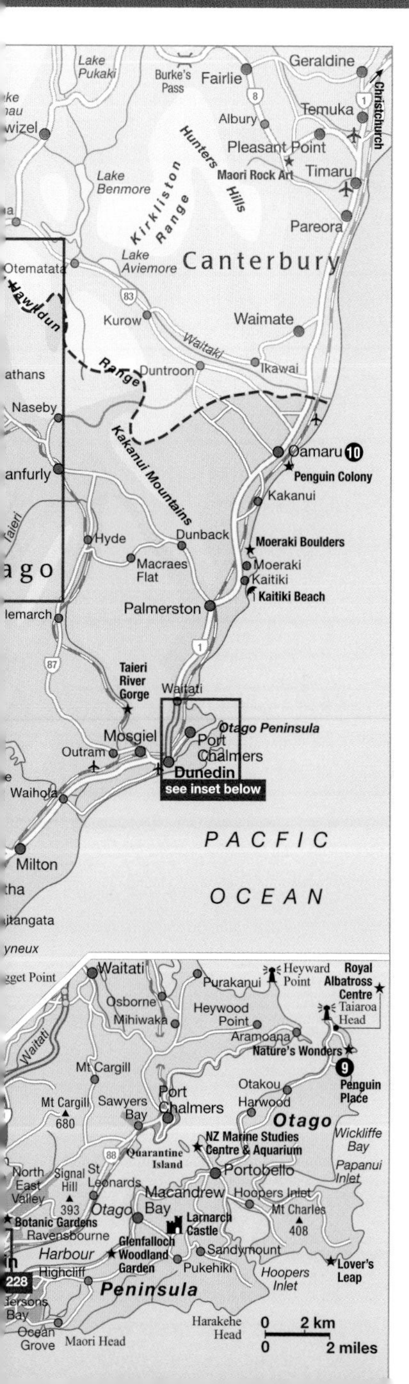

worthwhile. Another highlight is the 'tuatarium' where visitors can observe tuatara lizards, last survivors of the dinosaur era, roaming at leisure in a large, natural sanctuary.

Bluff

About 27km (17 miles) south of Invercargill at land's end is **Bluff ⓮**, an important port town. Large vessels tie up here and workers toil around the clock loading hundreds of thousands of frozen carcasses of lamb and mutton for export to markets across the globe. Aside from its busy port area, Bluff is famous, above all, for the plump oysters from the **Foveaux Strait**, the 35km (22-mile) stretch of water that separates Stewart Island from the mainland. Unique to New Zealand, this shellfish is not exported as the local market takes the full quota. The oyster season runs from March to August, with the highlight being the hugely popular annual **Bluff Oyster and Southland Seafood Festival** in April. To explore the workings of an oyster harvesting boat visit **Bluff Maritime Museum** (Mon–Fri 10am–4.30pm, Sat–Sun 1–5pm; charge) on Foreshore Road.

Gore

Northeast of Invercargill is **Gore ⓯**, the 'Trout Capital of the World', where the **Mataura River** teems with brown trout. Within an hour's drive, a number of other rivers can be explored with experienced local fishing guides. Other attractions in town include the **Hokonui Moonshine Museum** (Mon–Fri 8.30am–5pm, Sat–Sun 11am–4pm; charge), which celebrates the town's 130-year history of illicit whisky making, and the **Eastern Southland Art Gallery** (Mon–Fri 10am–4.30pm, Sat–Sun 1–4pm; free), where world-class Australian Aboriginal, African, and contemporary American art, plus works by New Zealand artists including Ralph Hotere, Rita Angus and Theo Schoon, can be seen.

For a bird's-eye view of Southland, make for the old Mandeville Airfield, a 10-minute drive northwest of Gore, where the **Croydon Aircraft Company** (tel: 03-208 9755) restores and flies vintage aircraft. Experienced pilots take passengers on scenic flights in the old de Havilland planes. Take-off and landing is cup-of-tea smooth and there's the option to loop the loop.

South Coast Towns

Invercargill may be flat, but westward lie the distant mountains that border Fiordland. This vast natural area can be reached in less than two hours, travelling across the central Southland plains via **Winton** through prime farmland, carrying several million head of stock. For those with more time, the coastal road from Invercargill to the mountains following SH99 – the western section of the Southern Scenic Route – makes for a more interesting drive. The historic town of **Riverton** ⓰, with its tranquil estuary and fishing port, was a key supply base for whalers and sealers in the 1800s, decades before Europeans settled elsewhere. Across the bridge the sandy shores of **Riverton Rocks** offer excellent swimming and fishing. A further 10km (6 miles) west is **Colac Bay**. Once a Maori settlement, it grew into a town with a population of 6,000 during the gold-rush days of the 1890s, and is now a popular surfing spot. A short drive away, a side trip leads to the salt-encrusted holiday cribs of **Cosy Nook** clinging limpet-like to a boulder-strewn shoreline. Next stop

Riverton Rocks

Clifden Suspension Bridge

on the SH99 is **Orepuki**, where you can search in the sands for hidden gems like garnets, jasper and quartz.

Tuatapere

Beyond Orepuki, the SH99 offers fine views of **Te Waewae Bay**, where Hector's dolphins and southern right whales are often seen, and of the rainforest-smothered mountains bordering the Fiordland National Park. Huddled beside the Waiau River is the old milling township of **Tuatapere** ⓱. In the heart of town stands the original **Waiau Hotel**, which serves tasty good-value meals and displays photos of the town's early days. Here you can visit **Waiau Downs Farm** (1609 Tuatapere-Orepuki Road Tuatapere; tel: 03-226 6622; charge 👪) for four-wheel-drive farm tours, demonstrations of shearing sheep, mustering dogs, milking cows and feeding lambs, plus the chance to ride on a horse or donkey, or shear your own sheep.

Tuatapere is also the starting point of New Zealand's newest walk, the **Humpridge Track** *(see p.26)*. Created and built by locals, the 53km (33-mile) track (a three-day circuit) meanders from sea to tundra, along an Alpine ridge and across Maori country, crossing the largest wooden viaduct in the world.

Te Anau and Fiordland

Wild waterfalls, forested valleys, granite peaks and crystal-clear lakes all clamour for attention along the edge of the Fiordland National Park; a fittingly inspiring journey to an unforgettable destination. Maori legends tell of the master carver who crafted these lakes and fiords with his adze, beginning in the south and working his way up the coastline to Milford Sound, his pièce de résistance.

Lake Hauroko

From Tuatapere, the road heads inland 12km (8 miles) to **Clifden**, notable for the nearby **Clifden Suspension Bridge** (built in 1899) and the spooky **Clifden Caves**. The caves can be explored without a guide, but make sure you have a good torch and follow the signposted instructions. From Clifden, a 30km (19-mile) unsealed side trip leads to New Zealand's deepest lake, **Lake Hauroko** ⓲, set amongst dense bush and steep slopes. The DOC campsite has an enviable location on a sandy beach

FARM LIFE

Farming, a way of life valued by close-knit rural communities throughout New Zealand, forms the backbone of the nation's economy. Amongst these smaller towns and villages visitors will find the warmth, friendly neighbourhood security and community spirit that once set the tone for the nation as a whole. There are many ways to experience the farming lifestyle, from farm stays and 'wwoof-ing' experiences through to sheep, beef and dairy farming demonstrations, and horticultural tours.

Farm stays are an ideal way to experience the farming lifestyle first-hand. Visitors stay in the rural homes of friendly New Zealanders and enjoy meals with the family. Accommodation is generally in the hosts' own home, or in separate private cottages, and guests are encouraged to roll up their sleeves and help with chores as part of the experience. Depending on what is happening on the farm at the time, this may include feeding the cows, pitching hay, mustering, dog handling and training, or even sheep shearing. Alternatively, you can simply soak up the wide-open spaces, and enjoy the peace and quiet.

If you are travelling on a budget you can also enjoy a farm stay by working for your keep as a Willing Worker on Organic Farms (WWOOF). WWOOF New Zealand (www.wwoof.co.nz)

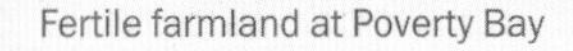

Fertile farmland at Poverty Bay

provides volunteers with the opportunity to live on a wide range of organic properties and learn about biodynamics, permaculture, urban organics, and alternative building and energy methods. It's an enjoyable and educational way to get to know New Zealanders, but it requires some forward planning as you can't just turn up on the doorstep. There is a wide range of organic farms to choose from – some are entirely self-sufficient – including sheep, cattle and deer farms, medicinal herb farms, and market gardens. Most ask for five half days of work per week in exchange for food and lodging. It is usually possible to negotiate flexible hours so that you have time to explore the area. WWOOF volunteers live on the property and gain hands-on experience with sustainable practices including companion planting, worm farming, composting, cooking and preserving, making wine or beer, cheese and bread making, and crafts. *For more information on 'Wwoofing' and farmstays, see p.260.*

A less intensive way to discover more about farming practices in New Zealand is to go on an agricultural tour or take in a farming show. These are available nationwide and popular experiences include the Agrodome in Rotorua *(see p.124)*, Waiau Downs Farm Adventures in Southland *(see p.245)*, SheepWorld in Auckland (www.sheepworld.co.nz), Kiwi 360 in Te Puke *(see p.110)* and the Feilding Stock Saleyard Tour *(see p.143)* to see the busiest yards in the southern hemisphere.

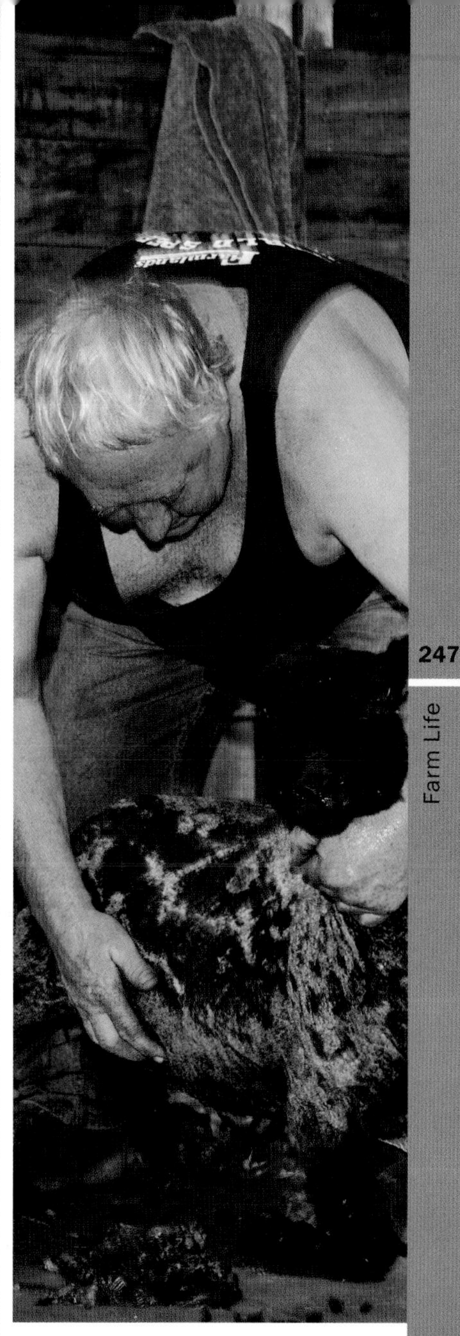

Sheep shearing in Hawke's Bay

fringed with beech forest, and the **Hump Ridge Jet** provides thrilling tours of the Wairaurahiri River. Hikers can organise a water taxi to the beginning of the **Dusky Track**, which journeys through Fiordland National Park to Supper Cove Hut in Dusky Sound.

Lake Manapouri and Doubtful Sound

Continuing north from Clifden, another side trip leads to the peaceful shores of **Lake Monowai**, where a DOC campsite offers a sheltered forest base for fisherfolk, hunters and trampers. Further north, **Lake Manapouri** is more populated, and its mirrored waters clearly reflect the snowcapped Hunter Mountains, Turret Range, and Cathedral and Jackson Peaks. Manapouri is the gateway to the deafening silence of **Doubtful Sound**, the deepest of Fiordland's sounds. Trips with **Real Journeys** depart daily from Pearl Harbour. The tours also a include a visit through the machinery hall of the massive **Manapouri Underground Power Station** located 200m (660ft) underground.

Te Anau Glow-worm Caves

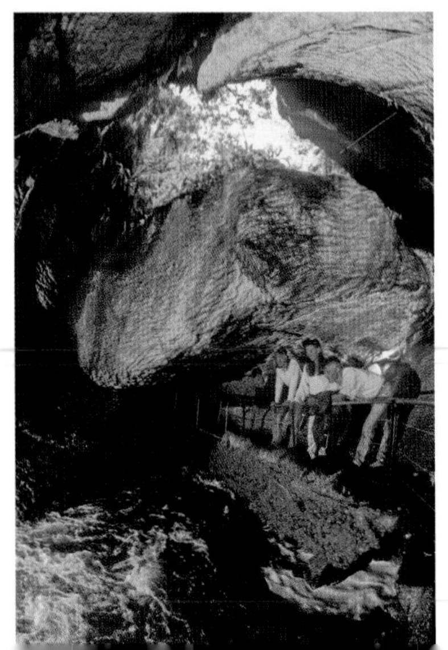

The Legend of the Lake

According to Maori legend, Lake Te Anau was created when local Maori chief Te Horo found a sacred spring. He asked his wife not to reveal its existence to anyone, but after he had departed on a journey, she nonetheless showed it to her lover. As soon as his face reflected in its waters, a torrent drowned the village and formed the lake.

Te Anau

At the hub of Fiordland's wilderness areas is **Te Anau** ⓳, which has a range of accommodation to suit all budgets. Scenic cruises with Real Journeys depart from the town wharf and visit the **Te Anau Glow-worm Caves** on the western shores of Lake Te Anau, where beech trees grow down to the waterline. The caves, believed to have been known to early Maori explorers, were rediscovered in 1948, and feature whirlpools, waterfalls and a glowworm grotto. The rare takahe makes its home in the Alpine tussock grasslands of the **Murchison Mountains** behind the caves, and these, along with other rare birds, can be seen at DOC's **Te Anau Wildlife Centre** (daily 24 hours; www.doc.govt.nz), on the lake shore.

Several short walks and hikes depart from Te Anau, including the **Kepler Track** *(see p.26)*. The full circuit takes

View from Milford Sound towards Mitre Peak

four days, but sections of it can be walked on organised day hikes.

Milford Road

Whether you choose to self-drive, join a tour, or hike in via the Milford Track *(see p.26)*, the journey to Milford Sound is spectacular. Those driving will discover lots of scenic highlights along the way including the **Mirror Lakes**, which offer perfect reflections of mountain scenery on a fine day, the **Avenue of the Disappearing Mountain**, where the mountain appears to shrink while driving towards it, and the **Homer Tunnel** ⓴. Work on this 1,240m (4,118ft) -long unlined tunnel, hewn from solid rock, began in 1935 as an employment project for five men who lived in tents and used only picks, shovels and wheelbarrows. It was completed in 1954, but not before avalanches had claimed the lives of three of the men.

From the Milford side, the road drops 690m (2,264ft) in 10km (6 miles) between sheer mountain faces to emerge in the **Cleddau Valley**, with its awe-inspiring **Chasm Walk**, a short stroll to a series of steep falls formed by the plunging Cleddau River. Back on the road, it's another 10km (6 miles) to the head of **Milford Sound** ㉑, where the iconic Mitre Peak rises in a ceremonial welcome.

Milford Sound

Cruises on the Sound depart regularly and can be booked at the wharf through Southern Discoveries or Real Journeys; a more energetic option is to join a kayak tour. However you choose to explore, highlights include **Mitre Peak**'s three-pointed glaciated slab which rises 1,692m (5,551ft) high from the Sound, the **Lady Bowen Falls**, which tumble 161m (528ft) from a hanging valley, and spotting bottlenose dolphins, fur seals and Fiordland crested penguins near Seal Rock. There is also the option to disembark at **Harrison Cove's Underwater Observatory** to peek below the shallow top layer of fresh water to spy on deepwater species and corals.

Back at base, the **Bowen Falls Track** is a good short walk. For comfort, pack a waterproof jacket, wear long trousers and cover yourself liberally with insect repellent before leaving your vehicle.

Stewart Island

Little known, even to New Zealanders, the country's 'third island' is a safe haven for many kinds of wildlife which would otherwise struggle to survive. It has just 28km (17 miles) of sealed roads and a grand total of 450 inhabitants. A paradise for trampers and nature-lovers, it has about 245km (152 miles) of walking tracks, all accessible from Halfmoon Bay.

Oban

Centred on Half Moon Bay and Horseshoe Bay, with its charming cottages almost hidden among the trees, **Oban** ㉒ is one of the most delightful settlements in New Zealand. The hub of the town is the local watering hole, the **South Seas Hotel** on the foreshore. **Rakiura Museum** (Ayr Street; Mon–Sat 10am–noon, Sun noon–2pm; charge) has displays relating to the island's maritime history, and is a good place to learn about local wildlife. Not far east of town, **Acker's Cottage** is New Zealand's oldest surviving dwelling, built by a whaler in 1835. Other attractions include a trip on a glass-bottomed boat, snorkelling or diving, visiting aquacultural farms at Big Glory Bay, deep-sea fishing trips, and visiting

Stewart Island Transport

Ferry: Stewart Island Experience; tel: 0800-000 511; **www.stewartislandexperience.co.nz**; daily departures to Stewart Island from Bluff aboard an express catamaran. The journey takes one hour. Tickets purchased online, by phone, or at the wharf.

Flight: Stewart Island Airlines; tel: 03-218 9129; **www.stewartislandflights.com**; daily flights from Invercargill Airport.

Oban, Stewart Island's main settlement

A weka on Ulva Island

Empress Pearls, an impressive aquarium and paua-pearl culture facility.

Around Oban are many delightful shore walks, and birdlife is prolific.

Ulva Island

Well worth a visit is **Ulva Island** ㉓, about 3km (2 miles) offshore and accessed by water taxi, or kayak. The island is covered in primeval forest and in recent years has been cleared of all predators, and a number of bird species have been introduced. The most conspicuous of these is the South Island saddleback, but there are also populations of Stewart Island robins, riflemen, weka and yellowheads. Signs discourage feeding the birds; however, weka are notorious for helping themselves to an unattended lunch. Ulva is also home to *tokoeka* (Stewart Island kiwi), and because they often forage during the day due to the short nights of midsummer, there is a good chance of seeing them here.

Rakiura National Park

Stewart Island has a mere 28km (17 miles) of public roads, which are treated by local pedestrians as a conveniently wide footpath. Where the roads end, the tracks of the **Rakiura National Park** ㉔ begin. A particularly good tramp is the 29km (18-mile) -long **Rakiura Track** *(see p.31)*, which starts and ends at Oban and takes three days to complete. There are huts along the way for overnight stays. Then there's the rugged wilderness experience of the 10- to 12-day **North West Circuit**, a 125km (78-mile) loop track; and lots of shorter walks which provide a taste of the natural qualities that have made Stewart Island a national treasure.

Island Birdlife

The waters around Stewart Island offer some of the best opportunities in the world for viewing sea birds. Over half the world's known albatrosses and mollymawks frequent the coastal waters here, and Acker's Point, 3km (2 miles) to the east of Oban, is a good place to spot them. In the evening, blue penguins call to each other as they float in rafts (groups) just offshore, waiting until it is dark before coming ashore to their burrows. During the summer breeding season, the sooty shearwater, or *titi*, nests in burrows here. Sooty shearwaters are generally known as mutton birds – the taste of their meat has a fishy mutton flavour. For the curious, the South Seas Hotel in Oban sometimes features them on its menu.

ACCOMMODATION

The regions of Southland and Stewart Island are renowned for their southern hospitality and here you will find New Zealand's most welcoming hosts whether you're camping, backpacking or staying in a luxury hotel or B&B. Te Anau, the hub of the magnificent Fiordland wilderness, has many hotels, motels and lodges to choose from.

Accommodation Price Categories

Prices are for one night's accommodation in a standard double room (unless otherwise specified).

$ = below NZ$30
$$ = NZ$30–75
$$$ = NZ$75–150
$$$$ = NZ$150–350
$$$$$ = over NZ$350

Invercargill and South Coast

Beersheba
58 Milton Park Road, Invercargill
Tel: 03-216 3677
www.beersheba.co.nz
Southern hospitality at its best. B&B guest rooms and a separate cottage set in 4 hectares (11 acres) of woodland gardens. **$$$–$$$$**

Hokonui Homestay
258 Reaby Road, RD4, Gore
Tel: 03-208 4890
www.bnb.co.nz/hokonuihomestay.html
Warm and inviting suites on a large rural property. Entertaining hosts. **$$–$$$**

Oraka Seaviews
16 Bungalow Hill Rd, Colac Bay
Tel: 03-234 9005
www.orakaseaviews.co.nz
Two self-contained cottages with sea views on a peaceful dairy farm at Colac Bay. **$$$**

Victoria Railway Hotel
3 Leven Street, Invercargill
Tel: 03-218 1281
www.hotelinvercargill.com
Cosy family-owned hotel in a beautifully restored historic building. **$$$–$$$$**

Waiau Hotel
47 Main Street, Tuatapere
Tel: 03-226 6409
www.waiauhotel.co.nz
Old-fashioned Southern country pub, where the locals are proud to welcome you into the fold. Tariff includes a cooked breakfast. **$$**

Te Anau and Fiordland

Lakeside Motel
36 Lakefront Drive, Te Anau
Tel: 03-249 7435
www.lakesideteanau.co.nz
Central motel with self-contained units, some with lake views. **$$$–$$$$**

Milford Sound Lodge
SH94, Milford Sound
Tel: 03-249 8071
www.milfordlodge.com
Accommodation ranges from campsites and dorm rooms, right through to brand-new riverside chalets. **$–$$$$**

Te Anau Hotel and Villas
Lakefront Drive, Te Anau
Tel: 03-249 7947
www.distinctionluxmore.co.nz
A range of rooms including deluxe suites and garden villas with spectacular lake and mountain views. Pool, spa and sauna. **$$$$$**

Stewart Island

Greenvale Bed & Breakfast
Kaka Ridge Road, Halfmoon Bay
Tel: 03-219 1357
www.greenvalestewartisland.co.nz
Small B&B offering two individually designed rooms with en-suite bathrooms. **$$$$**

Sails Ashore Luxury B&B
Halfmoon Bay, Oban
Tel: 03-219 1151
www.sailsashore.co.nz
Luxury boutique bed and breakfast with stunning views of Halfmoon Bay. **$$$$$**

South Seas Hotel
Foreshore, Halfmoon Bay
Tel: 03-219 1059
www.stewart-island.co.nz
A friendly country-style hotel with traditional hotel rooms and studio units. **$$–$$$**

Stewart Island Backpackers
Ayr Street, Oban
Tel: 03-219 1114
www.stewart-island.co.nz/backpackers.htm
Dorm, family, single and double rooms. Camping is also available here. **$**

RESTAURANTS

Blue cod and oysters are the region's speciality and once sampled you will hunger for more! Other Maori delicacies like mutton-bird can also be sampled in some parts.

Restaurant Price Categories

Prices are for a standard meal for one.

$ = below NZ$15
$$ = NZ$15–30
$$$ = NZ$30–50
$$$$ = over NZ$50

Invercargill and South Coast

The Cabbage Tree
379 Dunns Road, Otatara
Tel: 03-213 1443
www.thecabbagetree.com
A European-inspired restaurant and wine bar with delicious local seafood. **$$$**

Paddington Arms
220 Bainfield Road, Invercargill
Tel: 03-215 8156
Housed in a rambling old villa, this restaurant specialises in seafood but also caters amply to meat eaters. **$$–$$$**

The Pavilion
Seafront, Colac Bay
Tel: 03-234 8445
Fresh local fare including Colac Bay paua, Southland lamb, blue cod and chips, and Stewart Island salmon served from its beachfront location. **$$**

Te Anau and Fiordland

Blue Duck Cafe
SH94, Milford Sound
Tel: 03-249 7931
Café fare by day, pub-style fare by night. Great water views. **$–$$**

Olive Tree Cafe
52 Town Centre, Te Anau
Tel: 03-249 8496
Light meals, coffee and cake. **$**

Redcliff Cafe
12 Mokonui Street, Te Anau
Tel: 03-249 7431
A wide range of inspired New Zealand dishes, in a quaint cottage setting. **$$$–$$$$**

ENTERTAINMENT AND NIGHTLIFE

As the largest settlement in Southland, Invercargill has the most to offer in the way of nightlife; elsewhere head to the local pub, or join locals or a tour to spot kiwis.

Nightlife

Saints and Sinners
34 Dee Street, Invercargill
Tel: 03-214 4666
Prime live music venue.

Uncle Louie's Disco Bar
25 Tay Street, Invercargill
Tel: 03-214 4666
Pool hall and bar with disco Thur–Sat from 10pm.

Film

Fiordland Cinema
7 The Lane, Te Anau
Tel: 03-249 8844
www.fiordlandcinema.co.nz
Screens the stunning 30-minute locally produced film *Ata Whenua – Shadowland*, an unforgettable journey through Fiordland.

Theatre

Centrestage Theatre
33 Don Street, Invercargill
Tel: 03-218 4440
Home of the Invercargill Musical Theatre Company which stages frequent musical performances. Past productions include *Cabaret* and *Oliver*.

Te Anau Community Events Centre
20 Luxmore Drive, Te Anau
Tel: 03-249 7404
www.fiordlandcommunitycentre.co.nz
Community events centre where any local or visiting performances are staged.

SPORTS AND ACTIVITIES

Southland offers a wide range of activities in the great outdoors, most of which centre on and around the Fiordland National Park. Kayaking, is particularly popular in this region, while Stewart Island offers superb birdwatching.

Caving

Te Anau Glow-worm Caves
Lakefront Drive, Te Anau
Tel: 03-249 7416
www.realjourneys.co.nz
Guided tours of the Glow-worm Caves.

Fishing

B&B Sports
Main Street, Gore
Tel: 03-208 0801
Fishing trips on the Mataura River, where there are record numbers of brown trout.

Jet-boating

Hump Ridge Jet
17 Main Street, Otautau
Tel: 03-225 8174
www.wildernessjet.co.nz
Exhilarating jet-boating on the rock-strewn rapids of the Wairaurahiri River.

Kayaking

Adventure Kayak & Cruise
33 Waiau Street, Manapouri
Tel: 03-249 6626
www.fiordlandadventure.co.nz
Lake- and sea-kayaking on Lake Manapouri and Doubtful Sound with a local operator.

Fiordland Wildness Experiences
Milford Wharf, Milford Sound
Tel: 03-249 7700
www.fiordlandseakayak.co.nz
Four- to five-hour sea-kayak trips exploring Milford Sound and Doubtful Sound.

Rakiura Kayaks
Main Road, Oban, Stewart Island
Tel: 03-219 1160
www.rakiura.co.nz
Day- and multi-day trips on Stewart Island.

Ruggedy Range
Corner Main Road and Dundee Street, Oban, Stewart Island
Tel: 03-219 1066
www.ruggedyrange.com
Day- and multi-day kayaking trips.

Gore is a centre for trout fishing

TOURS

The most popular tours in the Southland region are scenic boat tours of its spectacular fiords – captivating Milford Sound and the eerily silent Doubtful Sound.

Boat Trips

Real Journeys Doubtful Sound Cruise
Lakefront Drive, Te Anau
Tel: 03-249 7416
www.realjourneys.co.nz
Day excursion/cruise to Doubtful Sound including a visit to the Manapouri Underground Power Station.

Real Journeys Milford Sound Tour and Cruise
Lakefront Drive, Te Anau
Tel: 03-249 7416
www.realjourneys.co.nz
Cruises on Milford Sound. Trips include bus journey to the Sound.

Southern Discoveries
Milford Wharf, Milford Sound
Tel: 03-441 1137
www.southerndiscoveries.co.nz
Departing from Milford Wharf, Southern Discoveries offer cruises of Milford Sound.

Underwater Explorer Cruises
Main Wharf, Stewart Island
Tel: 03-219 1134
www.stewartislandexperience.co.nz
Semi-submersible glass-bottom boat tours of sheltered Halfmoon Bay to see a range of marine life.

Doubtful Sound

Walking Tours

Kiwi Wilderness Walks
31 Orawia Road, Tuatapere
Tel: 021 359 592
www.nzwalk.com
Guided walks led by experienced New Zealand tramping guides.

Ultimate Hikes
Duke Street, Queenstown
Tel: 03-450 1940
www.ultimatehikes.co.nz
Guided hikes of the 53.5km (33-mile) Milford Track and other popular treks.

Ulva's Guided Walks
Tel: 03-219 1216
www.ulva.co.nz
Guided walks of Ulva Island with informative commentary on local legends, the traditional uses of flora and fauna, and rare birdlife.

FESTIVALS AND EVENTS

Southland's major event is its annual **Bluff Oyster and Southland Seafood Festival** (www.bluffoysterfest.co.nz), held in May. It's the highlight of the oyster season which runs from March to August and is a time when locals take part in a range of activities including oyster opening and eating competitions, and fashion design competitions using oyster sacks.

PRACTICAL ADVICE

Accommodation

New Zealand offers a wide range of accommodation options to suit all budgets, from low-cost campsites to high-end luxury lodges. The high season runs from December through to March and booking ahead is recommended during this period. If you are planning to visit New Zealand in January, it is essential to book accommodation prior to your arrival, as this is when New Zealanders are on holiday and prime holiday resorts fill fast. The shoulder seasons (Mar–May and Sept–Nov) offer good value and accommodation discounts apply. The low season (June–Oct) is the cheapest time to travel accommodation-wise, though prices remain high at resort towns with ski fields.

The New Zealand tourism industry uses the independent 'Qualmark' as a classification and grading system to help you find the best accommodation, shopping and activities to suit your needs. There are five levels of grading used in the system, from one star (minimum) to five stars (best available). Participation in the Qualmark system is voluntary, so if a motel or hotel doesn't have a grading, its location and tariffs will usually give a reliable indication of what to expect. You should expect to pay surcharges for additional occupants and peak season. The best way to book a room is directly, online, once you have arrived in New Zealand, through the official visitor information network, i-Site (www.newzealand.com/travel/i-sites).

HOTELS AND MOTELS

International-standard hotels are found in all large cities, in many provincial cities, and in all resort areas frequented by tourists. In smaller cities and towns, more modest hotels are the norm. Hotels range from larger central city hotels that provide full conference and recreation facilities to smaller boutique hotels. Most offer at least one licensed bar and restaurant with facilities to charge back to your room.

Motels (also commonly known as motor lodges and motor inns) are generally clean and comfortable, with self-catering kitchen facilities and in-room bathroom – ideal for families. Some motel units are able to accommodate up to six people, although most cater for two adults or a family of four. Studio motel units provide accommodation in a single room and are ideally suited for one to two people.

Lodges, such as Huka Lodge near Taupo, are a good option for longer stays

Accommodation Listings	Page
Auckland	79
Northland	94
Waikato/Bay of Plenty/East Cape	114
Rotorua/Central Plateau	131
Taranaki/Hawke's Bay	150
Wellington	165
Marlborough/Nelson/Tasman	182
Christchurch/Canterbury	202
West Coast	216
Otago	233
Southland/Stewart Island	252

Mixed dormitory in a youth hostel

BUDGET ACCOMMODATION

Budget accommodation in New Zealand includes backpacker and youth hostel accommodation which provides a mixture of shared accommodation from dormitory rooms through to double and twin rooms. Most backpackers and hostels also have a limited number of single rooms. Some provide linen, or it is available for hire. The bathroom, toilet, living room, dining room and kitchen facilities are shared. Shared rooms range from NZ$22–40 per bed per night, and double or twin rooms range from NZ$50–80 per room per night.

Youth hostels

The Youth Hostel Association of New Zealand offers an extensive chain of hostels to members throughout New Zealand. Details of membership and hostel locations can be obtained from its National Office at Level 1, 166 Moorhouse Avenue, PO Box 436, Christchurch; tel: 03-379 9970; www.yha.co.nz. BBH – World Traveller Accommodation also has a wide network of independent New Zealand-owned backpacker accommodation and provides discounts for its members when they purchase a Club Card. The card provides preferential rates – typically NZ$3–8 discount per night – cheap phone calls and discounts on rental cars and coach services. Details of membership and hostel locations can be obtained from its headquarters at 208 Kilmore Street, Christchurch; tel: 03-379 3014; www.bbh.co.nz.

Cabin accommodation

Cabin accommodation (NZ$40–60 per room per night) provides an alternative low budget form of accommodation and is available at many campsites and holiday parks. In its simplest form cabin accommodation consists of a bed in a room and guests are required to make use of the campsite's communal facilities. You may use your own sleeping bags or hire linen if required.

WWOOF-ing

Working farmstays are another option for those on limited budgets. The Willing Workers On Organic Farms (WWOOF) is a voluntary scheme. Participants from organic farms nationwide offer free accommodation and meals in exchange for four hours of work a day. Volunteers live with families and get hands-on experience with a wide range of organic and sustainable practices. No money changes hands – it's an educational and cultural exchange. Anybody aged 16 years of age or over can apply and the only prerequisite is a positive attitude. *See also pp. 246–7.*

Details of membership (NZ$40 for 14 months) and farm locations can be obtained from PO Box 1172, Nelson; tel: 03-544 9890; www.wwoof.co.nz.

OTHER ACCOMMODATION

Bed and Breakfast

B&Bs offer homely accommodation and, as an increasing number of New Zealanders are opening their homes to visitors, they are the perfect choice for those who wish to discover more about the Kiwi lifestyle. There is a wide choice of bed and breakfast accommodation in cities, towns, coastal and rural locations, from historic and heritage buildings to boutique inns and bungalows. Prices range from NZ$50–300 per room per night. The Bed and Breakfast book (online and print) provides an excellent search service and you can book direct with your hosts. Further details can be obtained from PO Box 6843, Wellington; tel: 04-385 2615; www.bnb.co.nz.

Farmstays

Farmstays are an excellent way for visitors to see the real New Zealand, which has been dependent on farming since the colonial days. This type of accommodation provides a unique opportunity to experience a slice of life in New Zealand's rural towns and on isolated high-country stations. Although guests have their own rooms, usually with an en suite or private bathroom, they share home-cooked meals with their hosts and can take part in sheep shearing, lambing, milking cows, working dogs and moving stock, or harvesting produce – whatever is happening on the farm at the time. Depending on the quality of the accommodation, farmstay visits range in price from NZ$80–350 per room per night.

The following companies provide further information and assistance to book farmstays: Rural Tours NZ, PO Box 228, Cambridge, North Island; tel: 07-827 8055; www.ruraltourism.co.nz; and Rural Holidays New Zealand, PO Box 2155, Christchurch 8140; tel: 03-355 6218; www.ruralholidays.co.nz.

Cottages and lodges

For longer stays in a coastal or rural region, rental accommodation is a good option. Simple self-contained cottages range from NZ$150–400 per night, while more up-market lodges offer the finest facilities, activities and standard of service to be found in New Zealand. Prices range from $500–3,000+ per room per night.

Further details can be obtained by visiting www.lodgesofnz.co.nz.

CAMPING AND CAMPERVANNING

Camping, caravanning and motorhoming is hugely popular in New Zealand and is an extension of New Zealanders' passion for the outdoors. October through to May offers the best conditions. Although, as yet, freedom camping (that is, camping in public places) has not been banned by all councils, care must be taken of New Zealand's environment; up-to-date information can be found at www.camping.org.nz.

Particularly good camping and campervan sites can be found in Department of Conservation (DOC) camps throughout New Zealand. Although facilities are fairly basic, with toilets (often long-drop or composting), cold showers (or solar heated) and drinking water only, locations are top-notch – many within National Parks, forest parks and scenic reserves. Prices begin at NZ$7 per person per night. For further information (including locations) visit www.doc.govt.nz.

Campsites and Holiday Parks provide facilities for campers and campervan travellers. All properties provide communal kitchens, toilets, showers and laundry facilities. The majority offer additional features which may include games rooms, children's playgrounds, swimming or spa pools, and dump stations (waste water disposal). Some also offer huts, dorm rooms, cabins or tourist flats. Most are in scenic and convenient locations. Prices for a tent pitch begin at NZ$10 and prices for a powered motorhome site start at NZ$30.

For a complete listing of registered Holiday Parks visit www.holidayparks.co.nz. For further information on Holiday Park umbrella groups which provide discount cards for multiple stays, visit www.familyparks.co.nz and www.top10holidayparks.co.nz.

Reputable companies to hire vehicles from include KEA Campers; tel: 0800-520 052; www.keacampers.co.nz; or Maui Motorhomes; tel: 0800-651 080; www.maui.co.nz.

Campervanning is an excellent way to take in the scenery

Transport

GETTING TO NEW ZEALAND

By Air

New Zealand has direct air links with the Pacific Islands, all major Australian cities, many Southeast Asian destinations, and cities in North America and Europe. Passengers arriving on long-haul flights should allow themselves a couple of rest days on arrival.

Most major airlines fly to New Zealand including Qantas, Emirates, Thai Airlines, Singapore Airlines and United Airlines. Air New Zealand is the national carrier.

Air New Zealand, www.airnewzealand.co.nz
Emirates, www.emirates.com
Qantas, www.qantas.co.nz
Singapore Airlines, www.singaporeair.com
Thai Airlines, www.thaiairlines.com
United Airlines, www.united.com

Direct flights are available from a number of key destinations bordering the Pacific Rim including Los Angeles (flight time 12 hours), San Francisco (13 hours), Vancouver (14 hours), Honolulu (8.5 hours), Tokyo (13.5 hours), Hong Kong (13 hours), Singapore (12 hours), Kuala Lumpur (12.5 hours), Bangkok (13 hours), and Seoul (14 hours). Direct flights are also available from Australian cities including Sydney (3 hours), Melbourne (3.5 hours), Brisbane (3.5 hours) and Cairns (5 hours), as well as several Pacific Island nations including Fiji (2.5 hours), Rarotonga (2.5 hours), Samoa (3.5 hours), Tonga (3 hours) and New Caledonia (3 hours).

As New Zealand is isolated, air travel is expensive. However, good deals are available for flying in the shoulder seasons or off-peak. Check out Air New Zealand's Grabaseat website (www.grabaseat.co.nz), as well as internet deals offered by other carriers who reward those who book well in advance. Note that a departure tax of NZ$25 (NZ$10 for children under 12) is payable on leaving New Zealand.

More than 99 percent of the 2.5 million tourists who visit New Zealand each year arrive by air

International airports within New Zealand include:

Auckland International Airport (**AKL**; tel: 09-275 0789; www.auckland-airport.co.nz) at Mangere, 24km (15 miles) southwest of downtown Auckland. International, domestic and scheduled and chartered flights operate in and out of Auckland International Airport.

Christchurch International Airport (**CHC**; tel: 03-358 5029; www.christchurch-airport.co.nz) in Harewood, 12km (7.5 miles) northwest of the CBD. International, domestic and scheduled and chartered flights operate in and out of Christchurch International Airport.

Hamilton Airport (**HLZ**; tel: 07-848 9027; www.hamiltonairport.co.nz) is located on Airport Road, 14km (8.5 miles) from Hamilton city centre. The airport services international flights arriving into New Zealand from Australia, and domestic flights.

Queenstown Airport (**QTN**; tel: 03-450 9031; www.queenstownairport.co.nz). Direct flights to and from Australia and domestic flights land and take off from this airport located 8km (5 miles) northeast of the town centre.

Wellington Airport (**WLG**; tel: 04-385 5100; www.wellington-airport.co.nz) has restricted access for most wide-bodied aircraft types because of the runway length so it only services international flights arriving into New Zealand from Australia and Pacific Island nations, and domestic flights. The airport is located on Stewart Duff Drive, 5.5km (3.5 miles) southeast of Wellington's Central Business District.

Transport Fact Files	Page
For detailed transport information relating to each major city, refer to the following pages:	
Auckland	*67*
Wellington	*157*
Christchurch	*188*

By Sea

A few cruise ships visit New Zealand, but there is no regular passenger ship service. Most cruises in the South Pacific originate in Australia, including P&O Line (tel: 0800-780 716; www.pocruises.co.nz) which regularly travels to New Zealand, mostly between November and April.

GETTING AROUND NEW ZEALAND

The best way to get around New Zealand is to hire a vehicle. However, coach services are regular and provide a good second option. Train services are extremely limited. Ferry crossings between New Zealand's two largest islands form a part of most visitors' travel plans so if you plan to rely on public transport, consider buying a travel pass that allows a combination of bus, train, ferry and plane travel nationwide at a substantial discount. One such deal is the New Zealand Travelpass from InterCity Group (NZ) Ltd (tel: 09-583 5788; www.travelpass.co.nz). The pass can be purchased online and used over 12 months. Tranz Scenic (tel: 04-495 0775; www.tranzscenic.co.nz) offers a 7-day and

14-day Scenic Rail Pass for train travel either in the North or South Island, or throughout both islands, with an optional ferry crossing.

Domestic Flights

Air New Zealand, Qantas and Virgin Blue/Pacific Blue are the main domestic carriers. Air New Zealand flies to every main centre nationwide, while Qantas and Virgin Blue/Pacific Blue provide flights between the cities of Auckland, Wellington, Christchurch and Queenstown. It takes 40 minutes to fly from Auckland to Wellington, and 1 hour to fly from Auckland to Christchurch. Wellington to Christchurch takes 30 minutes. Domestic flights can be expensive, but good deals are always available online.

Air New Zealand, tel: 0800-737 000; www.airnewzealand.co.nz
Qantas, tel: 09-357 8900; www.qantas.co.nz
Virgin Blue/Pacific Blue, tel: 0800-670 000; www.pacificblue.co.nz.

Domestic terminals within New Zealand include:

Auckland Domestic Terminal (AKL), tel: 09-275 0789; www.auckland-airport.co.nz
Christchurch Domestic Terminal (CHC), tel: 03-358 5029; www.christchurch-airport.co.nz
Dunedin Airport (DUD), tel: 03-486 2879; www.dnairport.co.nz
Hamilton Airport (HLZ), tel: 07-848 9027; www.hamiltonairport.co.nz
Hokitika Airport (HKK), tel: 03-756 8050; www.hokitikaairport.co.nz
Invercargill Airport (INV), tel: 03-214 0571; www.invercargillairport.co.nz

Entering Marlborough Sounds

Queenstown Airport (QTN), tel: 03-450 9031; www.queenstownairport.co.nz
Rotorua Airport (RTO), tel: 07-345 8800; www.rotorua-airport.co.nz
Taupo Airport (TOU), tel: 07-378 7771; www.taupoairport.co.nz
Tauranga Airport (TGA), tel: 07-575 2456; www.tauranga-airport.co.nz
Wellington Airport (WLG), tel: 04-385 5100; www.wellington-airport.co.nz
Whangarei Airport (WRE), tel: 09-436 0047; www.whangareiairport.co.nz

Ferries

Modern ferries operated by two competing companies, Interislander (tel: 04-498 3302; www.interislander.co.nz) and Bluebridge (tel: 0800-844 844; www.bluebridge.co.nz), link the North and South Islands. The ferries sail between Wellington and Picton and carry passengers, vehicles and freight. There are frequent daily crossings in both directions, but it is important to book vehicle space in advance during summer. The journey time takes about three hours depending on sea conditions. Ferry tickets can be purchased at NZ Post Shops, travel agents and visitor information centres.

A passenger ferry operated by Stewart Island Experience (tel: 0800-000 511; www.stewartislandexperience.co.nz) departs daily from Bluff, connecting Stewart Island with the South Island.

Passenger ferries (departing from the terminal behind the Ferry Building on Quay Street, Auckland) service Great Barrier Island and Waiheke Island as well as vehicular ferries. For further information on transporting your vehicle across to either island, contact SeaLink Travel Group (tel: 0800-732 546; www.sealink.co.nz).

Trains

By international standards the New Zealand rail network is extremely limited. The infrastructure is there, however rail is mainly used for freight. To travel the country completely by rail is not an option. The New Zealand government has set aside money to improve the rail network, so over time, things may change. In the meantime the following limited services are available.

Tranz Scenic (tel: 04-495 0775; www.tranzscenic.co.nz) offers three routes, one in the North Island and two in the South Island. Trains are outfitted with an onboard dining car serving light meals and beverages.

Tranz Alpine: This scenic train journey is also offered as a return one-day trip, and travels between Christchurch and Greymouth.

Tranz Coastal: This train travels along the coast and connects Christchurch with the inter-island ferries at Picton.

The Overlander: This service runs between Wellington and Auckland.

Tickets can be purchased online, and from travel agents and visitor information centres. A Scenic Rail Pass allows hop-on/hop-off travel aboard all Tranz Scenic trains.

Frequent ferry services link the North and South Islands

Intercity Coaches

There is an excellent inter-city coach network throughout the country, using modern and comfortable coaches equipped with toilets. The major bus operators are InterCity Coachlines (tel: 09-623 1503; www.intercitycoach.co.nz); the Naked Bus (tel: 0900 62533; www.nakedbus.co.nz); and Kiwi Experience (tel: 09-366 9830; www.kiwiexperience.co.nz). Travel and information centres throughout New Zealand can book bus tickets and multi-day pass tickets; alternatively, you can book online.

Cycling

If you are fit, cycling is another good way to get around New Zealand.

New Zealand's quiet roads and stunning scenery make it ideal for cycle touring

However, as the countryside is extremely mountainous, you may wish to sit some sectors out, and travel aboard a coach. Backpacker transport operators such as Kiwi Experience (tel: 09-366 9830; www.kiwiexperi ence.co.nz) can arrange bike hire and issue vouchers that allow you to transport your bike on their buses.

Bikes are hired out all over the country, and are a fantastic way to get around New Zealand's smaller towns. Ten-speed bikes and tandems can be hired for sightseeing in most cities, while resorts such as Queenstown and Taupo also rent out mountain bikes. Safety helmets are compulsory, and are included in the rental price.

The South Island's Canterbury Plains provide easy flat cycling, as does the city of Christchurch. Here bikes can be hired for NZ$15–35 a day. Alternatively, you can join multi-day guided cycle tours and your luggage with be transported by van to lodgings along the way. Cycling New Zealand (130B Montreal Street, Christchurch; tel: 03-982 2966; www.cyclingnewzealand.com) provide guided and independent cycling tours, plus excellent information on the sport. Another reputable company is Pedal Tours (45 Tarawera Terrace, Kohimarama; tel: 09-585 1338; www.pedaltours.co.nz) in Auckland, who provide cycling tours nationwide.

Driving

Touring the country by car or camper-van is one of the best ways to see New Zealand's extremely diverse landscape and on any single journey you can expect to enjoy a wealth of spectacular scenery. However, it is worth noting that some journeys travel on winding roads through hill country, and therefore the time to travel from one place to another can take a lot longer than you may expect.

Road Conditions

Multi-lane highways are very few – they only provide immediate access to and through major cities – and narrow, single-lane highways and roads are the norm. While traffic is light by European standards, the winding and narrow nature of some stretches of road means you can only go as fast as the slowest truck, so do not underestimate driving times. Main road surfaces are good and conditions are usually comfortable; the main problems you might encounter are slips, rock falls, dead possums, flocks of sheep and herds of cows, so go carefully. If you encounter animals, take your time and edge through them. Signposting is generally good.

Unleaded 91- and 96-octane petrol is sold, along with diesel, at all service stations. On most journeys you are never more than 50km (31 miles) away from the nearest station. New Zealanders, for the most part, are courteous drivers; however, watch out for their tendency to overtake on the inside lane (there is no law preventing this) and blocking what should be used as a passing lane.

Regulations

You can legally drive in New Zealand for up to 12 months if you have a current driver's licence from your home country or an International Driving Permit (IDP). You must be able to prove you hold a valid overseas licence and drive only those types of vehicles for which you were licensed in your country of origin. You must carry your licence or permit with you whenever you are driving.

Traffic keeps to the left. Drivers must yield (give way) to every vehicle approaching or crossing from their

Driving Times

NORTH ISLAND	
Auckland–Whangarei	2½ hours
Whangarei–Paihia	1 hour
Paihia–Cape Reinga	4½ hours
Auckland–Hamilton	2 hours
Hamilton–Rotorua	1½ hours
Hamilton–Whakatane	3 hours
Hamilton–New Plymouth	4½ hours
Hamilton–Taupo	2 hours
Taupo–Napier	2½ hours
Whakatane–Napier	5 hours
Taupo–Palmerston North	3½ hours
Palmerston North–Wellington	2 hours

SOUTH ISLAND	
Picton–Christchurch	5 hours
Christchurch–Greymouth	4 hours
Christchurch–Kaikoura	3 hours
Christchurch–Mount Cook	5 hours
Christchurch–Dunedin	5 hours
Mount Cook–Queenstown	4 hours
Queenstown–Invercargill	3 hours
Invercargill–Dunedin	4½ hours
Queenstown–Fox Glacier	7 hours
Fox Glacier–Greymouth	3½ hours
Greymouth–Westport	2 hours
Greymouth–Nelson	4½ hours

Driving is the best way to experience the beauty and diversity of the landscape

right. Seat belts are compulsory. Helmets are compulsory for motorcyclists and sidecar passengers. Maximum speed limits are 50kmh (30mph) in built-up areas unless otherwise indicated, 100kmh (60mph) on open roads. New Zealand's road signs follow the internationally recognised symbols.

Drink-driving penalties are tough, regardless of where you are from. Random breath tests by police are often conducted. Care should be taken not to exceed the limit of 0.8g of alcohol for each litre of blood.

Roadside Assistance

The Automobile Association (AA; tel: 0800-500 543; www.aa.co.nz) provides nationwide breakdown assistance as well as a comprehensive range of services for motorists. Reciprocal arrangements may be available for those holding membership of foreign motoring organisations.

The start of SH1, New Zealand's main highway

Vehicle Hire

To hire a vehicle, you must be 21 years of age or over and hold a current New Zealand or international driver's licence. Third-party insurance is compulsory, although most hire companies will insist on full insurance cover before hiring out their vehicles.

During the summer period from January to March it is wise to book in advance. Major international hire firms such as Avis, Hertz and Budget offer good deals for pre-booking, but better deals can be found through New Zealand-owned and operated companies. If you have not pre-booked, tourist information desks at most airports can direct you to an operator to fit your budget.

The average cost per day for rental of a mid-sized car is NZ$80–150, with competitive rates negotiable for longer periods. Campervans/motorhomes are very popular in New Zealand and are both an economical and flexible means of exploring the country. Campervans cost from NZ$90 or less per day in low season to NZ$375 for a six-berth in high season.

Apex Car Rentals, tel: 09-257 0292; www.apexrentals.co.nz
Avis, tel: 09-275 7239; www.avis.com
Budget, tel: 0800-283 438; www.budget.co.nz
Hertz, tel: 09-367 6350; www.hertz.com
KEA Campers, tel: 0800-520 052; www.keacampers.co.nz.

Accessibility

Law requires every new building or major reconstruction in New Zealand to provide 'reasonable and adequate' access for people with disabilities.

Most facilities have wheelchair access, but it pays to check when booking. Parking concessions are available for people with disabilities and temporary display cards can be issued for the length of the visitor's stay. For more information, contact Weka (tel: 06-353 5800; www.weka.net.nz), New Zealand's disability information website. Most transport operators can cater to people with special needs, although most urban transport buses are not well equipped. A few tour operators provide custom holiday packages for individual and group travellers with disabilities. Contact: Accessible Kiwi Tours, 1610 State Highway 30, RD4, Rotorua, New Zealand; tel: 07-362 7622; www.toursnz.com. Ucan Tours New Zealand Ltd, 8 Campbell Street, Sumner, Christchurch; tel: 03-326 7881; www.ucantours.com.

Health and Safety

MEDICAL CARE

No vaccinations are required to enter New Zealand and there are no endemic diseases to be aware of. New Zealand's medical and hospital facilities, both public and private, provide a high standard of treatment and care. However, visitors are charged for taxpayer funded health care so health insurance is highly recommended. To be eligible for the same health-care benefits as New Zealand residents, you must be a resident or be able to prove your eligibility with a NZ passport, residency permit, work permit for two years or more, refugee status, or proof that you are a Cook Islands-, Niue- or Tokelau-New Zealand citizen. In the case of visiting children under 18 years, the child's legal guardian must prove their resident status.

Any ineligible patient who seeks general specialist treatment at a hospital – whether it is a public or a private hospital – or any medical centre will be prioritised alongside eligible patients if there is spare capacity. The estimated cost must be paid in advance and any additional costs paid at the end of the treatment.

However, all visitors are entitled to initial, free acute (emergency) care following an accident, regardless of fault, and this is covered by the government-run Accident Compensation Scheme (ACC).

Free care is also provided by the NZ government for any visitor who has been admitted to hospital under a compulsory treatment order issued under the Tuberculosis Act, the Mental Health Act, or the Alcoholism and Drug Addiction Act.

Emergency Contacts

In an emergency dial **111** for ambulance, police or fire service, coastguard or mountain rescue. Emergency calls are free from public call boxes. Your call will be answered within 30 seconds by a person who speaks English and will be forwarded to the correct emergency services.

Always check weather conditions with the DOC before setting out on a trek

To acquire medical care for non-emergencies, full instructions for obtaining assistance are printed in the front of telephone directories. Hotels and motels normally have individual arrangements with duty doctors for guests' attention, and they can also assist in finding a dentist.

Pharmacies, or chemists, are found in most towns of a reasonable size and generally open 8.30am–5.30pm weekdays and until 12 noon on Saturdays. Some are also open for one late night a week. No single pharmacy remains open 24/7; this task is a shared responsibility and public hospitals, listed below, will advise which pharmacies are on duty on any given night. Some drugs sold over the counter in other countries may not be available without a prescription – this will involve a visit to a medical centre to obtain one.

North Island

Auckland City Hospital, 2 Park Road, Grafton; tel: 09-367 0000; www.adhb.govt.nz
Hawke's Bay Hospital, Omahu Road, Hastings; tel: 06-878 8109; www.hawkesbaydhb.govt.nz
Palmerston North Hospital, 50 Ruahine Street, Palmerston North; tel: 06-356 9169; www.midcentraldhb.govt.nz
Rotorua Hospital, corner Arawa and Pukeroa Road; tel: 07-348 1199; www.lakesdhb.govt.nz
Taranaki Base Hospital, David Street, New Plymouth; tel: 06-753 6139; www.tdhb.org.nz
Tauranga Hospital, Cameron Road; tel: 07-579 8000; www.pobdhb.govt.nz
Waikato Hospital, Pembroke Street; tel: 07-839 8899; www.waikatodhb.govt.nz
Wanganui Hospital, 100 Heads Road, Wanganui; tel: 06-348 1234; www.wdhb.org.nz
Wellington Hospital, Riddiford Street, Newton; tel: 04-385 5999; www.ccdhb.org.nz
Whangarei Hospital, Maunu Road; tel: 09-430 4100; www.northlanddhb.org.nz.

South Island

Christchurch Hospital, Riccarton Avenue; tel: 03-364 0640; www.cdhb.govt.nz
Dunedin Hospital, 20 Great King Street; tel: 03-474 0999; www.otagodhb.govt.nz
Grey Base Hospital, High Street, Greymouth; tel: 03-768 0499; www.westcoastdhb.org.nz
Nelson Hospital, Tipahi Street; tel: 03-546 1800; www.nmdhb.govt.nz
Wairau Hospital, Hospital Road, Blenheim; tel: 03-520 9999; www.nmdhb.govt.nz

Southland Hospital, Kew Road, Invercargill; tel: 03-214 7224; www.southerndhb.govt.nz.

NATURAL HAZARDS

New Zealand is noted for its high level of ultraviolet radiation and the brilliance of its light. This means you may develop severe sunburn resulting in sunstroke, even on days when there is cloud cover, or when the temperature may seem deceptively low. It is important to wear sunscreen lotions, a hat, sunglasses and protective clothing during the summer, particularly between 11am and 4pm when the sun's rays are most fierce.

There are no snakes or dangerous wild animals in New Zealand, although a bite from the native red-backed katipo spider and introduced white-tail spider may require medical attention. Sandflies and mosquitoes are prevalent in some areas, however insect repellents are widely available. As well as dispensing pharmaceuticals and medicines, chemists also sell insect and sun protections.

Apply sunscreen generously and regularly

Weather conditions can change very rapidly in New Zealand, so before setting out to explore a National Park, always check with the Department of Conservation (DOC) office and equip yourself with proper walking shoes and all-weather clothing (for more information on track safety *see p.29*).

Tap water in New Zealand is safe to drink and is of a high quality. However, it is not wise to drink untreated water from lakes and streams, or to fill up drink bottles in public toilets, as it may be plumbed from a stream. In National Parks, DOC signs will state whether water sources are safe to drink or if they require boiling first.

CRIME

New Zealand is considered to be one of the safer countries in the world for travellers and suffers only isolated incidences of serious crime. However, petty crime is a problem. Take precautions to secure and conceal your valuables at all times, and never leave them in a car. Make sure camper vans are well secured and don't leave valuable possessions on the beach while you swim.

To report a crime, contact the nearest police station where you will find police who are approachable and helpful. New Zealand police carry tazer stun guns, and the special force within the police known as the armed offenders squad, only called upon in emergencies, are heavily armed.

Drugs offences, particularly if they relate to harder drugs, are treated very seriously. Marijuana is widely available but remains illegal.

Hitchhiking alone or in isolated places is not advisable.

Money and Budgeting

High-street prices have risen in recent years

CURRENCY

The New Zealand dollar (NZ$), divided into 100 cents, is the sole unit of currency. Currency exchange facilities are available at Auckland, Wellington and Christchurch international airports, as well as most banks and bureaux de change in the larger cities and resorts.

There is no restriction on the amount of domestic or foreign currency (or traveller's cheques in New Zealand dollars) a visitor may bring into or take out of New Zealand. The New Zealand dollar is frequently called 'the kiwi' because the dollar coin features a kiwi, the national bird, on one side.

At the time of print, NZ$1 was roughly equivalent to GB£0.46; €0.52; and US$0.71.

CASH AND CARDS

The cheapest way to obtain currency is through an ATM or bank. Traveller's cheques are best changed at a bank, but are also readily accepted by most hotels. Credit cards, including Visa, American Express, Diners Club and MasterCard, are widely accepted throughout New Zealand. Banking hours are usually 9am–4.30pm Mon–Fri. Some branches open on Saturday until 12.30pm.

TIPPING

Tipping is becoming more widespread in New Zealand, particularly in restaurants, although it is still regarded as a foreign custom. In the major centres, tipping is encouraged but not expected. You should tip 5–10 percent of your restaurant bill if the service was worthy. Service charges are not added to hotel or restaurant bills.

TAX

A goods and services tax (GST) of 15 percent is applied to the cost of all goods and services and is included in all quoted and marked prices. GST is not charged on duty-free goods, on items posted by a retailer to an international visitor's home address, or on international air fares purchased in New Zealand. GST is added to accommodation, however, by law, and this is now included in the quoted price. There are no other hotel taxes or sales taxes.

BUDGETING FOR YOUR TRIP

Historically, New Zealand has always been less expensive for Europeans and North Americans, but at the time of going to press the New Zealand dollar was at a 30-year high against all major currencies, making prices a lot closer to those found in the UK/US. That said, with judicious budgeting, New Zealand can still be an economical destination.

Flights to New Zealand from the UK range from NZ$1,200 (£552; US$852) and from the US NZ$750 (£345; US$532) for an economy-class one-way ticket, through to NZ$5,000 (£2,300; US$3,550) for a first-class ticket, one-way. During the high season (December to March) the same tickets will cost an extra NZ$800–1,000 (£368–460; US$568–710) for economy-class travel, or an extra $1,000–1,500 (£460–690; US$710–1,065) for first-class travel.

For a budget, backpacker-style holiday (including transport costs) you will need to set aside NZ$500–700 (£230–322/US$355–497) per person per week. A standard family holiday for four will cost around NZ$2,000–2,300 (£920–1,058/US$1,420–1,633) per week. A luxury, no-expense-spared break can cost over $7,000–10,000 (£3,220–4,600/US$4,970–7,100) per person per week.

Budgeting Costs

Top-class lodge: NZ$500–3,000+ per person
Top-class boutique hotel: NZ$250–500 for a double room
Standard-class hotel: NZ$150–350 for a double room
Bed & breakfast: NZ$50–300 for a double room
Motel: NZ$80–200 for a double room
Youth hostel: NZ$22–40 per person
Motor camp: NZ$7–30 per person
Campsite: NZ$7–30 per person

Breakfast: NZ$8–15
Lunch in a café: NZ$7–25
Coffee/tea in a café: NZ$3.50–5
Main course, budget restaurant: NZ$12–20
Main course, moderate restaurant: NZ$25–32
Main course, expensive restaurant: NZ$35–45
Bottle of wine in a restaurant: NZ$25–150+
Beer in a pub: NZ$7–10

Domestic flight: NZ$65–120 one-way (Auckland–Christchurch)
Inter-city coach ticket: NZ$30–60 (Auckland–Rotorua)
Inter-city train ticket: NZ$39–80 (TranzCoastal Christchurch–Picton)
Car hire: NZ$80–150 per day
Camper van hire: NZ$90–375 per day
Petrol: NZ$1.80 a litre
10-minute taxi ride: NZ$20–30
Airport shuttle bus: NZ$15–35
Short bus ride: NZ$2
One-day travel pass: NZ$9–14

Museum admission: NZ$2–15
Daytrip to Cape Reinga from Paihia: NZ$118 adult, NZ$59 child, under 5 free
Kelly Tarlton's Underwater World: NZ$31.50 adult, NZ$15 child, under 3 free
Half-day ice-hiking in Franz Josef: NZ$105 adult, NZ$88 child, under 8 not permitted
Whale Watch, Kaikoura: NZ$145 adult, NZ$60 child, under 3 not permitted
Theatre/concert ticket: NZ$80–150
T-shirt from a shop: NZ$22–40
Nightclub entry: NZ$7–15

Money-saving Tips

- A number of coach companies offer passes along the routes they operate, either with unlimited stops along a fixed line or a certain number of travel days within a set time frame
- Look out for transport passes that include ferry and train journeys as these offer good value
- Discounts of up to 15 percent apply to seniors, students, backpackers and children on transport costs
- Early-bird coach fares starting from $1 are often available online
- Activity and museums discounts are offered to travelling students but you will need to ask. Acceptable identification is required such as an International Student Identity Card or International Youth Travel Card (www.isiccard.com).
- The Youth Hostel Association (www.yha.co.nz) is widely recognised in New Zealand and its members receive discounts of 10 to 25 percent on coach travel, adventure activities and shopping. Visit the website, click on membership, then on member discounts to see a sample list of savings.
- Make the most of every beach, National Park, Forest Park, scenic reserve and botanic garden as all are free to visit
- Look out for small country museums and community-run enterprises that request a gold coin *koha*/donation (a $1 or $2 coin)
- Choose adventure activities that include the cost of lunch or dinner as these are often good value
- Look out for special multi-attraction deals on offer in larger cities and key tourist destinations; the local i-Site visitor information centre will provide assistance
- Major discounts (sometimes up to half price or more) are available for children and senior citizens. Children under 5 are often free, while children under 3 years almost always are, so long as – where applicable – they are riding on your lap.

Responsible Travel

GETTING THERE

Flying is the best way to reach New Zealand, and many airlines, including British Airways, offer a voluntary passenger carbon offsetting scheme to minimise the impact of the journey. Alternatively, you can do it yourself; in the UK co2balance (www.co2balance.uk.com) offsets long-haul flight carbon emissions for £50 for one person. In the US, Terrapass (www.terrapass.com) is a reputable carbon offset firm and it costs US$17.85 to offset a return flight to New Zealand.

ECOTOURISM

New Zealand was the first nation to implement a fully integrated quality and environmental performance tourism assurance system. Known as the Qualmark Green grade, the system has three tiers: Enviro-Gold, Enviro-

Silver or Enviro-Bronze. Businesses displaying grades are sustainable with excellent eco-standards. These operators run a wide range of guided ecotourism activities within New Zealand's parklands from whale, dolphin and seal watching, through to bush walking, birdwatching, diving and sea-kayaking. Eco-accommodation options are varied.

For a list of sustainable ecotourism operators in New Zealand visit www.ecotours.co.nz.

ETHICAL TOURISM

To ensure money goes directly into local communities, opt to stay at smaller New Zealand-owned and operated accommodation rather than chain hotels. By eating locally produced food and wine, and purchasing souvenirs designed and manufactured in New Zealand (marked with a black and gold or blue, white and red sticker with a kiwi in the centre), rather than those manufactured in other countries, you can be certain that you are contributing to New Zealand's economy.

Support local producers and stock up on fresh provisions at a farmers' market

VOLUNTEERING/CHARITIES

The Department of Conservation (DOC) relies heavily on volunteers to run various environmental programmes in New Zealand. Details of upcoming volunteering programmes can be found at www.doc.govt.nz. Click on 'Getting Involved' and follow the links. To see the results of volunteer labour first-hand, visit TiriTiri Matangi Island in Auckland which provides a home to healthy populations of rare and endangered birds.

A worthy conservation cause is Operation Nest Egg, supported by the Bank of New Zealand, which operates a captive kiwi breeding programme. The project relies on the ongoing financial support of the New Zealand public; to make a donation or find out more visit www.savethekiwi.org.nz.

THINGS TO AVOID

With each new visitor arrival comes the risk of a new pest or disease entering New Zealand. Avoid bringing dirty outdoor gear or sports equipment into New Zealand and if you enjoy visiting natural areas, keep to the paths provided and take note of signposts providing guidelines on how to protect native plants and wildlife. Many ecosystems are fragile and may take years to recover from damage. For further tips on how you can help protect New Zealand's environment visit www.doc.govt.nz, click on 'Conservation' and follow the links through to 'Threats and Impacts'.

Family Holidays

PRACTICALITIES

New Zealand is well equipped to cope with the wide-ranging needs of families and provides plenty to keep children active and entertained in the great outdoors. For younger travellers, nappies and baby food are widely available at supermarkets, convenience stores and large petrol stations. However, nappy changing facilities are less common and are usually only found in large malls, and well-equipped rest rooms.

By law, children under 18kg must travel in a child seat and after that, up until eight years of age, 'booster' seats are recommended. If you are hiring a car you can request child seats – some companies provide these free of charge. While pushchairs and backpacks can be hired, the range and availability are limited, so it's best to bring your own.

ACCOMMODATION

New Zealanders love to travel so child-friendly accommodation is easy to find. Self-catering motels, apartments, holiday parks, and even some hotels provide one- and two-bedroom family suites. Apartments provide private laundry facilities, ideal when travelling with children, and motels and holiday parks have communal laundry facilities. Swimming pools, spa pools and playgrounds are common features at child-friendly accommodations. Some offer a range of board games. Kids' clubs are not that common; however, Top 10 Holiday Parks run children's programmes during the New Zealand school holidays.

Motels and other accommodation usually have a contract with a local babysitting service and can organise fully police-vetted sitters on your behalf. Expect to pay around NZ$18–25 per hour; many of the babysitters employed will be qualified nannies, so your children will be in good hands. Cots and highchairs are also widely available but should also be booked. Note that if you are travelling with twins or more than one child under two, some accommodations only have one cot, so it is essential to discuss your needs prior to your arrival.

FOOD AND DRINK

Western-style food is served in New Zealand along with a variety of ethnic foods, so child-friendly food, regardless of where you are from, is not hard to find. Most eateries welcome children and will provide a highchair; some also offer colouring-in equipment (activity

Many family-friendly accommodation options feature a swimming or spa pool

pads/paper and pens), outdoor areas, and sometimes even separate play areas. Picnic spots abound throughout New Zealand and provide a budget-friendly option for families.

ATTRACTIONS AND ACTIVITIES

Children's parks are found in every small town and at a minimum offer swings and slides, providing a chance for kids to let off steam, ready for the next leg. Outdoor playgrounds of note include Masterton's Kids Own Playground, Whangarei's Town Basin Playground, and Rotorua's Lakefront Playground. In larger cities, for a small charge, indoor playgrounds such as the franchised branches of Chipmunks and Lollipops provide children with access to bouncy castles, huge slides and adventure play. Rainbow's End in Auckland is the country's largest theme park, and Auckland, Hamilton, Wellington and Christchurch all have their own zoos. Small family-run petting zoos can be found on the outskirts of most major towns, and most towns also offer mini golf courses, mazes and nature parks of every description. Bush and beach walks abound. These range from 10–30 minutes for younger legs, through to longer hikes for the teens.

New Zealand's wealth of educational activities – thermal-pool walks, dolphin watching, glow-worm caves, farm tours and birdlife tours – is ideal for keeping young minds stimulated. The interactive exhibits at Wellington's Te Papa museum *(see p.156)* and the penguin habitat at Auckland's Kelly Tarlton's Underwater World *(see p.72)* go down well with children. Other novel

A luge ride in Queenstown, one of countless activities on offer to young thrill-seekers

activities include Puzzling World in Wanaka *(see p.226)*, and the Dannevirke Fantasy Cave *(see p.145)*, a magical grotto crammed full of scenes from nursery rhymes and fables.

Many of the adventure sports on offer have surprisingly low age limits: you can go rafting at age 3, bungy jumping at 10, tackle rapids at 13, and any age is considered suitable to swim with dolphins! Older kids (under 18) can enjoy horse riding, hot-air ballooning and even paragliding, so all young daredevils will be in their element.

As a general rule, children under 3 gain free entry to attractions, and this sometimes applies to under 5s. Most attractions offer reduced prices for older children, sometimes half-price or less. Special offers can also be found during off-peak school holiday periods (mid-April, the first half of July and early October).

SETTING THE SCENE

History

New Zealand is a young country in every respect. The North Island is still thermally active, as smouldering volcanoes, geysers and the occasional earthquake testify. While New Zealand's core landmass drifted north from the southern supercontinent of Gondwana over 100 million years ago, volcanoes have played a major part in shaping the land.

For millions of years, New Zealand was inhabited solely by plants and birds. The country's isolation kept it free of mammals, allowing flightless birds to thrive without threat of predators. The kiwi, an oval brown bird with a long curved beak, is the best known of these and has become New Zealand's national symbol. Others flourished too, like the gigantic extinct moa – taller than a man and able to kill with a single peck.

New Zealand's first incursion into the consciousness of humanity was in AD186, when the enormous volcanic explosion that created Lake Taupo in the centre of the North Island reddened skies over Rome.

New Zealand remained undiscovered until some time between AD800 and 1200. Anthropologists believe Polynesian navigators arrived by canoe in successive waves, having sailed from a Pacific home they called Hawaiki, most likely an island in the group that now forms French Polynesia.

THE MAORI

The Maori, who called their new land Aotearoa ('Land of the Long White Cloud', from its first appearance on the horizon), have their own account of creation and of the migration across the sea. Maori tradition holds that the Polynesian master navigator Kupe was the first to reach New Zealand. Finding the two large islands deserted, Kupe did not settle but returned to Hawaiki from the Hokianga, to provide directions for reaching the new land.

Maori lore also tells of the eventual 'Great Migration' to New Zealand in a fleet of large canoes. Once settled in their new land, the Maori lived mainly on birds, fish, ferns, roots and berries, cultivating taro and sweet potato *(kumara)*, sometimes supplementing their diet with human flesh.

Maori society was stratified. A few people were born into chiefly families *(rangatira)*; all others were commoners *(tutua)*. Communities lived in villages *(kainga)* or fortified settlements *(pa)*. The tribe *(iwi)*, presided over by a chief *(ariki)*, was divided into a number of smaller units *(hapu)*. Immediate authority in these sub-tribes was exercised by the elders *(kaumatua)* and *rangatira* families, whose authority was in part

Woodcarving

The New Zealand forests contained larger trees than Polynesians would previously have seen. This enabled them to build bigger-than-ever dugout canoes and resulted in a fine tradition of woodcarving.

Abel Tasman, the first European to sight New Zealand, is attacked by Maori at Massacre Bay

hereditary, and in part based on past achievement. Major issues affecting the tribe were debated in the *marae*, or village meeting place.

Warfare was an important feature of Maori life in most parts of the country. It was conducted to obtain territory abundant in food or other natural resources, to avenge insults, to obtain satisfaction from *hapu* whose members had transgressed the social code, or to resolve serious disagreements over authority. Combat was conducted hand-to-hand with spears, clubs and throwing sticks. Prisoners often ended up as slaves.

The Maori population were fiercely assertive of their ancestry and *hapu* membership. But what they shared strongly, no matter what tribe they were born to, was a deep and profound affinity with the land and its bounty.

EUROPEAN ARRIVAL

New Zealand was named by the Dutch explorer Abel Tasman, who in 1642 became the first European to sight the territory. Tasman had been sent by the Dutch East India Company to search for the great unknown southern continent, Terra Australis Incognita. Shortly after Tasman anchored off the northwest tip of the South Island, a Maori war canoe intercepted a party of his crew and there was loss of life on both sides. Tasman named the place Massacre Bay and the new country Staten Landt; the name was later changed to Nieuw Zeeland after the Dutch province of Zeeland ('Sea Land').

Over a century passed before serious exploration resumed in the region. In 1769, the English captain James Cook was dispatched to the South Seas aboard the *Endeavour*. The expedition circumnavigated New Zealand and

Captain James Cook was the first European to explore New Zealand in 1769

with brilliant accuracy made a chart of the coastline which proved reliable for more than 150 years. Many coastal sites still bear the evocative names Cook gave them. They include Doubtless Bay 'doubtless a bay', Mercury Bay, because an observation of the transit of the planet Mercury was made there, and Young Nick's Head, a prominent headland sited by a ship's boy, Nicholas Young. Overall, Cook's relations with the Maori were reasonably cordial. He admired their bravery but found them little inclined to trade. It was Cook who claimed New Zealand for Britain.

News of New Zealand's existence began to attract adventurers – traders, sealers, whalers and rampaging buccaneers – who based themselves largely around the Bay of Islands. They kidnapped Maori, broke their tribal laws and introduced disease, firearms and rum. In retaliation, Maori killed and ate the crew of two ships. Lurid reports of profligate and degenerate seamen battling heathen cannibals in the South Pacific began to circulate abroad, reaching the ears of the Reverend Samuel Marsden, a zealous clergyman and magistrate in the Australian colony of New South Wales.

MASS CONVERSIONS

Marsden set out for New Zealand as a missionary for the Anglican Church Missionary Society. His aim was to convert and 'civilise' Maori, and to save the souls of the various intemperate characters who were preying upon them.

Marsden established Church missions in New Zealand and preached the first Christian sermon on Christmas Day, 1814. Nine years passed before a single Maori converted. By this time, firearms were entering New Zealand in large numbers. Maori chiefs armed their tribes and taught them the art of musketry. Maori hostilities were directed generally not at Europeans but against each other. Guns gave chiefs new and more efficient ways of slaughtering tribal enemies. The 1820s and 1830s witnessed horrifying intertribal bloodshed.

Church influence expanded and the Maori began converting to the new religion in increasing numbers. A series of atrocities against the Maori and equally ferocious Maori reprisals helped missionaries to persuade a number of influential chiefs to ask the

British Government for protection. By 1831, fear of French annexation supplied another reason for Britain to intercede. The British appointed James Busby as 'resident', an official position similar to governor. Busby's aim was to reconcile all groups, but he failed to achieve this, and in 1838 the office was discontinued. Captain William Hobson was appointed lieutenant-governor, and British land in New Zealand was administered as a dependency of New South Wales.

Hobson drafted the Treaty of Waitangi, which was signed on 6 February 1840. In essence, the Maori ceded sovereignty to the British Crown in exchange for law and order and the rights of ownership to tribal lands. Discussion of the treaty and interpretation of its clauses continue to this day. About 50 Maori chiefs signed it initially, and by June 1840 over 450 additional signatures had been collected from outlying districts. Many chiefs may not have understood the meaning of their action.

Maori war dance

The treaty gave the British Crown sole right to buy land. Large-scale European settlement began, fostered by Edward Gibbon Wakefield, who established the New Zealand Company in Britain. Wakefield hoped to establish a utopian colony along the lines of English society, but excluding those on the lowest rung of the social ladder. The company bought land cheaply from the British Government and sold it to settlers, priced at levels that would appeal to the middle ranks of English society. Between 1839 and 1843, 19,000 British settlers headed to New Zealand under the company's auspices.

MAORI STRIKE BACK

Europeans underestimated Maori attachment to the land. Disputes over it, and other matters, led to the New Zealand Wars – about 30 years of intermittent battles between the Maori and Europeans. The British Empire did not commit significant troops to New Zealand until the early 1860s. Even without these reinforcements, troops outnumbered their Maori opponents in most battles. Skilled guerrilla fighters, the Maori fought tenaciously.

Tribal allegiances complicated matters, as some Maori occasionally sided with European forces attacking opposing tribes. The King Movement, started by a chief called Wiremu Tamihana, tried to achieve unity among the Maori by establishing a monarchy.

When the fighting ended, the Maori 'rebels' were punished by confiscation of land. The British Crown changed the rules, permitting settlers to buy land directly from the Maori, who were duped out of yet more land. The Pakeha (the Maori word for white settlers) acquired the most fertile land, and by 1892 the Maori people were largely confined to just 4.5 million hectares (11 million acres), much of it useless for farming.

The Maori population of the South Island has always been much smaller than that of the North Island, a consequence of the Maori having settled New Zealand from the north. The discovery of gold in the rivers of Otago province in 1861 triggered a gold rush. Thousands of immigrants poured into New Zealand, and gold became the country's main export. Dunedin – a Scots-dominated commercial and banking centre – grew into the country's largest town.

The boom was over by 1870, but for a brief period the Shotover was known as the 'richest river in the world'. Within a decade, foodstuffs replaced gold as New Zealand's main earner. The advent of refrigerated cargo ships made it possible to transport meat and dairy products to distant markets.

The Constitution of 1852, drafted by Governor George Grey, granted a measure of self-government with the introduction of an elected House of Representatives. Six Provincial Councils and the superintendents of the provinces were also elected directly. The British monarch remained the Head of State, and the governor, appointed by London, nominated members of the Legislative Council, who held office for life.

Gold diggers out prospecting in Otago, 1863

Richard John Seddon, much-admired prime minister who instituted liberal reforms

Only individual landholders were allowed to vote in elections held in 1855 and 1856, effectively excluding Maori, who owned their land collectively. The franchise, slightly liberalised in 1867, was later extended to all men aged 21 and over. Then, in 1893, New Zealand women became among the first in the world to gain the vote – more than a decade before the Suffragettes started campaigning for the same right in Britain.

KING DICK AT THE REINS

For more than 10 years, until his death in 1906, a benevolent liberal, Richard John Seddon, served as the country's prime minister. Familiarly known as King Dick, he made New Zealand famous as a humanitarian democracy. In addition to women's suffrage, old-age benefits and compulsory state arbitration in industrial disputes were introduced. Seddon coined the expression 'God's Own Country' to describe New Zealand.

In 1914, New Zealand entered World War I on the side of the Allies. New Zealand and Australian troops formed the Australian and New Zealand Army Corps (Anzac) to fight alongside other British Empire soldiers. On 25 April 1915, the Anzacs landed at Gallipoli, Turkey, in an ill-conceived diversionary operation that cost thousands of lives. The carnage, and Anzac heroism during the campaign, had a powerful effect on New Zealand's psyche. By the time World War I ended, almost 17,000 New Zealanders had lost their lives. Anzac Day (25 April) remains a national holiday.

FROM HUNGER TO HUMANITY

The Great Depression of the 1930s dealt a savage blow to New Zealand, a small country dependent on overseas markets. Exports fell by 40 percent in two years and the government slashed public expenditure, and unemployed men received the dole only if they took government-organised work.

When the Labour Party took power in 1935, New Zealand resumed its commitment to equality. It introduced a social security system, comprehensive medical services and state-financed housing schemes. Maori became eligible for all these benefits and were given extra help in an attempt to equalise standards of living.

In World War II, more than 140,000 New Zealanders served overseas, in Europe and the Middle East. Some 11,000 lost their lives.

In 1947, New Zealand gained the right to amend the Constitution without reference to Britain. The Legislative Council (Parliament's upper house) was abolished in 1950; Parliament now consists of a single chamber, the House of Representatives. New Zealand is a member of the Commonwealth, and a New Zealand governor-general represents the Queen. Support for a new flag, free of Britain's Union Jack, is growing, as is the suggestion that the country should become a republic.

The last two decades have seen New Zealand switch from a socialised economy, offering 'womb to tomb' benefits, to a highly deregulated market economy, producing an erosion of the country's former egalitarian ethic. 'Overseas' is still a magic word, holding promise of better jobs and salaries, of recognition for performers and artists, and a rather more cosmopolitan lifestyle. In 2005, the government initiated moves to encourage expatriates – estimated to number up to 1 million – to come home. Many did, following the global recession.

In the past two decades immigration has been encouraged, particularly from Asia and Great Britain, and New Zealand has begun to identify itself as an Asia-Pacific nation as well as a Maori-Pakeha one. Alongside this, global warming and other environmental issues have seen the Green Party become an increasingly important political force.

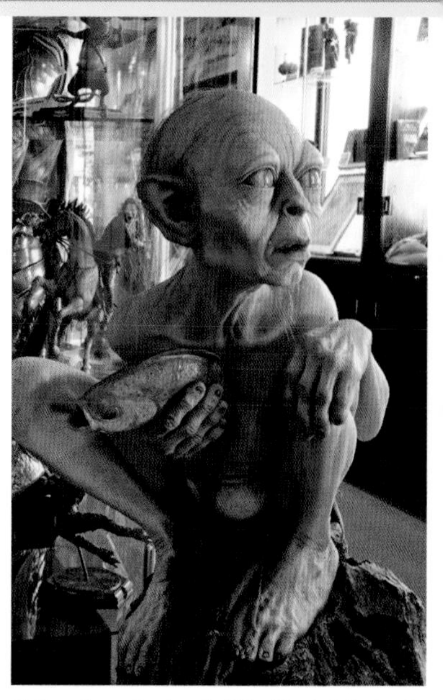

Gollum from the *Lord of the Rings* trilogy of films that ignited a tourist boom

Kiwi Innovation

For a small country with a small population, New Zealand punches well above its weight on the international innovation circuit. Locals are extremely proud of their 'firsts'. Some are well known: first person to conquer Everest (Sir Edmund Hillary), first person to split the atom (Sir Ernest Rutherford). Some will probably always be matters of dispute: did Richard Pearse really achieve powered flight before the Wright Brothers? But others are undoubted: Colin Murdoch invented the disposable syringe, which lessened the risk of cross-infections in mass vaccinations in the Third World, and Nobel Prizes include that shared by Maurice Wilkins with Watson and Crick for the discovery of DNA.

Historical Landmarks

1000–1200
Maori migrate by canoe from Polynesia.

1642
Dutch explorer Abel Tasman sights New Zealand, naming it Staten Landt.

1769
Captain James Cook is the first European to explore New Zealand and claims it for Britain.

1839–43
19,000 British settlers emigrate to New Zealand.

1840
Maori chiefs sign Treaty of Waitangi. Auckland becomes the capital.

1845–72
New Zealand Wars rage as Maori clash with settlers and troops.

1852
Governor George Grey draws up the Constitution.

1855
First elections held.

1861
Gold discovered in rivers of Otago province.

1893
Women granted the right to vote.

1911
New Zealander Ernest Rutherford, the 'father of nuclear physics', becomes first man to split the atom.

1915
New Zealand suffers heavy losses in Gallipoli campaign of World War I.

1930
Depression hits; exports plummet 40 percent.

1938
Health care and social security introduced.

1939
New Zealand enters World War II.

1947
New Zealand gains right to amend its Constitution without reference to Britain.

1953
Edmund Hillary and Sherpa Tenzing Norgay conquer Mount Everest.

1962
Maurice Wilkins shares Nobel prize in physiology and medicine for discovery of DNA.

1984
New Zealand refuses entry to nuclear-equipped US warships and adopts non-nuclear policy.

1995
New Zealand wins the America's Cup.

1997
The National Party's Jenny Shipley becomes New Zealand's first woman prime minister.

2001
Premiere of the first film in the *Lord of the Rings* trilogy sparks huge international interest in the country and its landscapes.

2003
Population hits the 4 million mark.

2005
Labour Party leader Helen Clark is elected prime minister for the third time.

2008
John Key's National Party voted into power following Helen Clark's nine-year reign.

2011
New Zealand hosts Rugby World Cup.

Culture

In this age of globalisation, New Zealanders – or Kiwis, as they are generally known – are as diverse as the people of any other Western nation. Kiwis share a passion for travel; at any one time more than 1 million reside overseas. The other 4.4 million live at home in one of the least crowded countries on the planet, yet most choose to live in the five main centres of Auckland, Wellington, Hamilton, Christchurch and Dunedin.

THE PEOPLE

The indigenous people of New Zealand, the Maori, were the first to arrive here; today they make up about 14 percent of the population. The Maori language *(te reo)* is spoken throughout New Zealand and the vast majority of place names are of Maori origin.

English, Scottish, Irish and Welsh settlers arrived in New Zealand six centuries after the Maori. The original settlement plan, mooted by the New Zealand Company, was to establish a 'Britain of the South.' However, unlike Australia, a criminal record did not provide a one-way ticket. Instead, industrious immigrants, respectable, hardworking rural labourers and cultured men of capital were determinedly sought. Where class was lacking, prosperity and respectability were promised in exchange for hard work.

In the early days, land issues were a constant source of conflict. The Europeans' land-grabbing ways did nothing to endear many of the new arrivals to the native population. The greatest conflicts arose over the mutual misunderstanding of what constituted land ownership. Even today, land issues surrounding the 1840 Treaty of Waitangi remain contentious. However, these are slowly being resolved.

Up to the 1960s, most immigrants were British, and those who were not, like the 30,000-strong Dutch community who arrived in the 1950s, were expected to adopt local ways. In the 1960s cheap air travel and TV opened New Zealand to the world. Traditional ties with Britain were broken in the 1970s when it joined the European Economic Community and assisted British immigration ended. A new wave of immigrants, from Asia and the Pacific, followed. Added to the mix are a growing number of refugees and asylum seekers, attracted by the

The annual Pasifika festival in Auckland is a celebration of Polynesian culture

Customs and Etiquette Tips

- If you are invited into a Maori family home, be aware that it is considered the height of rudeness to put your feet near tabletops (including coffee tables)
- Do not enter a *marae* unless you have been invited. If no invitation is forthcoming, join a *marae* visit tour in Rotorua *(see p.40)*.
- In many New Zealand homes whether Maori or non-Maori it is considered polite to remove your shoes at the door
- New Zealanders will not be slow in coming forward to tick you off if you leave the tracks provided in thermal parks or disturb native forest, birdlife, nesting penguins or any of New Zealand's marine mammals in any way
- If you are invited into a Kiwi home for a meal it is customary to take a token meal offering with you such as a bottle of wine or box of chocolates
- At larger gatherings such as BBQs it is customary to ask what you can bring along to contribute. The reply may range from 'just yourself' through to 'bring a salad'. In any case you should take something. If the answer, however, is to 'bring a plate', this actually means to make a dish of food to share with everyone, similar to 'pot luck'.
- Non-Maori increasingly have great respect for Maori rituals and places that are *tapu* (sites of sacred objects, historic events or burials), and Maori ceremonials are increasingly honoured by all New Zealanders. There are many places throughout New Zealand that are sacred to Maori. These will be signposted and visitors are urged to recognise the cultural significance of these places and treat them with respect.

country's progressive humanitarian stance, liberal politics and world-leading social welfare. Today, they continue to arrive from hotspots around the globe – Afghanistan, Iran, Somalia, South Africa and Zimbabwe. Overall, about 20 percent of New Zealand's residents were born overseas, with more of these living in Auckland than anywhere else in the country.

Auckland's distinctly multicultural character contrasts markedly with the rest of the country. South Auckland, in particular, is home to the largest Pacific Island population in the world. The largest group are the Samoans, whose payments to relatives back home provide half of Samoa's foreign exchange. Of the many tongues spoken in New Zealand, the most common after the official English and Maori is Samoan, followed by Tongan, Cantonese and Mandarin.

New Zealand has no state religion. However, more than half of New Zealanders affiliate themselves with a Christian religion; Anglican, Catholic and Presbyterian are the largest denominations. Non-Christian religions include Buddhism, Hinduism, Islam, and New Age religions.

Despite the overwhelming majority of urbanites, farming remains the backbone of the economy. It is a way of life valued by close-knit rural communities throughout the land. Many urban office workers are only one generation away from the farm.

Jane Campion, one of contemporary cinema's most distinctive directors

FILM AND THEATRE

Given New Zealand's multicultural make-up, there is much to experience in the way of cultural performances, literature, music, theatre and film. New Zealand's sumptuous landscapes provided local director Peter Jackson with the perfect fantasy backdrop for one of the most ambitious projects in cinematic history – the *Lord of the Rings* trilogy won 11 Oscars and has inspired a confidence in local talent that has resulted in a tremendous upsurge of all kinds of creative activity. Other notable directors include Niki Caro who followed her dazzling debut *Memory and Desire* with the international hit *Whale Rider*, based on a Maori legend as told by one of the country's foremost Maori writers, Witi Ihimaera, and Andrew Adamson, who has made his mark with blockbuster films *Shrek I*, *Shrek II*, *The Lion, the Witch and the Wardrobe* and *Prince Caspian*. Wellington-born Jane Campion, whose most famous film was the internationally acclaimed *The Piano*, was the first woman to receive the prestigious Palme d'Or for directing.

For its size, New Zealand seems to have given the world a disproportionate number of international film stars, notably Sam Neill, and the Oscar-winners Anna Paquin and Russell Crowe. Among the contemporary generation of film actors, Keisha Castle-Hughes, Danielle Cormack and Joel Tobeck are three stand-out performers.

Jane Campion's parents, Richard and Edith Campion, established professional theatre in New Zealand when they formed the New Zealand Players in 1953. Before this, theatre-lovers only had sporadic visits by British companies or community repertory groups. The New Zealand Players folded in 1960 but inspired a whole new generation of actors and professional companies. The first was Wellington's Downstage, which survives even though its position as the top theatre in the country's unofficial 'cultural capital' was lost to Circa, a reliable company of actors who perform international work and local plays. New Zealand's avant-garde theatre scene is less visible, but the works of Auckland's Silo and Wellington's Bats are daring and inspired.

Popular New Zealand playwrights include Hone Kouka and Briar Grace Smith, both of whom have also written about New Zealand history from a Maori perspective.

MUSIC AND DANCE

The New Zealand Symphony Orchestra (NZSO), which performs more than 100 concerts per year, is also based in Wellington. It was formed in 1946 amid a post-war optimism in which the nation's intellectuals, composers, painters and actors conspired to invent a national culture (groups like the Royal New Zealand Ballet and the New Zealand Players were born in the same era). New Zealand composers Jack Body, Hirini Melbourne, Gareth Farr and Philip Dadson have created a rich and diverse repertoire, and some of it draws upon Maori and Polynesian styles. However, New Zealand's most famous practitioner of classical music remains the soprano Kiri Te Kanawa. The nation is a prolific producer of good singers, including the sopranos Hayley Westenra and Malvina Major, and bass Jonathan Lemalu. A performance by New Zealand Opera (usually held at The St James in Wellington or Aotea Centre in Auckland) is first-rate.

The history of dance in New Zealand is one of struggle and perseverance. Dance is costly to develop and tour, yet the Royal New Zealand Ballet celebrated 50 years in 2003, and has built up a reputation for hard work and commitment. New Zealand's two leading modern choreographers, Douglas Wright and Michael Parmenter, have produced stunning and moving work, while Black Grace, an all-male troupe who combine the physicality of rugby players and the grace of ballet dancers, is renowned for its energetic blend of modern dance and Maori and Polynesian forms.

ART AND LITERATURE

In the past, many New Zealanders have had an ambivalent attitude towards the arts. Grants to artists and writers announced by Creative New Zealand – the state funding agency – once regularly aroused derision, as if wastrels and idlers were getting money for nothing. Today philistinism is never far from the surface of public life. But in spite of this – or perhaps precisely because of it – a robust indigenous culture has flourished. The very isolation of artists has forced them to forge their own way, without too much reliance on overseas models or local encouragement. It remains a scandal that there is no national art gallery in New Zealand. The remains of what used to be one have been squeezed into an upstairs space at Te Papa, and although this museum is a must, don't expect to find a truly representative display of New Zealand art. Instead trawl the fine range of city and provincial galleries – notably the Christchurch Art Gallery, Wellington's City Gallery, the Auckland Art Gallery, the Dunedin Public Art Gallery, the Suter Gallery in Nelson, the Eastern Southland Art Gallery in Gore, and the Govett-Brewster Gallery in New Plymouth. Look out for the works of the late W.A. (Bill)

Auckland-based dance troupe, Black Grace

The first Maori writer to be published in New Zealand was Witi Ihimaera in 1972

Sutton, whose spare semi-abstract landscapes seem to symbolise the artist's relationship with the land; the hugely popular realist landscapes of Grahame Sydney; and the works of Colin McCahon, Joanna Braithwaite, Shane Cotton, Dick Frizzell, Don Driver, Richard Killeen, Peter Robinson and Bill Hammond.

Many writers struggle in New Zealand to make a name, and, incredibly, it was only as recently as 1972 that the first book by a Maori writer was published in New Zealand – Witi Ihimaera's short-story collection *Pounamu Pounamu*. Ihimaera is now one of the country's leading novelists: his novel *The Whale Rider* was a hit film in 2003. Another work that was successfully adapted for the big screen was *Once Were Warriors* by Alan Duff, a sensational book that took the country by storm in the 1990s.

The field of history and biography was dominated for many years by the late Michael King, and the works of others, including Miles Fairburn, James Belich, Anne Salmond and Philip Temple, have helped to shape history writing into finely shaded explorations of society, culture and Maori-Pakeha relations.

Children's literature is spearheaded by such international successes as Lynley Dodd, famous for the *Hairy Maclary* series for younger children, and Joy Cowley, whose reading texts are widely used in education the world over. And then of course there is Margaret Mahy. Through her books, readings and public appearances, she has become a national treasure.

Surprisingly, poetry does well in New Zealand. Although the average volume of verse sells no more than a few hundred copies, dozens are published every year and poetry workshops and creative writing courses are booming. Only one poet has achieved the kind of stature that might be called legendary: the passionately nationalistic James K. Baxter, who was famous for wandering through the country barefoot with long hair and a Jesus-like beard in the last years before his death in 1972 at the age of 46.

Most Maori poets and novelists write in English, but there is a great deal of crossover between the languages. Read the self-deprecating poems of Glenn Colquhoun, and you'd be hard pressed to know if he was Pakeha or Maori. Chances are that you would conclude that it doesn't matter much anyway.

Food and Drink

NATIONAL CUISINE

New Zealand cooks have a love of vibrant flavours and working with fresh produce. Mediterranean influences are encouraged by the fact that peppers, aubergines, olives, asparagus and garlic are easily grown and readily available. Pesto and hummous are as popular here as anywhere in the world, as are the foods and flavours of Asia: curries, stir-fries, sushi, gouza and dim sum are commonplace. New Zealand keeps up to date with international trends, and in addition to this, the various cultural groups who call New Zealand home – Maori, Samoan, Indian, Korean, Chinese, Japanese, Malay, Indonesian, Greek, Cambodian, Croatian, Dutch, Thai, German, British and many others – have helped create New Zealand's unique form of fusion, each adding its own colour and flavours to the culinary melting pot.

National dishes include New Zealand lamb, *hangi* – a traditional Maori feast of meats, seafood and vegetables prepared in an earth oven *(see p.41)*, and pavlova – a delicious concoction of meringue, slightly sticky on the inside and crisp on the outside, topped with cream and fresh fruit. The latter, a summertime dessert, is often served following a barbecue, particularly on Christmas Day.

New Zealand's exceptional standard of local meat is showcased at a traditional Kiwi barbecue, when a variety of beef steak, lamb chops and sausages, and/or an array of freshly gathered seafood, is served with corn on the cob and salads.

New Zealand waters teem with fish and shellfish which may be freely harvested. Fishermen bring in excellent scallops, crayfish and oysters by the boatload, as well as a variety of fish. Restaurant menus nearly always feature snapper, and grouper (hapuka), a popular deep-water species. Kingfish is highly prized but is not widely available. You will also commonly strike blue cod (popular in the South Island), and kahawai, gurnard and tarakihi in the north.

Freshwater rivers produce delicate little whitebait, which are usually pan-fried as fritters and have become synonymous with New Zealand's West Coast. Salmon, fresh or manuka-smoked, is served widely. The rivers and lakes of both islands teem with

Mussels, a New Zealand favourite

Road-side fruit stall

brown and rainbow trout, but they are classified as game fish, and an eccentric law bans their purchase or sale. However, if you catch your own, some lodge restaurants, particularly, will usually cook it for you.

The superb selection of shellfish available in New Zealand includes varieties found nowhere else, such as the toheroa, a protected type of clam. However, note that only local Maori have a customary right to dig these restricted shellfish; visitors should seek out its plentiful smaller cousin, the tuatua, which taste delicious baked in its shell on the barbecue, or made into soup or fritters. Meal-size portions of cockles, pipis, mussels and oysters may also be freely gathered throughout New Zealand. Crayfish, mussels and oysters are found nationwide, and are often sold from small road-side stalls either fresh or smoked.

Game meats are popular in rural districts, and include tender and fragrantly seasoned wild boar, venison, wallaby, quail, pheasant and duck. Possum meat is also sometimes found on the menu, particularly on the West Coast.

The wide variety and abundance of New Zealand's fresh produce has helped build its world-class cuisine. Vegetables such as asparagus, globe artichokes and silver beet (Swiss chard) – luxuries in some countries – are plentiful here, as are pumpkins and kumara, the world's sweetest potato. Kiwifruit, apples, tamarillos, strawberries, passion fruit, pears, avocados, blueberries and boysenberries are shipped all over the globe, but while you are here, it's also well worth trying less famous fruits, such as feijoa, babaco and prince melons. In the subtropical far north of the North Island, pawpaw, papaya and banana grow happily in people's backyards. However, these fruits are not commercially grown. An enormous range of citrus fruits is grown locally, as are pears, and a range of stone fruits and berries.

All the familiar vegetables are grown in New Zealand – from leeks and carrots, through to lettuces, cauliflower and capsicums (green peppers). Thanks to the benign climate, vegetables tend to grow larger and have a stronger flavour.

New Zealand's celebrated dairy products include yoghurt and excellent cheeses. Among the latter, there's a choice of cheddar (mild or tangy), Camembert, Brie, blue-vein, Greek-style feta (packed in brine), and port-wine and smoked cheese, as well as cheeses and spreads flavoured with herbs, chives or sesame seeds.

Ice cream made using New Zealand's own dairy products is deliciously rich and comes in a range of subtropical flavours. Pavlova, meringue and cheesecakes are also popular, and British visitors will warm to home treats like hot apple pie.

WHERE TO EAT

Good restaurants and cafés abound in the cities of Auckland, Wellington, Christchurch, Hamilton and Dunedin, and in major resort towns like Queenstown and Rotorua. New Zealand has a large number of world-class restaurants, including those found at luxury lodges and vineyards. The variety of food is dazzling and inspiration is eclectic, drawing from the world's great cuisines. Competition is intense, which helps keep standards high. Many restaurants specialise in international cuisines, most notably Japanese, Thai, Indian, Chinese, Korean, Mediterranean and Italian. Restaurants and cafés range from formal through to extremely casual, and alfresco dining during summer months is common. Note that in New Zealand, the term 'entrée' on a menu means a starter, and the main course is usually referred to as the 'main'.

Throughout New Zealand there is a range of vegetarian restaurants and cafés, and health-food establishments. However, small villages are generally limited to European- or Chinese-style takeaway food and bakery items.

Seasonal Fruits and Vegetables

Each season brings with it an amazing range of fresh fruit and delicious tree-ripened fruit which can be bought direct from road-side stalls right where it is grown. Nationwide, weekend farmers' markets are an increasing phenomenon, as is the availability of organic produce. Varietal honey and locally grown chestnuts, walnuts, hazelnuts and macadamia nuts are other treats to look out for on your travels.

November–February: Strawberries, raspberries, blackberries, loganberries, boysenberries, gooseberries, blueberries, asparagus, peaches, apricots, plums, nectarines, cherries, beans, peas, tomatoes, sweet corn, chilli, eggplant, capsicum (bell peppers), rock melon, water melon, cucumber, parsnip, zucchini, avocado

March–May: Apples, pears, feijoas (a scented, oval green fruit with a taste reminiscent of pineapple and strawberries), tamarillos (a tart ruby-red fruit with a bright orange interior laced with black seeds), persimmons (glossy orange skins with bright non-astringent flesh), basil, marrow, passion fruit, kiwi fruit, avocado

June–October: Apples, oranges, lemons, limes, tangelos (a type of super-juicy orange), grapefruit, Brussels sprouts, broccoli, cabbage, beetroot, broad beans, cauliflower, kiwi fruit

Wither Hills winery and restaurant in the wine-growing region of Marlborough

International fast-food chains are well represented, but despite this, owner-operated fish-and-chip shops still provide the most popular take-away meal, comprising thick golden chips (french fries) and fish deep-fried in batter or crumbs, as well as seasonal oysters, scallops, paua fritters, sausages and other items. American-style hamburgers and milkshakes are popular – but beware of 'hot dogs', which are a sausage covered in batter, deep-fried, skewered on a stick, and, customarily, doused in ketchup. Wait while your meal is cooked to order, wrapped in absorbent paper or piled on a cardboard tray. Then take it to eat at a pretty spot by the sea.

Pubs serve simple, filling meals and offer good value at lunch time, as do cafés. The latter serve sandwiches, freshly prepared salads, and a variety of light hot dishes. The coffee is always espresso and is often made with beans roasted by small speciality businesses.

One takeaway snack meal that has a long local history is the meat pie. These are sold in convenience stores, bakeries and petrol stations, where they are heated to order. The single-serve pies are oval, round or square and most contain ground or diced beef in gravy. A layer of cheese is a popular addition, and some pies are topped with mashed potato instead of pastry.

Bakeries also offer well-priced food and are a great place to pick up picnic supplies including freshly baked bread and rolls, and sweet traditional treats such as Anzac biscuits, afghans, peanut brownies, ginger crunch, blueberry muffins and banana cake. Bakeries also offer a range of teas as well as local mineral water and fruit juices.

DRINKS

New Zealand wines win awards all over the world and are well worth trying. The country's summer maritime climate of long hot days and cool nights produces light, elegant, fruity white wines – and, in recent years, some very fine red wines. To sample fruity, fresh-scented Sauvignon Blancs from a range of award-winning vineyards, head to the notoriously sunny valleys of the Marlborough region (www.winemarlborough.co.nz). Pinot Noir has placed the southern North Island wine-growing region of the Wairarapa (www.wairarapanz.com) firmly on the map and other varietals including Shiraz and Pinot Gris are steadily increasing in popularity *(see p.148 – Food and Wine Trail)*.

New Zealanders, along with Australians, are among the biggest beer drinkers in the world, and many of New Zealand's beers – Steinlager, Speights, Tui, DB Draught, and boutique varieties like Black Mac and Monteiths – are very good. However, be cautious when ordering draught beer – it's often weak and fairly flat.

Most nightspots, restaurants and cafés serve liquor, and you can buy alcohol from liquor outlets (known as bottle shops), wine shops and supermarkets (beer and wine only), if you're 18 or over.

The majority of restaurants and cafés also serve alcohol. However, some are licensed for its consumption, but not for selling it. These eateries display a BYO sign which means 'Bring Your Own' bottle; generally you will be charged a small 'corkage' fee for supplying glasses and opening your bottle. Wine purchased with your meal at a licensed restaurant will be more expensive, adding roughly $10–20 extra per bottle. Look out for the restaurant's 'house' wine as these can be extremely good, often local, and offer significantly better value.

New Zealand produces its own range of freshly squeezed fruit juices. These include apple, orange, and other blends which incorporate locally grown subtropical fruits. An extremely popular fruit juice is feijoa, which served chilled, either sparkling or plain, is delicious.

New Zealand also has its own brand of lemonade known as L&P, or Lemon and Paeroa, which sells alongside international brands nationwide.

A range of water, bottled at source, can be purchased from supermarkets, petrol stations and all eateries. However, drinking tap water in New Zealand is perfectly safe and in most restaurants this will automatically be supplied to your table free of charge.

Café in Golden Bay

Index

Accommodation Index

Credits for Berlitz Handbook New Zealand

Written by: Donna Blaber
Series Editor: Alexander Knights
Commissioned by: Anna Tyler
Cartography Editor: Zoë Goodwin
Map Production: Apa Cartography Dept
Production: Linton Donaldson & Rebeka Ellam
Picture Manager: Steven Lawrence
Art Editors: Richard Cooke and Ian Spick
Photography: 4 Corners 8BL; Alamy 9BL, 87T, 107, 117, 140, 144, 164, 193, 200, 250, 251; Courtesy Air New Zealand; Tourism Auckland 9BR, 74, 76, 77; AWL Images 7MR, 55, 87B, 192, 221B, 222, 276; Axiom 14; Bay Of Plenty Tourism 5BR, 13, 40, 133; APA Andy Belcher 5TR, 6BL, 44, 53, 69, 89, 91, 99B, 101, 102, 105, 109, 113, 116, 118, 119/T, 121, 127, 128, 130, 134, 137, 146, 180, 187, 198, 209T, 211, 212, 217, 229, 232, 241T, 248, 249, 264, 270; Donna Blaber 6M; Courtesy Black Barn 150; Courtsy Blackball Hilton 216; Courtesy Cableway Restaurant 132Canterbury Tourism 3TR, 5BR; Phillip Capper 160; Courtesy Copthorne 233; Sean David 291; Destination Rotorua 2TL, 4TR, 6TL, 16, 45, 277; Dunedin Tourism 35; Courtesy Edgewater palms 94; Mary Evans Picture Library 57, 281, 282, 283, 285; Fiordland Tourism/N Dempe 4TL; Fiordland Tourism 255; Fotolia 198; Getty Images 54, 60/61, 209, 245, 290; The George 202; Courtesy Peter Gordon Dine 80; Glen Fergus 5BL; Haast River Safari 215; Courtesy Hanmer Springs 50; Courtesy Harbourside 81; Robert Harding 143; Courtesy Huka Lodge 258; Intercontinental 165; Istockphoto 43, 126, 201, 213, 219, 241, 244, 271; Koala bear 141; Brian Megaw 9TL; Messel Inn 184; Courtesy Millennium Hotel 131; New Zealand Tourism 5M, 7B, 7TR, 49, 65T, 79, 90, 93, 123B, 142, 153, 194, 209T, 210, 225, 237, 256/257, 258, 267, 268, 278/279, 293; NZT/Ben Crawford 92; NZT/Gareth Eyres 48, 106, 214; NZT/James Heremia 41; NZT/Jason Hosking; NZT/Fay Loney 38; NZT/Bob McCree 104; NZT/Chris McLenan 8BR, 30, 51, 78, 103B, 122; NZT/Nick Servian 42; NZT/Rob Suisted 8T, 18, 20/21, 22, 24, 84, 121T, 199; NZT/Ian Trafford 25; NZT/David Wall 27; NZT/Scott Venning 17, 75; Robert Nyman 205; Photolibrary.com 32, 96; QueenstownTourism 12, 15, 238, 239; APA Peter James Quinn 2TR, 3TL, 4B, 5tL, 9M, 10/11, 26, 28, 31, 33, 47, 56, 65B, 68, 71, 72, 73, 82, 85, 108, 110, 111, 112, 145, 147, 148, 149, 159, 161, 162, 163, 171/T, 174, 175, 177, 178, 179/T, 181, 183, 191, 206, 246, 261, 266, 271, 275, 286, 288, 294, 296, 297, 298; Courtesy Rainbow Springs 37, 125; Abi Skipp 204; Courtesy Sky Tower 83; Courtesy Speights 235; David Recordon 166; Courtesy Sign Of the Takahe 203; Courtesy Skyline 221; Courtesy Te papa Museum 9TR, 158; Topfoto 284; Coutesy Waitomo Caves Hotel 114Courtesy War Memorial Museum 7TL; Werner Forma Archive 123T; Wellington Tourism 155, 156, 167; Courtesy WFU 58; Courtesy WJet 6TR
Cover: AWL Images (front); iStockphoto (back left, right) BOP Tourism (back middle)
Printed by: CTPS-China

First Edition 2011

Contact Us: We strive to keep our guides as accurate and up to date as possible, but if you find anything that has changed, or if you have any suggestions on ways to improve this guide, please write to Berlitz Publishing, PO Box 7910, London SE1 1WE, UK, or email: berlitz@apaguide.co.uk;

Distribution: Worldwide: APA Publications GmbH & Co. Verlag KG (Singapore branch), 7030 Ang Mo Kio Ave 5, 08-65 Northstar @ AMK, Singapore 569880; tel: (65) 570 1051; email: apasin@singnet.com.sg
UK and Ireland: GeoCenter International Ltd, Meridian House, Churchill Way West, Basingstoke, Hampshire, RG21 6YR; tel: (44) 01256-817 987; email: sales@geocenter.co.uk
United States: Ingram Publisher Services, 1 Ingram Boulevard, PO Box 3006, La Vergne, TN 37086-1986; email: customer.service@ingrampublisherservices.com
Australia: Universal Publishers, 1 Waterloo Road, Macquarie Park, NSW 2113; tel: (61) 2-9857 3700; email: sales@universalpublishers.com.au
New Zealand: Hema Maps New Zealand Ltd (HNZ), Unit 2, 10 Cryers Road, East Tamaki, Auckland 2013; tel: (64) 9-273 6459; email: sales.hema@clear.net.nz

www.berlitzpublishing.com